Ranade and the Roots of Indian Nationalism

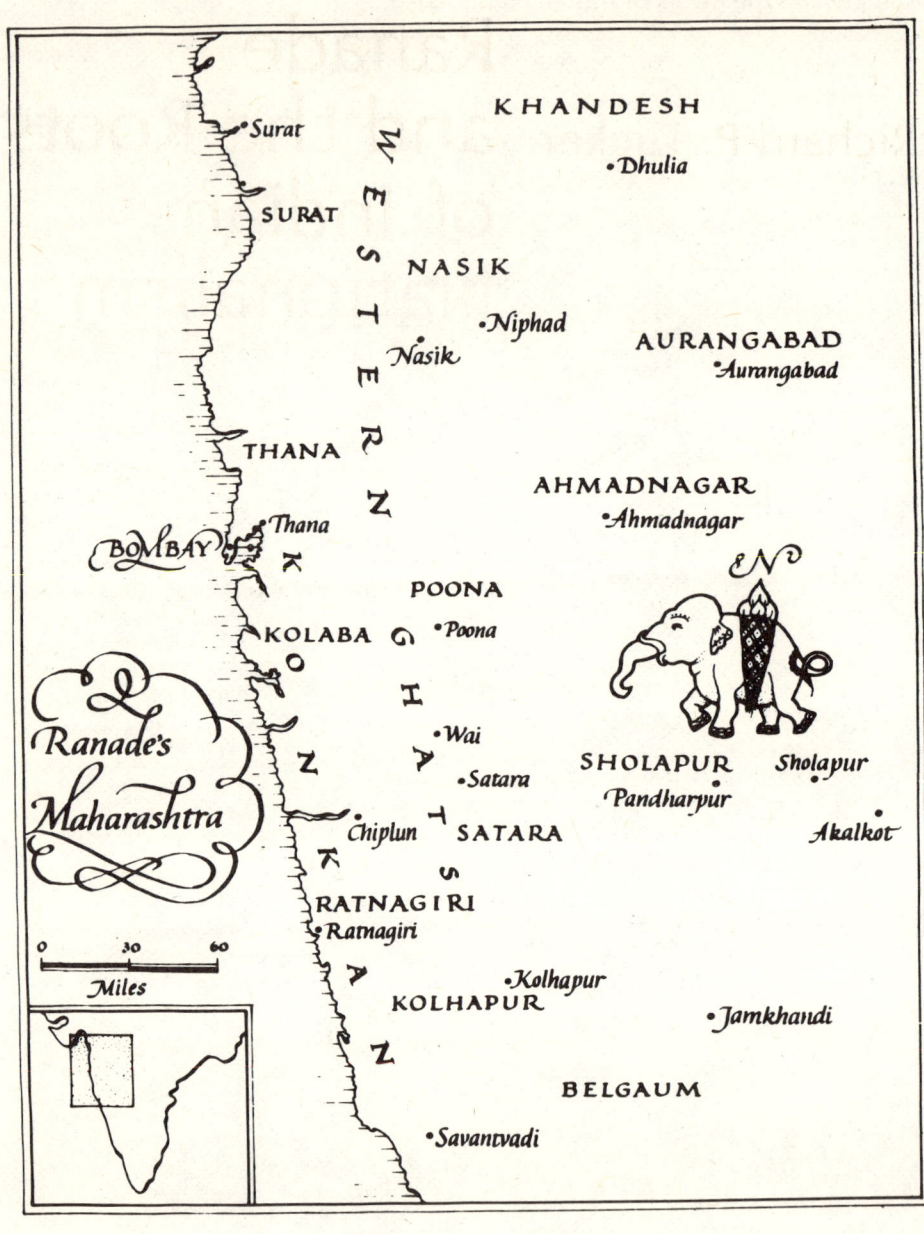

Ranade and the Roots of Indian Nationalism

Richard P. Tucker

The University of Chicago Press
Chicago and London

The University of Chicago Press, Chicago 60637
The University of Chicago Press, Ltd., London

© 1972 by The University of Chicago. All rights reserved
Published 1972. Midway Reprint 1976
Printed in the United States of America

International Standard Book Number: 0-226-81532-3

Library of Congress Catalog Card Number: 72-80683

For Sarah and Rachel

CONTENTS

MAP: RANADE'S MAHARASHTRA		Frontispiece
PREFACE		ix
KEY TO ABBREVIATED REFERENCES		xiii

Chapter

I. MAHARASHTRA: THE REGIONAL CONTEXT — 1

    The Pattern of Maharashtrian Society
    The Ranade Family
    Cultural Traditions of the Chitpavans

II. BOMBAY: THE APPRENTICESHIP OF A PUBLIC SERVANT — 16

    Society and Politics in Bombay City
    Education and Acculturation
    The Apprenticeship in Administration

III. THE REFORM BATTLES OF 1859-1875 — 41

    The Moral Foundations of Reform
    The Widow Remarriage Conflict
    The Tactics of Reform

IV. NATIONALIST POLITICS IN THE DESH, 1867-1880 — 68

    Factions, Alliances and the Sarvajanik Sabha
    The Ideology of Liberal Nationalism
    The Sarvajanik Sabha and Political Polarization
    The Crisis of Ranade's Loyalty

V. THE FOUNDATIONS OF POWER, 1876-1886 — 102

    The Deccan Agriculturists' Relief Act
    Economic Development and Social Harmony
    The Political Role of Social Elites
    The Powers of Indian Officials

VI. EDUCATION AND POLITICS IN POONA, 1880-1890 — 127

    Education and Social Renewal
    The Two Factions in Journalism and Politics
    The Last Round of Unity

VII. SOCIAL REFORM AND THE ROLE OF GOVERNMENT, 1884-1891 — 155

    Government and the Rights of Women
    All-India Reform: The National Social Conference
    The Spiritual Basis of Reform
    The Age of Consent Bill and Mass Movements

VIII. THE CRISIS OF THE MODERATES, 1891-1897 — 179

    Economic Development
    The Orthodox Counterattack
    Communalism and the Political Struggle
    Factions and Elections
    The Aftermath

IX. BOMBAY: THE LAST YEARS — 207

    The Many Facets of Politics
    The Reassessment of Maratha History
    Women, the Lower Castes, and Social Unity
    The Religious Matrix
    The Last Days

GLOSSARY	235
CHRONOLOGY	239
BIBLIOGRAPHY	241
INDEX	255

PREFACE

Many features of public life in Maharashtra today would be almost unrecognizable to the men who dominated the scene in the nineteenth century. The rapid growth of population and urban centers, the spread of technology and education, the liberalization of social patterns, and the removal of the Brahmin leadership from political power--all of these are ground swells of change. Yet the roots of these movements penetrate far back into the nineteenth century. They can be discovered in the years when Maharashtrians began to respond creatively to the new conditions which the imperial British had introduced into India. In the resulting process of modernization, the new Indian elite preserved some traditions from former times as well as circumstances permitted, while profoundly changing others. At no point, of course, could they control this process with the lucid rationality which hindsight sometimes suggests, for their work was attended with the turmoil and improvisation which accompany public events. They acted nearly always in a context of conflicting political powers, and they had one eye trained toward capturing the initiative from their British rulers.

This was so even for those most intimately associated with the imperial government. In the Moderate school of politics which they fashioned, Mahadev Govind Ranade was the dominant figure for twenty years after 1870, grafting liberal constitutionalism onto the framework of Hindu society. In Ranade's first twenty years in Poona after 1870, all sides acknowledged him as preeminent. He added structure and vitality to the fledgling voluntary organizations there, established a many-faceted ideology for their work, and prodded each of the many groups in question to accept the changes inherent in the new era. Most significantly, perhaps, he attempted to accomplish all these changes while simultaneously preserving the structure of traditional society as he understood it.

By 1890 Ranade's characteristic strengths had matured, but his limitations were also clear. His critique of imperial rule led inexorably to more fundamental attacks launched by the Extremists, who were beginning to displace him in political life. Equally significant, his claim to having articulated the genuine wishes of the people led implicitly to the popular politics of the market place, which Ranade feared as turbulent and irrational. These two factors in tandem led to a third area of tension between Moderates and Extremists: an elaborate dispute over the nature of Hindu and Maharashtrian traditions and their viability in a changing world. Conflicts over the genius of Hindu religion and the sanctity of her social arrangements were central to the political movements of the 1890's.

Within this cultural revival, though, debates on specific matters rested on the belief which all sides shared, that a primary task of modern leadership was to revitalize the characteristic genius of Hindu civilization. In this movement it was Ranade who most successfully mediated the internecine conflicts of Maharashtra's elites. Perhaps as much by this work as by any other side of his life Ranade's fame survived the political defeats of his last years. He became before his death one of the demigods of Brahmin affairs, not to be displaced before Brahmin dominance itself was reduced in Maharashtra in the 1930's. What was unclear to the Brahmin protagonists during his lifetime was that the dispute over cultural revival was largely a Brahmin preoccupation, which held little interest for the non-Brahmin majority of the populace. Hence the cultural revival and the associated political patterns of Ranade's lifetime helped give the era before World War I its distinctive style. Until well after Ranade's death in 1901 the public life of Poona was dominated by Brahmins, who had been the chief bearers of traditional Hindu culture. This is one reason why Poona presented many of the tensions inherent in political advancement and the modernization of Hindu society in more sharply delineated form than did Bombay, the capital of the Presidency.

Ranade's story, then, rests to a significant degree on the specific social structure of Maharashtra, and the cultural complex which flourished there. It also illustrates one variation on the relations between assertive regional traditions and the all-India unity which the men of Ranade's generation sought to construct. It was a mark of the Moderates that they searched for principles of political and social organization which would transcend regional boundaries and create a unified subcontinent. Ranade was for many years near the center of this liberal network. But at the same time he was almost uniquely creative in reconciling an all-India orientation with the effort to revitalize the regional life of Maharashtra.

Throughout most of his life Ranade held the sanguine hope that all these strands might be woven together harmoniously in the total pattern of India's modernization. The key to his strategy was to mobilize all productive energies, whether British or Indian, Hindu or Muslim, Brahmin or lower caste. But in a society prone to internecine conflict this fragile alliance could easily be shattered by narrow political rivalries. Here was the root of Ranade's deep pessimism in his last years: the momentum of public participation so painstakingly constructed over thirty years seemed on the verge of dissipation amidst the polarized loyalties of Englishman and Indian, reformer and orthodox, Moderate and Extremist. The entry of many groups into public life, which he had indefatigably encouraged, had led not toward his cherished vital harmony but to the intensification of the many social and ideological conflicts which he had tried to mediate.

This account, in sum, is an attempt to trace the interrelated patterns of Maharashtra's public life in the last half of the nineteenth century, as Ranade experienced and understood them. It is not a systematic biography of Ranade's personal life, which is explored more intimately in his widow Ramabai's Reminiscences of Our Life Together, and in N. R. Phatak's Nyayamurti Ranade, a detailed Marathi account written by one who shared Gokhale's profound admiration for the great preceptor. Ranade the private man appears in the present account at the dramatic moments of his career when his normally veiled personal impulses impinged upon his public bearing.

The staffs of several libraries contributed generously in making research materials available. They include Stanley C. Sutton and the staff of the India Office Library in London, G. L. Chandavarkar of the Prarthana Samaj of Bombay, P. M. Joshi and V. G. Khobrekar at the Bombay Secretariat Record Office, the Bombay Asiatic Society, and the National Archives of India in New Delhi. The archives of Poona were especially important. Unstinting support came from R. P. Patwardhan, curator of the Dadabhai Naoroji Papers, D. V. Ambekar and others at the Deccan Sabha, G. H. Khare, secretary of the Bharat Itihas Samshodhak Mandal, and the staffs of the Fergusson College Library and Poona University Library. M. V. Sovani, librarian of the Servants of India Society's library, and J. S. Tilak of the Kesari-Mahratta Trust Library provided welcome research facilities.

For what Ranade's public life signified, as well as the areas of Maharashtrian life which he failed to touch, the author is indebted to the criticisms and interpretations of many friends. Foremost, over a total of more than two years in Poona and Bombay, are Professors A. R. Kulkarni and N. R. Phatak. A fuller but still incomplete list must include Ram Bapat, D. K. Bedekar, N. R. Inamdar, Gordon Johnson, Stephen Hay, Iravati Karve, Mohan Khare, Ravinder Kumar, M. P. Mangudkar, S. R. Mehrotra, D. V. Potdar, John Roberts, Dietmar and Indira Rothermund, Suzanne Rudolph, G. B. Sardar, N. V. Sovani, and Stanley Wolpert. Portions of the manuscript at various stages received careful readings by Mahadeo Apte, Richard Cashman, Frank Conlon, Ellen McDonald, Maureen Patterson, and Eleanor Zelliot. And before any of these efforts were applied, the author learned something fundamental about humane scholarship from two others, Daniel H. H. Ingalls and Ewart K. Lewis.

Marian Wilson prepared the manuscript through an endless series of confusions thrust upon her; the author is grateful for her indefatigable care. The research and writing were supported by grants from the Danforth Foundation, the Foreign Area Fellowship Program, the National Endowment for the Humanities, the American Council of Learned Societies, the American Institute of Indian Studies, and Oakland University. Needless to say, neither these sources nor any of the individuals mentioned above are responsible for the failings or limitations of the present book.

This work has been published in an earlier version in two forms: a University of Chicago Press microfiche edition, 1972; and Popular Prakashan (Bombay), 1976. The present edition brings footnotes and bibliography up to date; I have made no substantial changes in the text.

KEY TO ABBREVIATED REFERENCES

DARA I and II
    Selections from the Records of the Government of India, No. 342. Home Department Serial No. 20: Papers on the Deccan Agriculturists' Relief Act, 1875-1894.

ERIE
    Ranade, M. G. Essays on Indian Economics.

IESHR
    Indian Economic and Social History Review.

ILR
    Indian Law Reports, Bombay Series. 1877-1901.

IOL
    India Office Library.

JPSS
    Quarterly Journal of the Poona Sarvajanik Sabha.

RDPI
    Bombay Government. Report of the Director of Public Instruction.

RMP
    Ranade, M. G. Rise of the Maratha Power.

RNP
    Government of India. Reports on the Native Papers Published in the Bombay Presidency.

RSR
    Ranade, M. G. Religious and Social Reform.

SMHFM
    Bombay Government. Source Materials for a History of the Freedom Movement in India.

A Note on Transliteration

    In the text Indian vocabulary appears italicized in the first instance but not thereafter. Each italicized word is included in the glossary, where terms common in Anglo-Indian usage are given in their familiar spelling. Less familiar terms are transliterated in the glossary according to the Library of Congress system. Similarly, transliterations in footnotes and the bibliography use that system.

Chapter 1

MAHARASHTRA: THE REGIONAL CONTEXT

> My employment . . . is to learn
> which system is in force, and
> to preserve it unimpaired.
> --Elphinstone

Mahadev Govind Ranade is celebrated throughout India even today, at least by the English-speaking, as one of the towering figures of her modern history. But like other members of the nationalist pantheon, he is more revered than understood or emulated. Only within the region of Maharashtra, where he spent virtually his whole life, is his story at all familiar to the vernacular-speaking populace. He was a product of the specific regional traditions of Maharashtra and the unique variation of Westernization which was Bombay. Although Ranade worked as systematically as any man of his generation to bind India's varied regions together in a common nationalism, his greater effort was spent in adapting European institutions to the specific circumstances of Maharashtra. The effort to understand Ranade, therefore, must begin with a consideration of the land and society which produced him.

The Pattern of Maharashtrian Society

Just as the monsoon storms off the Arabian Sea strike the Bombay coast well before they reach its hinterland, foreign seaborne intrusions have always been felt first and most intensely in the port cities of western India. Their immediate hinterland is no more than a few miles wide, blocked from the great Deccan plateau by the ghats, the coastal mountains which abruptly rise over two thousand feet to the plateau. Though the British were well settled in Bombay before 1800, their cultural influence beyond the ghats was fragmentary at most before Ranade reached adulthood. When the Great Peninsular Railway's passage over the ghats was completed in 1858 it was hailed as one of the engineering marvels of the century, a noble expression of British power and progress.

Behind the ghats lies the Desh, the northwestern segment of the Deccan plateau; this is the heartland of traditional Maharashtra. Within its broad unity of language and culture, the Desh saw significant variations in Ranade's times. Even after the British conquest of the old capital Poona in 1818, the southernmost Marathi-speaking districts remained autonomous princely states which guarded Maharashtrian traditions on the borders of Kannada-speaking northern Mysore. Northeast of there, Sholapur district, though dry and poverty-stricken, could yet boast the town of Pandharpur. Maharashtra's greatest pilgrimage still gathers annually there in praise of the god Vithoba, Vishnu's avatar. To the north of Poona as well, the present district headquarters towns of Nasik and Ahmednagar became cultural meeting grounds for Hindus and Westerners during the nineteenth century. Nasik, settled on the banks of the Godavari River, was one of the holy pilgrimage cities of India, while Ahmednagar, once the capital of the Nizamshahi kingdom, became in 1832 the seat of the aggressive American Marathi Mission.[1]

It was the society of the Desh which produced Ranade and with which he dealt in his mature years. In some regards this society was unusually homogeneous by Indian regional standards,[2] and Ranade assumed that this was a significant virtue. Several centuries of relative political autonomy had left Maharashtra with few non-Marathi speakers in its midst. The exception was among the trading and moneylending castes: in this commercially quiet region indigenous trading castes had never been wealthy or aggressive. By the beginning of British times in the Desh, numerous Gujarati Banias and Marwaris from Rajasthan had settled in the villages and market towns of the Desh. In Ranade's time they controlled a large segment of the money market.[3] They became the chief target of rural unrest as the century wore on. Ranade, like most Maharashtrian writers of the time, was explicitly troubled by the difficulty of integrating them into the ideal harmoniously stratified society of the Desh.

The rest of the populace outside Bombay city was almost entirely Marathi-speaking. It was divided into three major groups: the various Brahmin castes at the top of the status hierarchy, beneath them the non-Brahmin but still caste Hindu majority, and finally several important Untouchable castes. Most political and social movements in modern Maharashtra have been associated with one or another of these three groups, and relations between them have been a vexing problem for both political leaders and scholarly analysts.

Though the sense of social distance and resulting tension was never so great between Brahmins and non-Brahmins there as it has been farther south in India, through at least the nineteenth century there was a sharp demarcation separating Brahmins from all the other orders of Maharashtrian society. Even Shivaji, the charismatic Maratha[4] who forged unity and independence for his people in the mid-seventeenth century, had difficulty finding Brahmin priests who would consecrate his rule by performing the full Vedic investiture ceremony for a non-Brahmin. By the early eighteenth century his descendants were displaced by the Brahmin Peshwas, or prime ministers, in their new capital at Poona. Shivaji's family were effectively retired to their old home in Satara, though they remained the ultimate symbol of Maratha power. It was only after 1930 that the Marathas again became dominant in Maharashtrian politics, and during the two intervening centuries there remained undercurrents of competition between Brahmins and Marathas.

During those two centuries there were also subtle patterns of rivalry among the various Brahmin castes. In the nineteenth century, a period of almost total Brahmin domination of public life, these conflicts sometimes loomed large. Ranade knew these conflicts, for as a Chitpavan Brahmin he was not born into the ritually purest caste. This status was reserved for the Deshastha Brahmins, who, as their name indicates, had settled many centuries earlier in the Desh. In a total Marathi-speaking population of about ten million in 1901, the year of Ranade's death, they numbered 298,158.[5] They were the traditional kulkarnis, or village accountants of the countryside. By their literacy and control over local records they were a powerful force in the villages. They were often important landowners and officeholders in district and taluka (subdistrict) towns as well. Ranade came to know them well in the 1880's when he spent more than a decade as the Bombay government's special administrator of land revenue legislation in the Desh.

By contrast to the Deshasthas, the Chitpavan Brahmins were newcomers to the Desh and held a distinctly lower ritual status. They were a far smaller caste than the Deshasthas, numbering only 113,605 in 1901. Yet they had become vitally important in the affairs of Maharashtra, for they virtually dominated the Maratha government during the eighteenth century. Some centuries previously, the Chitpavans had settled in the Konkan, from which their alternative name, Konkanastha Brahmins, is derived. They established themselves there as khots, landowners who gained the rights to revenue collection over wide tracts of land. In the rugged, broken land of the Konkan and the isolation of its villages, the khots often exercised power over police and local courts as well. They also moved into trade and moneylending, further diversifying their social power.[6] Their aggressiveness was felt in the Desh from about the time of Shivaji, when Chitpavan administrator families began to serve the Maratha government. From their number the Peshwas were appointed. Under their patronage Chitpavan influence expanded steadily in the heartland of Maharashtra, and after about 1720 their numbers rose proportionately in the Desh. Their political primacy was now assured.

One other Brahmin caste exercised a vital influence in nineteenth-century Maharashtra, the Gaud Saraswat Brahmins. Their traditional home was south of the Chitpavans' home, in the coastal districts to the north and south of Goa. For some centuries they were isolated from the rest of Maharashtra, as attested by the fact that they spoke Konkani, a variant of Marathi so different from the language of the Desh that some today call it a separate language. The Saraswats had their own religious authorities or swamis, unlike other Maharashtrian Brahmins.[7] Unique among the region's Brahmins, they were fish eaters; this disqualified them in the eyes of some very orthodox from Brahmin status. Symptomatically, until well after 1900 the Saraswats were rarely invited to eat in the homes of higher-status Brahmins. Again unlike the Chitpavans, they never ventured in significant numbers into the Desh, but turned their energies to the expanding city of Bombay in the nineteenth century.

There they were already well entrenched in business and education by the time Ranade and other Chitpavans ventured to Bombay for higher education in the late 1850's. At Bombay University and thereafter in movements for social and educational reform, many of Ranade's closest associates were eminent Saraswats.[8]

The bulk of the non-Brahmin population lived on the land. They were dominated by several closely related Maratha castes, among whom those who worked the soil directly were known as Kunbis. Over the centuries they have tilled the thin and inhospitable soil of the Desh, and as Maharashtra's farmer-warrior castes they have provided generations of foot soldiers, first to the Hindu government and then to the army of British India. These were the "rural masses" whose interests Ranade attempted to articulate as an administrator and political spokesman.

The Marathas had their own traditional spokesmen in the great land-holding families of upper Maratha status. These <u>sardars</u> and <u>jagirdars</u> had once been the great landed feudatories of the Maratha rulers. They managed with partial success to maintain control over landed wealth and political influence throughout the nineteenth century. Some sardars were Brahmins who had been elevated to power and wealth under the Peshwas, but the majority were distinguished Maratha families. As a class they remained in the general estimation the "natural leaders" of Maharashtrian society in Ranade's time. Ranade himself never overlooked their importance or their wealth, yet he learned increasingly over the years that, preoccupied with landed status in rural society, they were rarely eager to take an active role in urban politics.

There were exceptions to the inaction of the sardars and princes. Well before the end of the nineteenth century two great Maratha princes began to take leading roles in non-Brahmin movements of the region. The princely house of Kolhapur, as the junior branch of Shivaji's family, remained autonomous until Independence in 1947; by 1900 Kolhapur was actively encouraging non-Brahmins in its service at the expense of Brahmin officeholders.[9] Events there during the nineteenth century touched on Ranade's life at several points and presumably gave him an awareness of both the relations of the British Raj to its subsidiary states, and the uneasy relations of Brahmins to non-Brahmins.

In Ranade's time the even more important example of a princely house active in Bombay Presidency affairs was the Gaikwads of Baroda, who remained one of India's great princely families from early Maratha times until 1947. Following scandals in the Baroda court in the early 1870's, in which Ranade narrowly missed involvement, Ranade formed a cooperative relationship with the young Maharaja Sayajirao upon his accession in 1881. Sayajirao was the chief financial support for Ranade's work on behalf of non-Brahmins in Poona from that time onward.

Leadership for the non-Brahmin movement had appeared long before Sayajirao's time, however, and from an unexpected source, the low-status

Mali or gardener caste. As early as 1848 Jyotiba Phule, a Mali, began schools in Poona for women and Untouchables. Until his death in 1893 he led a militantly anti-Brahmin and pro-British movement against the dominance of Brahmins in Maharashtrian affairs.[10] No Brahmin could express open cooperation with his radical educational experiments and the fury of his pen, but Ranade was generally considered to be in sympathy with Phule's goal of low-caste self-help.

The third great section of Maharashtrian society, the Untouchables, have also relied largely on leadership from among their own ranks for their dramatic self-improvement of recent years. They numbered well over ten per cent of the population in 1901, and of these the largest number were Mahars, the caste which has provided nearly all the initiative among Maharashtrian Untouchables since 1900.[11] Their entry into modern public life was just beginning when Ranade died. It was only in the 1890's that the first literate Mahar leadership appeared in Poona and Nagpur, and only a few Saraswat Brahmin reformers among Ranade's associates ventured to support them by attacking untouchability openly in public. Ranade himself held back from so controversial a position.

The significance of some of these social features was only beginning to emerge at the end of the century. The roots of Ranade's response to them lay in the circumstances of his earliest years, and particularly the political patterns of the early nineteenth century.

The Ranade Family

In the generation before Ranade's birth the administrators and landholders of the Maratha regime were largely deprived of their political influence. Under the last Peshwa, Baji Rao II, civil order and financial stability eroded steadily; competition for power became increasingly chaotic. In the countryside the mamlatdars, district revenue collectors who were the sinews of the administration, were often unable to function. In Poona Baji Rao resorted to auctioning the post of mamlatdar to the highest bidder, or even dividing its powers into two or more shares so as to increase dissension among the sardars.[12] The collectors in turn forced their subordinates to pay well for their positions, and in the end the cultivators themselves felt the pressure of heavy exactions.

When this pattern was destroyed following the British victory over the Peshwa in 1818, the elites of the old regime reacted ambivalently to the new order. They were now definitely deprived of political power, and their associated economic position was in jeopardy. The Chitpavans above all others suffered the uncertainties of the time, for their power in the Desh rested almost exclusively on the political patronage granted them by the Peshwas. Some Chitpavan families had risen by this route to great eminence, joining the ranks of the sardars, and many Chitpavan families filled the lower bureaucratic ranks as clerks and secretaries.

It was this latter group of Chitpavan administrator families, with little wealth but with education and firm social status, which provided a large percentage of the political and educational leaders of Maharashtra until well into the present century.[13]

Ranade's family was one of these. His ancestral home was in the Chiplun taluka of Ratnagiri district in the Konkan.[14] The family had gained land there under khoti tenure and eventually became moderately prosperous landlords. For several generations they had also been bureaucrats, and their recorded family history shows that they experienced the usual difficulties of the late Peshwa period. Ranade's great-grandfather Bhaskarrao was the first to serve in the Desh. Sometime in the late eighteenth century he became chief clerk to one of the Peshwa's great jagirdars, Appasahib Patwardhan, the Chitpavan chief of Sangli state. In his later years Bhaskarrao Ranade rose to the position of political agent to the British Resident in Sangli, thereby establishing the family's connection with the British. In consequence, the Ranades gained the _inam_ right to collect the revenue from a modest parcel of land in Sangli, and joined the ranks of local gentry there.

The family's association with British administration was strengthened in the next generation, when Ranade's grandfather Amritrao joined the British revenue service, living at one time or another in several important towns of the Desh, including Ahmednagar and Poona. Ranade's father Govindrao in turn chose administrative service; his career was marked by shifts back and forth between British districts and princely states. He was stationed in the British taluka town of Niphad as clerk to the mamlatdar there, when his first child, whom he named Madhav,[15] was born on January 18, 1842. When the boy was two years old Govindrao left the British service and moved to Kolhapur, where he became a revenue clerk under the Maharaja.

Thus the Ranades, like other Chitpavan families, maintained a modicum of continuity in their professional lives. Much of Ranade's work throughout his career can be seen as an attempt to reinforce the role of the administrator castes as the primary agents of both continuity and change in Maharashtra's affairs. This might never have been possible had it not been for the policies of Mountstuart Elphinstone, the first British successor to the Peshwas. As Governor of Bombay Presidency from 1819 to 1827, Elphinstone systematically maintained the social order in roughly its former pattern, while cautiously introducing long-range Westernization through a rationalized administration and English-language education. He reserved effective power for British officers at the higher levels, but below them he relied on Indian officers and institutions wherever feasible.[16] He hired Indians for most subordinate positions in the revenue service and for a while attempted to resuscitate the former judicial panchayats with Indian members.[17] This strategy met with some initial success, especially on the revenue side, but by the late 1820's the Maratha holdovers generally proved inept in salaried positions and uninterested in purely voluntary work on the panchayats. Simultaneously, British aspirants for employment pressed the Presidency government for subordinate positions in the Deccan, on the grounds that they were better qualified to run a British administration than Indians, who had no experience of Western institutions.[18]

Despite the increasing competition with British administrators, however, many Maharashtrians maintained one position or another in the new regime. There were now fewer opportunities for great personal aggrandizement than before 1818, but as the British administration expanded, there were steadily more positions open for men of talent and education to fill.[19] Many of the former mamlatdars were reemployed as immediate subordinates of British Collectors, responsible for areas sometimes as large as talukas, in both revenue and judicial matters. As their subordinates, others found continued employment in taluka towns and villages. By the time of Ranade's birth in 1842, it was clear that the region's administrative cadres had found continuity in their occupations.[20]

The surface stability of British overlordship was not the entire story during these years, for Ranade's childhood years in Kolhapur were marked by periodic civil unrest in southern Maharashtra. The year 1844, when his family arrived in Kolhapur, witnessed a dangerous crisis in the state's history, and demonstrated the inherently unstable relations of a princely state to its British neighbors. From its establishment after Shivaji's time, Kolhapur had been in periodic conflict with neighboring jagirs, leaving a legacy of turmoil in the region. The British established paramountcy in Kolhapur in 1825, but left its internal administration under the Maharaja Bawa Saheb. When he died in 1838 his heir Shivaji was still a minor. The next six years saw bitter conflict. On one side was the Maratha-caste family of the Bhonsles led by the Maharani Tara Bai. On the other was the British-nominated Chitpavan regent, Daji Krishna Pandit, who used his position to disband several of the hill forts still garrisoned by Maratha troops. Other Maratha troops, fearing additional encroachments, rebelled in 1844. They were joined by bands of mercenaries, including irregular Persian troops who had lingered in the region from the last years of the Peshwas. It required nine months of fighting and severe reprisals by ten thousand troops of the British Raj. The Maharani, who was implicated in the revolt, was deported, and the offending states were forced to pay all costs. Henceforth, the Resident pressed British influence more forcefully in the affairs of Kolhapur.[21]

One of the determinative lifelong facets of Ranade's character, a punctilious respect for order and authority, may well have been conditioned by his childhood memories of turbulence like this in the princely courts.[22] The Ranade family arrived in Kolhapur at about the time of the rebellion. Identified with the newly ascendant Chitpavan faction which had firm British backing, Govindrao survived the subsequent disruptions and purges, settling there for the rest of Madhav's childhood. The Ranades lived in the extended household of Janardan Hari Kirtane, who had succeeded Daji Krishna Pandit as <u>karbhari</u> or chief administrative officer of the state. In both families the fathers' occupations determined those of the sons; the sons in turn captured great honor and eminence for their families. In addition to Ranade himself, his younger half-brother became an official in Indore, one of the large remaining Maratha states.[23] And the two Kirtane brothers, Ranade's closest friends in childhood and university days, also served in princely states' administration as chief ministers of Indore and Baroda.[24] This powerful current within Ranade's family and caste help to explain why he more than once nearly left British employ for the princely states. It also sheds light on his systematic efforts as Poona's leading political strategist to link the states with political movements in British districts, despite the periodic disapproval of his British superiors.

<u>Cultural Traditions of Maharashtrian Brahmins</u>

This indicates something of the political context of Ranade's early years, but it reveals little of the more intimate personal patterns of his family or the pervasive cultural values which helped determine the direction of his reforming crusades. For this we must sketch the complex pattern of his cultural inheritance. In some regards it was duplicated throughout most of the Hindu world, and in others it was specific to the regional heritage of Maharashtra.

Most Chitpavan families, like the Ranades, practiced secular occupations hereditarily. In the early nineteenth century perhaps ten per cent of them followed religious callings, either as family and temple priests or as scholars of the Vedas and <u>dharmashastra</u>. Most priestly Chitpavan families were still located in the ancestral district of Ratnagiri, and even there they practiced only the daily and customary life-cycle rituals, not the elaborate Vedic ceremonies which required more profound learning and were largely the preserve of other Brahmin castes.[25] Most Chitpavan families who had ventured to the Desh, where Ranade spent his adult life, were secular. In a pattern which has become even more pronounced in the twentieth century, it was they who claimed dominant prestige within the caste.

The Ranades, then, were not limited as priestly families were to the rigorously traditional pattern of ritual specialization. Nonetheless they considered themselves strictly orthodox. This was expressed through the daily rituals carried out in their household. Ranade's first and most rigorous training as a child was in these daily recitations; his stepmother recalled later that whenever he was interrupted in the <u>sandhya</u> recitation he petulantly demanded the right to finish.[26] The family's social role as guardian of Brahmin traditionalism went beyond this. Ranade's grandfather Amritrao was an avid student of Sanskrit philosophy, and in his later years he turned in the traditional way to concentrated religious study and meditation. He lived on, a powerful presence in his family, until 1868 when Mahadev, his eldest grandson, was already twenty-eight.

The social values implicit in these patterns were hierarchical and paternalistic. Amritrao was an avid student of the Vedas, the sacred literature of learned Brahmins. He once wrote a commentary on the Purushasukta, a creation myth in the Rig-Veda which envisions human society as a harmonious organism of separate but interdependent parts. The myth teaches that each order of society has its own function, yet each is responsible to the others in a pattern of mutual well-being, guided by the Brahmins at their head. Ranade learned this notion of Brahmin trusteeship well. The social reform movements which he later led, however deeply they challenged the power of orthodoxy at specific points, never clearly questioned this view of the Brahmins as leaders and responsible exemplars in society.

Had the traditions of Sanskrit learning and Brahmin ritualism been the only side of the Ranades' culture, there would have been little possibility of flexible response to the changing conditions of the nineteenth century. But they were complemented by the rich Maharashtrian regional expression of the bhakti tradition, which emphasized spiritual devotion as superior to all other forms of religious practice. From the time of Dnyaneshwar in the thirteenth century a succession of Marathi poet-saints had composed vernacular literature in praise of the god Vishnu in his many incarnations. These varied poetic forms, suffused with devotional fervor, are still the richest possession of the Maharashtrian people, regardless of caste. Their creators were both Brahmin and non-Brahmin, men and women. Most of the poets, in fact, were non-Brahmins, including Tukaram, the most beloved of all, who was a Sudra. Tukaram's songs are still sung by thousands from many castes on the great annual pilgrimage to the temple of the god Vithoba in Pandharpur.[27]

Adherence to bhakti relieved its followers of the burdening commitment to ritual as a total value system. Yet families like the Ranades found social ritual and spiritual devotion perfectly compatible: as long as men were equal only in the spiritual realm, the detailed prescriptions of caste dharma could be accepted as valid in the social sphere.[28] Nonetheless Maharashtrian Brahmins varied widely in their appreciation of the bhakti movement; the Ranades were devoted bhaktas. Amritrao was a well-known kirtankar or preacher. In his discourses in Kolhapur temples he described the way of life of a devotee and exhorted his listeners to purify their spiritual lives. Although there is no record of Ranade's ever publicly acknowledging his grandfather as a pattern for him, the parallels in his own career are too marked to ignore. He too, while a lifelong government servant, became a celebrated exponent of devotional religion, though characteristically in a reformed and liberal mode. In both Bombay and Poona he was for thirty years a leader of the Prarthana Samaj, western India's foremost theistic organization, in which he preached a Christian-influenced but basically Hindu version of the bhakti movement.

Ranade's training for this role began as a young child. Like other Maharashtrian boys he imbibed the poetry of Tukaram and the other saints, who provided him with sharply etched psychic and intellectual ties with traditional Maharashtrian culture. His own protégé, G. K. Gokhale, described many years later how as late as 1897 Ranade found deep solace in times of discouragement by singing to himself two songs of Tukaram:

> He who befriends the weary and the persecuted--
> he is a true saint and God himself is to be found there.

and,

> Be you humble and seek the favor of saints.
> If you want to meet God, this is an easy way.[29]

Ranade inherited from his father Govindrao many of the same elements of the complex culture of Maharashtrian Brahmins, but in a somewhat different pattern. Accounts of Govindrao portray him as systematically and sternly orthodox. In 1842, shortly after his son's birth, he undertook the traditional pilgrimage to Karvir, a Shaivite temple complex outside Kolhapur which has long been a pilgrimage center for the region.[30] As Madhav grew older, his first lessons in Marathi and Sanskrit came from his father. Likewise his father instructed him in the family religious rituals, in the time-honored way. After these first lessons the young boy continued his education in the more formal Brahmin schools of Kolhapur.

It must be noted that Ranade did not inherit an entirely rigid style of orthodoxy from his father, for in one regard Govindrao was tentatively progressive against the current of his time. He insisted that the women of his household be given basic education. Here was the germ of concern for the welfare of high-caste women, the central emphasis of the social reform movement which Ranade guided in the last half of the century. Yet Govindrao set strict limits to this, as his son was to discover in the bitter personal conflicts of later years. The widow-remarriage movement was on the horizon in the 1850's, but Govindrao was not prepared to sanction such a radical reform. In 1854 he arranged marriages for Madhav, then aged twelve, and the boy's sister, who was two years younger. Madhav was married to Sakhubai Dandekar, the daughter of an orthodox <u>inamdar</u> who lived on the revenue from villages granted his family by the Peshwa. As her family home was in Wai, the Brahmin center south of Poona, Ranade's ties with the traditional gentry of the region were thereby strengthened.

Ranade remained under his father's strict authority in personal matters until Govindrao's death in 1875. Despite his own more liberal social views he never challenged that paternal authority as long as Govindrao lived, for in his earliest years Ranade developed a solemn respect for the august integrity of both his parents. Even after he moved to Bombay for college, in an atmosphere which loosened many students' ties with their homes, Ranade described the psychological power of the orthodox mold. In a college essay entitled "Respect to Old Age," he judged with grave disapprobation some students' casual disregard of their parents. Obedience to elders was a duty which "everyone confesses to be an obvious and an important duty, yet it is to be regretted that few follow it. Everyone knows that he is to become old and everyone desires to be respected and to be duly treated in his old age by his sons. But how many are there who though cognizant of this fact, who though they toil and moil for this sole end, how many are there who treat their old parents with scorn. . . . Happily our India affords few instances of this sort."[31]

Ranade's childhood attested that education was designed to reinforce traditional family relationships. He had only one sister and his younger half-brothers were born when he was nearly grown. The household of his boyhood was dominated by adults, and Madhav himself seemed to observers a miniature adult from the time he was a small boy. He was remembered as somber, silent and slow, the condescendingly loved "baby elephant," as the household nickname had it. He was physically awkward, and for several years he possessed a slight speech defect which the family found amusing. He suffered by contrast with his effervescent younger sister and became the butt of family jokes. His mother sometimes wondered aloud whether Madhav would ever be clever enough to support both himself and a wife.

Nor was Ranade's father a refuge from teasing and condescension, for Govindrao was stern and remote. The young Madhav carried to an extreme the traditional deference toward his father: in a mixture of respect and fear, he rarely spoke directly to Govindrao but preferred to communicate through another family member as intermediary. The impact on him may be mirrored in the self-deprecating and undemonstrative manner which pervaded his public life in later years. He too, though admired by many, was often described as a remote and even impersonal guide for younger men. In his adult manner there was a subtle sense of isolation, of a man moving self-contained and stoically through a life of complex pressures. The Victorian call to Duty was entirely congenial to such a man. It became one of his common themes as a preacher for the Prarthana Samaj: that life was a set of tasks to be carried out conscientiously without thought of praise or reward.

Ranade's experience in the Kolhapur English School reinforced this pattern. He began to grow into the world of English civilization when at age eleven he entered the school in its first English class in 1851.[32] He was a competent but undistinguished student, sitting in the shadow of his more brilliant friend Vinayak Kirtane. He preserved his dignity by never speaking of his modest successes and developing a quiet self-sufficiency and indifference toward praise when it came from his family. Long hours of study and a determined seriousness in his work compensated for the lavish praise which Kirtane elicited.[33] Yet ultimately this pattern took its toll: Ranade's self-discipline was so intense as to impair his eyesight sharply during his college days, and his self-control masked an impetuous temper which he learned to subdue reliably only during his years at Elphinstone College.[34] Even in later public life, Ranade's sense of carefully cultivated righteousness reappeared in a political context at moments of high pressure when he felt outraged distress at unjustified criticism. His unwitting self-revelations at those moments revealed far more about his deeper ambitions than his coolly dignified public bearing was intended to show.

The arena of Ranade's mature actions was a far more complex misture of European and Hindu elements than the traditional patterns of his early life at home. His efforts to reconcile the two began when he first left home. After three years of study he and Vinayak Kirtane completed the syllabus of the Kolhapur English School, and their fathers decided to send them together to Bombay for more advanced English-medium studies. Colonel Reaves, the British Resident, suggested that they enroll in the celebrated high school run by John Wilson, the most eminent educational missionary of nineteenth-century Bombay; but the two fathers, wary of missionary schools and practical in intent, chose instead the secular, government-sponsored Elphinstone High School.[35] The young Ranade thus joined the ranks of the Anglicized Indian elite who were intended by their mentors to transform Indian civilization. In the coming years his adherence to traditional ways would be put to subtle and severe tests.

Notes

[1] The eastern sections of Maharashtra experienced a very different fate in the nineteenth century. Then as now they were far less oriented to Poona and Bombay; they rarely entered the events of Ranade's life. Five modern districts, collectively called Marathwada, were the northwestern portion of the princely state of Hyderabad until 1948, looking to the Nizam's capital for leadership. The northeasternmost districts of the Marathi-speaking region, Vidarbha, still look to Nagpur. They were in the autonomous Nagpur state until it was annexed by the British in 1854. See R. M. Sinha, Bhonslas of Nagpur (Delhi, 1967). Even now Vidarbha protests the preferential position allegedly granted Bombay and Poona in Maharashtrian affairs.

[2] For fuller treatment of the social structure of Maharashtra, see Irawati Karve, Maharashtra—Land and Its People (Bombay, 1968), ch. ii; and R. E. Enthoven, The Tribes and Castes of Bombay, 3 vols. (Bombay, 1921).

[3] See the analysis of the moneylender class in Ravinder Kumar, Western India in the Nineteenth Century (London, 1968), passim.

[4] The term "Maratha" has two meanings. During the British period it was often spelled "Mahratta" and usually meant a member of Maharashtrian society or the preceding government, the Maratha Confederacy. The term now has a more precise usage, indicating a member of the Maratha caste cluster. For Shivaji both meanings of the term applied.

[5] For these statistics, see Census of India, 1901 (Bombay, 1902), IX (A), Part 2, 192-196.

[6] Maureen L. P. Patterson, "The Changing Patterns of Occupations Among Chitpavan Brahmans," IESHR, VII (September 1970), 377-380.

[7] For further detail on the three Saraswat swamis, one of whom was notably liberal in his social attitudes in the late nineteenth century, see Frank F. Conlon, A Caste in a Changing World: The Chitrapur Saraswat Brahmans (Berkeley, 1976).

[8] The only non-Brahmins who shared something of the professional status and traditional literacy of the Brahmins were Maharashtra's two resident writer castes, the Pathare Prabhus and the Chandraseniya Kayastha Prabhus, who numbered only about 25,000 in 1901. The latter, usually known as the C. K. P., had competed for administrative positions in the Desh during the Maratha period, but in the nineteenth century their influence was limited largely to Bombay, and they played only an incidental role in Ranade's story.

[9] For details of the Brahmin/non-Brahmin conflict in Kolhapur at the turn of the twentieth century, see A. B. Latthe, Memoirs of His Highness Shri Shahu Chhatrapati, Maharaja of Kolhapur, 2 vols. (Bombay, 1924).

[10] For details of Phule's life, see Dhananjay Keer, Mahatma Jotiba Phooley (Bombay, 1964).

[11] See Eleanor M. Zelliot, "Dr. Ambedkar and the Mahar Movement" (Ph.D. diss., University of Pennsylvania, 1969).

[12] Mountstuart Elphinstone, Report on the Territories Conquered from the Peshwa, 2nd ed. (Calcutta, 1821), p. 3; and Kenneth Ballhatchet, Social Policy and Social Change in Western India, 1817-1830 (London, 1957), ch. ii.

[13] Patterson, "Changing Patterns," pp. 380-386; Ellen E. McDonald, "English Education and Social Reform in Late Nineteenth Century Bombay," JAS, XXV (May 1966), 454.

[14] Most of the biographical information on Ranade comes originally from his widow's reminiscences: Ramabai Ranade, Āmcyā āyuṣyāntīla kāhīṅ āṭhavaṇī (Some Reminiscences of Our Life Together), (Poona, 1910). His family background and childhood are treated in ch. i.

[15] As if to symbolize the fact that Maharashtrian Brahmins largely ignored the South Indians' tensions between followers of Shiva and devotees of Vishnu, Ranade used both a Vaishnavite and a Shaivite name. At birth he was given the Vaishnavite name Madhav; but he was known as Mahadev, a Shaivite name, from his college days onward. In the present text he is referred to by whichever name is appropriate to the time in question.

[16] For a detailed analysis of the early fate of the administrators, see John Roberts, "The Movement of Elites within the Bombay Presidency under Early British Rule" (unpublished, 1969).

[17] For Elphinstone's experiments with panchayat courts, see Ballhatchet, Social Policy, pp. 106-115, 193-200.

[18] Ibid., ch. ix.

[19] Ibid., pp. 96-99.

[20] A similar trend was evident for village officials, both the patils and the kulkarnis. Elphinstone had attempted to cushion the impact of the new government on these officials as well, but the exigencies of efficient administration plus his scepticism regarding the competence and loyalty of the old village officers, began a transformation of their status as well. As the new courts penetrated to the villages, the old judicial and mediating powers of the patils were encroached upon. The need for efficient revenue collection produced a new class of kulkarnis, salaried agents of the Collectors now, whose control of landownership records and whose literacy often made them more powerful in the villages than the headmen themselves. Furthermore, as revenue collection became more efficient and the demands higher under the Utilitarian revenue systems after 1827, many well-to-do peasant and gentry families became progressively impoverished. In terms of caste patterns this proved a blow to the numerically dominant non-Brahmin Kunbis, who owned much village land and provided most village headmen. The Deshastha Brahmins who controlled kulkarni positions seem to have been more able to adapt to the new conditions. As the dominant Brahmin caste of the villages of the Desh, they had more mixed fortunes for the following century. See Kumar, Western India, passim.

[21] G. B. Malleson, An Historical Sketch of the Native States of India (London, 1875), pp. 254 ff.; George LeG. Jacob, Western India Before and During the Mutinies (London, 1871), pp. 156-160.

[22] For a detailed treatment, see Jacob, Western India, passim.

[23] Bombay Gazette, January 18, 1901, p. 5.

[24] D. V. Kirtane, in Indian Worthies (Bombay, 1906), p. 9.

[25] See Patterson, "Changing Patterns," pp. 393-395, for detailed analysis of the Chitpavans' secular and religious vocations.

[26] Ramabai Ranade, Reminiscences, p. 22.

[27] The sect is studied in G. A. Deleury, The Cult of Vithoba (Poona, 1960). The pilgrimage itself is also described in Irawati Karve, "On the Road: A Maharashtrian Pilgrimage," JAS, XXII (November 1962), 13-20.

[28] In recent years some have argued that since the saints emerged from various castes and sometimes dismissed the value of Sanskrit ritual, they were in effect anti-Brahmin and socially democratic. But this was at most a secondary possibility, whose social implications remained dormant until they received a transfusion of nineteenth-century liberalism. Bhaktas out of tune with their society characteristically retreated to the inner world of spiritual solace. Dnyaneshwar himself, who was probably an outcast Brahmin, fervently worshipped his god as a bulwark against orthodox society's condemnation.

[29] G. K. Gokhale, Speeches (Bombay, 1920), p. 783.

[30] M. S. Mate, Temples and Legends of Maharashtra (Bombay, 1962), ch. ii.

[31] M. G. Ranade, "Respect to Old Age," Second Essay Book at Elphinstone College, 1858.

[32] The Kolhapur English School later grew into Rajaram College, the only Maharashtrian college outside Poona and Bombay which was to be affiliated with Bombay University before 1900. Designed to give English education "mainly to the sons and wards of the Chiefs and Sardars of the Southern Mahratta Country," this was one more link for Ranade with the landed elite whose political fortunes he helped to guide throughout his career. S. R. Dongerkery, "Higher Education in Modern Maharashtra" (unpublished, 1969), pp. 5 ff.

[33] Kirtane's originality was demonstrated again when, as a student at Bombay University, he created a new literary genre, social drama, with his play, Thorle Madhavrao Peshwe. See Pramod Kale, "From Epic to Polemic: Marathi Drama and Theatre in a Period of Social Change" (unpublished, 1969), pp. 13-14.

[34] G. J. Agashe, The Third Anniversary of Mr. Justice M. G. Ranade's Death, address at the Hindu Union Club, Bombay, January 16, 1904 (Bombay, 1904), p. 4.

[35] N. R. Phatak, Nyāyamūrti Mahādev Govind Rānaḑe (Poona, 1925), p. 10.

Chapter 2

BOMBAY: THE APPRENTICESHIP OF A PUBLIC SERVANT

> The character of your whole
> people is to a great extent
> in your hands.
>   --Sir Bartle Frere

Ranade lived for nearly all the next fifteen years in Bombay, a period as long as his childhood in the mofussil. He never again spent so long in the Presidency capital, nor was he ever again so decisively Anglicized as he became under the powerful influences of his university years. This was the time of his early manhood, when he first framed a reasoned understanding of the challenges of his times: the decline of his own culture, the presence of an alien government, and the contest of values characteristic of Bombay city. His ties to the Desh became weaker now than they would ever be again, just when he was most deeply immersed in the life of an aggressively self-confident and westward-oriented city.

Society and Politics in Bombay City

Like Calcutta, Bombay was a recent city; it lacked the centuries-old ties to its hinterland which other ports of western India had developed. A century before Ranade's youth, Bombay had been only a small port on the west coast, and during the eighteenth century it competed with Surat for first position in India's external trade to the westward.[1] Its subsequent development was in an international commercial network in which the British were latecomers. By the late eighteenth century they ousted their European competitors from these waters, but a complex of Indian trading communities--Hindus, Muslims and Parsis alike--was firmly entrenched along the coast. The British quickly learned to work with them, first in joint commercial ventures and later in other aspects of public life. British power and prosperity henceforth rested to a significant degree on this cooperation; Ranade's career was one of the most productive examples of its patterns.

From 1818, when the Desh was annexed to the earlier districts of Bombay Presidency, the city's importance rapidly grew. After the opening of British trade with China in the 1830's, Bombay served as a major link in the commercial lifeline of the East India Company stretching from Liverpool to Canton. By 1864 it was the largest city in India, with a population estimated at 816,000, attracting students, laborers, investors and adventurers from all parts of the subcontinent.[2] The key to its character was this heterogeneity. Calcutta was a largely Bengali city, as Madras was largely Tamil. But Bombay was the capital of a bilingual

Presidency; its public life was shared between Maharashtrians and Gujaratis. Moreover, Bombay was not predominantly Hindu in its public life, for its leading Hindu castes shared influence with Muslims and especially Parsis.

The Parsis, a small community of Zoroastrians who had been transplanted to western India from their homeland in Persia as the Islamic world expanded, had become one of the dominant commercial communities in Gujarat by the time the first Europeans arrived in Surat. Parsi entrepreneurs helped build the English East India Company's ships and finance its operations, first in Surat and later in Bombay. By the time of Ranade's birth they were the most powerful Indian interest in the commercial life of Bombay and were very active in cultural and educational affairs as well.[3]

The Parsis provided much of the articulate leadership for the Indian commercial interest which began to assert its demands in the local politics of Bombay in the 1850's. Unlike the political leadership of Poona a generation later in Ranade's time, the commercial lobby of Bombay could not be considered the voice of any single caste or religious group. There were strong Hindu commercial groups in Bombay as well, notably the Gujarati Bania castes who had long shared both social and ritual dominance with Brahmins in their region.[4] By 1850 many of their leading shets, rich merchants who doubled as arbiters of intracaste affairs, had moved to Bombay where they henceforth played a major role.[5]

Muslims too were active in Bombay, in small numbers but in important positions. They came from several heterodox Muslim sects--Memons, Khojas, and Sulaimani Bohras. Their most powerful families had been engaged for centuries in the trade with the Persian Gulf, the Red Sea and East Africa.

The divisions among Maharashtrian Hindu castes in the city were no less complex. Until at least mid-century relatively few ventured down from the Desh; the coastal districts of the Konkan provided most of Bombay's Maharashtrian population. The bulk of her work force came from middle-ranking castes of the Konkan, especially before the influx of Maratha and Kunbi workers into the rapidly developing mills and factories late in the century. Prabhus in turn exploited the growing demand for clerical workers. Among Brahmins until mid-century it was Saraswats rather than Chitpavans who took advantage of the growing city. From that time onward their energies were focused in Bombay rather than the Desh; among Ranade's colleagues in Bombay the Saraswats were a vital lifelong influence.

This was partly by default, for until the 1850's very few Chitpavans moved to Bombay. The reasons are not entirely clear, but an important factor which is often overlooked was the cultural aversion of orthodox Brahmins to the corrupting influences of the big city. Like other turbulent ports Bombay had its seamy side, which shocked both Victorian and Brahmin proprieties. Evangelical missionaries and their friends both European and Hindu established temperance societies in Bombay and the district towns by the 1850's, in agreement that drunkenness was rapidly on the rise.[6] Vernacular speeches and newspapers dwelt constantly on the varieties of social promiscuity in Bombay, and spokesmen for high-caste morality decried the materialism and laxness of self-discipline there.[7] By contrast, the more ordered purities of rural life seemed a safer guarantee against the physical danger and cultural corruptions of the city. As we shall see, Ranade became a beneficiary of these views. While he adopted Western values in many ways, he permanently maintained the personal patterns of a traditional Brahmin, in clothing, daily ritual and social propriety, unlike a few of his Brahmin contemporaries. He became in effect one of Bombay's distinguished Victorian Brahmin gentlemen. In this way he managed to resolve the cultural dilemmas which faced anyone of his time and place.

For all the leading castes and religious communities of Bombay an important test of success was their ability to coexist profitably with the Europeans. The British there were in many regards less abrasive in their relations with Indians than were their counterparts in Bengal. Bombay was spared the influx of so large a private community of planters and traders as that which gave British society in Bengal a more overtly imperious and racist tone.[8] Further, Calcutta was the imperial capital, the focus of British power and splendor, and Bengal was the first province to undergo radical structural reforms, beginning with Cornwallis' attempts to plant British institutions on Indian soil. Long after Mountstuart Elphinstone's departure from Bombay in 1827, the western Presidency resisted Calcutta's efforts to transform Indian society and culture abruptly. The aggressive reformers of Bentinck's time had their counterparts in Bombay, but never so many or with such influence as in Bengal.[9]

The most distinguished exemplar of Bombay's delicate balance between cultural aggressiveness and social pluralism was John Wilson. Like Alexander Duff, his friend and counterpart in Bengal, Wilson was a product of the evangelical revival of the 1820's in Scotland. He arrived in Bombay in 1829 in search of converts for Christ. With his remarkable zeal for learning Indian languages he soon was studying the Hindu, Muslim and Zoroastrian classics and using that knowledge to challenge the orthodox spokesmen of all three religions. But his youthful abrasiveness quickly modulated, as he became more deeply involved in constructive relationships in Bombay. With a crusader's belief in the transforming power of education, he founded the most celebrated English-medium high school in Bombay, which attracted students from several Indian communities. And by the middle 1830's his interest in Indian traditions led him to become the leading member of the Bombay Branch of the Royal Asiatic Society.[10] Over the following thirty years he dominated the society, publishing learned papers on the antiquities of western India and leading the fight which finally opened its membership in 1836 to Indians. His ethnographic studies, begun informally on preaching tours in the mofussil, were supported by the society and resulted in *Indian Caste*,[11] one of the major ethnographic studies of its era. Not surprisingly, it was his Indian protégés who followed him into the Asiatic Society and became its leading lights in the following generation. They and others in Bombay remembered Wilson, when he finally returned to Edinburgh in 1871, as stern and rigorous, evangelical to the last, but soft-spoken in his massive dignity and dedicated to the advancement of his Indian students.

John Wilson was Bombay's most eloquent advocate of India's deliberate and orderly westernization under the unchallenged power of British political authority. It was that authority which stood its severest test in the year after Ranade arrived in Bombay, and which became one of the most vivid lessons of his student years. In the years before 1857 the relative calm of Bombay's political life stood in contrast to the more unsettled conditions of the mofussil. Between 1818 and 1857 there were sporadic revolts in remote parts of the Desh against the still recent imposition of British rule. Social disruptions in the countryside of Bombay Presidency followed rigorous collection of land revenue by British officers after the late 1820's.[12] The princely states felt a severe threat after 1848 when the Viceroy Lord Dalhousie temporarily reversed Elphinstone's policy of restraint toward them. Dalhousie believed it a British responsibility to annex and reorganize states which were corruptly and inefficiently administered. His policy hit the successor states of the Maratha empire with special force. He annexed Satara in 1848, depriving Shivaji's family of its ancient if largely ceremonial patrimony. Six years later he also annexed Nagpur, which had been ruled by another branch of Shivaji's family.[13] Tensions were running especially high in these annexed states by the beginning of 1857.[14]

Ranade arrived in Bombay only months before the Great Rebellion began that June. From that vantage point the rebellion seemed a stark threat to the forces of enlightenment and progress. Ranade's lifelong commitment to orderly and deliberate political processes must surely have been conditioned by the rebellion, which was simultaneously the seminal political event of his life and the greatest crisis of British rule. From the plains of northern India it spread rapidly to the borders of Bombay, and for most of the year both the city and its countryside faced the imminent possibility of violence.[15] Only decisive action by the governor, Lord Elphinstone, preserved peace there. Lord Elphinstone, the nephew of Mountstuart Elphinstone, had served previously as governor of Madras and had experience in military campaigns on India's northern borders. Faced with incipient mutinies in the old trouble spots of Satara and Kolhapur, he moved troops quickly, captured the leading mutineers and publicly blew them from guns.[16] His intelligence network served with equal efficiency in Bombay city, which narrowly avoided an explosion during the Muslim festival of Mohurram.[17]

By the end of the year calm returned to Bombay, and with it a general surge of relief from danger.[18] The power of the British Raj had been triumphantly vindicated, while the backward-looking sardars of the Deccan led by Tatia Saheb the would-be Peshwa, received their final discredit. Canning, the Viceroy, and Lord Elphinstone applied a policy of restraint in the settlements which followed. Their conciliation was reinforced by the Queen in her Proclamation of November 1, 1858, when she promised India:

> We desire no extension of our present territorial Possessions; and while We will permit no aggression upon Our Rights to be attempted with impunity, We shall sanction no encroachment on those of others. We shall respect the Rights, Dignity, and Honour of the Native Princes as Our Own. . . . And it is Our further will that, so far as may be, Our Subjects, of whatever Race or Creed, be freely and impartially admitted to offices in Our Service, the Duties of which they may be qualified, by their education, ability, and integrity, duly to discharge.[19]

In that moment no one in Bombay doubted for a moment the seriousness of Britain's magnanimous promises, for the Queen entrusted her liberal Viceroy, Canning, with implementing them. It was a time of unqualified and grateful support of the Raj. The commercial leaders who dominated Indian opinion in Bombay responded on December 15 with a public meeting at which they expressed their grateful loyalty. The memorial which they adopted proclaimed:

> No Empire has been more consecrated by time, none more perfectly consolidated, none more great in intellect, more overwhelming in power, more infinite in resources; and yet it is not on its awful might that it is founded, nor on the force of its naval and military greatness, but supremely in the devotion of its people.[20]

The atmosphere was reminiscent of the days of the first Elphinstone, who still lived in England. By coincidence he died in late 1859, giving Bombay an occasion for reaffirming loyalty to his policies. Ranade, then a student at Elphinstone College, undoubtedly attended the memorial meeting of the college on January 11, 1860, when speakers praised "the enlightened policy originated in this Presidency by that venerated nobleman [who was] the first patron of native education in Bombay . . . one whose philanthropy was unlimited by caste or creed."[21]

Bombay emerged from the rebellion into the most buoyantly optimistic years of its history. Communal harmony had survived, political stability was restored, and a cotton boom brought almost frantic economic growth. When the American civil war cut off England's access to raw cotton in the New World, an immense temporary market was created for Bombay cotton. Between 1861 and 1865, the years of Ranade's post-graduate studies, some £80,000,000 beyond normal receipts flowed into Bombay. The crash of the market in 1865 caused only a temporary decline in commercial activity.[22]

Sir Bartle Frere, governor of Bombay during this period, was a worthy figure to preside over the new era of optimism. Frere was to have the greatest political impact on the Indian community since Mountstuart Elphinstone, and in many ways he continued a similar policy tradition. His initial appointment had been in 1835 as a survey settlement officer in Indapur taluka in southeast Poona district, where he brought a modicum of prosperity out of chaos and depopulation.[23] He was later posted as British agent to the court of Satara, where he unsuccessfully opposed British annexation of the state in the 1840's.[24] The experience gained in these positions made him openly sympathetic to Indian interests, from peasants to princes, and his sympathy was rewarded by the admiration of the Indian population.

In his years as governor, Frere gave new substance to the tradition of liberal paternalism which had first been visible in Elphinstone. He shared the assumption that Indians were inherently capable of governing themselves if given proper training. And he provided a link with the radical liberals of later years, maintaining that it was folly for the British to rule India without consulting Indian representatives. He supported the principle, established in the Indian Councils Act of 1861, of adding Indians to the Legislative Councils. In his words, any respectable Indian "would give us the most valuable aid by looking at questions from a Native point of view, and this is aid of a kind for which I know no substitute and it certainly could not be obtained from any European."[25] The old paternalist belief in the empire as a trust held for the subjects' welfare was being transformed in Frere's time into the Liberals' belief in representative government, or at least constitutionalism.

University students who would become the chief beneficiaries of the trend toward representative government lionized Frere. Several years later, after Frere departed from Bombay, Ranade wrote an introduction to a collection of his speeches, in which he praised Frere's "generous ambition to help the native population to elevate themselves, to teach them self-reliance and the strength of lawful combination."[26] It was this combination of liberal principles and transparent sympathy which impressed Ranade most forcefully. He went on to describe Frere's "varied intellectual gifts and an imagination which enabled him to realize the men and manners of times the most removed as though he saw them and lived in them, a native simplicity of heart, familiar acquaintance with native speech and usage, affable manners, and a rare gift of speech which communicated its own earnestness to the most indifferent listener."[27] Like some of Ranade's other writings this eulogy was a vivid expression of the personal and political ideals which he was then adopting for his own. They were all the more forceful for being embodied in Frere, who, like John Wilson and a handful of others over the years, provided a living paternal example of an enlightened and liberal Victorian gentleman. Beyond this, Ranade's indirectly expressed relation to political and intellectual gurus like Frere provides a powerful clue to the unshakable support which Ranade and his allies henceforth gave to the Liberal party in imperial politics. There was to be no clearer expression of their Moderate nationalism than this support.

Education and Acculturation

Ranade's adherence to the Liberals' political principles cannot be explained, though, except against the background of his education in Bombay. Frere's encouragement of Indian ambitions under the British umbrella reflected a cultural policy which was already well rooted in the Bombay system. Missionaries and civil servants had worked closely together to develop Bombay's schools from 1815, when they jointly founded the Bombay Education Society. Though their emphases differed in degree, they shared the desire to create a new class of "educated Indians," based on what they assumed were the complementary truths of scientific rationalism, Victorian moral probity and Christian spiritual truths.[28] During his tenure as governor, Elphinstone helped clarify the purpose of this system, to produce an elite class of cultured gentlemen who would collaborate with the British to shape India's ultimate destinies.[29] Bombay was well prepared for the victory of Anglicist educational views under Macaulay in 1835.

Macaulay's orotund and contemptuous dismissal of Indian traditions expressed the basis for the Westernizing of educated Indians. But his fundamental purpose, "to form a class who may be interpreters between us and the millions whom we govern,"[30] could be used as the basis of a policy more sympathetic to Indian tradition. And so it was in Bombay, where even in Macaulay's time the conflict between Anglicists and Orientalists was less severe than in Calcutta. John Wilson and others, though confirmed advocates of Western values, were simultaneously rediscovering the richness of India's ancient past. In applying the new imperial education policy, they moderated its most abrasive qualities. As a partial consequence, Ranade and his older contemporaries never faced the intensity of cultural conflict which their Bengali counterparts often did.

In order to facilitate the creation of an Indian administrator class the Bombay government established a Board of Education in 1840 to coordinate both missionary and government schools. Sir Erskine Perry, who dominated the board for the following decade, placed first priority on producing teachers for English-language government schools, as well as lawyers and other professionals.[31] These men, in return for advancement in the British service, would collaborate with their rulers in conveying the purposes of British rule to the vernacular-speaking masses. In the mid-1850's this "Downward filtration" policy was further implemented by closer coordination of the school system. In 1855 the position of Director of Public Instruction was established, to coordinate all schools in the Presidency and watch over their standards. E. I. Howard, the director for the rest of the decade, continued Perry's policy, completing the system in 1857 with the founding of Bombay University, one of India's first three modern universities.

From the time the university accredited its first B.A. candidates in 1859, a university degree became the passport to membership in the English-educated cultural elite. The university was built in part on the existing foundation of the Elphinstone Institution, where Ranade enrolled in 1856. Founded as a parting testimony to Mountstuart Elphinstone in 1827, it had later become both a high school and a college. Before the university opened, trends in the composition of the student body were not entirely encouraging to those who envisioned steadily strengthened ties between Bombay and its hinterland. The fact that most of the city's growing population came from the coastal districts was reflected in the pattern of graduates from the Elphinstone Institution in its first fifteen years. Of 152 graduates, seventy-one or nearly half were Prabhus, twenty-eight were Parsis, twelve were Saraswats, and only sixteen were members of other Brahmin castes.[32] The British were displeased that this group numbered no Gujarati Banias or Muslims, and almost no sons of the landed aristocracy. There were suggestions among them that the policy of imparting a literary culture was having little impact on the commercially and bureaucratically oriented students who dominated the schools.[33]

Had the British clearly foreseen the Chitpavan dominance of public life in the Desh in the last third of the century, they might have been equally dismayed by the fact that few Chitpavan students experienced Bombay's influence until well into the 1850's. The arrival of large numbers of Brahmin students in Ranade's time changed the pattern decisively, as Ranade himself preeminently demonstrated. Just as Ranade was joining the ranks of the English-educated in Bombay, a rapid shift occurred in the student composition of colleges there. Between 1856 and 1861 the number of scholars in English-language higher studies more than doubled, and nearly all of the additional students were either Parsis or Maharashtrian Brahmins.[34] A majority of them now were Bombay Parsis, and from this time onward the second largest group were Brahmins from various parts of the Konkan and the Desh. They were not from the wealthy landed aristocracy whom conservative British hoped to attract, but were in most cases sons of government clerks or educated Brahmins. As a group they were tied like Ranade to the British in two vital regards. They depended on the Raj first for scholarship grants during their student years and then for administrative careers thereafter.[35] Equally important, they represented not only the administrative elite but the cultural elite of Hindu society as well. They were more receptive than earlier students to the British vision of a class which would establish not only modern administration but Western civilization in the towns and countryside.

It was Sir Bartle Frere who expressed this vision most eloquently. As Governor of Bombay from 1860 he was Chancellor of the University at its first convocation in 1862, when Ranade and three others became its first graduates. In his speech to them Frere depicted the grand destiny and sober responsibility which awaited them. He saw their places in the university as a singular privilete designed to prepare them for service to their people.

> What is here taught is a sacred trust confided to you for the benefit of your countrymen. The learning which can here be imparted to a few hundreds, or at most to a few thousands, of scholars, must by you be made available through your own vernacular tongues to the many millions of Hindustan. . . . The character of your whole people is to a great extent in your hands.[36]

Ranade, the outstanding student in the first class, later remembered that Frere's annual addresses to the students were "state documents . . . rare treats, and their moral influence upon the hearts of the listeners will never fade away."[37] The other students shared Ranade's intense excitement at participating in one of the great adventures of the new age.

There were factors within the university itself which contributed to the prestige of the West. The early bachelor of arts syllabus included the major English authors in world history, English history and literature, the moral sciences, political economy, logic, mathematics, and natural sciences.[38] The academic atmosphere was further Anglicized when a reading room was established where the latest periodicals from England were available to all students.[39] There was also a sustained effort to staff the faculty with distinguished scholar-teachers from the universities of England and Scotland. These men were expected to cultivate sustained personal contact with their students, so as to exercise the pervasive moral and political influence of modern-day gurus.

The first graduating classes of the university produced probably the most illustrious group of scholars and statesmen ever to pass through its doors. Many of them were soon thereafter immersed together in a variety of campaigns to reform Indian society. As if to symbolize this new trend, the first four graduates in 1862 were two Chitpavans, Ranade and V. A. Modak, and two Saraswats, B. M. Wagle and R. G. Bhandarkar, both of whom worked closely with Ranade in the subsequent widow-marriage controversy and many other liberal campaigns in later years.

As a student Ranade was at every point first among equals in this company. He was associated with the university as student and then as teacher for its first twelve years, and during that time he compiled academic records which set university standards for many years.[40] In contrast to his merely competent record as a student in Kolhapur, he entered the first class to pass the university matriculation examination in 1859 and stood first when that class graduated in 1862. He thus gained the distinction of receiving the first B.A. ever granted by

Bombay University. In the following year he again stood first in the M.A. examination. Finally, he became the first law graduate of the university in 1866, passing the examination with his customary honors. By this time he was already a member of the teaching staff, having been named one of the first Dakshina Fellows of the university in recognition of his success in examinations. In return for a regular stipend Ranade had considerable tutoring responsibilities. He initially taught mathematics, logic and composition, but later spent most of his time teaching Indian and world history. This work provided him with the great breadth of competence which was the outstanding characteristic of his mature writings. He was also appointed as a university examiner for the college examinations of younger students. In this connection he was closely associated with several of his British professors, as well as several of the leading Indian scholar-reformers of his generation. Dadoba Pandurang, the leading religious reformer among Ranade's older contemporaries, was an examiner with him. M. M. Kunte, who later took a leading role in religious and social reform movements in Poona, was another.

The significance of Ranade's achievement was seen by the Vice-Chancellor, Sir Alexander Grant, who came closer than any other Englishman to becoming Ranade's guru. Grant was a distinguished scholar of the Greek classics who had recently come to Bombay from the University of Edinburgh to serve as professor of Greek history and literature and Director of Public Instruction. Grant was a champion of close relations between students and professors,[41] and he took particular interest in Ranade as a model scholar. In his annual report to the Director of Public Instruction in 1862-63, Grant praised Ranade's report of his past year's studies as demonstrating that both morally and intellectually Indian students were prepared for the trust placed in them. "As far as my experience goes, nothing can be more untrue than the common notion that English education is injurious to the moral principles of Natives. In the college I have invariably found that students improve in trustworthiness and respectability, in direct ratio to their improvement as scholars."[42] Ranade reciprocated Grant's praise; he reminisced many years later to a friend that his academic success was largely attributable to Grant, whose encouragement had given him the inspiration responsible for his own famed achievements.[43] The role which his father Govindrao had played in his childhood, that of exacting but honored taskmaster, was assumed in Bombay by Grant. In intensely personal form they embodied the polarity between Hinduism and the West which Ranade spent his life reconciling.

Ranade's success at the university was achieved as much by diligence as by innate brilliance. The steadfast determination of his childhood studies in Kolhapur was repeated in his university career, where his compulsively rigorous study habits soon became legendary. Several of his classmates later reminisced on his unremitting effort to master every detail of every subject. The familiar Ranade traits appear in the urbane Dinshaw Wacha's portrait:

> Unconscious himself, and unsophisticated in urban manners, he would sit on one of the benches with his massive legs stretched on the desk opposite, and would, turbanless, go on reading in a loud voice, from noon to dewy eve. He took no breath and no pause. His reading so absorbed him that he did not know what was passing around him. Dress or food never troubled him.[44]

Wacha remembered him as "simple in his habits . . . and above all fitted with a spirit of shyness which never left him till the day of his death."[45] The simplicity and modesty of manner which Wacha noticed resulted in Ranade's never being fully at ease in the social life of Bombay with its men of elegance, ostentation and brilliance. As R. G. Bhandarkar later wrote, "He never became very intimate with anybody, nor did he ever seek any introductions."[46]

One unanticipated testimony to Ranade's endless hours of reading was damage to his eyes. His sight failed almost entirely in 1862 and was never fully regained. For six months he was forced to live with bandages over his eyes and employ a student to read his lessons to him. Ranade's consolation was that his attending doctor was Dr. Bhau Daji, the most eminent Indian doctor of his time in Bombay and a leading member of the Bombay Royal Asiatic Society. Bhau Daji, author of numerous Indological studies, helped to stimulate Ranade's interest in the civilization of ancient India. Not long thereafter Ranade began his duties as a teacher of history.

These months of living with crippled eyesight also undoubtedly reinforced that strand of stoicism which had protected Ranade as a child from the vicissitudes of praise and censure. Ranade was defining for himself in this period nearly unattainable standards of excellence and thoroughness, in an effort to surpass the most rigorous standards which his superiors might set. His fellowship report for 1862-63 contained a list of his reading during the previous year whose length and complexity awed the other students.[47] Yet even here he prefaced his report with the apology that his weakened sight had been partially responsible for the inadequacy of his performance! This uncertainty about his own academic accomplishments was closely linked to his passionate regard for legitimate authority. In his report for 1863-64 he emphasized his nearly perfect attendance at classes, and added:

> The utmost I can hope now is to stay here a year more, and enjoy the protection and the privileged life of these walls. By that time I shall be qualified to be a candidate for the Bachelor of Laws Examination. If I am unhappily prevented from trying my chance sooner, I will no longer claim a protection for which I can make no worthy return.[48]

Self-punishing toil, doubt about his own adequacies in the face of his many solemn responsibilities, indifference to popular acclaim--all these aspects of Ranade's character as a student conditioned his later role as a leader in Maharashtrian society. Perhaps more fully than he himself knew, he had absorbed the moral earnestness and self-taxing conscience which was a common attribute of British public figures in Victorian times. In later years Ranade became known throughout India for his uniquely broad and balanced understanding of public issues. This reputation indicated the limits as well as the strengths of his public following: he was admired with a sentiment approaching awestruck reverence such as the public granted to solemn eminence. Those who knew him indicated that Ranade was never as approachable or immediately at ease with his followers as were some other leading figures of his time, nor did he inspire the enthusiasm of intimate familiarity which his later antagonist Bal Gangadhar Tilak did. Ranade's search for excellence and dispassion suited well his career in government and his efforts to construce modern public institutions for Maharashtra. But his affinity for scholarship and administration left him ill at ease with the turbulent conflicts and harsh rhetoric which accompanied the mass politics of his later years.

Ranade's preference for council chamber over market place reflected his adoption of Victorian British methods and philosophy of public life. For the factors which gave him this supporting ideological orientation, we must survey the content of his university studies. Here his extant writings express with singular vividness the transformation of a mofussil Brahmin into an Anglicized scholar-gentleman.

Ranade arrived in Bombay with the views of a Maharashtrian patriot which he had learned at home and in school in Kolhapur. In a competitive essay written in 1858 he revealed a view of his region's past which contained many of the themes familiar in later nationalist historiography of the region. This essay is one of the earliest extant examples of modern Maharashtra's self-image, all the more striking because of its unsophisticated manner. Wrestling with the intransigeant syntax of Victorian English, Ranade began:

> To write the history of one's own country is always a pleasing task. The felicity and the pleasure (though a little alloyed with pain when our former power and glory have departed from our nation, when the land knows not its sons for its Masters) are yet still great when one sits to write the rise and progress of his own nation.[49]

There was a poignant note to his patriotism, for he knew it was a time when Maharashtrian traditions were under attack. Ranade turned to the myth of a happier golden age as a compensation for the degradation of recent times. He continued:

> Misanthropy may like to brood over the mishaps which hastened the ruin, the pusillanimity and the dissensions which precipitated the downfall of one's own country. Amidst a sickness so deadly, and a destruction so complete, as now prevails through the land, a warm and patriotic bosom may prefer to breath [sic] for a time the purer air of more distant ages when wealth, honour, liberty were the possessions of his nation.[50]

In later years as Ranade travelled in other parts of India and worked with men from other regions, he began to draw on the cultural traditions of Bengal, the Punjab, and Tamilnad to enrich his sense of national identity. But in his student days his patriotism was exclusively Maharashtrian, and it centered on the figure of Shivaji. Envisioning a time before 1650 when Maharashtra had lain in subjection to the rule of the Mughal foreigners, Ranade described Shivaji and his followers as patriots whose self-sacrificing devotion to public duty swept the enemy from the land. The anti-Muslim tone of much Maharashtrian writing on Shivaji is present in Ranade's essay, as is an impulse to defend the whole fabric of Maharashtrian tradition against threats from the outside:

> When the intolerant followers of Mahomet confident in their complete conquest, believed in the utter prostration of their subjects, began as is customary with heated and bigoted nations to insult our prejudices, to kick at a distance our venerated idols, to rase [sic] to the dust our venerated temples and sanctuaries, to drive before our sight the humble, the useful (and still more the sacred) cow to the slaughter-house and to dash the gods to pieces for the treasures they contained, when thus our most venerated objects were used it roused the peasantry. And it was this peasantry (who had tilled the soil and fed their flocks in the country lying near the ghauts thus peacefully and contentedly so many years,) that became within a century the dreaded Marathas.51

British writers from Grant Duff onward, while fascinated with Shivaji, had portrayed him as a plundering opportunist. Challenging this bias, Ranade saw (both now and in the historical writings of his mature years) selfless patriotic dedication as the essential character of Shivaji and his lieutenants.

> Shivaji hoped that a persevering in his plans would at last prove to the Mahomedans their utter inability to hold the awakened country and force on them the necessity of abandoning the Kingdom. Thus originated the rise of the Maratha nation--a band of robbers (if robbery be the proper name for what Shivajee did) led by a successful chief laid the foundation of an immense empire. Shivajee was forced to rob for no other plan promised the slightest success under the eaglelike sight and tyranny of Aurungzebe. Shivajee lived to see his plans nearly realized. . . . The spirit had been awakened. All the former chiefs had tasted liberty and therefore were not willing to exchange it for slavery.52

Ranade was clearly considering suggestive parallels between the Mughals and the British Raj, the two foreign powers who had sought to humiliate his nation. His transparent implication in this essay became something of a cause célèbre in the college. Alexander Grant was indignant at the implied disloyalty and chastised Ranade by temporarily withdrawing his scholarship. Grant's next annual report stated that "the writer of one essay, Mahadev Govind, has thought fit to indulge in foolish and impertinent expressions about the Government which is educating him, and has forfeited the marks attached to the . . . essay."53 In compensation to Ranade he then added praise for an accompanying essay which he considered more restrained and perceptive. Faced with Grant's combined praise and discipline, Ranade quickly learned the limits of acceptable criticism of the regime; henceforth he practiced impeccable tact and moderation in dealing with his British superiors.

Juxtaposing these patriotic essays with Ranade's other writings of his undergraduate days we can sense his lifelong ambivalence between Maharashtrian pride and adherence to the glories of Western civilization. Basic to the Western glories was the "rule of law," without which no civic virtue might flourish. The university curriculum laid heavy emphasis on the study of classical Greece, whose history and philosophy were Grant's special subjects. In an essay 1859 he mirrored the British portrayal of the Greeks as "the most singular and intelligent people that inhabit or did inhabit" the earth, and suggested that the greatness of Greece derived from its republican constitution and active cultivation of civic responsibility.[54]

Even more than ancient Greece, modern England seemed the home of political genius. In 1858, in an ironic "Essay on William the Conqueror," Ranade fused his Indian patriotism with respect for English constitutionalism, musing on the theme of an inferior civilization submitting to the despotic but potentially just power of a superior nation. At the battle of Hastings the Saxon and Danish tribes "submitted without striking [any] blow for freedom," and in return the Conqueror granted them amnesty "with the moderation which characterizes all usurpers."[55] But amnesty was no compensation for the disaster which the landed aristocracy faced:

> The whole old landed proprietors [sic] were almost annihilated, and foreign upstarts raised in their stead. Not satisfied with ruining the proprietors or immovable property, he tried to ruin the others also. On the simple charge of rebellion versus the state he desolated the whole country between the Humber and the Tyne. . . . What a degraded state must man have reached when he succumbed . . . under such a galling and intolerable tyranny.

No military rule, whether indigenous or foreign, could be beneficent in itself, but at least a higher level of civilization might gradually emerge. Ranade wrote didactically of William I that "although his reign considered in itself was surpassed by none in atrocity yet as good cometh out of evil so his reign was beneficial in its results." The results included the introduction of more polished manners into England, the infusion of new and badly needed words into the language, the advantages of foreign commerce, and the seeds of revolt against military rule.

> Finally it made the British what they are. This severity of his reign and that of his successors too created in the mind of the British such an abhorrence of despotism as has been nowhere seen. It enabled them to demand the Magna Charta, to enforce the assembling of Parliament and in short to defend the Right of Man. In conclusion it is William's invasion and his reign only and no others that enables the modern Briton to defy the whole world.

Central to these notions was the view of the present as a transitional era, in which alien rule, though basically objectionable, was at least paving the way toward self-rule and liberal constitutionalism, the political benchmarks of modernity. England of course seemed the model of constitutionalism at home, however authoritarian she had to be in

India. She provided an example for future generations which even other European nations had not yet achieved.

Ranade's views of continental Europe during this time indicate by contrast how effective his teachers were in communicating anglocentric values. Ranade's student essays on continental Europe were almost invariably derogatory. On one occasion in 1858 he claimed that on the continent "the great principles of government [are] totally unknown. [That] those who obey laws have authority to change or modify them, those who are taxed must be represented, that power rests with the people, are principles totally lost sight of by all continental countries of Europe."[56] Again in 1861 he decried the lack of self-reliance in French society specifically:

> The French colonies have suffered on account of the excessive patronage the French monarchs were pleased to extend towards them--which crippled all self-energy and reliance. I think the French colony in Canada to be a success. Perhaps it is on account of Canada being an English dependency. . . . Moreover the French are always desirous to make political capital out of their possessions. They will settle in Algiers not for the same reason that the English settle in New Zealand or New Holland--but to turn the Mediterranean into a French Lake.[57]

Ranade's praise of the principles of English government had within it the seeds of discontent over the actual practices of the British, especially in their Indian empire. But in most of his early essays he rather naïvely accepted the British self-evaluation as patently disinterested. This uncritical attitude would not stand unequivocally for long against Ranade's accumulating experience, but one element of it never left him. The paternalistic idea that India must be ruled as a trust for its silent millions was to be as useful a rationale for Ranade and his Western-educated contemporaries as it was for the British. This in turn expressed another traditional value of the Whig liberalism which underlay both his cultural background and his political perspective: the assumption that self-rule for a society meant government by those leading classes who best understood the people's interests. From his earliest essays onward, Ranade frequently articulated the usual respect of his age for the landed aristocracy, the "natural leaders" of the people, as well as for the educated. As his later life revealed, he saw little conflict between this social conservatism and the liberal belief in self-government. His subsequent career can be seen as the construction of a grand strategy to weld together the traditional aristocracy and the new educated elite into the governing class of a new India.

This complex evolution of society and politics would require many years under British tutelage. For justification of this assumption, Ranade was becoming an Indian counterpart of John Stuart Mill, the most influential liberal theorist of the 1860's. Mill's essays, On Representative Government and On Liberty, which were becoming known in Bombay, reinforced the growing belief that representative institutions would not be feasible in India for some time to come.[58] By the 1860's Ranade clearly shared the ambivalent liberalism of this tradition. In a review of Frere's administration in Bombay, he wrote of the early British rulers in India that their

> tremendous power for working mischief was joined to a resolute determination to hold that power as a trust,--a benignant black cloud which intervened to protect the country from evils worse than anarchy, and which in its own time would dissolve after vivifying the land with the seeds of a higher and manlier life. Strong personal Government thus found favour with them as being most in accordance with native habits, and the exigencies of foreign sway. Graduated authority, the division of the functions of sovereignty, free admission to the natives of the country to advise and co-operate in their government as unfranchised fellow-subjects,--these wants of the present times are of later growth, and it will be years before these ideas take deep root in the soil. This generous ambition to help the native population to elevate themselves, to teach them self-reliance and the strength of lawful combination, animates only a few of the more advanced Indian statesmen even in the present day, notably Frere himself.[59]

By 1870 Ranade had had enough experience with the realities of British administration to share the reformers' discontent over the lack of Indian representation in the government, but he still accepted his teachers' view that Indians must be far better prepared to accept political responsibility before they could be granted representation. He shared with Mill both the ultimate ideal of representative government and the belief that the critical weaknesses of Indian society included its lack of individual dignity and self-reliance and its lack of experience in running a constitutional government.

The Apprenticeship in Administration and Politics

By 1866 Ranade's formal education was complete. In the ten years since he had arrived in Bombay, he had adopted many British perspectives on India's condition. The 1860's were the most fully Anglicized years of his life, yet the second half of the decade differed decisively from the first. Until 1866 his life had been sheltered within the university's walls. In the following five years he began to test his adopted world view against the realities of administrative responsibility and political action.

With the completion of his studies Ranade was appointed in 1866, at the age of twenty-four, to be karbhari of the former princely state of Akalkot. Akalkot was a small state southeast of Sholapur which dated from the early days of the Peshwas.[60] In 1866 the British deposed the degenerate ruler and assumed the administration of the state, appointing Ranade as its first chief administrator.[61] Little is known of the year he spent in Akalkot, but some significant incidents have been preserved relating to his transfer a year later to a similar post in his old home of Kolhapur. In 1867 Ranade was appointed karbhari in that more important state, and further judicial responsibilities were added to his duties a few months later when he was promoted to nyayadhish.[62]

These two years' experience in the administration of princely states took Ranade back to the mofussil for the first time in a decade. Here he faced his first opportunity to test his political views, and on the whole they showed their durability. In contrast with the years of his childhood, he was now in mofussil towns as a representative of the British system, pledged to uphold that system rigorously. There were subtle difficulties in his way, for unlike Bombay the old Maharashtrian towns forced upon him complex conflicts of social status. Ranade's father Govindrao had returned to Kolhapur in 1862 from another position to become secretary to the Maharaja, a post which he held five years later when his son returned home. In 1868, shortly after Ranade's reappearance, his grandfather Amritrao died. As the new head of the family, Govindrao held personal authority over his returned son, although the son's official status was superior to the father's. Facing an irreducible status conflict, the younger Ranade chose to arrive at his office before anyone else each morning so as to avoid the dilemma of bowing to his father or not, in passing the older man's desk.[63]

This symbolic conflict pointed to more concrete conflicts of interest as well. Ranade was aware of the difficulty of working where his father was well known. He feared that in Kolhapur he might be compromised by requests for special favors from his father's influential friends. To guard against misunderstanding he announced to his father on arriving that there must be absolute impartiality in his work. When one friend came to Ranade's house to discuss his side of a pending lawsuit, Ranade refused to see him, despite the social embarrassment which his father consequently faced.[64] Ranade felt the pain of being caught between the old system and the new: when a question of public probity arose, as with the neighbor who came to talk, he was uncompromisingly impartial. However, when a conflict arose between official propriety and deference to his father, Ranade made every effort to circumvent the dilemma. In the following years he was not always able to resist the claims of tradition in his family life, even though these claims sometimes violated his firmest social principles and weakened his standing as a leader of the reformers.

Ranade's experience in the politics of princely states ultimately produced a similar tension in his writing between traditional and British values. His later articles on the administration of the states express sympathy with their autonomy, balanced by an eagerness that they emulate the British system. This perspective repeated the principles which Ranade's political mentors, Elphinstone and Frere, had always pursued. Many of the states, as he well knew, were corrupt and inefficient, and he believed that adopting Western ways was their only means of self-preservation. By now he had firsthand experience of resistance to new ways in the societies of Akalkot and Kolhapur. The difficulties attending his work there may have influenced his decision to turn down several invitations later in his career from greater princely states, which frequently tried to enlist him as either chief justice or prime minister.

After less than a year in Kolhapur Ranade resigned his post and returned to Bombay. He went back to his academic pursuits as Assistant Professor of English and History at Elphinstone College, where he remained for three years. During this time he finished his legal studies and an apprenticeship as reporter at the High Court. In early 1871 he passed the Bombay advocates' examination which qualified him to practice law in Presidency courts. Rather than taking up private practice, Ranade chose to enter the judicial branch of the government, following his family and caste tradition of government service. His biographer and associate in the judicial department, G. A. Mankar, speculated later that Ranade's decision was taken also because a judgeship was a safer and more regular form of employment.[65] However that may be, Ranade would not have felt comfortable facing the social demands of a private practice, and the lucrative possibilities of that profession had no appeal for him.

It soon became clear that he had chosen wisely. In his early years his progress up the judicial ladder was more rapid than that of any Indian judge before him in Bombay Presidency. He was appointed to the Small Cause Court of Bombay in early 1871, and the following November he was transferred to the Small Cause Court in Poona, a position which he retained for many years. As a Small Cause judge Ranade was granted first-class rank at the early age of twenty-nine, in contrast with most Indian judges, who spent many years before rising above second-class rank.[66]

The work of the Small Cause Court was well suited to Ranade's propensities as a judge. The court dealt with civil suits involving sums under Rs. 1000. Its presiding judge was given unusual breadth of discretion in settling disputes; the court was therefore separate from the regular judicial system. Because of its emphasis on equity rather than the mechanical application of law in determining the judge's decisions, the government was reluctant to offer the position to Indian judges. Ranade was the exceptional case. Some of his Indian colleagues, notably K. T. Telang who was to precede him on the Bombay High Court, established reputations for total command of the detail of Hindu law. Ranade's strength lay more in his application of the principles of equity. His superiors often pointed to his consistently reliable discretion as his most valuable service.

Their trust in appointing him to the Small Cause Court was demonstrated from the time he first took up his duties, for on the court he had the daily experience of adjudicating cases presented by English barristers.[67] This was concrete experience of the Queen's pledge in 1858 that Indians and Englishmen would be treated alike by the government of India. Here was the policy standard; the moments of Ranade's most bitter disillusionment with the British in later life arose when he believed they were betraying their own cherished principles. Fortunately he never lost the trust of his judicial superiors in his integrity, even when the executive officers of the government and their allies in the press doubted his political loyalty.[68]

As he began his career in government, Ranade experienced a benign regime. He had not as yet begun to probe the limits of its tolerance of criticism. His discovery of how narrow this tolerance was emerged over the following decade, through his work with the political associations of Bombay and later of Poona. There were restraints on Ranade's ability to participate actively in organizations designed to influence official policy. As a government servant he was required to abstain from any agitation which severely criticized the government. But to an extent which many have called unequalled in his time, Ranade insisted on playing the dual role of servant and critic. He and his contemporaries saw voluntary organizations as the reasonable embodiment of the principle which they had learned in the university: that Indians should gradually learn to take responsibility themselves for public life. The liberal tradition from Macaulay onwards had implicitly foreseen the emergence of organized interest groups as an outgrowth of higher education in English. Yet most British had anticipated that educated Indians would serve the government so as to implement policies handed down from their superiors. It was a different matter when the educated class organized movements outside the government's aegis and designed to pass judgment on its policies.

The first political associations in Bombay were largely very discreet and decorous, dominated as they were by the same commercial interests which collaborated intimately with the British. The rather scanty record of Ranade's participation in them between 1869 and 1871 indicates that he shared this caution as he painstakingly learned the details of political organizing from the political leaders of the city. As yet he took no independent initiatives, for the implications of a government servant's working closely with its critics were still unclear. In any case, Ranade was only an apprentice, whereas the leading citizens of Bombay had been actively constructing associational life for years.

The first of Bombay's modern political associations, the Bombay Association, had been active for three years from 1852 to 1854. It was founded to articulate Indian interests to the government at the time of the East India Company's charter renewal. As its constitution defined its ambitious aim, "The object of this Association shall be to ascertain the wants of the Natives of India living under the Government of this Presidency, and to represent, from time to time, to the authorities, measures calculated to advance the welfare and improvement of the country."[69]

The Bombay Association strove to be more than the mouthpiece of a particular interest in the community. Later, during the 1870's, Bombay and other cities saw the rapid rise of professional groups and, far more important, caste associations whose chief purpose was to champion the limited interests of specific social groups.[70] In those years political action penetrated to wider segments of the populace, but at the expense of universality. The Bombay Association in the 1850's at least claimed to represent all Bombay with one voice. It included members of various communities and was sensitive to British scepticism about its representing a broad segment of the populace. At the second annual meeting one of the Parsi founders articulated these beginnings of the search for national political unity as he pointed out the large numbers of Hindus and Muslims as well as Parsis present: "With what pleasure do we not witness for the first time a cordial and sincere union of the Parsis, Hindus, and Mahomedans of respectability and intelligence."[71]

Nonetheless the association was effectively dominated by the Parsi and Hindu shets whose commercial alliance with the British presupposed political caution. Preoccupied with trade and other local issues, they were staunch defenders of the Raj. Typically, their work resulted in discreet requests for more widespread employment in the government. For example, in a petition of 1852 the association suggested to the Presidency government that "the cost of administration in India is unnecessarily great and great reductions might be made . . . by abolishing sinecure offices,"[72] which were largely held by Englishmen.

In financial issues such as this the association's memorials held the seed of the broader political conflicts which Ranade understood by 1870. As early as 1852 Dadabhai Naoroji, the rising spokesman of the young Western-educated generation and Ranade's lifelong associate,[73] sounded a more challenging note. He asserted in a speech to the association that British officers were generally ignorant of conditions in India. He then suggested ominously that the British were doomed to ineffectiveness unless a larger number of Indians held genuinely influential positions in government.[74] Twenty years later Ranade broadened this critique into the more far-reaching assertion that since Indians were always more familiar with their society than were Englishmen, they were better qualified to understand their country's needs.

The early Bombay Association did not become a vehicle for the younger, more impatient generation. Differences of orientation between them and the senior shets prevented the association from speaking with a unified or sustained voice for Indian opinion in Bombay.[75] A first attempt had been made to fuse the interests of various groups in a common platform, yet the diversity of Bombay's social and political interests insured that no single group could mobilize a disciplined segment of the population behind a steady political challenge to the British.

After thirteen years of intermittent activity, the years which coincided with Ranade's education in Bombay, the shets revived the Bombay Association in 1867. They were careful this time to enlist the support of the growing Western-educated class by admitting a number of young.

lawyers and others.[76] The association also adopted a bolder tone on some issues, such as criticizing the Indian Civil Service for excluding Indians from its ranks in violation of the principles affirmed by the Queen's Proclamation of 1858.[77] It was at this point that Ranade joined the association in 1869, after his return from Kolhapur. He began contributing financially in 1870, and from 1871 was a non-resident member of the managing committee for several years.[78] By now the Bombay leaders saw him as a rising star among Maharashtrian Brahmins and an important link with the affairs of Poona. But Ranade's direct participation in the Bombay Association was necessarily limited. His claim to influence rested on his leadership in the educated class which was only a minor partner in the association, and as a Maharashtrian Brahmin from the mofussil he had no caste constituency in the city. His roots were elsewhere, and like the educated class as a whole he was concerned with broader political issues than the purely local matters which the Bombay Association dealt with.

Far more congenial to Ranade's temper and position was the Bombay Branch of the East India Association, founded in 1869 by Dadabhai Naoroji and others to publicize the needs of India to Parliament and the English people. Unlike the Bombay Association, the East India Association had an all-India program; its broader range of politically sensitive positions attracted many recent graduates of the university. True to his administrator's instincts Ranade was a founding member of the Managing Committee. His work was mostly behind the scenes, presumably both to protect his position within the government and to express his personal reluctance to dominate the public platform. The most notable public record of his work is the text of a rather conventional speech which he gave to the members in 1871. He reviewed the chief function of the branch as raising money for the work in London and in providing England with persuasive facts and suggestions regarding public questions in India. At first the effort had been a failure because "the sympathy of the public . . . was not shown in a manner to encourage spontaneous action. The public seemed to be listless and indifferent on these points."[79] There were reasons for optimism, however; Ranade expressed pleasure that funds were coming from a variety of sources, including the southern Maratha sardars.

> All this shows that the sympathy for the work of the East India Association is not confined to the classes who have partaken of the benefit of an English education, but that the leading Chiefs and Princes of India, either of their own accord, or under the guidance of wise ministers, have come to perceive that the usefulness of the East India Association for promoting the interests of India was great beyond measure.[80]

Significantly, Ranade's speech revealed no strong personal views. He was working systematically in the cause of liberal politics, but he had not yet found an effective base of operations. It was only when he moved to Poona in 1871 and found the smaller city lacking in Western-educated leadership that he became a powerful and independent voice. As long as he stayed in Bombay he was still young in a city where there was already mature leadership for well-organized non-Maharashtrian constituencies. Poona lacked such a network, but its public life was dominated by his own caste. Ranade had the necessary qualifications by now to fill the political vacuum there: experience in financing and organizing associational politics, established friendships with the political elite of western India, a maturing ideology to justify liberal constitutionalism, and concrete experience of factionalism and the resulting need to forge coalitions of diverse interests.

Ranade's commitment to moderation and coalition was based not only in political events, however. During the late 1860's he became even more active in the sphere of social reform, where divisions in Hindu society were even more rancorous than in politics. One of the ironies of his career was the fact that he was immediately accepted as a political spokesman in Poona, within a year after he first confronted that city as a vigorous proponent of Brahmin social reform. In his social liberalism he was even more decisively influenced by his student years in Bombay than in his political views, and he arrived in Poona in the controversial role of critic of Hindu traditionalism. In the social reform movement he had become a more belligerent crusader than in any other sphere; his transition to the role of a cautious, diplomatic reformer was nearly as abrupt as his transfer from Bombay to Poona. The transformation in Ranade's experience was to reveal how vast the difference was between the society of Bombay and that of Poona.

Notes

[1] See Holden Furber, *Bombay Presidency in the Mid-Eighteenth Century* (Bombay, 1965).

[2] M. D. Morris, *The Emergence of an Industrial Labor Force in India: A Study of the Bombay Cotton Mills, 1854-1947* (Berkeley, 1965), ch. ii, traces the early economic development of Bombay.

[3] D. F. Karaka, *History of the Parsis* (London, 1884).

[4] For further background, see Kenneth L. Gillion, *Ahmedabad* (Berkeley, 1968), chs. i-ii.

[5] Christine Dobbin, *Urban Leadership in Western India* (Oxford, 1972), ch. i.

[6] For typical examples, see *Dnyanoday*, July 1, 1850, p. 247; and November 1, 1852, p. 338.

[7] See, for example, the lectures of Krishna Shastri Sathe in Bombay, 1852-53, as reported in *Dnyanoday*, beginning in October 1852. For the broader context of these discussions, see Richard P. Tucker, "Hindu Orthodoxy and Nationalist Ideologies in Maharashtra, 1850-80," *Modern Asian Studies*, forthcoming.

[8] For the background of this development, see Percival Spear, *The Nabobs* (London, 1963).

[9] See, for example, Bombay's reluctance to implement Bentinck's directive on sati. Ballhatchet, *Social Policy*, pp. 275-305.

[10] For details of Wilson's career, see George Smith, *The Life of John Wilson* (London, 1878).

[11] John Wilson, *Indian Caste* (Bombay & London, 1877).

[12] Kumar, *Western India*, ch. iii.

[13] G. B. Malleson, *A History of the Indian Mutiny, 1857-59* (London, 1880), III, 23; Sinha, *Bhonslas*, ch. xii.

[14] Jacob, *Western India*, pp. 147-156; T. R. E. Holmes, *The Indian Mutiny* (London, 1891), ch. xiii.

[15] The most complete study is J. M. Surlacar, "1857 in Maharashtra" (Ph.D. diss., University of Bombay, 1964).

[16] Jacob, *Western India*, pp. 147-151.

[17] Charles Forjett, *Our Real Danger in India* (London, 1877), pp. 100ff.

[18] Dinshaw Wacha, *Shells from the Sands of Bombay* (Bombay, 1920), pp. 76ff.

[19] Quoted in Atul Chandra Banerjee, *Indian Constitutional Documents*, 3rd ed. (Calcutta, 1961), II, 26-28.

[20] Smith, *Life of John Wilson*, p. 511.

[21] *Elphinstone School Paper*, February 1860, p. 79.

[22] Morris, *Emergence of an Industrial Labor Force*, pp. 24-26; R. P. Masani, *Evolution of Self-Government in Bombay* (London, 1929), p. 173.

[23] W. W. Hunter, *Bombay: 1885-1890* (London, 1892), p. 234.

[24] M. G. Ranade, "Introduction" to *The Speeches and Addresses of Sir H. B. Frere*, ed. Balkrishna Nilaji Pitale (Bombay, 1870), p. x.

[25] Frere, *Speeches*, p. 263.

[26] Ranade, "Introduction" to Frere, *Speeches*, p. viii.

[27] Ibid.

[28] The conflict between spiritual and secular aims was never so sharp in Bombay as it sometimes became in Calcutta during these years. See

David Kopf, *British Orientalism and the Bengal Renaissance* (Berkeley, 1969), pp. 116-124.

[29] See Ballhatchet, *Social Policy*, pp. 248-275. And for a rigorous analysis of the educational system which resulted over the years, see McDonald, "English Education," pp. 453-470.

[30] W. T. DeBary, ed., *Sources of Indian Tradition* (New York, 1958), p. 601.

[31] Dobbin, *Urban Leadership*, pp. 27-33.

[32] *Ibid.*, p. 31.

[33] *Ibid.*, pp. 31-35.

[34] See statistics in the annual volumes of *RDPI*.

[35] *RDPI*, 1861-62, pp. 106-108.

[36] Frere, *Speeches*, p. 110.

[37] Ranade, "Introduction" to Frere, *Speeches*, p. xiii.

[38] *RDPI*, 1856-57, pp. 25-28.

[39] Wacha, *Shells*, p. 675.

[40] G. A. Mankar, *A Sketch on the Life and Works of the Late Mr. Justice M. G. Ranade* (Bombay, 1902), I, 23-26. Greater detail on Ranade's progress through the university can be traced in the annual volumes of *RDPI*.

[41] As he put it in 1863: "On the learning of the professors in the colleges of the Presidency the success of the Bombay University depends, and how much depends on the success of the University. Little else than the regeneration of the minds of the people. When it is reflected that the native University students furnish, or will ere long furnish, the school teachers, the pleaders, the practitioners of European medicine, the subordinate revenue and judicial officers, the overseers of public works, and above all, the newspaper writers, who are constantly disseminating, wise or foolish, disaffected or loyal, criticisms of the acts of Government, it cannot but be felt that it is of the utmost importance that the fountainhead of all this stream of influence, namely, the professors and principals of colleges, should be as high and as pure as possible. Without solid and special learning in the professors there is no saying what subversive sentiments may become associated with European learning." Quoted in Bruce T. McCully, *English Education and the Origins of Indian Nationalism* (New York, 1940), p. 158n.

[42] *RDPI*, 1862, p. 94.

[43] T. V. Parvate, *Mahadeo Govind Ranade: A Biography* (Bombay, 1963), p. 15.

[44] Dinsha E. Wacha, "Introduction" to *The Miscellaneous Writings of the Late Hon'ble Mr. Justice M. G. Ranade* (Bombay, 1915), p. vi.

[45] *Ibid.*

[46] Parvate, *Ranade*, p. 10.

[47] The full list is printed in Mankar, *Ranade*, I, 28-32.

[48] *RDPI*, 1863, p. 115.

[49] M. G. Ranade, "English Essay Beta," *Elphinstone School Paper*, May 1858, p. 53.

[50] *Ibid.*, p. 54.

[51] *Ibid.*, p. 55.

[52] *Ibid.*, p. 56.

[53] *RDPI*, 1857-58, p. 5.

[54] M. G. Ranade, "The Progress of Mankind in Civilization," December 12, 1859, in "Second Essay Book" (unpublished).

⁵⁵This and the following quotations are from "An Essay on the Reign of William the Conqueror, Its Character and Its Effects upon the Future History of England," June 23, 1858, in "First Essay Book" (unpublished).

⁵⁶"Compare the Civilization of Ancient Greece and Modern Europe," 1858, in "First Essay Book."

⁵⁷M. G. Ranade, essay for Senior Scholarship examination, Elphinstone College, April 20, 1861, RDPI, 1860-61, p. 62.

⁵⁸Eric Stokes, The English Utilitarians and India (Oxford, 1959), pp. 252-253.

⁵⁹Ranade, "Introduction" to Frere, Speeches, p. vii.

⁶⁰Malleson, Historical Sketch of the Native States of India, p. 366.

⁶¹Gazetteer of the Bombay Presidency, Vol. XX: Kolhapur (Bombay, 1885), 509-510.

⁶²M. G. Ranade, Statistics of Criminal Justice in the Bombay Presidency (Bombay, 1874), p. 35.

⁶³An incident which Ranade related to G. K. Gokhale, who passed it on to R. P. Paranjpye. Recounted by Paranjpye in a speech at Poona University, February 7, 1964.

⁶⁴Ramabai Ranade, Reminiscences, pp. 17-18.

⁶⁵Mankar, Ranade, I, 35.

⁶⁶Conversation with the Hon. V. A. Naik, Associate Justice of the Bombay High Court, February 4, 1965.

⁶⁷See the scattered reports of cases over which Ranade presided; in Times of India during these months.

⁶⁸See below, pp. 91-95.

⁶⁹Bombay Association, Minutes of the Proceedings of the Founding Meeting (Bombay, 1852), p. 11.

⁷⁰Dobbin, Urban Leadership, chs. viii-x.

⁷¹Bombay Association, Minutes of the Proceedings of the Second Annual General Meeting, January 1855 (Bombay, 1855), p. 4.

⁷²Bombay Association, Petition to Parliament, 1852 (Bombay, 1852), p. 10.

⁷³R. P. Masani, Dadabhai Naoroji (London, 1939).

⁷⁴Bombay Association, Founding Meeting, pp. 17-18.

⁷⁵James C. Masselos, Towards Nationalism (Bombay, 1974), pp. 51-52.

⁷⁶Dobbin, Urban Leadership, pp. 88-90.

⁷⁷Bombay Association, Minutes of a . . . Public Meeting . . . on March 5, 1868 (Bombay, 1868), p. vi.

⁷⁸See the annual reports of the association for these years.

⁷⁹Journal of the East India Association, Bombay Branch, V (1871), 11-14.

⁸⁰Ibid., p. 12.

Chapter 3

THE REFORM BATTLES OF 1859-1875

> One resolute pull and the bonds
> of centuries will be shattered
> into harmless toys.
> --Vishnu Shastri Pandit

It would be mistaken to suggest, as some authors have, that Ranade's career as a public servant was the center of gravity in his life. To be sure, he was to attract both increasing prestige and increasing criticism over the years for his role in government, and the political context of his other work became an increasingly determinative factor as time went on. But this was only one level of his experience. Even at the outset of his public life Ranade insisted that politics and administration were only the surface of a much broader movement, the total effort to remodel Indian culture in line with the pressures of modernity. His duties and powers as an employee of the government were strictly limited, whereas his duties, if not his power, as an emerging leader of Hindu society were potentially far broader. He and the other members of the new Western-educated elite were responsible in a way that no outsider could be for reforming the fabric of their own society; without that transformation they understood that even their limited political goals were unattainable and their criticisms of the British regime were built on quicksand.

The Moral Foundations of Reform

The English-language colleges from very early in their development encouraged their students to become active social reformers. Not long after its founding in 1815, the Bombay Education Society organized a debating society which discussed issues of social reform and mass education. Like other cultural institutions initiated by the British, its founding members included Englishmen, Parsis and Hindus. The dominant Indian member was Bal Shastri Jambhekar, whose brilliant academic career in the 1820's and 1830's and multiple efforts in journalism and social reform during his subsequent short career provided a powerful model.[1]

The Native Improvement Association was reconstituted in 1848 as the Students' Literary and Scientific Society, which became the chief means of recruiting student reformers in Bombay for many years. Bombay University professors were its guiding lights, and during the 1850's the society's Indian officers included many of the men whose names appear prominently in the social and religious reform organizations of the same years. It was thus no accident that participants were imbued with a missionary zeal to elevate the backward masses around them.[2] At the society's monthly meetings students read papers (in English) on a broad range of religious, social, moral and scientific topics, since scientific reason and rigorous morality were considered twin doors to the modern age. The society was a hothouse in which students could test their radical ideas in temporary isolation from the surrounding city. One of Ranade's fellow students later reminisced on their sense of living in a closed and purposeful community: "We were like members of a small family, inspired with a joint-family desire of working for the good of the compact body, which cannot be the case when the numbers are overflowing."[3] The debating society intensified their enthusiasm. As early as a meeting in 1852 one speaker articulated their social attitudes by pointing to "that sluggish and indolent disposition which keeps the people of this place aloof from the Society;--making it as it were an oasis in the desert, where alone a resting-place is found for parched pilgrims in their search after knowledge."[4]

The florid rhetoric of their meetings did not prevent the students' society from initiating concrete and controversial educational reform programs. It opened several vernacular primary schools, including girls' schools. In 1862 it declared its support for equal education for women, and by that year it was supporting nine free schools for women.[5] In order to assist the government in stocking the schools with books, the society translated and published vernacular textbooks and other materials at a time when very little vernacular material was published.[6]

Like most leading students of Bombay University, Ranade was an active member of the society for several years after 1859. The papers he presented at the monthly meetings have not been preserved; only the titles of some of them have been recorded. They include: "The Duties of Educated Young Men" (1859), "The Future Prospects of the Marathas and the Bengalees Compared" (1863), and "The Theory of Population" (1864).[7] The titles alone indicate the combined evangelical and utilitarian content of their cultural offensive.

In order to reach a broad segment of the educated public, Ranade like other reformers turned simultaneously to journalism. Here too, Jambhekar established the pattern when in 1831 he founded the first native newspaper in Bombay, the short-lived Mumbai Durpun (Bombay Mirror) and dedicated it to spreading Western knowledge among his countrymen.[8] The most influential Bombay reform newspaper of Ranade's time, Indu Prakash (Moonlight), was founded in 1862 by the well-known Brahmin reformer, Gopal Hari Deshmukh, or "Lokahitawadi," the Advocate of the People's Welfare, as he called himself. Like the Mumbai Durpun, the Indu Prakash was bilingual in Marathi and English. The first Marathi editor was Vishnu Shastri Pandit, who emerged as the leader of the widow-remarriage movement later in the decade. Ranade accepted an invitation to edit the English columns, a singular honor for a student barely twenty years old.[9] This post marked the beginning of Ranade's close lifelong cooperation with both Vishnu Shastri and Lokahitawadi. Ranade was forced by family affairs and the pressure of studies to resign the editorship after a few months, but he continued to write articles for the paper for a few years afterward. Again the extant titles of his articles give some indication of a scope which mirrored the university curriculum: "The Anniversary of the Battle of Panipat," "Maharaja Scindia," "The Cotton Fraud Bill," "India in England," "Bengalee Journals," "Christianity in America," and "Government and Idolatry."[10]

But whether through schools or newspapers, the educational reform crusade was only the surface of a deeper commitment which Ranade held in common with many of the Bombay reformers. In itself, the secular education of the new era threatened to destroy all moral and spiritual values, whether Hindu or Western, especially when its Benthamite elements came to the fore. The challenge then was to reform secular society while reinforcing spiritual values. Many of the reformers resolved this challenge by participating in religious reform organizations as well. As a student Ranade was not directly active in the life of reformed Hinduism, but he entered both the social and religious reform movements actively on his return from Kolhapur in 1869. Both movements were then in the process of reorganization. He found the Prarthana Samaj, or Prayer Society, Bombay's religious association for liberal Hindus, more cautious in its criticisms of Hindu society than its missionary acquaintances might have wished. This resulted in large part from the experience gained from the Prarthana Samaj's antecedents, most notably the Paramahamsa Sabha (usually translated as the Eclectic Society), which was founded in Bombay in 1848.[11] The earlier sabha's founders were inspired in part by Christian missionaries. One leading member, Atmaram Pandurang, was a close friend of John Wilson, and other founders were in intimate social contact with other British educators and missionaries. More important, perhaps, the sabha's members saw themselves as Bombay's iconoclastic counterparts of De Rozio and Young Bengal in Calcutta. The Paramahamsa Sabha practiced intercaste dining at dinners prepared by non-Hindu cooks. Members signed pledges opposing idolatry; it is said they were evicted by the owner of their meeting room when he discovered their purposes. In retaliation they broke into his home at night and overturned his family gods.[12] Such bold violations of traditional dharma necessitated that they keep their membership and activities semi-secret, though orthodox society was aware of what seemed a dangerous atheistic plot. The sabha seems to have grown steadily, however; it claimed to have established branch societies in Poona, Ahmednagar and other towns with a total membership of some five hundred by 1860. Disaster struck in that year when a member revealed the sabha's membership. The resulting uproar in orthodox society destroyed the sabha within a few weeks.[13] Ranade could hardly have missed the scandal, for he was then at Elphinstone College under the tutorial guidance of some of the sabha's members.

After 1860 there was no reformed Hindu organization in Bombay until the Prarthana Samaj was founded in 1867, far less iconoclastic or belligerent than the Paramahamsa Sabha. The Prarthana Samaj was organized only under prodding from the Brahmo Samaj of Bengal. Under the leadership of Keshub Chander Sen in the 1860's, the Brahmo Samaj began to send missionaries to propagate their cause in other parts of India. Keshub himself visited Bombay in 1864, encouraging the formation of a Brahmo Samaj out of the remnants of the Paramahamsa Sabha. Bombay was obsessed with the cotton market boom at the time, and had little time for spiritual matters. The new samaj was founded only after Keshub's second visit in 1867, on his return from a triumphal tour of England.

The Prarthana Samaj first met that March in the home of Dadoba Pandurang. Dadoba, his two brothers and fourteen friends, most of whom had been active members of the Paramahamsa Sabha, were the founding circle.[14] Its membership from then onward was entirely Maharashtrian, though it had financial support from numerous Parsi and Gujarati Bania sympathizers. Nearly all the active members were Chitpavans and Saraswats, and they included almost every close Maharashtrian associate whom Ranade had in the political affairs of Bombay.[15]

Sen hoped that the Prarthana Samaj would become a branch of the Brahmo Samaj, and relations between the Calcutta and Bombay groups were cordial. P. C. Mozumdar, the Brahmo Samaj missionary, made regular visits to Bombay, assisting reformers there with organizational activities. He was associated with most of their educational efforts, giving public lectures and conducting classes for as long as six months at a time.[16] Nevertheless, the Prarthana Samaj carefully maintained its separate identity, and never joined the Brahmo Samaj. The Brahmos had long since split off from orthodox Bengali society, becoming a separate and religiously isolated sect. The Prarthana Samaj was determined not to follow that path, for its members had already attempted that course once, with dismal results. By now they were older and more pragmatic. As one commentator later suggested, "In Bombay's heterogeneous population there were degrees of revolt from tradition and custom, and great caution was exercised not to drive away any of them" from the new samaj.[17]

In contrast with the Paramahamsa Sabha's fascination with symbolic details of dharma, the Prarthana Samaj under Dadoba's leadership emphasized the importance of social amelioration. In principle they still denounced the caste system and idolatry, but like Christian evangelicals they expressed their piety through social action, advocating widow remarriage and women's education and an end to child marriage.[18] Many of them had been members of the Students' Literary and Scientific Society; hence the schools were one of their major concerns. By 1876 the samaj was supervising three night schools with some forty low-caste students. It opened girls' schools as well, but had little success in finding either students or teachers.[19]

This emphasis reflected another contrast between the Prarthana Samaj and its Bengali forebears. The older generation in the samaj, the men around Dadoba, failed to develop a systematic philosophy like that of the Brahmos. Their creed was little more than the Paramahamsa Sabha's opposition to caste and idolatry, and this was a major weakness in an age of acute ideological controversies. The samaj came of age as a religious organization only after Ranade and other young university graduates joined it.[20] Only they had an adequate educational background to respond systematically to its critics, both orthodox Hindus on one side and Christian evangelicals on the other.[21] Ranade expressed the worry of the philosophically minded when he admitted in 1872 that "our friends of the Prarthana Samaj seem to be perfectly satisfied with a creed which consists of only one positive belief in the unity of God, accompanied with a special protest against the existing corruption of Hindu religion, viz., the article which denounces the prevalent idolatry to be a sin and an abomination."[22] But on what sources could he rely for a doctrine which would challenge the orthodox resistance to social reform yet avoid both evangelical dogmatism and secular scepticism?

The position which Ranade formulated by the early 1870's took the form of an eclecticism which never fully satisfied anyone, but reflected the complex crosscurrents of his times. It was summarized in his essay of 1872, "A Theist's Confession of Faith," which could only have been written by a university graduate. The most evident influence on him in these years was the natural theology of eighteenth-century England. The leading exponent of this school was Bishop Joseph Butler, whose <u>Analogy of Religion</u> and <u>Three Sermons on Human Nature</u> dominated the moral philosophy syllabus of Bombay University in the 1860's.[23] Bishop Butler's writings combined a belief in a natural moral order with a confidence that social justice could be achieved under God's providential decree.

> It is intuitively manifest that creatures ought to live under a dutiful sense of their Maker; and that justice and charity must be his laws, to creatures whom he has made social, and placed in society. . . . Religion is a practical thing, and consists in such a determinate course of life, as being what, there is reason to think, is commanded by the Author of Nature, and will, on the whole, be our happiness under his government.[24]

Consequently, a man's duty was to express in his life the divine moral command, disregarding the suffering which might result. In this way a man's spirit would be purified. "The known end [for which] we are placed in a state of so much affliction, hazard, and difficulty, is, our improvement in virtue and piety, as the requisite qualification for a future state of security and happiness."[25]

Ranade found Butler an ideal and urgently needed philosophical basis for the Prarthana Samaj, enabling it to deepen its theological commitments while neither jeopardizing the commitment to social crusades nor capitulating to the missionaries. In the "Theist's Confession of Faith," he argued that since both the natural order and the moral order are often hidden by the prevailing confusions of life, only spiritual insights can reveal them both and point the way to a more just society. Moral government of the world has been established by Divine Will, which "has its sanctions in the misery and happiness which follow as the physical consequences of moral or immoral conduct."[26] The fact that men face moral temptation demonstrates that they are under a divine charge to prepare themselves for a higher existence by constant, sober striving in the affairs of the world.[27]

Ranade's clearest exposition of the relation between devotional piety and commitment to the world of human society had come some five years earlier, in a critique of the best of Maharashtrian bhakti literature. In a review of Moropant's devotional poem, Kekavali, which he and many others considered the finest literary expression of the Marathi language, Ranade praised Moropant's description of "those attributes of the Deity which have a prominent bearing on the devotional aspect of human faith, his all-forgiving temper, his zeal to serve those who seek his help and place their faith in him, bountifulness and extreme condescension." But he felt that the poem was fatally weakened because

> there is no awe about the Deity, nothing of terror surrounding his glory, no humiliation of spirit on the devotee's part, no dazzling of sight at the awful vision. . . . [This] can be understood, if not relished, in a country where both the prevailing philosophy and theology place man almost on an equality with God, and advocate either his present unity with or his future absorption in God. This kind of philosophy is destructive of all real devotion.[28]

Here was a direct attack on the Hindu monistic tradition, which provided him with no reason for diligent moral striving and no expression of his experience that men stand under judgment of authorities higher and more just than themselves. In effect, Ranade had accepted an uneasy truce between bhakti devotionalism and evangelicalism.

By accepting one broad strand of Christian thought, Ranade faced the challenge of coming to terms with other elements of Christianity. Like his forerunners in the Brahmo Samaj he found its moral idiom congenial, but rejected its central theological beliefs, especially as the fundamentalist missionaries expressed them. Their emphasis on the incarnation of Christ as God's only son, Christ's physical resurrection after death, and man's original sin resembled the superstition and anthropomorphism of the Puranic Hinduism to which the samaj objected. His eclecticism rejected the demand that man undergo conversion and pledge exclusive loyalty to Christ; he preferred the more benign and imprecise doctrines of Bishop Butler's natural religion, with its focal emphasis on prudential morality.

Nonetheless, Christian doctrine in a modified form provided Ranade and the liberal Hindus with a means of challenging the prevailing orthodox belief that social reform was metaphysically wrong. Many orthodox Hindus used the doctrine of karma, which was thought to imply that individual destinies were predetermined, to resist any change in the existing pattern of society. Rather, they insisted, a pious and spiritual man should withdraw into the asceticism of the sannyasin. Ranade challenged this quietistic view insistently,[29] but here he faced a delicate dilemma. Asceticism at least was an expression of spiritual purity; in this sense the Hindu tradition was at one with Bishop Butler in condemning the materialism of the age. In the early 1870's he was witnessing his father's final years; hence it seemed perfectly appropriate to grant in "A Theist's Confession" that "retirement from the world at the proper season of life may be . . . a duty, after all our worldly engagements are fulfilled."[30]

The uneasy compromise which Ranade attempted to establish among all these conflicting forces was reflected dramatically in the succinct creed of the Prarthana Samaj which he and others prepared for the foundation ceremony of its new meeting hall in 1874. A Christianized version of Vedanta appeared in its legalistic phrases.

> Every day, at least every week, the One only God without a Second, the Perfect and Infinite, the Creator of all, Omnipresent, Almighty, All-knowing, All-merciful, and All-holy, shall be worshiped in these premises. . . . No carved or painted image, no external symbol which has been or may hereafter be used by any sect for the purpose of worship or the remembrance of a particular event, shall be preserved here.[31]

Yet as if to mitigate the attack on traditional Hinduism and preserve tolerance, the document proceeded to condemn religious bigotry.

> No created being or object that has been or may hereafter be worshiped by any sect shall be ridiculed or contemned in the course of Divine service to be conducted here. No book shall be acknowledged or revered as the infallible word of God; yet no book which has been or may hereafter be acknowledged by any sect to be infallible shall be ridiculed or contemned. No sect shall be vilified, ridiculed or hated.[32]

These regulations reflected a continuing tension within the Prarthana Samaj between the aggressive iconoclasts and men like Ranade who insisted on maintaining a rather more diplomatic relation with Hindu society. During the following years Ranade suffered considerable criticism from some of his more militant co-workers for his willingness to give discourses on the bhakti poet-saints in the orthodox Thakurdwar temple in Bombay, much as his grandfather had once done in Kolhapur. But as his protégé G. K. Gokhale later commented, "Mr. Ranade thought that the discourses were everything--the place where they were delivered was nothing."[33]

These were the years of Ranade's broadest critique of traditional Hinduism, but even now he revealed a characteristic determination to find worth on both sides of every issue. He was never the radical iconoclast that some Prarthana Samaj members were, and consequently he was more able to pursue the difficult balance of protesting against Hindu society without leaving its fold, a task to which all Prarthana Samaj members pledged themselves. Yet he was finding it difficult to achieve a satisfying balance in these years; for as a thinker he was emerging as a moderating force, while as a social reformer he was still as militant as any.

The Widow-Remarriage Conflict

The first expression of Ranade's mature view of Hinduism appeared in the widow-marriage controversy, which dominated the social reform movement in Bombay in the late 1860's. The Prarthana Samaj did not take the lead in this movement, although it encouraged widow-marriage among its members. Instead, individuals, including Ranade, pledged their support. For Ranade it presented a challenge to the moderation of his theistic beliefs, but more significantly the controversy catapulted him to the front ranks of reformers in Maharashtra.

Like other social issues there, the widow-marriage movement grew out of earlier debates in Bengal. The leader of the Bengali movement was Pandit Ishwarchandra Vidyasagar, who had been principal of the Calcutta Sanskrit College since 1851. Vidyasagar used his profound knowledge of the Vedas to attack the prevailing ban on widow-marriage from an ostensibly conservative position. In 1856 he published a volume, Marriage of Hindu Widows, in which he maintained that the oldest and purest texts allowed the remarriage of widows. Vidyasagar appealed beyond the orthodox leaders when he demanded that the government make remarriage fully legal, following the precedent set by its abolition of sati. A campaign of petitions and counter-petitions to the government followed Vidyasagar's plea. In July 1856 the government passed the Hindu Widows Remarriage Act over the bitter opposition of the Bengali orthodox forces.[34]

The fight over remarriage was as yet largely polemical in Bombay. Christian missionaries denounced the ban as barbarous, and Bal Shastri Jambhekar advocated remarriage in the Mumbai Durpun in the 1830's. Later, Baba Padmanji, a member of the Paramahamsa Sabha who subsequently became a leading Christian, wrote two books on the subject.[35] Organizational support for the Bengali reformers began only in the 1860's. After Keshub Chander Sen's first visit to Bombay, Vishnu Shastri Pandit and a few friends formed the Vidhavāvivāhottejaka Maṇḍalī (Widow-Remarriage Association) in 1866. Like the other reform organizations of the time in Bombay, the Mandali was predominantly a Saraswat and Chitpavan venture. But unlike the Prarthana Samaj, it made no formal distinction between member and contributor; this was a deliberate and successful attempt to attract leaders of both old and new elites. In addition to university graduates there were liberal shastris, one or two sardars of the Desh, and Parsi and Gujarati reformers.[36] Vishnu Shastri Pandit was one of the leading liberal pandits of Poona.

Ranade, who had first known him when they were co-editors of Indu Prakash, soon emerged with Bhandarkar as the spokesman for the Western-educated group. Ranade was uncompromisingly dedicated to the cause; for like many others he had personal experience of the suffering of women in their own homes. Children were usually betrothed at an early age, and some child brides whose intended husbands died even before the wedding ceremonies were considered widows. The child widow was required to remain permanently unmarried; she shaved her head and in other humiliating ways was excluded from full participation in family life. Ranade's own sister, married at the age of ten, was widowed a few years later; henceforth she lived in seclusion in her father-in-law's household. She was rarely allowed even to visit her brother.[37]

Ranade's eagerness to challenge the old order in its inner bastions was evident in his earlier writings, for he had learned in college to hold the priestly order in contempt. He wrote in one college essay:

> I know very little of Brahminical schools--either their method or their scope. Still I know this much that they are diametrically opposed to Bacon's method--and are full of the restless agitation and the dogmatic tendency which Bacon has censured. They despise that knowledge of nature which they derive from observation as being mean and sordid. They have recourse to mental abstraction and contemplation and spun [sic] a web out of their own brains which astounds us all and is intelligible to none.[38]

Yet despite such depth of hostility to "the priestly establishment," the reformers chose to challenge the orthodox view of women's rights not by reference to abstract ideals of justice and morality but by invoking the dharmashastra itself. Announcing the attack, Vishnu Shastri asserted that the society would "take into consideration the best means of reintroducing the practice of remarriage of females of the high caste community who have or may become widows, and to advocate the cause on the authority of the Hindu Dharma Shastra."[39] The reformers thus deliberately chose to occupy the home ground of the shastris. The orthodox party responded to the new society by forming its own group, the Hindū Dharma Vyavasthāpaka Maṇḍalī (Society for the Protection of Hindu Religion), which sponsored meetings at the great temple at Thakurdwar in Bombay and elsewhere to rally support.[40] When Vishnu Shastri published a Marathi translation of Vidyasagar's book in Indu Prakash in 1868, he precipitated a debate between the two sides which grew into a bitter three-year conflict. The struggle demonstrated the patterns of social power in Maharashtra and the means which were used both to defend stability and to initiate change.

The shastris were the arbiters and exemplars of traditional caste behavior, and the British courts had clearly enunciated that the dharmashastra had jurisdiction over family life. The reformers, who were already suggesting that Indians should control a larger share of their political life, agreed that in religious matters Hindu society must initiate reform for itself. Justification for more liberal social practices had therefore to be found in the traditional order itself. Maharashtrian Brahmin orthodoxy, as a social structure, was decentralized and flexible. Traditionally, when disputes arose within the caste as to the proper standards of orthodoxy, they followed the dictates of the shastris. Whenever authoritative texts or traditions were contradictory or unclear, any member of the community could call a public meeting presided over by local shastris. For important disputes they convened either in a political center such as Poona, or in a temple and pilgrimage city such as Nasik or Wai.

The ultimate arbiter of these deliberations in the Desh was the Shankaracharya of Karvir and Sankeshwar, a Deshastha Brahmin who was elected for life from among the distinguished shastris.[41] He presided over gatherings of shastris whenever a major dispute arose, determining with their advice which rules and penalties should be invoked. His powers blended those of a legislator with those of an executive, for he often functioned more as an enforcing authority than as a maker of decisions in his own right. He was the embodiment of continuity in the orthodox tradition; through his ability to adjust the Hindu law texts to slowly changing social conditions, he maintained the Brahmin tradition in a living and flexible form.[42] His final sanction against deviates from orthodoxy was the power of excommunication, but he lacked the civil authority's power of police enforcement. The general consent of the community to his decrees was his only effective power, and this was to be seriously challenged for the first time by nineteenth-century social liberals led by Ranade.

Out of combined strategy and conviction the reformers portrayed themselves as only moderate reformers, eager not to dismantle the whole fabric of traditional ethics. M. M. Kunte, one of Ranade's long-time associates and secretary of the Poona Prarthana Samaj, wrote in 1870 that the shastras "lay down rules for the guidance of society and maintenance of order, justice and purity of affections and sentiments. Their proper function is to save society from impurity and degradation, to prevent it from sinking in vice, . . . to inculcate correct principles of religion, to teach proper methods of worship, and thus to regulate all the general social affairs."[43] Kunte felt obliged to distinguish between reformers, who advocated gradual change and based their actions on "the social constitution," and revolutionaries, who "seek to turn everything upside down." The wise course of reform, he wrote, "does not hold out imaginary and celestial hopes. It is humble in its ambition and cautious in its policy. The legitimate basis of its action then is the removal of direct, positive, and definite evils in conformity with the social conservative constitution and principles."[44]

Vishnu Shastri and his co-workers recognized that the later shastras had been written in a period when caste Hinduism had developed many of the repressive practices which were still in force. They chose therefore to appeal to earlier times, when social practices were more fluid. They made their appeal to the Vedas and other early texts, urging the people to put aside the practices which had appeared more recently. In this way they hoped to appear more purely traditional than the shastris themselves.

Vishnu Shastri published several essays on remarriage in <u>Indu Prakash</u>. The shastris responded with a series of detailed questions, which he printed with his answers. He then decided to tour the mofussil to give public lectures. He travelled to Nasik and other orthodox centers, where he distributed placards inviting the public to attent his talks and challenging the orthodox to debate him.[45] Vithoba Anna Daftardar, an orthodox leader of Poona, accepted the challenge by giving lectures opposing remarriage. Vishnu Shastri also lectured in Poona, but as yet the two men did not face each other directly.

The clash of opposing ideas was followed avidly by the Brahmin segment of the public, especially when the reformers arranged a direct challenge to the orthodox by finding a widow whose family would allow her to remarry. An advertisement in <u>Indu Prakash</u> brought forth a willing groom, a teacher from northern Maharashtra. The Widow-Remarriage Association undertook arrangements for the marriage ceremony and sent printed invitations to important people to attend. The invitations were signed by seven men, including Ranade, Vishnu Shastri and Lokahitawadi,[46] who persevered with their intentions despite anonymous threats of violence or murder. The marriage was celebrated on June 15, 1869, in full traditional style. Among the guests were the leading Englishmen and Indian reformers of Bombay.[47]

The orthodox retaliated quickly, organizing a mass meeting at the Thakurdwar temple at which a resolution was adopted excommunicating the sponsors of the marriage. Since the meeting was attended by hundreds of people, confusion developed over the wording of the resolution. A few men sympathetic with the reformers attended; after the meeting four of them asserted somewhat dubiously that since no resolution had been passed unanimously this invalidated the excommunication. They too were then excommunicated, and the public began to take sides. The reformers in Poona, Nasik, and other cities organized meetings which passed resolutions asking the Shankaracharya to intervene and preside over an orderly debate over the question of widow marriage before anyone was excommunicated.[48] Simultaneously, the leading reformers went around the Presidency seeking to rally support. They appealed to the leaders of public opinion, including the native Princes. Ranade joined a committee which went to Baroda in November 1869 to talk with the Gaikwad, but they were unable to win his support.[49]

The orthodox party agreed that the Shankaracharya should adjudicate, in the face of the several hundred signatures on the petitions. So broad a challenge to traditional authority was unprecedented. Yet the Shankaracharya had frequently adjudicated conflicting interpretations of the shastras. His authority rested on general consent; this was not the first time he attempted to preserve his position by searching for a compromise acceptable to both sides. He is said to have agreed privately to support remarriage of child widows if the reformers would not advocate remarriage of adult widows. But the reformers refused to agree to the compromise, sensing a surge of public support. They preferred a full-scale debate in the traditional style, the winning side's views to be adopted as standards for the whole community. The antagonists then agreed that each side would select five judges, with an eleventh to vote in case of a tie; they would listen to the arguments of both sides and then pass their decision. The Shankaracharya agreed to invoke his authority on the majority side.[50]

The debate took place in Poona beginning March 20, 1870. Vishnu Shastri Pandit presented the reformers' views with Ranade as his associate; Narayanacharya Gajendragadkar took the orthodox side with Daftardar as his associate. The debate was attended by hundreds of people; one witness described it as "a spectacle which had not been witnessed for centuries, a spectacle which most probably will not be witnessed again. The race of Shastris, perfect in the schoolman's art of discussion, profound in religious learning and research, has nearly died out and will never revive. . . . The Shastris who took part in the late controversy at Poona, were the product of the last days of Hindu ascendency untouched by the influence of Western education."[51]

With such high stakes the orthodox party applied pressure on those who had signed the petitions, and the reformers found many of the signers deserting the ranks. In the heat of the fight Ranade wrote to one of them, saying:

> If there is any truth in you--you must stand by your word. . . . You will see from the enclosed which is a copy of a draft sent by the orthodox side how weak their whole position [is]--and the undignified conduct of such as you--simply is unreasonable to the last degree. . . . As it is, what you propose to do has no other name by which people will call it than simply disgraceful. If you can bear that, it is wonderful you cannot muster courage to say--I have signed it I must stand by it.[52]

Yet the reformers gauged that the debate was progressing well for their side. They were dismayed when at the end of the ninth day the Shankaracharya abruptly closed the debate and called for a decision. In an unexpected change, Vyankat Shastri Mate, one of the reformers' judges, voted against Vishnu Shastri, giving the orthodox a six to four victory. The amazed reformers questioned him privately as to his reasons for changing his vote. He admitted having responded to pressure from the orthodox, who had told him among other things that any move was legitimate in the pursuit of religious purity. Shortly thereafter, Mate's admission was published in <u>Dnyan Prakash</u> (Light of Knowledge), the weekly voice of the Poona reformers. The orthodox responded with bitter criticisms of <u>Dnyan Prakash</u> and its editors. The reformers finally took the ominous step of appealing to the British courts where they prosecuted an orthodox spokesman for defamation. The Poona court sentenced him to a thirty-two-day prison term. The unsatisfied reformers continued their campaign by charging that witnesses for the orthodox side had given false evidence in the first trial; they should be taught by further prosecution that such acts were not permissible under the new political system. In a second trial the defendant was convicted of perjury and given a three-month prison term.[53]

In the course of the first trial, Ranade published his interpretation of the shastras in a pamphlet entitled "The Texts of the Hindu Law on the Lawfulness of the Re-marriage of Widows," which was widely circulated. Shortly after, his article, "Vedic Authorities for Widow Marriage," reiterated many of the same points. The two became basic texts for the reform movement, both for their specific arguments and for their broad assumptions about the worth of Indian social traditions in the modern world. The body of the articles was an extended review of texts which Ranade interpreted as allowing remarriage. He argued that some texts permitted widows to remarry under specified conditions of distress; others from different times permitted a long list of exceptions to a general practice forbidding remarriage.[54] He concluded that the injunctions were meant only as a general endorsement of monogamy and did not specifically apply to widows.[55] His views amounted to a wholesale attack on the Puranas, the texts which reflect caste society in its most rigid development. He insisted that the Puranas were corrupt by comparison with earlier texts; they should be disregarded when they conflicted with the pure traditions described in the Vedas, to which Hindu society must now return.[56] His approach closely paralleled that of contemporary Parsi and Muslim reformers in India, who likewise invoked the authority of the early, pure age of their religions against the unwelcome accretions of later times.

By now it was evident that the reformers had overreached themselves in the heat of conflict, for their recourse to the courts turned public opinion against them. At about the same time, their cause was weakened by Lokahitawadi, who had been under pressure because his son, Krishnarao, had taken the forbidden sea voyage to England for his law studies. Upon returning to India, Krishnarao learned that he would not be readmitted into caste unless both he and his father did proper penance. They had shared in the remarriage party's excommunication and now faced a second charge. The orthodox party had been speaking to Lokahitawadi, promising that the Shankaracharya would grant him readmission if he first took certain actions conciliating the orthodox. Ranade doubted the reliability of their promises and wrote to his friend:

> Beware of Satan and his temptation. I fear they are trying your soul, and according as you yield or stand up will be the measure of your glory. Do not listen to Vishnu Bhat's overtures. Swami [Shankaracharya] is not inclined--he is decidedly opposed to admit men in your Krishnarao's position back into the caste. In fact our troubles on that head will be far more numerous than what we experience now. You did well to send the man back with a message that you would think what you should do to satisfy them in the present after they had satisfied you about the future. Stand to that--till you see in black

and white under the Swami's own hand and seal the letter of license to Krishnarao's admission. . . .

I for my part, and the part of many more undertake [with] Krishnarao's coming back to continue to hold with him and with you and your family intercourse in every way as thorough and intimate as we do now.

I know you have your family troubles--who has them not. Here I am with a poor orphan sister who is kept away from me for months together. My father is sick--and I am prevented from going to him by this consideration only that I might bring troubles on him. This is the lot of us all. We must however stand together for more time to come. Our standing together is our strength and their defeat--and this lesson will bear its fruit.[57]

Ranade's admonitions were not fully effective, since in the following week Lokahitawadi publicly did penance, although he stated in a letter to <u>Indu Prakash</u> that he did not mean a word of it.[58] Despite this assertion, his action compromised the moral position of the reformers. His defection, added to the public criticism of the prosecution, severely weakened the popular support for the reform movement.

The orthodox too had been damaged in the fray. Their methods of private pressure and public dishonesty had been exposed. The Shankaracharya had shown himself willing to bargain with his challengers. Kunte gloated afterwards: "The spell of the Shankaracharya is broken. Newspapers have written of him as if he is a common man, pointed out his faults, exposed his ignorance, and proved him incompetent to be where he is."[59] The reformers could show no great substantive victory, but their ranks had been momentarily strengthened.

In the general re-evaluation Ranade too must have questioned where events had led him. The debate had placed him in the second most important position among the reformers and brought him publicity in Poona, much of it unfavorable. In his youthful enthusiasm, Ranade had denounced the orthodox disputants as dishonest and devious. In their hands, he wrote, the texts were "twisted and tortured in all manner of ways, some of them most ridiculously absurd, and absolutely no attempt was made to show that the only true and natural meaning of the text was not the one contended for by the advocates."[60] Like the other participants, Ranade had been severe, compromising his pledge to the Prarthana Samaj to maintain contact with orthodox society even while pressing for reform. He soon concluded that in a conservative stronghold like Poona, reforms must come gradually and only when the basis for them was carefully prepared.

The Tactics of Reform

Ranade was appointed subordinate judge in the district court of Poona in November 1871, shortly after the end of the widow-marriage battle. When he moved to Poona he confronted a very different city from Bombay. Whereas Bombay was large, socially varied and cosmopolitan, Poona was almost wholly Marathi-speaking and far smaller, numbering under 90,000.[61] Located in the Desh, it was far less exposed to Western ideas and institutions than Bombay. Poona was an old town whose village temple, still in use, dates from perhaps the thirteenth century.[62] In the ensuing centuries the city had built traditions of its own which resisted the European cultural advance. These traditions revolved around the memory of the Peshwa, who had built his capital there in the eighteenth century, causing Poona to grow from a small town to the most powerful city in Maharashtra. Sinhagad, one of the strongest of the Maratha hill forts, loomed to the south of the city. Closer to the edge of the city, Parvati hill rose from the plain, supporting the Peshwa's temples. On the opposite edge of the city lay the ruins of Shanwar Wada, the great palace of the Peshwas, whose affairs had attracted leading groups from all over Maharashtra to settle near its walls. Its remains were a constant reminder of past glory to the inhabitants of the nineteenth-century city.

The public life of Poona was dominated by the Brahmin quarter, which spread south and west from Shanwar Wada. Compact, densely populated and homogeneous, this quarter was the home of the orthodox forces. Unlike Bombay there were no language barriers or great distances in the city to inhibit the spread of public moods. The intensity of feeling which arose here concerning the widow-marriage reformers was likely to recur in other debates over high-caste practices. In Poona, and even more in the mofussil towns which looked to Poona for leadership, a small group of men could dominate the public scene.

Ranade's awareness of this potential was demonstrated by his reform work during the next decade, much of which dealt with educational programs, both formal and informal. Of necessity much of this work was carried out in Marathi, for the task now was to transmit Western values into the vernacular culture. There was much painstaking groundwork to be done, for when Ranade arrived in Poona, there was an almost total absence of public institutions. The only exception was the Native General Library, which badly needed new quarters and more reliable financing. One of Ranade's first efforts in Poona was to provide both by finding land for a new building and organizing a campaign to raise funds for the library's activities.[63]

In a more direct contribution to the rapid development of his influence in Poona, he also founded two annual public gatherings whose purpose was to encourage students to debate vital social questions. The Vaktratvottejaka Sabhā, or Elocution Encouragement Society, was Ranade's means of adapting the Literary and Scientific Society to the Poona scene; it sponsored annual oratory contests on topics designed to bring modern learning to the public eye.[64] The second and more important organization was the Vasanta Vyākhyānamālā, or Spring Lecture Series, in which leading public figures addressed a wide range of topics in public affairs and modern science. Its importance arose from the fact that most influential men of the Desh came to Poona for the hot months of April and May. The lecture series soon became the outstanding cultural event of the season. Ranade remained chairman of the series for nearly twenty years, using this platform as one of his important means of influencing public opinion in the city. His own speeches and his extensive comments on other lectures were discussed in both Marathi and English newspapers.[65]

Both of these series were extensions of Ranade's expanding campaign to enrich vernacular literature. He had embarked on this work as a result of his university education, which included requirements in Marathi language and literature designed so that students might study their own traditions in the light of Western critical standards. Ranade's views on Marathi literature were stated most clearly in his reports as Marathi Translator in the Education Department. This post, which he held simultaneously with his positions in Akalkot and Kolhapur in 1867-68, required him to evaluate which works were worthy of publication or translation. His reports revealed deeply Anglicized standards, which he summarized in a rhetorical flourish worthy of Macaulay: "There can be no mistake that to any one who looks at [it] from a stranger's standpoint our existing literature will appear for the most part either superstitious or childish. Many centuries of earnest effort are needed before this reproach can be washed away."[66]

Since the regional culture required a new infusion of Western content, Ranade stressed that Western-educated men must not lose contact with their vernaculars or they would become gradually isolated from society and their responsibilities to it.[67] By the 1870's this was an increasing danger, for shortly after Ranade finished his studies Bombay University eliminated Marathi from its list of required subjects. He at once began a lifelong campaign to reinstate the language, a campaign which ironically achieved success in 1901, shortly after his death. Ranade also worked on a non-official basis to encourage the modernization of Marathi. After several years of informal effort, he successfully established in 1878 the Society for Promoting Marathi Books, with branches in Poona and Nasik.[68]

These efforts were carrying Ranade steadily deeper into the mofussil culture. Most reformers of his time were preoccupied with affairs in Bombay or Poona, but one of Ranade's notable initiatives was in the educational affairs of smaller towns and villages. Characteristically, he exploited both governmental and private channels in this work. He defended government grants to rural schools in which the traditional Sanskrit curriculum was taught, on the grounds that rigorous study of Sanskrit would elevate the moral character of the students.[69] Again combining official and non-official work, on his regular tour of the districts as judge he systematically lectured in mofussil villages and towns on his favorite topics, such as the value of Western learning and the lessons of American social history. The surviving report of one speech which he gave in the orthodox stronghold of Nasik indicates his campaign against the parochialism of the unreformed vernacular culture:

The English language must be understood as not solely an English matter, but rather as an expression of all the advanced nations of the West. If it is asserted that there is no need to go to a foreign language, because India has its own language and learning, the answer is that Indian learning even in its most flourishing period must be pronounced immature, whereas today European knowledge has reached maturity. The important thing about any body of knowledge is that it should tell us what we are, what our duty is, what we are to do in this world, what our rights are, and similar matters. This is the knowledge we ought to seek, no matter whether it originated in our own country or in a foreign country. That knowledge has been discovered by the Europeans, whereas even in the greatest flowering of our Indian learning there was no trace of it. . . . English rule should be regarded as a fortunate occurrence for India, and not as a reason for refusing the proffered knowledge.[70]

To paraphrase Gokhale, Ranade's theme was often Western, but his techniques were traditional. When he arrived in a village he lectured in the traditional fashion before the Maruti temple. This temple, dedicated to the monkey-god, was the usual location of village meetings; it provided Ranade with an implicit symbol of cooperation and unity to reinforce the substance of his talks.

In Poona Ranade was similarly sensitive to conservative feelings. Working to give women elementary education, he generally did little teaching himself, but left the work to his wife and other women, encouraging them from the sidelines. Classes were held in Ranade's home, so as not to offend tradition-bound women who would not consider attending a public school. The first step in women's education often took the form of the traditional haḷḍi-kuṅkū parties for women only, at which his wife and the other educated women would tell stories of the virtuous heroines of the Puranas to illustrate their ideals of womanhood. Only after gaining the other women's confidence in this way could they go on to further teaching.[71] Beyond arranging for the Puranic discourses, Ranade maintained his ties with a variety of orthodox establishments by giving financial aid to Sanskrit schools and the Vedaśastrottejaka Sabhā (Society for Promoting the Veda).[72] He was also well known among the orthodox for his support of pilgrim rest houses at temple centers in Kolhapur and in Alandi, the birthplace of Dnyaneshwar.[73]

A striking feature of this work is its quiet persistence and lack of drama. Ranade never developed the charismatic appeal of a powerful platform oratory which some of his adversaries achieved. He preferred not to bend public proceedings to his will by the force of rhetoric, but to remain subdued, reasonable and patient. One friend wrote:

> At all informal or public meetings and gatherings Mr. Ranade would invariably and studiously keep himself in the background, and he would not open his mouth until all others had had their say. . . . There was never a man more unassuming, more unconscious of self, more simple, more childlike, than Mr. Ranade. Extremely severe and even unjust to himself, his leniency and justice to others leaned to a fault.[74]

Ranade was averse on principle to the dangers of demagogy, and as a liberal educator he based his hope for India's future on the assumption that men would respond to the quiet appeal of lucid reasoning. His personal idiosyncracies reinforced the development of this singular public style. Lord Reay, later governor of Bombay, and a firm supporter of Ranade, once called him "the ugliest man in the Presidency," and described him as leading "a hermit life."[75] Many British were disconcerted because Ranade always chose to wear the simple traditional dress of the region, even in Bombay, and on his bulky frame it often gave an unkempt impression.[76]

Maintaining traditional patterns in his personal life increased Ranade's accessibility to members of numerous factions in the city. He thus made his influence felt in both liberal and orthodox circles. Ramabai reported that "important people of orthodox groups, Brahmins, Maratha, Gujerati, Bhat and other castes came to consult him, and he treated each one according to the manners of his caste."[77] He paid a price for this effort. His many-faceted involvement in the city's affairs and his constant accessibility were tiring, and pressures were increased by life in a joint family which was itself torn between orthodox and reformed practices.[78] These combined with his recurring weakness of sight to intensify the nervous strain under which he worked. Hence he seemed remote and uncommunicative to some.[79] One writer remembered him as having been "deficient in social agreeableness."[80] Yet no one questioned Ranade's exemplary moral dignity, which recommended him to orthodox and reformed camps alike. At home he practiced the Vedic rituals which his father had taught him and studied the songs of the bhakti saints morning and evening. He was totally oblivious to the temptations of ostentatious or luxurious living, unlike some of his associates in Bombay; to the orthodox this could be a sign that his impressionable years in Bombay had not undermined his moral standards. On the contrary, Ranade's natural impulse had been heightened in Bombay, where he developed a Victorian moral fastidiousness. One incident is reported from these years, which reveals his expression of moral tastes common to the Victorians and the Brahmins. When Ranade once attended feativities at Deccan College and a dancing girl appeared, he indignantly left the party and obliged several friends to leave with him in protest.[81]

Ranade's involvement in conservative society ran deeper than strategy or philanthropy; it was rooted in the compulsions of his own family. In 1873 his father moved from Kolhapur to Poona. Until he died three years later, he exercised orthodox controls over his son. He arrived shortly before a crisis in his son's life, for in October of 1873 Ranade's first wife, Sakhubai, died of tuberculosis after months in which Ranade personally attended her every night.[82] He expressed his depression in a subsequent letter to G. A. Mankar, his friend and, later, biographer who had suffered a similar loss.

> My own loss has been equally bitter, and at times these mishaps so puzzle one's understanding that the most devout are tempted into sinful despondency and disloyal rebellion. You are, however, too soundly grounded in virtue and piety to be shaken in your faith

permanently, whatever may be the temporary shock you suffered. It is not good of friends to give permanent advice in this spirit. Such consolation is only liked when the heart, saddened by its loss, finds out the truth that the world was not intended to be a bower of roses.83

After Sakhubai's death, Ranade wanted to seek diversion by a visit to Europe, which he had long been contemplating. His father forbade him to go, on the grounds that prolonged exposure to foreign air might corrupt his values.84 Meanwhile, Govindrao was eager to arrange a marriage for his son, to avoid the possibility of being disgraced by a widow-marriage in the family. The question of Ranade's remarriage became the ultimate test of the two men's wills. Ranade resisted his father for some time but finally yielded when Govindrao threatened to return to Kolhapur and break all ties with him. A marriage was arranged with Ramabai, the daughter of the Kurlekar family of Satara. Her family were respectable gentry who had ties to the Patwardhan family, jagirdars of Sangli.85 Govindrao was pleased with this good marriage, although his new daughter-in-law was as yet totally illiterate. Faced with the inevitability of the marriage, Ranade expressed his frustration by making it as useful to the reform cause as possible. He insisted that the marriage ceremony be reduced to its simplest form, and after the wedding he simply walked home with his bride, avoiding the usually elaborate procession. He abruptly began her education the same evening, requiring her to pronounce his name to him in violation of a woman's traditional submissiveness.86

The reformers of both Poona and Bombay criticized Ranade harshly for the marriage, insisting that he had betrayed all his professed social values. When the marriage contract was announced, <u>Indu Prakash</u> stated in an editorial:

> He has been one of the foremost leaders in all the social and religious reforms that are being seriously tried in the Hindu community. He has been one of the leaders of the Prarthana Samaj, and in the great widow marriage movement, he has been one of the foremost, if not <u>the</u> foremost, leader. . . . This is the man that now, when God has pleased to put him to the crucial test of showing by his deeds whether he is prepared to act up to his advocacy of widow-marriage, is going to marry, not a widow, but a virgin girl of eleven or twelve years, hardly before it is two months since the death of his first wife.87

The social reform movement in the following years was damaged by similar defections by its leaders, but none was more constantly exploited by critics than Ranade's marriage to Ramabai. The significance of Ranade's capitulation to his father ran deep, for reform and orthodox Hindus alike placed great importance on practice as the confirmation of ideals. It was generally agreed that a leader in public life should not so much describe as exemplify his beliefs; the purity of his acts was far more persuasive than the clarity of his ideas. Ranade's acute discomfiture was hardly relieved by the knowledge that Bishop Butler had insisted on the same principle.88

Ranade's failure to resist his father's will was associated with his sense of filial responsibility. This relationship undergirded his whole conception of a reformer's often isolated life in orthodox society and supported his efforts to conciliate the conservatives. He is quoted as having warned his followers, with strikingly revealing metaphors:

> Conservatism is a force which we cannot afford to forego or forget. You may talk and act in a way that appears to be the result of your voluntary efforts, but you are unconsciously influenced by the traditions in which you are born, by the surroundings in which you are brought up, by the very milk which you have drunk from your mother's breasts or influenced by the other things of the world. To say that it is possible to build a new fabric on new lines without any help from the past is to say that I am self-born and my father and grandfather need not have troubled for me.[89]

Once more before Govindrao died he successfully restricted his son's social contacts with reformer friends, but this time at a high cost. Vishnu Shastri Pandit came to Poona to visit Ranade after marrying a widow in 1875, and shortly before his own death. Govindrao refused to sit at dinner with them and sent the women from that part of the home. The next morning he packed his bags and prepared to return to Kolhapur. He was dissuaded only by a burst of bitter sobs from his son, who ran from the room, crying, "Obviously, I am an orphan since my mother died."[90] Ranade had reached the point of fearing that his father no longer shared the family loyalty which ran deeper than differences of social principle.

The final irony in the complex tensions of their relationship appeared not long afterward, for Govindrao was in Kolhapur on a pilgrimage when he became seriously ill. Ranade took leave from his work in Poona for two months to nurse him, but he was required to return to Poona at the end of that time, despite his father's fears. A new leave was arranged in Poona, but in the interim Govindrao died. Ranade was so grief-stricken that he decided not to go at all to Kolhapur, even to carry out the funeral rites which were traditionally incumbent upon the first son. He had gained a certain release from orthodox influence in his life, but in a deeply traumatic fashion.[91] There could hardly have been a more mutely eloquent expression of his emotional crisis during this period, and the depth of his ambivalence toward both his father and the orthodox tradition. This crisis may help to explain the rapid decline of the social reform movement for a decade to follow.

Throughout the early 1870's Ranade had pursued the work of social and religious reform as well as educational construction, despite the severe restrictions of his orthodox milieu. As in Bombay previously, his basis of social and organizational cohesion was the local branch of the Prarthana Samaj. Its roots in Poona can be traced to The Friendly Meeting, a similar group formed in 1862, which in itself may have replaced the defunct Poona branch of the Paramahamsa Sabha.[92] Its few members, isolated from their surroundings far more than the reformers in Bombay, gathered quietly through the 1860's. When V. A. Modak, Ranade's fellow member of the Bombay samaj, lectured on "The Necessity of Religion" in Poona in 1870, he inspired nine men from several castes to found the Poona Prarthana Samaj that December. Ranade arrived in Poona the following year and immediately became a leading member; he was responsible for acquiring land and constructing a meetinghouse for the samaj in 1877.[93] The Poona organization, which remained tiny in numbers throughout Ranade's life, nonetheless provided a basis for constructing institutions like the Huzur Paga School, the first school for high-caste women in Poona. It was founded in 1884 by Ranade and his close friend, the Saraswat Brahmin Shankar Pandurang Pandit, in the face of severe criticism from the orthodox.[94]

True to its strategy of embracing allies wherever they could be found, the Bombay Prarthana Samaj welcomed the appearance of a new samaj in Bombay in 1875, the Arya Samaj, which was founded by Swami Dayananda Saraswati. Shortly thereafter, Dayananda visited Poona for nearly two months to propagate his teachings. In Poona he gave a series of fifteen lectures on historical and religious topics.[95] The core of his doctrine was the belief that the Vedas were the sole and complete revelation of divine truth, and on this ultra-orthodox basis he denounced idolatry and all caste distinctions.[96] Some of Ranade's friends in the Prarthana Samaj were reluctant to sponsor Dayananda, since his iconoclasm and opposition to caste were more outspoken than their own; they feared an orthodox reaction as taxing as the uproar over widow marriage. They further rejected his view that the Vedas were divinely inspired to the exclusion of all other scriptures. Ranade was more tolerant of different views and advised, "What does it matter if Dayananda Saraswati says the Vedas and the Vedas alone are the revelation of God? Be that his faith. But let us go deeper and see if, apart from that principle, there is anything which is in accord with our principles."[97] Undeterred by the failure of 1871, Ranade continued to encourage a variety of reform movements. His decision was also an effort to engage all shades of both orthodox and heterodox opinion in reasoned debate.

Ranade's tenacity had not diminished since his arrival in Poona, although the belligerence he displayed in the widow-marriage debate had subsided. As he expected, the orthodox once again found a champion, this time in Ram Dixit Apte, one of the most eminent shastris of Poona, who gave a series of lectures attempting to refute Dayananda. This in itself pleased Ranade, for Apte was a close associate in political and educational affairs.[98] Their cooperation in civic affairs, across the barriers of religious orthodoxy, was only the first of many crosscutting relationships which Ranade constructed over the years in Poona, and it undoubtedly dampened the conflict in 1875. But the debate nearly precipitated a violent confrontation in the streets, for on the day of his last lecture the reform group arranged for a procession to wind through the city, led by an elephant carrying the swami. Hearing of the plans, the orthodox party formed a countermarch honoring a donkey as a mock saint. Ranade had been warned that violence might result, but he refused to cancel the procession. He evidently took this as an occasion to demonstrate his own commitment to social reform, for the criticisms which he had borne at the time of his remarriage were only three years old. He insisted to his followers that they must be prepared to face persecution and blows from the orthodox in the service of their cause.[99] On the day of the procession the reformers were showered with mud and stones despite police protection; they escaped into the courtyard which was their destination barely in time to avoid a riot.

Dayananda's visit to Poona was one of a series of events which weakened the social reform movement. Later in the same year Vishnu Shastri Pandit died, leaving the reform movement without its militant senior leader.[100] Perhaps as a result, the Prarthana Samaj faced the first great split in its ranks in the following year. A small group led by S. P. Kelkar wished to follow Dayananda's path of rejecting all caste rules, but Ranade and others disagreed, fearing that this might lead to the internal factionalism and external isolation which marked the Brahmo Samaj groups in Bengal. This time the difference of principle could not be mediated successfully, and Kelkar's group departed to form a new society, the Brahmo Samaj of Bombay, which lasted only eight years.[101] Kelkar later returned to the Prarthana Samaj to become its leading missionary,[102] but in the meantime the social reform movement was fragmented for nearly a decade. Concurrently the late 1870's were a time of increasing political turmoil for the Presidency as a whole, and Ranade was in the vortex. When he was temporarily transferred away from Poona for two years, from 1878 to 1880, his leadership was lost to the social reform movement. In any event, the focus of public attention was shifting to a developing political crisis in which all factions within Hindu society found themselves united against the hostility of the imperial regime.

Notes

[1] See Memories and Writings of Acharya Bal Shastri Jambhekar, ed. G. G. Jambhekar (Poona, 1950), I, i-lxiv.

[2] See the annual reports of the Students' Literary and Scientific Society for lists of officers.

[3] J. A. Dalal, in Vasant N. Naik, Kashinath Trimbak Telang (Madras, n.d.), p. 15.

[4] Students' Literary and Scientific Society, Third Report (Bombay, 1852), pp. 50-51.

[5] S. Natarajan, A Century of Social Reform in India (London, 1959), p. 39; Masani, Evolution of Self-Government, p. 341.

[6] Students' Literary and Scientific Society, Third Report, p. 26.

[7] V. V. Thakur, "Kai. Nyā. Mu. Rānaḍe" (The Late Justice Ranade), Vividhadnyānavistāra, February 1913, p. 41.

[8] Jambhekar, Acharya Bal Shastri Jambhekar, I, xxiv-xxxv.

[9] G. L. Chandavarkar, Maharshi Karve (Bombay, 1958), p. 53.

[10] Thakur, "Ranade," pp. 43-44.

[11] A. K. Priyolkar, Paramahaṃsa sabhā va tice adhyaksha Ramchandra Baḷkrishṇa (The Paramahamsa Sabha and Its President Ramchandra Balkrishna) (Bombay, 1966).

[12] "A Political Rishi," Indu Prakash, May 25, 1885, pp. 2-3.

[13] Baba Padmanji, Once Hindu: Now Christian (London, 1890), p. 79.

[14] Mumbaī ethīla prārthanāsamājācī hakīkata (Account of the Prarthana Samaj of Bombay) (Bombay, 1883), p. 3; A. K. Priyolkar, Rao Bahadur Dadoba Pandurang (Bombay, 1947), p. 262.

[15] As in most civic associations of the period, some of the leading Southern Maratha sardars lent their names as titular officers of the Prarthana Samaj, though none took an active role. The caste composition of the samaj changed very little by the time of a detailed 1877 report, when its official membership list of 46 names, all Hindu, included 19 Chitpavans and 18 Saraswats. In addition, there was a list of 164 contributors, which included nearly every well-known Indian reformer in Bombay, both Hindu and Parsi, and many from the mofussil. B. H. Bhagwat, Prārthanā mandīrāca saṅkshipta vṛttānta (A Brief Account of the Prarthana Mandir, Bombay; with a list in English of the subscribers) (Bombay, 1877), pp. 12-16.

[16] V. R. Shinde, The Theistic Directory (Bombay, 1912), p. 135.

[17] S. Natarajan, A Century of Social Reform in India (London, 1959), p. 61.

[18] Sivanath Sastri, A History of the Brahmo Samaj (Calcutta, 1911-12), II, 411-412.

[19] The Brahmo Yearbook, 1876, ed. S. D. Collett (London, 1876), p. 38.

[20] Sastri, Brahmo Samaj, II, 414.

[21] For polemics of the following decade directed against the Prarthana Samaj, see K. R. Kirtikar, Two Addresses on the Theistic Movement in Western India (Bombay, n.d.). Kirtikar was a Brahmin convert to Christianity; he shared the missionaries' frustration that the Prarthana Samaj members held many Christian views but refused to accept conversion.

[22] M. G. Ranade, "A Theist's Confession of Faith," in Religious and Social Reform, ed. M. B. Kolaskar (Bombay, 1902), p. 252.

[23] RDPI, 1859, p. 3. The report singles out Ranade for his careful study of the work.

[24] Joseph Butler, The Analogy of Religion, Natural and Revealed, to the Constitution and Course of Nature (London, 1878), pp. 311, 320. For a fuller discussion of Butler's place in the university curriculum, see McDonald, "English Education," pp. 459-466.

[25] Butler, Analogy, pp. 139-140.

[26] Ranade, "Theist's Confession," p. 265.

[27] Ibid., p. 266.

[28] M. G. Ranade, "Keka Dursh," Bombay Educational Record, III (1867), 247.

[29] For an analysis of the same problem at a later stage in the nationalist movement, see D. M. Brown, "The Philosophy of Bal Gangadhar Tilak: Karma vs. Jnāna in the Gītā Rahasya," Journal of Asian Studies, XVII (February 1958), 197-208.

[30] Ranade, "Theist's Confession," pp. 268-274.

[31] Bhagwat, Brief Account of the Prarthana Mandir, p. 10.

[32] Ibid.

[33] Gokhale, Late Mr. Justice Ranade, p. 10

[34] Charles H. Heimsath, Indian Nationalism and Hindu Social Reform (Princeton, 1964), p. 85.

[35] W. M. Kolhatkar, "Widow Re-Marriage," in Indian Social Reform, ed. C. Y. Chintamani (Madras, 1901), Part I, p. 293.

[36] The leading members, most of whom were also active in the Prarthana Samaj and other reform organizations, included Atmaram Pandurang, Bhau Daji, V. A. Modak, B. M. Wagle, R. G. Bhandarkar, N. M. Paramanand, J. S. Gadgil, and Ranade. The Raja of Jamkhindi, Honorary President of the Widow-Marriage Association, was shortly to become Vice President of the Poona Sarvajanik Sabha, indicating another link in the pattern of liberal reform. As a social reform organization the Widow-Marriage Association could also attract English support directly in a way which a religious body like the Prarthana Samaj could not. Justice J. B. Peile of the Bombay High Court was a major contributor, and other British took part in the association's activities. See The Two Half-Yearly Reports of the Widow-Marriage Association, from 1st February 1869 to 30th January 1870 (Bombay, 1870), passim.

[37] Phatak, Ranade, p. 154.

[38] RDPI, 1860, p. 6. Ranade's viewpoint was pervasive among the liberals. Lokahitawadi had initiated in his Satapatre the Brahmin reformers' attacks on priestly obscurantists. And during the remarriage turmoil M. M. Kunte excoriated the priests, writing that "the clergy try to rule over the rest of society and oppose every reform likely to enlighten the people. Their education is contemptible: their habits are irregular and irreligious." The Reform Question (Bombay, 1870-71), I, 3.

[39] Quoted in Masselos, Towards Nationalism, p. 89.

[40] Kolhatkar, "Widow Re-Marriage," p. 294.

[41] In earlier times Maharashtra had fallen directly under the jurisdiction of the Shankaracharya of Sringeri, the center in northern Mysore. This Shankaracharya, also traditionally a Deshastha, was one of the four swamis who divided the subcontinent into four regions under their authority. But some centuries ago the shastris in parts of Maharashtra had established separately a Shankaracharya of Karvir and Sankeshwar. Though nominally subordinate to Sringeri, he thereafter held de facto authority in the Desh, and it was to him that the Chitpavans turned for guidance. Personal communication from V. V. Paranjpe, July 1969. See also Census of India, 1911 (Bombay, 1912), VII, Part 1, 245.

[42] See Richard P. Tucker, "From Dharmashastra to Politics: Aspects of Social Authority in Nineteenth-Century Maharashtra," IESHR, VII (September 1970), 325-346.

[43] Kunte, Reform Question, I, 20.

[44] Ibid., pp. 14-15.

[45] Kolhatkar, "Widow Re-Marriage," pp. 298ff., gives the most detailed narrative of the affair.

[46] The text of the invitation is printed in Marathi in The Two Half-Yearly Reports, pp. 7-10.

[47] Bombay Gazette, June 18, 1869, p. 3. The guests included John Wilson, High Court Justice Melvill, William Wedderburn, W. W. Hunter, Bhau Daji, Atmaram Pandurang, V. N. Mandlik, Dadoba Pandurang, R. G. Bhandarkar, and Naoroji Furdoonji. This was not the first remarriage in recent times in Maharashtra, but the first which caused a public stir. About 1853 a Gaud Saraswat Brahmin from Ahmedabad married a widow in Poona, but his first wife was still living, so few reformers were willing to champion his position. Kolhatkar, "Widow Re-Marriage," p. 294. One or two other remarriages had also been celebrated privately.

[48] Report of the Widow-Marriage Association includes the text of the marriage invitation, the details of the reformers' efforts to gain public support, and the petitions to the Shankaracharya. The pattern of this conflict between the orthodox and the Western-educated had already emerged over twenty years before. See Dnyanoday, November 1, 1849, pp. 401-403.

[49] Report of the Widow-Marriage Association, pp. 13-14; Parvate, Ranade, p. 50.

[50] Each side chose five men known to favor its views, but the reformers had some difficulty finding their representatives. Krishna Shastri Chiplunkar, an associate of Ranade in the government as well as the reform movement, was forced to do penance for having taken tea and fruit at English homes in Bombay before the orthodox would sit with him. R. G. Bhandarkar was totally disallowed, despite his already impressive reputation for Sanskrit scholarship, since he was a Saraswat Brahmin. See Parvate, Ranade, p. 51.

[51] C. V. Vaidya, The History of Hindu Social Reform Agitation (Poona, 1890), p. 12.

[52] Ranade to Gopalrao, possibly Gopalrao Tilak, a student at Poona Engineering College, November 25, 1869. Quoted in Masselos, Towards Nationalism, p. 267, n. 51.

[53] Kolhatkar, "Widow Re-Marriage," p. 304.

[54] M. G. Ranade, "Vedic Authorities for Widow Marriage," Religious and Social Reform (Bombay, 1902), pp. 55ff.

[55] Ibid., pp. 75ff.

[56] M. G. Ranade, The Texts of the Hindu Law on the Lawfulness of the Remarriage of Widows, with a Note on the "Punarbhu" (Bombay, 1870), p. 18.

[57] Ranade to Deshmukh, May 11, 1870, in Kesari-Mahratta Trust Library.

[58] Kolhatkar, "Widow Re-Marriage," p. 306.

[59] Kunte, Reform Question, I, 30.

[60] Ranade, "Vedic Authorities," p. 90.

[61] D. R. Gadgil, Poona: A Socio-Economic Survey, Part I: Economic (Poona, 1945), p. 19.

[62] Gazetteer of Bombay State, Vol. XX: Poona District (Bombay, 1954), 586.

[63] Mankar, Ranade, I, 82.

[64] Ibid., I, 83.

[65] Ibid., I, 82-83. From 1881 onward there are scattered reports of these gatherings each year in Mahratta.

[66] M. G. Ranade, "Remarks on the Marathi Portion of the Catalogue," Catalogue of Native Publications in the Bombay Presidency, up to 31st December, 1864 (Bombay, 1867), p. 29.

[67] Agashe, Third Anniversary, p. 11.

[68] See below, p. 132.

[69] India Office Library, Private Papers: William Lee-Warner, Finance, Politics, etc., Series IV: 1885-89, p. 125.

[70] From a report in Indu Prakash, quoted in Marathi in Phatak, Ranade, pp. 302-305.

[71] Ramabai Ranade, Reminiscences, pp. 74, 140.

[72] Puṇe vedaśāstrottejaka sabhecā śake 1808 sālacā vārṣika riporṭa (Poona Society for Promoting the Veda: Annual Report for 1883-84) (Poona, 1884), p. 12.

[73] Agashe, Third Anniversary, p. 7.

[74] D. V. Kirtane, in Indian Worthies, pp. 23, 26.

[75] Reay to Dufferin, May 24, 1885, Dufferin Papers, 47 Reel 528, quoted in Anil Seal, The Emergence of Indian Nationalism (Cambridge, 1968), p. 237.

[76] Phatak, Ranade, p. 262.

[77] Ramabai Ranade, Reminiscences, p. 188.

[78] A constant theme in Ramabai's account is her conflicts with the orthodox women in the family; Ranade often had to intervene to maintain a modus vivendi.

[79] N. G. Chandavarkar, Speeches and Writings (Bombay, 1911), pp. 348-349.

[80] N. C. Kelkar, Pleasures and Privileges of the Pen (Poona, n.d.), p. 112.

[81] Agashe, Third Anniversary, p. 6.

[82] Ramabai Ranade, Reminiscences, p. 19.

[83] Mankar, Ranade, I, 22.

[84] James Kellock, Mahadev Govind Ranade (Calcutta, 1926), p. 59.

[85] Ramabai Ranade, Reminiscences, pp. 21-22.

[86] Ibid., p. 34.

[87] Indu Prakash, quoted in Times of India, December 18, 1873, and Bombay Gazette, December 17, 1873.

[88] The idea of the public hero as a source of moral inspiration to his followers was a widespread notion common to Hindu tradition and Victorian culture. For the Victorian cult of heroism, see Walter E. Houghton, The Victorian Frame of Mind (New Haven, 1957), pp. 316-324.

[89] D. V. Krishna Rao, "The Methods of Social Reform," Hindustan Review, VIII (September 1903), 224-225.

[90] Parvate, Ranade, pp. 69-70.

[91] Ramabai Ranade, Reminiscences, p. 45.

[92] The Poona samaj held "Divine Service" on Sunday morning and a "Tukaram Service" on Friday evening; both were usually in Marathi. Its membership grew from 47 in 1870 to 89 in 1875, four years after Ranade joined. Shinde, Theistic Directory, pp. 138, 147-148.

[93] Ibid., pp. 148-149.

[94] G. C. Bhate, History of Modern Marathi Literature, 1800-1938 (Poona, 1939), p. 147.

[95] Bawa Chhajju Singh, The Life and Teachings of Swami Dayanand Saraswati, Part I (Lahore, 1903), p. 256.

[96] Two accounts of Dayanand's visit from sources close to Ranade are in Agashe, Third Anniversary, p. 8, and Phatak, Ranade, pp. 230-234. Other detailed accounts of the affair from the orthodox side present very different narratives and interpretations, leaving many facts open to question. The controversy was heated for many years after the event, indicating the depth of feeling which the events produced.

[97] Chandavarkar, Speeches and Writings, p. 543.

[98] Masselos, Towards Nationalism, pp. 176-177.

[99] Agashe, Third Anniversary, p. 8.

[100] Chandavarkar, Karve, p. 56.

[101] Sastri, Brahmo Samaj, II, 423-424.

[102] Shinde, Theistic Directory, p. 134.

Chapter 4

NATIONALIST POLITICS IN THE DESH, 1867-1880

> There is one class among the Brahmins
> who indirectly foment all troubles
> . . . and they are 'in' with every row
> in the Deccan. --Sir Richard Temple

Most writers who have assessed Ranade's political work in Poona in the 1870's have shared the prevailing British assessment from that time: that he moved there when the society of the former capital had been totally demoralized and disorganized for a half century, and that he single-handedly constructed the institutional basis of modern life there. This assessment portrays him as almost superhuman, and his fall from unchallenged pre-eminence in later years has seemed correspondingly monumental. This view cannot be substantiated; for the society of Poona was already loosely grouped into disparate political interest groups, and modern public associations had existed there in their infancy for at least a generation before 1871. Ranade's achievements were two: first, to revitalize a series of existing organizations and thereby to overcome for a time the factional differences which plagued the city beneath its surface. In the process he revealed himself as a man of considerable administrative genius. Second, he provided a coherent and balanced ideology of moderate nationalism through which he gave the movement a sense of direction. In this he provided the same strength which he was imparting to the religious reform movement, but his political writings were far more substantial and broad-reaching than his spiritual essays. In these ways he earned his well-known title, "uncrowned king of Poona." His claim to this status was more as a unifier than as an originator. In order to assess his role more accurately, we must first describe briefly the pattern of public life which greeted him that chill November of 1871.

Factions, Alliances and the Sarvajanik Sabha

Public life in Poona before 1870 was dominated by fragile alliances of the traditional social leaders, the shastris and sardars, and the newly appearing group of modernizers, the students educated at Poona College who were known in the press as "Young Poona." These three groups faced a complex task of reconciling their interests, both before and throughout Ranade's time.

Ever since the early eighteenth century, when the Peshwas made Poona their capital, many of the landed aristocrats of the Desh had owned homes there. Most of their wadas, elegant buildings with spacious central courtyards, still stand in the old neighborhoods on three sides of

Shanwar Wada palace. In Ranade's time these were the usual locations of schools, public meetings, voluntary organizations and exhibitions. Their owners were the traditionally accepted arbiters of power; they inevitably played a major supportive role in public life, even when they chose not to initiate movements. Their interests were always taken into account.

The British from Elphinstone onward courted the sardars' loyalty and attempted to associate them, at least symbolically, with new ventures. These new initiatives took the form of an interlocking series of schools and public institutions, closely modelled on those of Bombay, which were nearly all founded by 1852. British officers, both military and civilian, with the support of the local missionaries, maintained careful control over them until the time of Ranade's arrival. In the single instance when Indian initiative threatened to be too independent, the British quietly and firmly discouraged it. This is not to say that the representatives of the empire did not welcome cooperation from the luminaries of Poona. They made it abundantly clear that the key to progress was the sardars' participation in the schools. But like their counterparts in Bombay, the British in Poona faced constant discouragement in their efforts to share Western enlightenment with the leading classes of the Desh.

Under Elphinstone the dakshina subsidies which the Peshwas had given to learned Brahmins had been used to establish Sanskrit College along the lines of the older Sanskrit College in Benares. The college was located in the heart of the city, using for wuarters the Peshwas' palace, Vishrambag Wada.[1] At first the curriculum was confined to the classical Sanskrit learning, but by 1840 it began to be replaced by a secular Western curriculum. By 1850 the British increased pressure on the Brahmin teachers to admit non-Brahmin students into all branches of its curriculum, and simultaneously encouraged the sardars to send their sons to the college and grace its public functions with their presence. Several Brahmin sardars, men like Abasaheb Dhamdhere and the Rastes, who were leaders in every public association of the time, willingly lent their prestige.[2] But on the whole, the sardars responded little to Western education itself. After all, schooling was more attractive to sons of pandits and Brahmin administrators than to those whose wealth and status were not dependent on formal education. When Erskine Perry retired from the Board of Education in 1852, the sardars and others united behind the initiative of English professors at the college to send him a loyal memorial, and in return he wrote: "It has been a matter of . . . regret that the old aristocracy of the Deccan is withering under British rule, and the efforts of some of our most distinguished statesmen have been directed . . . to propping up those ancient houses, whose good swords made the name of Maharashtra famous throughout India."[3] But when they failed to contribute significantly to scholarships in his honor, the British editor of the Poona Observer scolded them candidly:

"We positively blush for the meanness of these so-called Sirdars of the Deccan."[4]

The task of cooperating more steadfastly with the British mentors thus fell by default, as it largely did in Bombay, to the sons of less aristocratic Brahmins. These were the early graduates of the English curriculum of Poona High School, a tightly knit group of intellectually Anglicized crusaders much like Ranade a decade later, who appeared in the years around 1850. Gopal Hari Deshmukh was the best known of them, partly through his "Lokahitawadi" essays from 1848 onward, and partly through his editorials in Poona's first Marathi weekly, Dnyan Prakash (The Light of Knowledge), which he and his associates founded in 1849. Deshmukh also helped to organize virtually every public meeting and voluntary organization in Poona during the following decade.[5] Ranade's style of leadership in later years owed a profound debt to Deshmukh, his friend and mentor.

Others, too, with whom Ranade later worked intimately were active in Young Poona. Vishnu Moreshwar Bhide, a leading light in political organizations for the rest of the century, appeared by 1852, as did Krishna Shastri Chiplunkar, the outstanding student of the college and the leader of the subsequent movement for literary revival. These young crusaders eagerly followed their British mentors when they established the Deccan Vernacular Translation Society in 1848. The society was designed to diffuse useful knowledge throughout the Deccan, and implicitly to inculcate the proper loyalty to British rule among its Indian protégés. This society's work was furthered by the Poona Native General Library, founded in 1849, with which Deshmukh was closely associated, and then by the Deccan Institute in 1853, which was a replica of the Students' Literary and Scientific Society in Bombay.[6] Although the fruits of these efforts were meager indeed in these years, they provided institutional and occupational patterns which the new Western-educated class pursued from then onward. When Ranade arrived in the city he found the same men somewhat older and less aggressive, yet ready to make new efforts in familiar directions.

From the beginning both the sardars and the educated faction confronted delicate political implications in their work. The sardars were faced in the 1850's with the government's challenge to the validity of their traditional inams, or grants of tax-free land. The Deccan Inam Commission, whose offices were situated in Poona, began in 1848 a systematic examination of the validity of all inams granted by the Peshwas. The sardars feared that if their rights were stripped from them any British protestation of sympathy such as Perry's would stand as cynical pretense.[7] Consequently, for the decade of the commission's active investigations, relations between the sardars and the Raj were unavoidably guarded. At the same time, every leading member of the educated group took up positions in the educational or judicial service of the British. This difference of orientation among potentially powerful allies was an important safeguard for British interests. That they were aware of the fact was indicated by their subtle but firm response when both groups jointly organized in the early 1850's to further their mutual political interests.

Modern associational life as initiated by Indians began in Poona in May of 1850, when Mor Shastri Sathe, one of the city's leading pandits, founded the Kalyāṇonnāyaka Maṇḍalī (Society for General Amelioration). Sathe's major interest lay in the revival of moral and religious vitality in the community, but he attempted to adopt the organizational procedures which the British were introducing and apply them to the full range of public issues. The mandali proposed in its manifesto both to "make known the real meaning of the shastras" and to "discuss all new projects having relation to the good of the community."[8] A chairman and treasurer, as well as an executive committee of the traditional five members, were to be appointed, and members were expected to pay voluntary dues. Initially, the mandali seems to have gained little support, as Sathe was involved in factional conflicts among the shastris, and there was no precedent anywhere in western India for his organization. But by 1852 the mandali was transformed into a far more secular form, with the active participation of both the sardars and the educated.

Following the lead of the British Indian Association of Calcutta, Poona established its first predominantly political association, the Deccan Association, in February 1852. The association was designed to press its political interests before Parliament, in time for the East India Company's charter renewal.[9] Bapusaheb Raste for the sardars and Deshmukh for the educated seem to have been the prime movers. Its salient demands included security for all existing land rights and other prerogatives of the sardars, and the reservation of far more government posts, especially for educated Indians. Its meetings were presided over by Indians, not Englishmen. No Englishman could be sure how far the association's demands might escalate, or how serious the political threat might become, in a region where British rule still seemed precarious. When after a few public meetings the association fell into quiescence that summer, its leaders had no doubt of the reason. The English-language press began to suggest that the government, perhaps through R. Keays, its Agent for the Sardars in Poona, was discreetly opposed to the movement. At the annual prize-giving ceremony of Poona College that July, he pointedly urged leading citizens to pursue their political interests by accepting government positions: "It rests entirely with you to shorten the period when . . . you can be allowed to take a part in the administration of the affairs of your country in higher appointments."[10] By September the reformers' voice, Dnyan Prakash, stated the public's belief that the Bombay government was threatening to destroy the Deccan Association if necessary. The rumor alone had already been responsible for the withdrawal of several members from the association.[11] As an alternative strategy, several members joined the newly founded Bombay Association, whose purposes were identical but whose leaders were more fully trusted by the government.[12]

For the next several years political life was quiescent in Poona. During the rebellion of 1857, which swept over the northern plains and nearly ignited the Desh as well, the Hindu elite of Poona cautiously refrained from political activity, and the only plot which seriously concerned the British centered about a small group of Muslims.[13] Political life revived in the following year with the establishment of the Poona Municipal Committee, the forerunner of Poona's present city government. A regulation of 1850 had enabled any town whose citizens petitioned the government to have a municipal committee with Indian members appointed by the government. Although some of Poona's leading men petitioned Bombay to this effect in 1850 or 1851, their interest was soon diverted to the Deccan Association. It was only after the initiation of new municipal taxes in 1857 that the committee was formally established. Its chairman was the British district magistrate, and it included eleven Indian members. Significantly, most of those eleven were non-Maharashtrian residents of the city; only one was a sardar and only one had been active in Young Poona.[14] For many years thereafter, corporation administration was open largely to the most cautious government servants; it was an insignificant aspect of political life in the city.

In the following decade there was little independent political action in Poona, for the educated class was preoccupied with professions in government and responsibilities as heads of families. But this new Western-educated cadre had gained considerable experience in public life by the late 1860's. They had become accustomed to providing the organizational leadership which the sardars quietly supported but rarely initiated. It was no surprise, given this alliance, that whatever modernizing the professionals envisioned, they had no intention of significantly changing the existing patterns of social prestige and wealth. Ideologically and politically they were advanced; socially they were conservative.[15]

In the four years immediately preceding Ranade's arrival in Poona, a new round of organizational activity occurred. The British had maintained their posture of cautiously encouraging self-reform within the Indian community, and once again in 1867 Poona anticipated Bombay by six months in reviving its political association. The new Poona Association's leaders included many familiar names among the sardars and professionals of the former Deccan Association. This time, though, there were new recruits to the educated circle, notably men trained as lawyers. One of the most prominent, K. P. Gadgil, was destined to play a leading role in Moderate politics through the rest of the century.

The Poona Association, like its predecessor, pledged itself to the dual role which Frere and others envisioned for India's new leaders:

loyal critics of the Raj and the government's political apologists to the masses. In its three-year lifetime, the association concentrated on local affairs, studying municipal problems and reporting on economic and commercial conditions.[16] But the sporadic character of its work showed that it still lacked sustained leadership. It was superseded in 1870 by the Sarvajanik Sabha, which derived its membership from both the fragile political interests and the more deeply rooted religious interests of the city.

The Parvati temple was one of Poona's most important religious sites, having formerly been favored by daily visits and financial subsidies from the Peshwas. After 1818 the British Raj continued to give financial support to the temple but exercised no direct control over its administration. This was left to a committee of five, who held life tenure and chose their own successors. The government only required unanimous agreement of the five on major policies before the monthly subsidy was released to them. During the 1850's this led to sometimes bitter personal feuds among the committee's members over its financial management.[17] In 1858 sardar Ganesh Ballal Natu, the chairman, charged some of its members with fraudulent use of funds, whereupon the British Collector suggested for the first time that the committee be elected by the citizens of Poona. The conflict was informally resolved at the time, but in 1869 it flared again. This time the chairman of the Parvati temple panchayat was Natu's son, Ramchandra Ganesh, who was simultaneously president of the Poona Association and later a member of the managing committee of the Sarvajanik Sabha.[18] In March 1869 Natu repeated the charges of fraud against other committee members. Joining with friends he appealed to the public through Dnyan Prakash to found a broadly based association to oversee the management of the Parvati temple. After a year of discussion with the Poona Association, the two groups united to establish the Poona Sarvajanik Sabha on April 2, 1870. Traditional public concerns were henceforth united with modern political techniques in Poona, and for the next twenty-seven years the resulting association was prominent on the political map of western India.

The Sarvajanik Sabha was dominated by the familiar elites of the Desh and Poona; its manifesto made pointedly clear that it intended to speak with one voice for the people as a whole. In describing its members as "men of position and respectability, inamdars or proprietors of land, savkars or moneylenders, merchants, pensioned government officers, pleaders, professors, and most of the ruling chiefs of the Southern Maratha country,"[19] it defined with some precision the social and professional groups whom it became Ranade's lifelong task to weld into effective and unified leadership for Maharashtra. Its claim to have representatives of all interest groups in the Deccan was more a hope than a reality, for it had only token representation of Parsis, Muslims, the commercial castes, and non-Brahmins.[20] But the sabha's claim to systematic representation of the society reflected a highly significant innovation: it established a precise procedure for membership. Each candidate was required to gain the power of attorney from at least fifty people, allowing him "to act . . . in our name and on our behalf in all public matters."[21] By September 1871 the sabha had 141 members who represented, on paper at least, some 17,000 citizens.[22] This gave the sabha a firmer basis for claiming to represent the people as a whole than any of its predecessors in Poona or Bombay, though the Bombay government was reluctant to acknowledge the fact.

The Sarvajanik Sabha made a systematic appeal to conservative groups. Its titular leadership came predominantly from the sardars. Whether or not they took an active role in its affairs, it needed both their financial support and their social authority. As long as the sabha articulated their interests as well as others, it could claim their support. Further, the sabha gained the participation of the religious conservatives, who showed by their participation in its affairs that orthodoxy and modern political activity were not necessarily incompatible, so long as the political leaders avoided religious controversies. The only religious question on which the sabha took a stand was its support of the existing government policy regarding religious endowments. Before long, its interest even in the management of Parvati temple faded. Its policy of religious neutrality gained important recruits. Its first president was the Pant Pratinidhi, the jagirdar of Oundh, who was a champion of the orthodox party in the concurrent religious reform debates.[23] Shortly thereafter, Ram Dixit Apte, who later presented the orthodox lectures rebutting Dayananda Saraswati, became a member of the sabha's managing committee and thus a political associate of Ranade.[24] In contrast, aside from Ranade, few of the religious and social liberals were active in the sabha. For the time being, the two streams of reform pursued separate courses. One reason for the increasing breadth of Ranade's influence in Poona was that he more than any other figure was able to sustain both social and political reform efforts simultaneously.

During its first two years the Sarvajanik Sabha placed primary emphasis on local affairs around Poona, acting in effect as the independent adjunct of the municipal committee. Its usual method was the well-tried practice of memorializing the government, with a plea to reduce the number of legal liquor shops in Poona, suggestions on the local revenue courts, and a protest against new commercial and police taxes.[25] These initiatives provoked no strong British opposition. But in 1872 a decisive change occurred in its character, a permanent transformation which was largely the work of two men, Ranade and Ganesh Vasudev Joshi. Joshi was one of Poona's most respected lawyers, a native of Satara who had acted as legal representative for various sardars in the two towns for many years. In this capacity he more than any other man bridged the gap between the sardars and the newer professional class. Since he held no governmental position, he was able to supply the week-to-week administrative sinews of the sabha until his death in 1878. And since he was truly comfortable only in the simplest traditional dress and speaking Marathi, he provided the common touch which linked the sabha with the society at large. In consequence, he soon became known as "Sarvajanik Kaka," the uncle and guardian of the people.[26] Ranade, in contrast, was the brightest young star among the Bombay-educated. By 1872 he was already well known in Poona for his executive ability and his aggressive championing of reform causes. He was soon welcomed by all those who trusted Joshi, for he could provide the links with Bombay's politics and the detailed ideological base which the Sarvajanik Sabha needed in order to transcend its purely local interests.

Ranade and Joshi soon brought the sabha into the liberal political alliance which stretched from Calcutta to London and was already actively lobbying on the foremost issue of the day: increased representation of Indians in the government. Official encouragement of this action had come in 1870 when the viceroy, Lord Mayo, decentralized administration of portions of the imperial budget, giving the provincial governments control over receipts and expenditures for police, jails, education, and other items. While financial economy was the principal motive for this change, the viceroy hoped that the change would "afford opportunities for the development of self-government, for strengthening municipal institutions, and for the association of Natives and Europeans to a greater extent than heretofore in the administration of affairs."[27] The Queen had promised in the Proclamation of 1858 that Indians and Englishmen should be treated alike as government employees. But Mayo's resolution, put forth in the context of a concrete policy decision, brought to the test the fundamental principle on which Indian loyalty rested. From this time onward the question of representation was rarely absent from public debate. The reformers' preoccupation with it indicated not only their desire to gain avenues to power but their concern for the integrity of the British political system.

As early as 1848, Lokahitawadi had proposed in some detail a system of admitting Indian representatives to the Indian legislative councils and the imperial Parliament. In Bombay, Dadabhai Naoroji and others had subsequently kept the proposal alive. Acting in this tradition, the Sarvajanik Sabha memorialized the Bombay government on July 28, 1872, suggesting a revised system of selecting Indian representatives to the Presidency Legislative Council. At the time, four were appointed from Bombay and only one from the rest of the Presidency. The memorial suggested that two should be appointed from Bombay, two from elsewhere in Maharashtra, one from Gujarat, and one from the Southern Maratha country. More care should be taken to appoint at least one Muslim and to obtain some members with high-level education.[28] The sabha also repeated the demand that Parliament in London include seats for India, as the two associations in Bombay were suggesting. In a petition to Parliament in 1874 it requested that eighteen seats be reserved for Indian members, who would be elected by all citizens of British India who paid annual taxes of Rs. 50 or more.[29] Ranade and the sabha organized a campaign throughout the Desh to gather signatures for the petition; it is said that the number of signers was approximately 200,000, an astounding figure for the time. The petitions elicited no official response, so Ranade warned his associates that they must not expect rapid changes from the British but must be sure that Indian society was prepared for representation when it appeared. He saw the primary purpose of the petitions as educating the people in modern political processes. In the long interim before representative institutions became a reality, India must satisfy itself with indirect representation.[30]

Anticipating the failure of the campaign to gain seats in Parliament, Ranade had already induced the Sarvajanik Sabha to raise funds to support the East India Association's work of publicity and pressure in London.[31] Their optimism concerning the efficacy of this work rested on the assumption that Parliament and the English people were sincerely committed to safeguarding India's interests, even against the policies of Conservative governments and the Anglo-Indian bureaucracy. This was their means of coming to terms with the obvious conflict between the principles of English constitutionalism and the existing authoritarianism of the political system of India. Their hopes, now and later, rested on the Liberal party, which harbored the few members of Parliament who presented the East India Association's views in Commons.

This campaign brought the Indian political associations into fresh confrontation with detailed issues of finance and administration, the area of Ranade's growing professional competence. When Gladstone's Liberal government instituted a parliamentary committee in 1871 under Henry Fawcett to investigate the chronic defects of the Government of India's finances, the associations of Bombay and Poona decided to send material and representatives to aid the committee. Poona finally sent no representative to London, allowing Naoroji Furdoonji from the Bombay Association to represent them instead. The Sarvajanik Sabha was content to send an address to Professor Fawcett, praising him as a true representative of India's interests in England.[32]

Their view of the Liberal party as India's steady defenders was negatively confirmed with the Conservative victory in the elections of 1874. One of Disraeli's first moves was the adjournment of the Fawcett Committee, confirming Ranade's belief that the Conservatives were the parliamentary support of "the entire herd of officialdom," as he called the Anglo-Indian bureaucrats.[33] Two lessons were becoming clearer to Ranade: that the English career bureaucrats in India had little patience with any Indian criticism of their rule; and that they had the consistent support of the imperialist Conservative party.

The Ideology of Liberal Nationalism

These experiences of the pattern of power in British India led Ranade in the early 1870's to formulate an ideology of moderate but systematic opposition to the Raj. This he presented in a series of writings and speeches; each of them was designed for a specific occasion, but in their total pattern they provided a heightened sense of direction for the political movement of the Desh. Many of his views were already familiar to Bombay audiences from the work of his older contemporaries, but Ranade presented them with a coherence and substance which demanded attention and helped make them commonplace in the Moderate school of nationalist politics. Further, in these years when the British had experienced little or no articulate dissent, the impact of Ranade's writings was unsettling to both government officials and journalists.

As the Fawcett Committee's work indicated, some of the outstanding controversies of the early 1870's concerned fiscal issues, an area in which Ranade had had considerable training. The committee's work centered on the problem of imperial taxation. The Government of India's budget between 1867 and 1869 showed a total deficit of £5,774,000. Pressure consequently arose within the government to raise the rates of existing license, salt and land taxes, establish an unprecedented income tax, and retrench on spending for education and public works.[34] The Indian political associations saw these trends as uniformly inimical to their interests; on their side Dadabhai Naoroji and others were at work defining the "Drain Theory" of India's financial and political condition.[35] Ranade had begun a lifelong association with Dadabhai at Elphinstone College. Through the 1870's Ranade generally followed the older man's thinking on financial and administrative affairs. At the time of the Fawcett Committee's work, Ranade established his authority in Poona on economic affairs with two Marathi lectures on Indian economic conditions, in which his critique of imperial policies roughly reflected Dadabhai's position. On December 8, 1872, he dealt primarily with the drain of wealth from India to England, producing the sharpest criticism of England's economic policy that he ever published. He charged the government with primary responsibility for India's poverty, stating that each year one third of India's tax revenues went to England as Home Charges, and that great amounts of raw materials were being shipped to England, primarily for the profit of Englishmen. In return, by shipping its manufactured goods to India, England was undermining the Indian market for indigenous goods.[36]

In the second lecture Ranade argued that this competition had resulted in a rapid decline of Indian manufacturing, throwing many workers back on the strained resources of the soil. This was a disaster for the entrepreneurial class, who held the key to India's future economic development. India possessed considerable potential in its raw materials and agricultural products, but English initiative and English capital were depriving Indians of their own wealth. Foreign capitalists were setting up farms and businesses and paying Indian laborers only a subsistence wage for helping them exploit the country.

It was in this lecture that Ranade's habit of self-criticism appeared. He pointed to a major weakness in his own society, which he felt must be faced directly and not blamed on the imperial government. Ever the Victorian moralist, he vowed that the uplift of India must finally come through its own efforts, admonishing the people for wasting investment capital by burying it in the earth or purchasing expensive jewelry. Having seen the prosperity which trade and industry had brought to Bombay, he insisted that Indians change their habits and use this wealth to start indigenous industries.

Here in embryo was the swadeshi strategy, the belief that India would become economically strong and independent only if she relied on her own industrial products and refused to buy European imports. Ranade was not the first in Poona to raise the flag of swadeshi, for Lokahitawadi had suggested this strategy before 1850, and G. V. Joshi became famous in the Desh in the 1870's for wearing only swadeshi clothes. Ranade's endorsement of the position gave it increased weight. Swadeshi for him was not a matter of rejecting British expertise; India must study Western industrial processes carefully and then use them for its own purposes. Only a receptivity to Western methods, combined with determined self-reliance in their application, could bring new wealth to India.[37] That he meant to implement these views directly became clear in April 1874 when he and Joshi organized the first annual exhibition of swadeshi industries in Poona in the name of the Sarvajanik Sabha.[38] The exhibitions were attended by large numbers of both Indians and Englishmen; they featured a wide range of products of modern small-scale factories owned by both Brahmins and non-Brahmin sardars throughout the old Maratha domains.

In the same years, Ranade's selective critique of the British Raj came to bear also on the Anglo-Indian bureaucracy of which he was a part. In 1871 and 1872 he wrote an attack on the increasingly rigid and bureaucratic structure of the British Raj which, though little known, is one of the first and most incisive of many nationalist attacks. It also reveals the strong influence of Whig principles of government on his mind. The 1860's had seen systematic codification of law in India. Standard systems of procedure were established between 1859 and 1861 by the Penal Code, the Code of Civil Procedure, and the Code of Criminal Procedure. These codes, which provided the basis for Ranade's work as a judge, were in his eyes the final guarantor of the subjects' rights against the threat of despotic government. His pamphlet on the system of civil justice has been lost, but enough appears in his critique of the system of criminal justice, published in 1872, to indicate the full range of his views. The essays were designed as a rebuttal to the proposals of Sir James Stephen, Law Member of the Viceroy's Council. On grounds of political prudence,

Stephen favored retention of the Non-Regulation system of administration wherever possible, in which executive and judicial powers were combined in the hands of district revenue officers. Stephen claimed that the grant of these powers to local officers was necessary as a means of guaranteeing the political stability of India.

When Ranade received a copy of the proposals with a request for his comments, he wrote the response which marked his first appearance on the stage of all-India administration. Ranade warned against giving the district collector undivided and therefore authoritarian power. No other British officer was both so powerful within his sphere and so intimately in contact with the daily life of the people as the district officer; hence the tendency toward despotism inherent in the British Raj must be checked at this point. Stating a theme to which he returned frequently throughout his career, Ranade attacked the all-powerful collectors for their lack of understanding of local conditions and their discouragement of Indians from acting responsibly for themselves. The most effective step toward checking these abuses, he suggested, was to ensure the courts full autonomy, for under a modern political system only the courts could act as disinterested defenders of Indian society.

> The disparity between the power represented by the governing classes and the capacity on the part of the subject millions to influence the exercise of this power for good, and to check its evils or abuses, is so great that, in the interests of a good and progressive liberal Government, it is essential that the two functions of sovereignty represented by the Judge and the collector of revenue must be entrusted to separate officers. The judicial courts are emphatically the only institutions in the land which serve the purposes of a formally guaranteed constitution to conserve the rights of the subject population; and the education they give in the habits of constitutional obedience to the law, as distinguished from abject submission to the individual will of the officer declaring and executing the law, is of a sort which can never be too highly esteemed.[39]

Ranade's negative view of the Non-Regulation system also contained a historical dimension: he saw it as perpetuating the evils of the former Indian tyrannies in a more dangerous form. In contrast to his early essays on Shivaji, Ranade by now was acutely aware of the deficiencies of pre-British governments in India. His years in Bombay had convinced him of the superiority of constitutional government; an independent judiciary seemed the decisive innovation of the British. Without the courts Ranade feared a dangerous continuity between the old Hindu rule and the authoritarian strand in British administration. In contrasting the new authoritarianism with the old, Ranade revealed his view of both the weaknesses and the strengths of the Hindu political system.

> The old native model in which civil, military, revenue, police and judicial functions were united in one and the same hands, each petty officer representing the full absolute sovereign within his own domain, has brought the nation into its present plight of helpless dependence. In the case of native rulers, common sympathy and the restraints of religion offered some guarantees against the worst evils of this absolutism. As both these checks are wanting under the British rule, the perfect independence of the courts of justice is the only security provided by the constitution.[40]

Despite his commitment to the values represented by the judicial system, Ranade reserved severe criticisms for the courts, echoing the minority view of British justice in India which both Indians and a few Englishmen had been expressing for years. However much the new courts had improved over the former panchayat system in principle, their cumbersome procedures made it impossible to guarantee justice in practice. The complex procedures of trials and the long appeal process deprived the people of effective legal protection and corrupted those whose living depended on the courts.

> The waste of powers involved in the present arrangement is simply frightful to contemplate; the weakening of responsibilities, the encouragement given to frivolous complaints, the demoralization of the people caused by this frequent recourse to the police courts, and the inefficiency generally of the work done, are all of a sort which demand a radical change.[41]

In order to reverse this trend, the courts must be given a flexibility which would allow the judge not a despotic power over the people but adequate discretion to tailor laws and regulations to the circumstances of each case. Codified law, however brilliantly conceived, was incapable in practice of securing full justice, and must be supplemented by the judge's detailed knowledge of legal and social traditions. It was at this point that Ranade wrote in clearest sympathy with the virtue of the traditional Hindu judicial system, which was the arbiters intimate knowledge of the conditions underlying legal conflicts.

Bombay Presidency approximated his ideal in some regards. It was more flexible in its regulations than either Bengal or Madras, yet at the same time it did not share the authoritarian evils of the Non-Regulation provinces. At the higher levels, the Bombay courts were autonomous and judges were given wide areas of discretion in arriving at decisions.[42] Nonetheless, at subordinate levels the Bombay system still assigned judicial powers to the collectors,[43] and here lay its greatest offense. The subordinate judges' close contacts with local conditions were largely vitiated by the appeal system in which, as Ranade interpreted it, "the first appeal is always an appeal from a well-informed to an ill-informed tribunal--from a Judge of considerable standing and experience, versed in native languages and perfectly acquainted with native character, and hearing and recording the story as told by the witnesses before him, to a Judge often his junior in years and standing, unversed in native languages and manners."[44] This was implicitly a defense of the prerogatives of Indian subjudges against their British superiors, since most of the judges like himself sitting on original hearings were Indians, while their superiors were universally English.[45] The political implication of Ranade's argument was clear: if intimate understanding of the circumstances surrounding conflicts was a precondition of justice, Indian rather than foreign judges should be appointed wherever possible. He further maintained, as did most of the Indian political leaders of his time, that for judges of equal rank and training it was discriminatory to pay lower salaries to Indians than to Englishmen.[46] This was the point at which the British Raj seemed most transparently caught in a contradiction between avowed ideals and the actual application of its power. This contradiction was the source of Ranade's growing ambivalence concerning the power and responsibilities of a paternalistic regime.

The Sarvajanik Sabha and Political Polarization

The increasing candor of Ranade's critiques, and the growing precision of his argument evidently alarmed not only conservative British but older men in the Sarvajanik Sabha as well. Fragmentary evidence indicates that both sardars and government servants educated in the pre-university era, felt that Ranade was threatening both political harmony and their authority within the sabha. This faction was led by K. L. Nulkar, the chairman of its managing committee during most of the 1870's. In contrast with Ranade's stance, Nulkar continued to stress the sabha's task of interpreting the Raj to the populace.[47] Although these differences of strategy were never allowed to endanger the unified action of the association during the decade, they did presage the more divisive conflicts among nationalists in later years. They kept firmly before Ranade the realization that unified political action was a difficult matter indeed to achieve.

Another factional difference with which Ranade had to contend was the contrast between the Western-educated and the landholding classes. The petition to the Bombay government in 1872 outlining a more equitable system of representation in the provincial legislative council included a plea for more reserved positions for the educated class; previous uneducated nominees, it asserted, had not proved either useful or representative of true Indian interests.[48] The Western-educated men who had assumed leadership of the Sarvajanik Sabha appreciated the support of the otherwise inert landholding class, but they were becoming impatient of the British government's policy of appointing sycophantic landholders to the legislative council. The incipient divergence of interests between the two Indian elites posed a serious threat to their combined strength. Both for the sake of unified action, and in order to extend their role as effective spokesmen for their whole society, Ranade and the educated group led the movement from 1873 onward to challenge the agrarian policies of the Raj. In the extent to which they succeeded in forging unified action against official policies, they contributed to a steady polarization between imperial British and subject Indians as the decade wore on. In this pattern Ranade was the central figure.

The Sarvajanik Sabha was well placed to spearhead this trend, for by 1873 the political associations of the Presidency cities were once again in decline,[49] while the Poona sabha had many and intimate contacts with the mofussil. For the rest of the decade the sharpest conflicts between the sabha and the Bombay government were directly related to the debate over the condition of the ryots, or agricultural castes, of the Desh.

Agricultural conditions in the Desh were chronically depressed, for the soil of the Deccan plains was poor and the monsoon rains inadequate and unpredictable. Exacerbating the situation were caste and ethnic conflicts in the countryside. The vast majority of the farmers were Marathas and Kunbis, the middle-caste backbone of the Maharashtrian population. However, the savkars, the moneylenders who provided the funds which sustained them from year to year, were not their caste fellows. Some were local Brahmins, but as the British revenue system stimulated the expansion of the money market, an increasing number of outsiders appeared, both Marwaris and Gujarati Banias.[50]

The chaotic conditions of the last years of the Peshwas left the ryots deeply in debt to their creditors. The first British revenue settlements, carried out according to abstract Utilitarian formulas, established disastrously high rates and thereby only exacerbated the trouble.[51] When these rates were adjusted downward, some thirty years of general prosperity ensued, postponing further troubles until the late 1860's. A reconsideration of the tax rates was due in 1867, and recent prosperity led the government to raise rates in many areas. In this it failed to anticipate the severe drought of the following year and the poor seasons and steadily falling price levels which followed.[52]

The Bombay Association began a survey of mofussil conditions after 1870, recognizing that its protest against the new income tax was connected to the rural tax grievance.[53] The Sarvajanik Sabha, however, was in a better position to conduct the survey, since its members had closer contact with the mofussil. This survey, carried out by a committee working under Ranade's guidance, was closely related to the formation of branch sabhas during this period in Sholapur, Satara, Karhad, Wai, Dharwar, Nasik, and Dhulia.[54] The committee's summary report, submitted to the Bombay government in mid-1873, described far more serious rural dislocation than the government had ever admitted, and pressed its case with unprecedented boldness. Referring to the 1867 tax rates as a "measure of confiscation," it charged that high, inaccurate and rigid assessments were forcing large numbers of ryots off the land and even threatening the solvency of large landholders. Poor soil conditions and recent inadequate rains in the Desh only exacerbated troubles for which the sabha held the government largely responsible. The British, it charged, had ignored the traditional custom of remitting taxes in times of stress: "When . . . the assessment is levied indifferently in all seasons under penalty of forfeiting the land, is it any wonder that the ryot is involved in bondage to the sowcar?"[55] By direct implication the sabha had found a dramatic example of the impact of bureaucratic rigidity: the harmonious fabric of a well-ordered, hierarchical society was in danger of unravelling unless policies were quickly changed. Bania and Marwari moneylenders, interlopers who cared little for that harmony, were the only beneficiaries of existing rates, for "the sowcar . . . sinks no capital in the land itself, but speculates . . . upon the improvident habits of the peasantry."[56] Under these conditions, the cooperative development of the economy which Ranade's economic lectures of these same months envisaged was out of the question.

The sabha's report did succeed in eliciting an official inquiry into the condition of the Deccan, but in the short run this was little consolation. The inquiry admitted the seriousness of the trouble, but no policy changes resulted, and meanwhile British officers in the districts began charging the Sarvajanik Sabha with what amounted to seditious agitation among the peasantry.[57]

Two years later the tensions of rural Maharashtra exploded in the most severe agrarian riots in many years.[58] In late 1874 Koli tribesmen revolted against Marwari moneylenders in several villages, where they were known to press without restraint for recovery of debts. Rumors quickly spread that the savkars were going to foreclose on large amounts of property, and on May 12, 1875, the Deccan Riots began. Cultivators in many parts of Poona, Satara, Sholapur, and Ahmednagar districts attacked the homes of their creditors, destroying the financial papers which recorded their debts. In most cases there was little serious crime or destruction of property. Most of the victims were Marwari and Gujarati savkars; local Brahmin moneylenders were usually spared.[59] The upheavals died out within about a month, yet they dramatized to the government the degree of dislocation in the countryside.

The difficulty centered on the fact that many peasants believed the government and the savkars to be allied. Some violence had been precipitated by rumors that Marwari moneylenders were about to extort bonds from helpless ryots with the help of government officers and the courts. Investigators found that peasants had been victims of fraud in court because the complex procedures of the courts left the peasants open to oppression by the more wily and wealthy savkars.[60] The Deccan Riots Commission was quickly appointed to conduct an exhaustive inquiry; its report followed the argument of the Sarvajanik Sabha and others by suggesting that the rigid revenue system did not respond adequately to crop and price fluctuations. The commission shared the sabha's basic contention that the ryots needed legislative reforms to improve their position.[61]

But before any preventive action could be taken, a still greater disaster struck the countryside: a drought and famine which lasted from September 1876 well into 1878. The failure of the monsoon in 1876 led to a crop failure which threw thousands of agricultural workers out of work. By December many Kunbis began to migrate from the famine areas looking for work.[62] Governor Wodehouse was prepared to institute large-scale relief works, but the new viceroy, Lord Lytton, wanted to minimize famine relief for the sake of economy, since the famine was spreading over large parts of India. Lytton replaced Wodehouse with Sir Richard Temple, a former finance member of the Viceroy's Council. Temple arrived in Bombay at an inauspicious time, for the conflict was growing between his government and the Indian political associations of which he was inveterately suspicious.

Lytton refused to sanction large public works such as railroad building to employ famine victims unless absolutely necessary. For those on famine relief he instituted a policy of rewarding long hours of work with a standard one pound of grain per day per man, which he considered adequate for subsistence. Many workers protested that this food allowance was not even sufficient to prevent starvation, much less to allow hard work. Early in 1877 some 120,000 workers abandoned relief works in protest against the regulation. An official report of the strike insinuated that covert influences were at work, stating that the strikers "are acting in bodies and in concert, and are probably under influences which are not apparent."[63] Before long the Bombay Gazette, which represented the conservative British interest there, openly charged that the Sarvajanik Sabha was responsible for the strike. On January 29 and 31, 1877, telegrams from the Sholapur Sarvajanik Sabha to the government confirmed the sabha's role: they described a mass protest meeting under its auspices which demanded that the government revert to a traditional wage rate which was much higher than a pound of grain per day.[64]

The famine was becoming steadily more severe, and the conflict between the sabha and the government deepened. In August 1877 the sabha submitted an extensive Famine Report to the Bombay government, in which it attempted to show that the official mortality rate estimates were far too low. It charged that in the famine districts up to fifty percent of the population had migrated, nearly eighty percent of the cattle had died, and as much as sixty-five percent of the arable land had been deserted. "The prime cause of all the destitution and death that has occurred has been the persistent adherence of the Local Authorities to the sufficiency of the one pound subsistence theory," a policy contrary to practices followed elsewhere in India. The extent of the sabha's antagonism toward the government was suggested in a detailed catalogue of the callous acts of the famine commissioners toward the people.[65]

Another dimension of the dispute, which had far-reaching policy implications, emerged clearly by 1877. Following the principles of free trade and laissez-faire government, the Raj had refused to open fair-price shops or to prevent the export of grain from famine areas. Instead it encouraged private charity in conformity with classical economic doctrine. The Sarvajanik Sabha had initially supported this approach, though for somewhat different reasons. Its first such effort had been in 1872 when it sent substantial relief to flood victims in Khandesh and Nasik.[66] When the famine began, the sabha opened privately financed grain shops to provide food at low cost to the ryots, supplementing this by private charitable donations. This solution was consonant with a long tradition of philanthropy among wealthy Hindus, but now it had political implications as well.

The sabha's hope in the efficacy of private famine relief was soon discouraged. During 1877 as the famine worsened it became clear that no amount of private relief would be adequate. The sabha therefore demanded that the government save lives with no thought to the cost rather than continue to administer relief on the basis of available resources. In the August Famine Report, the sabha sent a plea for bold government intervention at whatever sacrifice of economic principle, adding:

> We need hardly urge that the people of this Presidency have manifold claim upon the liberal support of Government in these sad times. The Government is the State Land-lord in this Presidency, and monopolizes all the rents and profits of agriculture which, in other countries, are in the hands of the middle-class. In return for this great benefit it becomes the duty of Government to regard the people as a landlord regards his tenantry, and the ordinary principles of noninterference by the State have no place in such a relationship.[67]

Under these harsh conditions laissez-faire principles seemed but a shield for callous self-interest.

Ranade published his first personal statement on the famine experience in July 1878, summarizing the sabha's data once again. He then repeated the attacks on the administration, for the first time specifically singling out Governor Temple. He quoted contemptuously a Minute by the governor in which Temple congratulates the ryots for their "strong self-supporting power and the resolute spirit of self-help," counts up their boundless "stores and stocks of foodgrains," gloats upon their "extensive credit" and "great means of purchasing supplies from a distance," and finally winds up with a challenge to other countries to show "a better-behaved peasantry," blessed with a more "careful revenue settlement and just administration."[68]

But according to Ranade, no amount of facile rhetoric could disguise the gravity of the situation, and the financial burden of the famine belonged squarely with the government. "The money question ought to be entirely subordinated . . . for famines like wars can never be made to pay themselves."[69] As long as the famine lasted, there seemed little possibility of avoiding the collision course between the government and its Indian critics.

The Educated Class and the Native Princes

The famine gradually subsided during 1878, and the specific issues at stake between the sabha and the government lost their intensity. Nonetheless, a residue of distrust remained to exacerbate new conflicts. Hostility was simultaneously developing in a second area in which the sabha's interests were increasingly at stake, namely, the relations of the Raj with the Princely States. Official policy toward the princes changed after 1857 when Dalhousie's attack on their autonomy was discredited. The great states remained loyal to the Raj during the rebellion, contributing substantially to the British victory. The viceroy, Lord Canning, soon reaffirmed the autonomy of the states and granted the princes their first unequivocal guarantee of the right to adopt heirs when necessary. And the Queen proclaimed that in the future the princes would once again play their rightful role in the moral and material progress of the land.[70] By the early 1870's Ranade and the Indian political reformers took up this principle in hopes of mobilizing the princes' support for their work of reform. But the political atmosphere in which they worked was fraught with ambivalence: the British Raj followed a fluctuating policy, leaving to the states autonomy in internal affairs but reserving the right to intervene should a state's administration break down.

Bombay Presidency was charged with diplomatic relations with the powerful princely states of western India. While Ranade was still a student in Bombay, the details of the new policy were in the hands of Bartle Frere, a governor whose sympathies with the princes endeared him to all segments of Indian opinion. To the Maharashtrian reformers the states provided living examples of Indian self-rule in the midst of foreign domination and a ready alternative to the British Raj for professional employ. The network of administrative posts, encompassing both British and princely districts, which had been evident in Ranade's earliest years had subsequently expanded. With it the interests of the political associations expanded, after the late 1860's, across the borders between British and Princely India. The states provided a sense of national identity for the reformers and financial support for their campaign of political self-help.

Ranade's interest in the affairs of the states had never diminished during his time in Bombay. It focused on the fate of Satara, the seat of Shivaji's descendants, which Dalhousie had annexed in 1849 over the protests of Frere, then the British Resident in Satara. The aggrieved prince, Pratap Singh, had become a martyr in the eyes of many Englishmen as well as the Indian populace, and the controversy over what his family's compensation would be was as hotly discussed in the press as any issue of the 1850's and 1860's. When in 1869 Ranade returned to Bombay from his experience in Akalkot and Kolhapur, he discussed the fate of Satara in his introduction to a volume of Frere's speeches. The official policy behind the annexation, he wrote, had been based entirely on "the greed of territory" and "the ordinary claptrap of native misrule and disorder." Pratap Singh had been a firm and liberal prince; "a more self-denying prince, a more considerate prince, never sat on any royal throne. The order and discipline he maintained all over his territory was the marvel of his times."[71] There were further conflicts ahead over the right of Britain to interfere in the internal affairs of the states; the memory of the Satara controversy helped fuel the bitterness of the 1870's.

In Bombay the leaders of the East India Association disagreed among themselves as to the wisdom of working with the princes. Bhau Daji, K. T. Telang and others doubted that they would assist the association's work actively, seeing them as sycophants of the British. But Dadabhai Naoroji insisted that their power and especially their purses must not be ignored.[72] There was no such disagreement within the Sarvajanik Sabha, which attempted from the first to recruit the active support of the princes, for their prestige, their financial contributions, and their potential for enacting reforms within their own domains. The sabha consequently had established close ties with the princely states of western India by the time the Baroda controversy exploded onto the all-India scene in the early 1870's.

Malharrao, the ruling Gaikwad at the time, was dominated by his favorites, and his administration was notoriously corrupt.[73] Governor Wodehouse of Bombay, an energetic opponent of princely misrule, moved against Malharrao in 1873 by appointing Colonel Robert Phayre as his Resident in Baroda. Phayre, a forceful and undiplomatic man, threatened to depose Malharrao on grounds of gross misrule. Malharrao thereupon called on Dadabhai Naoroji, who was known for his administrative ability and his sympathy toward Baroda. Dadabhai agreed to become the <u>dewan</u>, or chief minister, and accept the difficult task of purging Baroda of corruption. As he later wrote to Allen Octavian Hume: "The interests of the Native States are intimately connected with those of the subjects of British India. Any improvement in Native States is a gain to all India, and the very success of Native States will by comparison shame and expose the failures in the British System."[74]

Dadabhai attempted to bring Western-educated men with him from British India to carry out the necessary reforms. A friend in Bombay recommended that he recruit Ranade and others from the old university circle there. "If you have men like these about you, the administration of Baroda will . . . become within one year a model for others to imitate and will prove what good a purely educated native Government is capable of accomplishing."[75] After some consideration Ranade declined the offer, perhaps out of a commitment to his work in Poona, or perhaps from wariness of the political intrigues at the Baroda court.

Dadabhai's efforts achieved momentary success, but eventually the opposition of the entrenched forces at the court plus Phayre's hostility to his growing influence obliged Dadabhai to resign. He did so in 1875, shortly before the British deposed Malharrao and imprisoned him on charges of plotting to poison Phayre. Public opinion in Bombay and Poona had heretofore opposed Malharrao, but it now turned to excited sympathy for his plight. The Indian reformers were indignant at his summary arrest, since the government refused to allow him funds for hiring defense lawyers.

The Sarvajanik Sabha immediately organized a campaign to raise the necessary funds for Malharrao's defense. At a public meeting in Poona on January 15, 1875, they adopted a memorial to the government, which expressed the sabha's kinship with the states by saying:

> Your memorialists, as the inhabitants of the Capital of the Peshwas, are bound by diverse ties of interests and relationship with the outlying conquests of the once great Maratha Confederacy, represented by the states of Baroda, Indore, Gwalior, etc. They feel legitimate interest in the progress and well-being of those states, which maintain in their various service and by means of their large charities a considerable number of their fellow-countrymen, . . . The Gaikwar kingdom, as being the oldest, richest and nearest, has always been regarded as having greatest claim upon the affection of the people.[76]

The sabha recognized the corruption of Baroda and other states, but feared a return to Dalhousie's times. Annexation would amount to depriving the people of Baroda of their independence solely because of the weaknesses of one man. "So long as the subjects of a Native State are not guilty of hostility toward the British Government, it will not be just to punish them for the errors of vices of their chiefs."[77]

Such outspoken opposition startled the government, which took steps to discover what influences lay behind the organization's actions. At about this time a stranger took up residence near the homes of the sabha's leaders. When he refused to reveal his background of purposes, the sabha investigated his mail and discovered secret correspondence with the police. He vanished one night, but the sabha now knew that it was being carefully watched.[78] From this time onward the attitudes of even the most moderate Indian politicians were conditioned by their wary truce with the Criminal Intelligence Department.

Ultimately the sabha did not have to finance Malharrao's defense, for the British released funds from his coffers. After a thorough investigation by the government in London, Malharrao was permanently deposed, but in compensation to Indian opinion the administration of Baroda was immediately returned to Indian hands with the appointment of a new and distinguished dewan, Sir T. Madhavrao. Phayre was replaced as British resident by Sir Lewis Pelly, an outspoken sympathizer of the princes. Until Malharrao's permanent successor, the young Sayajirao, ascended the throne in 1881, Madhavrao and Pelly jointly administered the state, to the satisfaction of the political associations.

The Baroda affair reinforced in the eyes of the Sarvajanik Sabha the notion of the states as sources of power independent of the British and potentially able to become an effective alternative to alien rule. The sabha first announced this vision formally in January 1877, when the princes gathered in Delhi at a darbar to celebrate the Queen's assumption of the new title, Empress of India. The Sarvajanik Sabha memorialized the Queen at the darbar, asking that the native princes be constituted as an assembly which would advise the government on administrative affairs, especially in relation to the states. Simultaneously the delegation presented the princes with an address, probably written by Ranade, urging them to press the government to establish the assembly. It called them "the first Parliament of the united Indian nation, the first Congress of the representatives of the diverse states and nationalities which make up the body politic of India."[79] The educated class was still small in numbers and unsure of its legitimacy as spokesmen for the Indian people. Ranade, Joshi and others saw alliance with the princes as their surest way of linking their new style of leadership with traditional authority and thereby reinforcing the putative unity of Indian interests. This alliance helped to generate the most explosive conflict with the British regime which Ranade ever faced.

The Crisis of Ranade's Loyalty[80]

Under the prevailing conservative trend of the post-Mutiny British Raj and image of traditional India, "the real India," came to dominate the minds of many British administrators.[81] Reacting against the increasingly articulate ambitions of the educated class, they claimed that the only legitimate spokesmen for India's masses were the landed gentry. It was for the masses in turn, the study yeomanry of the countryside, that England held India in trust. There was no place here for the liberal hope that a Western-educated class could share responsibility for the country's future. The pretensions of this class were the folly of the deracinated and culturally hybrid. To the conservative mind Ranade's class represented no one but themselves; their agitations were disruptive and potentially seditious.

In this myth of Indian society the Poona Brahmins were a uniquely problematical group. Their university-educated leaders, most notoriously Ranade, fell into the category of unrepresentative intelligentsia. Yet they were also suspected of organizing every revolt against British authority in the Desh since 1818. This British ambivalence contained a germ of truth, for men like Ranade had the combination of university education and close ties to mofussil society in which liberal Europeans placed their hopes and conservative Europeans their fears. Their genuine social and professional ties made them all the more suspect. This conservative ideology was influential within the Government of India throughout the last third of the century, and twice it became the dominant note in British policy: first under Lord Lytton in the late 1870's and again at the very end of Ranade's life. In 1878 and 1879 Ranade came perilously close to political martyrdom as a result. By 1877 he and his associates had clashed directly with the government on two vital questions: revenue policy and the princely states. Their opposition was intensified by the fact that the darbar of 1877 was held with great splendor and expense at the peak of the famine. The criticism of Lord Lytton's regime which Indian journalists wrote during this time led conservative British circles to fear that criticism was lapsing into sedition. The government's anxiety was heightened by tensions between

England and Russia on the northwest frontiers of the Indian Empire. Memories of 1857 were not far beneath the surface; hence, to protect India from enemies both within and without, the government passed the Vernacular Press Act on March 30, 1878. The act provided severe penalties for any vernacular journalist who published material considered either politically seditious or communally unsettling.[82]

As in the Baroda affair, Indian opposition to the law was immediate and widespread. Before the act became law, the Sarvajanik Sabha organized a meeting in Bombay to protest it. However, it failed to gain the support of the more conservative Gujarati press in Bombay. In heightened protest, the Sarvajanik Sabha organized a second meeting in Poona on May 2, denouncing the Press Act as "retrograde, unnecessary, severe, unjust and subversive of all constitutional freedom and progress."[83] It denied that there had been the slightest trace of disaffection in the native press at any time since 1835, when the principle of a free press was established in India, and it rejected assertions that the native press ever aroused race, caste, or religious tensions. The meeting supported a petition to Parliament which outlined in detail the sabha's major grievances against Lytton's administration. In summary, the sabha called for repeal of the act in the spirit of British principles of justice.[84]

Two months later the sabha published the first issue of the _Quarterly Journal_, which began a series of detailed studies of official policy in India. Its scholarly tone was modeled after the English political quarterlies rather than that of the daily or weekly newspapers. The _Journal_ became the sabha's chief means of political education, and in its pages Ranade published articles on political, economic, and administrative affairs over the next fifteen years.[85] The _Journal_ shortly developed into one of the most influential and controversial Indian periodicals of its time. To publish it in the repressive atmosphere of 1878 was an act of calculated political courage.

The sabha was not directly affected by the press censorship, since the _Journal_ was published entirely in English. Nonetheless, it again articulated Indian opposition to the Press Act in September, after Parliament had sanctioned the act. In a new memorial the sabha condemned the act and asserted that "the repressive influences of the Act . . . leave the Government no resource to ascertain the genuine wishes of the people through their recognized organs."[86] This led the British proponents of press censorship to conclude that native English-language newspapers should also fall under the act. Lionel Ashburner, a leading member of the Bombay Executive Council, expressed official suspicions of the sabha by stating ominously:

> To be effective, the press law must be . . . thorough and if we tolerate sedition in English, the _Sabhas_ which are springing up all over the country will find no difficulty in translating it into the vernacular. The seditious associations . . . are doing much mischief

and I would take this opportunity of suppressing them by making it penal to pay subscriptions to agitate political questions without the sanction of Government. Holkar and other Native Chiefs subscribe largely to the Sarvajanik Sabha which it is not unfair to say is a seditious Association.87

Some of the British antipathy to the sabha in the press and elsewhere was directed toward Ranade personally because of his conspicuous role in the sabha's recent activities. The government too feared Ranade's growing influence in the sabha. As a precautionary measure Temple issued an executive order transferring Ranade from Poona to the smaller city of Nasik in January 1878. This move failed to achieve its purpose, for the sabha continued to consult Ranade in its campaign against the Vernacular Press Act.

When the press attacks became heated, Ranade was bitterly surprised; he feared the consequences of rumors that he was fomenting sedition. He wrote to his old school friend, N. M. Parmanand, in Bombay, saying:

> I am now too much weighed down with the cloud of evil rumours that have been wafted from Bombay hitherwards to be in a mood to write much to any friend. I had hardly any idea that the force of prejudice could go to such a length. Cannot any kind friends be got to undertake the duty of explaining the truth about these matters or pleading the excuse of the hot controversy which made every body lose his temper for a month and more?88

Ranade's controversy with an increasingly repressive government had brought him to the point of a depression in which his trust in British justice was severely shaken. The British of all people should be dispassionate enough to trust his integrity, but perhaps even this was too much to expect.

Still more shocks were to come in the following year. In early 1879 a series of <u>dacoities</u>, or robberies, occurred in the countryside surrounding Poona. By March it was clear that a Chitpavan Brahmin named Vasudev Balvant Phadke was leading the robbers, most of whom were low-caste ryots who had not yet recovered from the effects of the famine.89 At first Phadke's raids were directed against moneylenders and other wealthy men in the towns. But his exploits took a sinister turn when, obsessed with the wrongs that Britain had perpetrated on India, he proclaimed a revolt against British rule in the name of the Peshwa.

The British found in Phadke's movement proof of their suspicion of natives. Temple wrote on March 8 to Ashburner: "I have . . . seen some Police reports; actually attributing these little events to treason hatched by Poona Brahmins, who organized Ramoosees . . . against the British Raj. This is almost <u>too</u> audacious to be true; but it is the old story of our always being on the brink of little volcanoes."90 He dispatched a special military force against Phadke, but the rebel moved quickly over the countryside, remaining at large through the hot season.

The Sarvajanik Sabha recognized that it was under surveillance as the probable source of the unrest. In self-defense it gathered information to assist the government in capturing Phadke, preparing a series of

"Dacoit Letters" which used the occasion to renew its criticisms of the revenue administration. The letter of April 25 laid the blame for the robberies not on an undercover sedition campaign but on the disastrous state of the rural economy. "The dacoits belong chiefly to the criminal classes who have been impoverished and thrown out of employment by the famine and scarcity for the last two or three years, and the stoppage of the great public works."[91]

The implication that the government was indirectly responsible for the trouble was not well received in Bombay. Meanwhile, Ranade arrived in Poona for his annual holiday on May 5. On the night of May 13 the two great palaces of the Peshwa, Budhwar Wada and Vishrambag Wada, burned in spectacular fires. Members of the Sarvajanik Sabha assisted in putting out the flames and immediately began inquiries as to the cause of the fires. The Deccan Herald, the conservative British newspaper in Poona, charged that Phadke and other Poona Brahmins were involved in setting the fires. But the vernacular press of the entire Bombay region refuted the charges, upholding the exemplary loyalty of the educated men of Poona.[92] The Bombay Gazette, however, viewed the fires as proof of a Brahmin conspiracy:

> The rumours that have been flying about Western India for the past few months to the effect that a certain clique of Poona Brahmins were attempting something more than the mere talking and writing of sedition have now apparently received ample confirmation. . . . The foolish Brahmins of Poona, who have been educated up by ourselves to a ridiculous conception of their own capacities and importance think, it is said, to repeat in the nineteenth century and against British power the events that, although possible, were even wonderful two hundred years ago.

The Gazette asserted that the cowardly Brahmins were instigating desperate, half-starved people in the mofussil to take up arms. It went on: "Some men must lie under suspicion--it is always so in India although there may not be actual proof against them. . . . A little martial law would do Poona and its Brahmins a great deal of good."[93]

The Sarvajanik Sabha discovered the arsonist to be a government clerk named K. K. Ranade (no relation of M. G. Ranade). On questioning from M. G. Ranade and other leaders of the sabha, the arsonist admitted that he had burned the palaces to destroy evidence of his theft of money from his office. He explained that excitement over Phadke's deeds had given him the enthusiasm to light the fires.[94] Phadke, however, was still at large. As late as June 2 Lytton stated: "If Temple can bring home to some of the Brahminical literati at Poona, complicity with the recent incendiary fires and dacoities, I sincerely hope he will make a severe example of them."[95]

Ranade's position had already been damaged before the arsonist was captured. On May 19, 1879, Ranade was summarily ordered to a new post in Dhulia, a small district town on the northern border of Maharashtra.[96] The order came to Ranade as an executive letter, for Temple had moved quickly; he had bypassed Ranade's superiors in the judiciary, from whom such orders would normally come.[97] In his first weeks in Dhulia Ranade received several letters from Poona, seemingly from the dacoits. He immediately turned them over to the police, suspecting a police trap. He was relieved of suspicion by the police, but his dignity had been deeply affronted.[98] He later wrote to Temple protesting the summary order which forced him to leave Poona in the summer heat. He requested transfer to Nasik in July when an opening would occur there, but there was no immediate reply from Bombay.[99]

Extreme tension continued between the English and their Indian subjects until Phadke was captured in July, ending the rural unrest. At his trial a few months later, it became evident that Phadke's campaign, although it exploited the unrest of the times, was basically the quixotic flourish of one individual. Phadke had been educated in English schools in Bombay, but he detested the drudgery of his work as a government clerk. He attended Ranade's lectures in 1872 when Ranade advocated economic self-reliance and the purchase of Indian rather than imported goods.[100] Ranade's qualified patriotism had become transmuted in Phadke's mind into insurrection. For his trouble he was sentenced to life imprisonment in the stronghold at Aden, where he died a short while later.

The public crisis was over, but the question of Ranade's employment in British India was more difficult to resolve. His work with the Sarvajanik Sabha had tested to the limit the regime's tolerance of criticism, or more precisely its view of the fine line between criticism and sedition. Conservative members of the government insisted that Ranade had overstepped the restraints which should govern a servant of the Raj, but liberals countered that this conclusion rested on the unfounded allegations of the British press. A test of strength soon developed within the government over the question of Ranade's reinstatement to a major judicial post. Ranade and his friends saw its outcome as determining whether the Raj would tolerate any significant criticism of its policies. After the repressive legislation of Lytton's regime it was doubtful to them whether Indian political associations would henceforth be allowed any useful role as a loyal opposition.

The personal issue at stake for Ranade was whether to remain in the service of the British. This would be intolerable if the cloud of suspicion was not decisively removed. An alternative was at hand. In late 1879 he received a lucrative offer from the dewan of Baroda to become Chief Justice of the state with which Ranade had been so closely involved since 1875. His sympathizers among the liberal British advised him against accepting the offer, warning that tenure in the states was often short and a reformer's enemies unscrupulous.[101] But when no positive indication came from Bombay, Ranade provisionally accepted the offer from Baroda in early 1880. He then turned to Sir Michael Westropp,

Chief Justice of Bombay, in a letter of disillusioned protest. Ranade believed now, he wrote, "that there was no reasonable prospect before me of getting promotion in the Judicial service here."

> I was led to take this despondent view of my prospects from the fact of my unaccountable transfer from Poona to Nasik followed shortly after by my transfer from Nasik to Dhulia, under circumstances which evidently suggested the idea that I did not stand well in the good opinion of the authorities. I have been however assured by the European well-wishers whom I consulted that the apparent prejudice to which popular rumour ascribed these transfers did not in fact exist, and that there was nothing in the way of my claims being duly recognized when the proper opportunity should come for such recognition.102

He ended his letter with a request to be considered for rapid promotion to district judge in Thana or Nasik, either of which appointments would have been open at the time.

As Ranade had hoped, Westropp continued his long-standing support of his ablest Indian subordinate, strongly recommending Ranade for the position at Thana in June 1880.103 By this time the Liberal election victory in England brought to power forces favorable to Ranade's reinstatement. Lord Ripon soon replaced Lord Lytton as viceroy and Sir James Fergusson replaced Sir Richard Temple as governor of Bombay. Fergusson was sympathetic with Ranade's position, although he too carried a rather narrow tolerance for criticisms from Indian reformers. He wrote to Ranade on June 9, assuring him somewhat prematurely that he stood well with his superiors, but warning him against future indiscretions.

> With regard to the estimation in which you are held by Government, the Governor thinks you would do well to consider that the liberty of expression which is permitted by the British Government to its subjects may not always be suitable for one in a judicial office, in which a prudent reticence and abstinence from political controversy is specially becoming. From your connection with the Government you have opportunities of bringing to the notice of the authorities, through the usual channels, the wants and troubles of the people: of such opportunities you would do well to avail yourself, rather than to employ your talents and influence in such a way as to encourage agitation or discontent.104

He then pledged that there should be no difficulty in arranging for the appointment to Thana or Nasik. But the cautionary note nettled Ranade's pride. Fergusson's conception of proper political activity left little place for the role of political educator which Ranade claimed in his work with the Sarvajanik Sabha. Defending his concept of public action, Ranade replied:

> I shall strive to the best of my powers to regulate my conduct in the future, as I most conscientiously affirm I have done in the past. . . . Brought up as I have been, it is impossible for me to be forgetful of my duty to the rule I serve under, and . . . those who know me best, and have seen my work, feel no hesitation in absolving me in this respect from all blame and discrediting all aspersions to the contrary.105

Yet Ranade was satisfied for the moment; he decided to decline the Baroda offer in hope of the promotion. His defenders, after all, were the executive and judicial heads of the Bombay government.

Ranade's reinstatement did not come in the anticipated way, for Fergusson was unable to overcome the unremitting opposition of Conservative council members who remained from Lytton's time. Lionel Ashburner and others were especially annoyed by a confidential government report of a meeting in Surat on June 2, 1880, which Ranade had addressed, at the height of his alienation from the British government. At that time, Ranade had "proceeded to dwell on the necessity of united action among natives in order to create a strong public opinion. He dwelt on the increased force of public opinion, and contrasted the annexation of Oude twenty years ago with the dealings of Government with Baroda recently, which, he said, but for public opinion, would have been likewise annexed. He complained of a want of any association in Surat with which leading members of other societies could correspond, and said they heard from Ahmedabad but never from Surat."[106] It was precisely this sort of agitation, at the height of his disfavor in government circles, to which the Conservatives objected. But Fergusson had no objection to a government servant "who ventures to hold political opinions and to express them with ability and freedom." He warned that "nothing would be so short-sighted and indeed so impossible as to close the minds and the mouths of the acute thinkers whose intellects we have quickened and who have learned what liberty means from their contact with our civilization."[107]

The decision was passed to the Imperial Council in Calcutta, where Lord Ripon likewise failed to overcome the opposition of his council; Ranade's promotion was vetoed in July. Learning of the decision, Fergusson wondered whether a whole generation of Indian leaders, rigorously trained and loyal to the Raj, would be deprived of the professional rewards of mature years.[108]

Fergusson finally salvaged Ranade's loyalty in December, when he transferred Ranade to Bombay as Second Presidency Magistrate.[109] This was a demotion in rank but a transfer to a far more desirable location. Three months later, on March 3, 1881, he reappointed Ranade to his old position in Poona, as First Class Subordinate Judge of the district court. He thus absolved Ranade of any further suspicion of complicity in the events of 1879 by stating that his transfers to Nasik and Dhulia "may be held to have served as a warning to him not to take a prominent part in political agitation."[110]

Whether or not Ranade remained prominent in political agitations thereafter became a matter of heated dispute in later years. That he was somewhat sobered by these events seems clear from the fact that he did turn his major center of attention now to administrative matters within the government. He had learned that the government held pervasive power to influence the pattern of society, and that effective use of that power depended on nurturing the fragile alliance between Indian nationalists and their liberal sympathizers among the British. The task of encouraging this alliance was far more congenial to Ranade than engaging in confrontations, in any case. He was willing to go to some lengths to avoid further conflict with men like Temple, for he had barely survived one of the British Conservatives' most vituperative campaigns.

In a retrospect on Temple's administration that April, Ranade framed his critique of British autocracy as a disillusioned personal attack on Temple, unique in all Ranade's writings for its subjectivity and emotion.[111] Temple was sycophantic toward his superiors and supercilious toward the representatives of the Indian people. He affronted India with "his theatrical exaggeration of speech and action, his ultra-Englishism, the absence of all sincere love of the people, his positive dislike of all free institutions, the total absence of any large lines of statesman-like actions, the strongly retrograde character of his land and famine policies, his impatience of all opposition, and his often successful efforts to make words play duty for deeds." No governor of Bombay had been so universally unpopular in Ranade's lifetime, and when Temple left India it was, in Ranade's words, "as though the incubus of a great weight had been removed."

Temple and Lytton suffered specifically in contrast with the new Liberal regime of Lord Ripon and Sir James Fergusson, on whom Ranade and most reformers placed effusive hopes. The issues between the Indian reformers and the imperial government, which had emerged under the Conservative regime, were not forgotten. But for Ranade and the Moderates they caused less basic crises of confidence after 1880. For the rest of his career, Ranade asserted that the British Raj was not so autocratic as it might be, and excessive criticism of the British could only elicit their oppressive tendencies. In any case, it was time after 1880 for the elaborate and undramatic work of building representative institutions which would function well on Indian soil.

Notes

[1] For partial accounts of the story, see Ballhatchet, Social Policy, ch. x; Kumar, Western India, pp. 51-55; and Tucker, "The Defense of Dharma," passim. The official name of the college changed twice: from Sanskrit College to Poona College in the reorganization of 1851, and then to Deccan College in 1864.

[2] Dnyan Prakash, September 27, 1852, p. 311.

[3] Poona Observer, July 10, 1852, p. 33; November 20, 1852, pp. 110-111; December 18, 1852, p. 127. Dnyanoday, April 6, 1849, pp. 145-148.

[4] Poona Observer, November 20, 1852, p. 110.

[5] See the author's article, "Hindu Traditionalism and Nationalist Ideologies in Nineteenth-Century Maharashtra," Modern Asian Studies, forthcoming, July 1976.

[6] Poona Observer, February 5, 1853, p. 23; Dnyanoday, April 2, 1849, pp. 121-122; September 16, 1850, pp. 331-333; and February 1, 1853, p. 48.

[7] For a retrospective account of the commission's work, see Bombay Government, Selections from the Records of the Bombay Government: New Series, No. 30, A Selection of Papers Explanatory of the Origin of the Inam Commission (Bombay, 1856). One source of serious factional suspicions in the 1850's was that Deshmukh, scion of a landed family himself, worked as assistant inam commissioner for some time, and periodically wrote scathing critiques of the sardars' backwardness in the Marathi press.

[8] The manifesto is published in Dnyanoday, June 15, 1850, p. 218.

[9] Its founding charter is published in Marathi in Dnyanoday, April 1, 1852, pp. 109-112. Mor Shastri Sathe was a contributing member of the new association, helping to provide continuity with its predecessor.

[10] Poona Observer, July 10, 1852, p. 33.

[11] Dnyan Prakash, September 27, 1852, pp. 310-311.

[12] Dnyanoday, September 1, 1852, p. 263; and November 15, 1852, p. 374.

[13] Dnyanoday, November 15, 1852, p. 374.

[14] Dnyan Prakash, March 7, 1858, p. 110; and July 22, 1858. A similar report of 1864 shows that the individuals had changed somewhat but their constituencies had not.

[15] For some time in the 1850's Young Poona experimented with social radicalism by helping to organize Jotiba Phule's schools for low-caste children and by teaching in them. This emphasis evidently lasted only a few years, however. See the author's forthcoming article, "Ideologies of Intercaste Relations in Maharashtra, 1848-75."

[16] Pūnā asosiesana mhanje punyāntila sārvajanika sabhā hyā sabhecī niyama (Rules of the Poona Association or the People's Association of Poona) (Poona, 1867), pp. 1-2. See also S. R. Mehrotra, "The Poona Sarvajanik Sabha: The Early Phase (1870-1880)," IESHR, VI (September 1969), 293-322.

[17] Dnyan Prakash, August 5, 1858, p. 372. In 1853 a similar conflict had swirled around the then chairman, Abasaheb Dhamdhere, the Deccan Association's leader. Dnyanoday, December 1, 1853, p. 371.

[18] Pūnā asosiesana, p. 10.

[19] Puneṅ yethīla sārvajanika sabhecī racanā va niyama (Poona People's Association: Procedures and Rules), (Poona, 1870), p. 1. Translations of excerpts appear in Mankar, Ranade, I, 203.

[20] See membership lists in Puneṅ yethīla, pp. 2-5. The chief non-Brahmin voice was the well-known Maratha pleader and former Young Poona activist, Gangaram Bhau Mhaske.

²¹Masselos, "Liberal Consciousness," p. 286.

²²Ibid., p. 287.

²³Vithoba Anna Daftardar, who led the orthodox forces against widow-marriage in 1870, was in his service. Times of India, January 12, 1870, p. 2.

²⁴Masselos, "Liberal Consciousness," pp. 480-481. Apte and Ranade also worked together for years in the Society for Promoting the Veda.

²⁵First annual report of the Poona Sarvajanik Sabha, quoted in Native Opinion, May 11 and 18, 1873.

²⁶See R. G. Borvankar, Gaṇeśa Vāsudeva Jośī urpha Sārvajanika Kākā yāṅce caritra (The Life of Ganesh Vasudev Joshi alias "The Uncle of the People"), (Poona, 1924).

²⁷Quoted in Metcalf, Aftermath, p. 258.

²⁸Quoted in Native Opinion, August 18, 1872, p. 262.

²⁹A Marathi description of the petition is in Phatak, Ranade, pp. 216-217.

³⁰Twenty years later Ranade still used similar reasoning to overcome his friends' discouragement. See Gokhale, Speeches, pp. 779-780. How complex the origin of this central assumption of Moderate politics was can be intimated by a Marathi examination which Ranade had previously administered at Bombay University. Students were required to translate the following passage into Marathi: "I find that much has been given man to enjoy, yet still more to suffer. . . . In this life . . . it appears that we cannot be entirely blessed, but yet we may be completely miserable. Why man should feel pain, why our wretchedness should be requisite in the formation of universal felicity . . . these are questions that can never be explained, and might be useless if known. On this subject Providence has thought fit to elude our curiosity, satisfied with granting us motives to consolation." University of Bombay, Matriculation Examination Papers in Marathi from 1859 to 1866, ed. G. M. Pitale (Bombay, 1867), pp. 33-34 (examination of November 17, 1863). These teachings may have had an indirect influence on Ranade's steadfast assumption that India must accept very slow political evolution and indefinitely long foreign domination. In his later years Ranade used the idea that Providence works mysteriously and demands patient forbearance to counsel moderation to his younger compatriots whose education did not include these teachings, and who were growing restive under the British yoke.

³¹H. P. Mody, Sir Pherozeshah Mehta: A Political Biography (Bombay, 1921), p. 169.

³²The address was printed in Native Opinion, May 18, 1873, p. 309.

³³M. G. Ranade, A Revenue Manual of the British Empire in India: An Epitome of the Fawcett Committee Report (Poona, 1877), p. 2.

³⁴Masselos, "Liberal Consciousness," pp. 297-299.

³⁵See Dadabhai Naoroji, Poverty and Un-British Rule in India (London, 1901).

³⁶M. G. Ranade, Vyāpārasambandhī vyākhyāneṅ (Lectures on Trade and Commerce), (Poona, 1963), pp. 5, 9.

³⁷Ibid., pp. 24-25, 62-63.

³⁸See Native Opinion, January 18, 1874, pp. 43-44; April 5, 1874, p. 220; May 30, 1875, pp. 343-344; and June 27, 1875, p. 408.

³⁹M. G. Ranade, Statistics of Criminal Justice in the Bombay Presidency (Bombay, 1873), p. 6.

⁴⁰Ibid.

⁴¹Ibid.

⁴²G. C. Franklin, Background to Indian Law (Cambridge, 1946), p. 196.

[43] Ranade, *Statistics*, p. 36.

[44] *Ibid.*, pp. 47-48.

[45] C. A. Kincaid, *Forty-Four Years a Public Servant* (Edinburgh, 1934), pp. 31-32.

[46] Ranade, *Statistics*, p. 50.

[47] N. C. Kelkar, *Lo. Tilaka yāñce caritra* (The Life of Lokamanya Tilak), (Poona, 1923-28), I, 88; see also, Gokhale, *Late Mr. Justice Ranade*, pp. 26-29.

[48] Quoted in *Native Opinion*, August 18, 1872, p. 262.

[49] Seal, *Emergence of Indian Nationalism*, p. 230.

[50] See *Report of the Committee on the Riots in Poona and Ahmednagar, 1875* (Bombay, 1876), ch. 1.

[51] R. D. Choksey, *Economic Life in the Bombay Deccan, 1818-1939* (Bombay, 1955), pp. 13-35; Kumar, *Western India*, ch. iii.

[52] G. Keatinge, *Rural Economy in the Bombay Deccan* (London, 1912), pp. 23-26.

[53] Masselos, "Liberal Consciousness," p. 14.

[54] *Native Opinion*, May 18, 1873, p. 310.

[55] *Report of the Poona Sarvajanik Sabha on Matters Relating to India* (Poona, 1873), p. 28.

[56] *Ibid.*, p. 66.

[57] Kumar, *Western India*, pp. 180ff.

[58] For detailed analyses, see *ibid.*, and I. J. Catanach, "Agrarian Disturbances in Nineteenth-Century India," *IESHR* (March 1966), pp. 65-84.

[59] *Gazetteer of the Bombay Presidency*, XVII: *Poona* (Bombay, 1885), Part II, 106, 119-123.

[60] *Report . . . on the Riots*, pp. 109-110.

[61] *Ibid.*, pp. 110-112. A series of proposals concerning the legal responsibilities of debtors and the structure of the courts were designed to provide the ryots with greater justice. Many of these recommendations were passed into law four years later.

[62] *Poona Gazetteer, 1885*, Part II, 87-89.

[63] Quoted in Masselos, "Liberal Consciousness," pp. 495-496.

[64] William Digby, *The Famine Campaign in Southern India, 1876-78*, 2 vols. (London, 1878), II, 345.

[65] Poona Sarvajanik Sabha, *A Memorial to the Right Honourable Lord Lytton* (Poona, 1877), pp. 10-16.

[66] *Native Opinion*, May 18, 1873, p. 309; Digby, *Famine Campaign*, I, 11-13, 25.

[67] Poona Sarvajanik Sabha, *A Memorial*, p. 6.

[68] M. G. Ranade, "Famine Administration in the Bombay Presidency," *JPSS*, I (July 1878), 4-5, 8, 26. There is some uncertainty in the attribution of articles in the *Journal* to Ranade or any other specific writer, since they were not signed and the records of the Sarvajanik Sabha were burned in 1925. However, the list of articles which G. A. Mankar gives as written by Ranade and advised or supervised by him is generally accepted as correct, with certain notable exceptions which will be mentioned. See Mankar, *Ranade*, I, 82-83. N. R. Phatak, who studied the files before they were burned, supports Mankar's list, with certain reservations.

[69] Ranade, "Famine Administration," p. 26.

[70] See Metcalf, *Aftermath*, ch. vi.

[71] Frere, *Speeches*, p. ix.

[72] Masani, Dadabhai, p. 116.

[73] The most detailed narrative of the affair is D. A. Taleyarkhan, The Revolution at Baroda, 1874-75 (Bombay, 1875). See also E. C. Moulton, Lord Northbrook's Indian Administration, 1872-1876 (Bombay, 1968), ch. v.

[74] In a letter of January 5, 1888, in Masani, Dadabhai, pp. 301-302.

[75] S. S. Bengalee to Dadabhai, January 1874, ibid., p. 146.

[76] This and the following extracts from the petition are included in a partial reprint of the text in Phatak, Ranade, pp. 220-223. Ranade is said to be the author.

[77] Ibid.

[78] Ramabai Ranade, Reminiscences, pp. 57-59.

[79] The Petition to the Queen and the "Deccan Address to Her Majesty," which was also given to the princes, were republished in Native Opinion, December 10, 1876, pp. 787-789. See also J. C. Masselos, "Lytton's 'Great Tamasha' and Indian Unity," Journal of Indian History, XLIV (December 1966), 731-760; and Mehrotra, "The Poona Sarvajanik Sabha," pp. 313-316.

[80] For a fuller treatment of the following events, see the author's "The Proper Limits of Agitation: The Crisis of 1879-80 in Bombay Presidency," JAS, XXXVIII (February 1969), 339-355.

[81] See Francis G. Hutchins, The Illusion of Permanence (Princeton, 1967).

[82] The provisions of the act are discussed in detail in S. Gopal, The Viceroyalty of Lord Ripon (London, 1953), p. 67.

[83] Poona Sarvajanik Sabha, "A Memorial . . . on the Bill to Amend the Vernacular Press Act," September 19, 1878, JPSS, I (October 1878), 20. Ranade made clear his association with these memorials in a letter to N. M. Parmanand of May 5, 1878. He wrote that "the memorials though not drafted by us were glanced over to see that they read well and facts are put together well." P. B. Kulkarni, Māmā Paramānaṅda āṇī tyāñcā kālakhaṇḍa (The Life and Times of Mama Parmanand), (Bombay, 1963), p. 491.

[84] Poona Sarvajanik Sabha, "Memorial," pp. 20-27.

[85] Ranade also advised and edited articles written by others, thereby extending his influence over the Journal to an extent which cannot be precisely determined. The effect of his advisory and editorial work was to give a unified view to nearly all of the Journal's contents.

[86] Poona Sarvajanik Sabha, "Memorial," pp. 29-33.

[87] Quoted in Mahratta, June 26, 1898, p. 4.

[88] Letter of May 1, 1878, quoted in Kulkarni, Māmā Paramānaṅda, p. 492.

[89] V. S. Joshi, Vasudeo Balvant Phadke, First Indian Rebel Against British Rule (Bombay, 1929), pp. 30-56.

[90] Temple Papers, F 86/191.

[91] Poona Sarvajanik Sabha, "Letters to Government on the Deccan Dacoities," April 25, 1879, JPSS, II (July 1879), 70.

[92] See Bombay Government, Report on the Native Papers Published in the Bombay Presidency, for May 1879.

[93] Bombay Gazette, May 15, 1879, p. 2.

[94] Gokhale, Late Mr. Justice Ranade, pp. 13-14n.

[95] Lytton to Cranbrook, Lytton Papers, E 218/3/4.

[96] Gokhale, Late Mr. Justice Ranade, pp. 13-14n.

[97] Mankar, Ranade, I, 47. The order came during Ranade's holiday. Several of his friends insisted that he protest the move, but he was in no mood to ask for favors. He responded, "As long as I have to serve, I shall not put forth any excuse. I would rather resign than beg for

anything." Ramabai Ranade, *Reminiscences*, pp. 80-81.

[98] Gokhale, *Speeches*, p. 775.

[99] Gokhale, *Late Mr. Justice Ranade*, pp. 13-14n.

[100] Joshi, *Phadke*, p. 22. Ranade's work thus had some effect, however unintentional, in unsettling the countryside. This gave the Bombay conservatives' charges against him a certain plausibility.

[101] Mankar, *Ranade*, I, 70.

[102] Ranade to Westropp, May 4, 1880. Government of India, Home Department, *Judicial A Proceedings*, August 1880, Nos. 203-205. Henceforth *GOI 1880*.

[103] Westropp to Hart, Secretary to the Government of Bombay, June 4, 1880. Bombay Government, *Judicial Department Proceedings*, 1880, No. 797. Henceforth *Bombay JD 1880*.

[104] Fergusson to Ranade, June 9, 1880, *GOI 1880*.

[105] Ranade to Fergusson, June 16, 1880, *Bombay JD 1880*.

[106] Quoted in Ravenscroft, Minute of July 11, 1880, *GOI 1880*.

[107] Fergusson, Minute of July 23, 1880, *GOI 1880*.

[108] C. Gonne, Chief Secretary to the Bombay Government, to C. Grant, Officiating Secretary to the Government of India, September 15, 1880, *Bombay JD 1880*.

[109] Bombay Government, *Judicial Proceedings*, 1880, p. 1257.

[110] Bombay Government, *Judicial Department*, 1881, XV, No. 71.

[111] The following quotations are taken from M. G. Ranade, "Sir Richard Temple," *JPSS*, II (April 1880), 40-54.

Chapter 5

THE FOUNDATIONS OF POWER, 1876-1886

> From one end of India to the other, it is the same sad tale of old institutions decayed, old associations severed by the hand of violent innovation. --Ranade

By 1880 Ranade had already entered a new phase of his life, both as leader of public life in Poona and as an Indian spokesman in the government of Bombay Presidency. In Poona he was becoming a senior adviser for a new generation of young men who entered public life in the early 1880's. An analysis of his influence over them and their criticisms of his leadership must await the next chapter, for this rested largely on the other dimension of his public career, his new roles in the government. Here he rose to a position of considerable visible influence in the Bombay administration by the middle 1880's, becoming one of the few Indians so highly placed. He was emerging now as a major spokesman for the leading classes of Maharashtrian society, organizing and articulating their efforts both to preserve their social influence and to expand their political leverage.

These events largely concerned rural society and its development, which had been at the forefront of events in Maharashtra ever since 1873. They centered first on issues of local administration but expanded under Ripon to encompass political matters as well. Ranade wrote on all these issues in careful detail. In the course of these writings his mature social strategy became clear: a belief that cooperative alliances among both professional and landed elites were the only meaningful counterpoise to the vastly ramified power of the Anglo-Indian bureaucracy. In this he reserved a special place for the Western educated in their putative ability to harmonize the traditional interests of the "influential classes," and to prod them into progressive, enlightened public service. The result was liberalism at a deliberate pace, a commitment to the evolutionary growth of institutions limited by his fear of turbulent or irrational processes of change. This decorum, so typical of Ranade, in the long run was to frustrate nearly every one of his colleagues and protégés. But in the cooperative, optimistic atmosphere of the early 1880's, the tensions of the decades before and after seemed remote. These were perhaps the most satisfying years of Ranade's life.

The Deccan Agriculturists' Relief Act

From the time the Sarvajanik Sabha's _Journal_ was begun in 1878, it carried a series of articles on local administration, most of them written or supervised by Ranade. His reputation as an Indian spokesman on rural affairs steadily grew after 1879, when the Bombay government substantially revised its revenue administration. From 1881 onward, Ranade was closely associated with the adjustment of the system to the realities of rural society. His work thereafter demonstrated in great detail a strategy for rebuilding the social harmony of the Desh.

Village society was roughly divided into three categories: wealthy landed families, Kunbi cultivators, and moneylenders. In the towns, in addition to a wider variety of traditional castes and occupations, there was now an emerging group whose livelihood depended on the British presence: vakils who prospered in the courts, pensioners who had once worked in local government offices, and others. This growing class of men were associated with the Raj, yet still tied closely to mofussil society. Before the 1870's they were rarely mentioned as a possible source of future leadership; the worth of their experience in local administration was as yet untested against the coming demands of self-rule. Ranade championed their legitimacy as spokesmen for Indian society in the 1880's. He was, after all, from a family in this professional class. But before the role of the professional classes in the towns could be determined, conflicts among the major classes of rural society had to be resolved; the riots of 1875 and the subsequent famine focused primary attention on the villages.

The vaunted harmony of village life was disrupted most acutely in terms of relations between ryots and savkars. The Deccan Agriculturists' Relief Bill, an attempt to regulate their relations more equitably, elicited an elaborate debate on both the facts of rural life and the appropriate social and economic principles to follow in addressing those facts. Since the first Utilitarian revenue settlements, the Raj had encouraged the growth of capitalist agriculture through the enforcement of contracts and the free transfer of land ownership. In pursuit of a dynamic farm economy it had encouraged the trends which by 1875 went too far toward destroying the integration of village life. The Civil Procedure Code of 1859 had established strict rules for litigation of debts, eliminated the power of local courts to determine the equity of debt contracts, and made the ryots' tools and cattle liable to sale for debt payment. The Limitation Act of the same year had further strengthened the moneylenders' hands by changing the legal debt-recovery time limit from twelve to three years, thereby ending long-term loans to the ryots. Caught in the enforcement of these regulations, the ryots had been confronted with court decrees in such numbers by the early 1870's that their only self-defense lay in violence. The rate of land transfer and the level of social disruption by now endangered the stability of the government, and by 1878 the Bombay government was prepared to sanction extraordinary measures on behalf of the ryots.[1]

The debate over new legislation centered on the extent to which government policies had been responsible for the turbulence, and whether it was willing to abandon its reliance on laissez-faire principles in order to redress relations between savkars and ryots. The Deccan Riots Commission, which investigated the violence of 1875, reported that the ryots' debts resulted from a combination of many factors: the poor soil and climate of the Desh, the ignorance and improvidence of the ryots, the rigid revenue system which took no heed of poor harvests, and the corruption of the local courts.[2] The commission's findings implied that trusted Utilitarian policies had had an excessively disruptive impact on the countryside.

The Deccan Riots Commission led the way to new legislation by its recommendations in two areas. First, the ryots should be given more effective legal defenses against their creditors. Imprisonment for unpaid debts should be abolished, and their cattle and tools should be immune from sale for recovery of debts, as their land then was. The time limitation on lenders' suits to recover debts should be returned from three to twelve years for suits involving over Rs. 500, since the three-year limitation statute then in effect forced the lender to recover his debts quickly even in poor seasons.[3] In a second area the commission suggested two means by which the government could make its legal institutions more responsive to the needs of mofussil society. It should establish a new set of courts in small towns to adjudicate minor debts, in the hope that ryots would easily attend these courts and their neighbors' presence would encourage honest testimony from witnesses. To buttress the courts' legitimacy, the village patils would be made officers of the courts, responsible for enforcing their decrees. This would associate internal village authority more closely with the government's courts imposed from the outside.

With Governor Temple's support the commission's proposals in revised form became the Deccan Agriculturists' Relief Act of 1879. The act gave local courts discretionary powers to intervene in the economy on the ryots' behalf by rewriting the terms of inequitable debt contracts and by defining lower interest rates or more reasonable schedules of repayments. The act also ended imprisonment for debt, limited the sale of property for debt payment, limited the maximum cumulative interest on any contract to the traditional one hundred percent of the principal, and returned the limitation period for recovery of debts to twelve years. It went beyond the Riots Commission's report by also requiring the savkars to keep accurate records of debts and interest payment and to file contracts with village kulkarnis.[4] In themselves these provisions did no more than adjust the balance of legal procedures somewhat in the ryots' favor; they did not touch the broader demands of Ranade and his associates that the basic rate of revenue assessment be lowered or that the government make major tax remissions in lean years. But the act did represent a challenge in principle to the laissez-faire doctrine that government should refrain from manipulating the economy in detail. This meant an opening for further efforts by Indian reformers.

The Relief Act provided for Ranade's entry into policy-making levels of the government. A Special Judge was established with a full-time assistant for each two districts to administer the new regulations. Dr. A. D. Pollen was appointed Chief Special Judge, and Fergusson, the new governor, resolved to appoint Indians to the two posts of Assistant Special Judge. Continuing his campaign to placate Indian interests within the administration, he chose Ranade in 1881 to assume responsibility for Poona and Satara districts.[5] As Pollen's subordinate Ranade had only an advisory influence on policy, but Pollen praised the quality of his work so unqualifiedly that on his retirement in 1885 Fergusson's successor, Lord Reay, proposed that Ranade be appointed Chief Special Judge.

Even at this late date, the old intragovernmental controversy over Ranade's qualifications flared up again. Conservatives within the executive council insisted that such an important position should be reserved for members of the Covenanted Civil Service, which meant in effect Englishmen, and that the appointment of Ranade would be considered a capitulation to Indian political pressure. Reay nonetheless announced Ranade's temporary elevation on November 30, 1885. A year later he wrote to Courtenay Ilbert that he intended to make Ranade's tenure permanent, "<u>not</u> because he is an eminent Native but because the previous Judge Pollen says and we believe him to be the <u>best</u> man for the place. I am of opinion that Natives are especially well fitted for Civil Judicial employment and I attach <u>very</u> great importance to this appointment."[6] Despite bureaucratic opposition Ranade was permanently confirmed on May 15, 1887.[7] The government was eager to avoid a repetition of the tensions of 1879, and its success demonstrated that power patterns within the Bombay government had perceptibly shifted in the years since Temple's departure. Ranade was never again faced with public criticism of his political work from the Anglo-Indian community. For the eight years after 1885, until he was further elevated to the Bombay High Court, he was the single most influential person associated with the Relief Act.

Relief Act work took Ranade out of Poona on tours of the districts for up to eight months of each year. In his first year he set an energetic pattern for the whole decade by visiting all talukas twice, and inspecting carefully the records of subordinate judges and village registrars, "personally instructing them and discussing all changes in the law and all questions of procedure," as he matter-of-factly expressed it.[8] When his wife Ramabai advised him to work at a less torrid pace, he answered rather severely that his thoroughness was designed to contrast with the sedentary habits of most British district officers:

> The Government has not sent us so that we may enjoy an outing and demand the travelling allowance. . . . If I send for the records, the cleverer sort of person gets an undue advantage over others. He misleads the inspecting officer about the condition of the

villages. The object of the Government is to find out the truth about the condition of the farmers, their problems and difficulties. And this is not possible simply because the officers are too lazy.[9]

What he found on his tours he summarized in his annual report for 1882, a document written just a year after his appointment, in which he firmly defended the social impact of the new legislation. Ranade reported that the first purpose of the Relief Act, amelioration of the ryots' financial position, was succeeding emphatically well. The courts were functioning more efficiently and justly, no longer acting by default as debt collectors for the savkars. Many ryots were now freed from the fear of prison, indebtedness in general was declining, and a more orderly system of credit was emerging. In summary he wrote in sanguine tones that the act had helped the ryots to "a growth in the standard of life, more variety of pursuits, a more assured sense of property in land, greater self-control, greater intelligence to cope with the Savkars, and increased facilities to borrow money when needed."[10] Ranade had to admit that the total amount of credit had declined, since creditors were less willing to lend on the security of personal property, but he argued that this was primarily the aftermath of famine, a necessary transition to a more secure system of rural credit.[11]

In assessing the moneylenders' role in village society, Ranade suggested restricting their powers in favor of the Kunbis, but he was careful to leave them a social function, for he was no Utilitarian social leveller. The moneylender class had powerful advocates in the Bombay government, which saw them as the key to future prosperity. According to laissez-faire analysis, government should be limited to providing the legal framework within which capitalists, regardless of their place in village society, could freely accumulate capital. Sir Raymond West, the most influential theorist in Bombay on these matters, believed that the Relief Act had stimulated social and economic disruption in the Deccan.[12] In 1881 he charged that most savkars had been ruined by the act, which had made it impossible for them to recover their debts and consequently had made the ryots financially reckless. He maintained that many savkars had left the Deccan, leaving the ryots with less credit available than before.[13] Two years later West wrote an elaborate denunciation of the act, summarizing his opposition with the view that restrictions on the competitive flow of capital could only worsen rural conditions. Only time, aided by the enforcement of contracts, could bring prosperity.[14]

Ranade's reply to this position rested on the perception that laissez-faire as a description of the government's policies was a grossly ironic misnomer. The only era in which the government had truly not interfered in the economic relations of the countryside was under pre-British regimes, which tacitly approved a static economy with small-scale moneylending in the villages. The British system of law and administration had systematically altered social patterns, usually to the detriment of traditional landholders. The government could not possibly return now to an unregulated economy; it could only use its power more wisely. "The mistake was made when all traditionary protection of person and property was done away with, when the panchayats were abolished, and the periods of limitation reduced. The Deccan Agriculturalists' Relief Act is one of a series of measures in which this mistake has been acknowledged and an attempt made to rectify it."[15] The act, in other words, was a vital step on the path toward reconstructing the hierarchical and harmonious village society which had served Maharashtra's past and which was the surest foundation for a dynamic future. This conservative social stance was the basis for all of Ranade's subsequent attempts to revitalize society; without this his progressive paternalism cannot be understood.

The views of Pollen and Ranade, which committed the government to intervene actively in the economy in the name of social conservatism, resulted in the decline of West's opposition by 1883, for West was in effect calling for a return to the policies which had already proved ineffectual in the 1870's. The Relief Act went further than new regulation of property relations, too; it adjusted the local courts so as to function in a more traditionally Indian manner. The controversial clause of the act enabling a judge to go behind the terms of a contract to determine its equity was modelled on one of the most important recent initiatives of the Sarvajanik Sabha. Ranade, Joshi and others, using the traditional panchayat as a model, founded the Poona *lavad* (arbitration) court in January 1876.[16] Its purpose was to arrange informal but effective compromises in both private and public conflicts, thereby obviating the need for men to rely on British courts. As such, the lavad court was a prototype of the swadeshi institutions which burgeoned around India after 1905. With or without the cooperation of the Raj, Indians would begin to take a greater role in their own affairs. The Poona lavad court was comprised of men from several castes and communities in Poona; its authority, like that of the old panchayats, was based entirely on the prestige and influence of its members. Parties to a suit could voluntarily approach the court, which would provide one or more conciliators to resolve the dispute. The lavad court's best-known success was its discovery of the clerk who burned Budhwar Wada in May 1879. The Poona court was imitated in other towns of the Desh where the panchayats displaced in 1859 by official revenue courts were revived as lavad courts. Their procedures of examining all materials relevant to a case was borrowed by the Relief Act's provision for a judge to "arrive at decisions on grounds of equity rather than formal legal considerations."

This innovation in the courts' procedures led further still to the most controversial feature of the Relief Act. The act established a new class of "conciliators," men of local influence before whom all suits were to be heard before they could be taken to court. The conciliators were supplemented by a second new class of semi-official agents, village munsifs who dealt informally with cases involving less than Rs. 10. The two groups had the purpose of relieving the immense load of trivial case work which the courts faced, a difficulty which Ranade had stressed as early as 1872 in his <u>Statistics of Criminal Justice</u>. They were to be an extension of the courts into the villages, embodying the traditional virtues of discretion and equity. Ranade saw these men as the key to reconstructing harmonious social relationships in the mofussil.[17]

Most of the conciliators appointed in the first two years had practiced as members of lavad courts before their Relief Act appointments.[18] The Sarvajanik Sabha predictably praised the conciliation system as an imaginative variation on the panchayat system and suggested that opposition to the plan "seems chiefly to come from the Local [Presidency] Government who have expressed a want of confidence in the honesty of purpose of the native gentry."[19] Coming in September 1879 this was a barbed assertion.

Ranade took pains to describe the conciliators' effectiveness in his reports as Assistant Special Judge, since these men were chosen from the very groups in which he placed his hopes for progressive leadership. As early as 1879 he had written that in selecting a conciliator "regard will be had chiefly to his local standing and personal influence over the people. . . . It is to be hoped that amongst the numerous classes of old pensioners, non-practising Vakils, and respectable bankers or traders there will be found men who, by their position, character, and influence, will prove themselves fit to discharge the duties of the honorary office."[20] This list did not emphasize the ascriptive leaders of village society, the patils, kulkarnis and landholders. Their position was assured in any case, and in emphasizing an expanded role for the commercial and professional groups Ranade was broadening the definition of the "respected leaders" of mofussil society to include those who were more likely to be in direct contact with new currents in the outside world.

The first group of conciliators produced work of uneven quality. Their number was somewhat reduced in 1882 so as to correct inefficiencies, as Pollen diplomatically phrased it. He praised the general effectiveness of the conciliators, their popularity among the populace, their accessibility to debtors, and the relief which they gave to the courts. Ranade went even further, asserting that the conciliators were serving well in situations where the courts could not function at all.[21]

The support of the Special Judges in the early years was necessary for the survival of the conciliators, for some circles in Bombay assumed that they would prove inefficient, unjust, and even corrupt. The first official review of the Relief Act proposed in 1883 that the conciliators be replaced by a new group of official subordinate judges.[22] Accordingly a commission was formed that year to examine the matter. Its report commended the conciliators, on the basis of statistical studies presented by Ranade which showed that the ryots had access to the conciliators and that the conciliators were more effective in resolving disputes than the courts.[23] Ranade summarized his defense by asserting:

> The conciliators are like the panchayats of old, only with no power to arbitrate in cases of contest. They save the parties and the Courts much useless expense, delay and trouble. They are certainly not distrusted. Their social position is better than that of any other class of voluntary public servants. They enjoy the confidence of those among whom they live. They bring justice to the doors of the ryots in a way no adaptation of the stipendiary machinery can secure. To entrust the work to Subordinate Judges would be to defeat the main object of the institution, namely, to moderate the heat and passion of litigating parties by honest mediation.[24]

Here was a time-honored tradition reinterpreted and made to serve modern putposes. This was Ranade's most decisive policy victory in the twelve years in which he was associated with the Relief Act.[25]

By 1883 the Relief Act was well established. Over the following decade, as long as Ranade was associated with it, no major changes were made, and the relief administration became a permanent part of the rural economy of the Desh. A review of the act conducted by A. F. Woodburn in 1889 showed that although rural indebtedness was still endemic, it had steadily declined to a point considerably below the level in surrounding regions unaffected by the act. Further, land revenue in the four Relief Act districts was more easily and regularly collected than elsewhere in Maharashtra.[26]

Three years later a new commission made a more exhaustive survey of the Relief Act and produced a favorable report in all major respects. In commenting on this report, Ranade noted that his defense of the conciliators had gained almost unanimous support. Even Justice West had finally complimented the quality of their work, now that enough time had elapsed to eliminate unqualified men.[27] Ranade could take satisfaction that before he left the Relief Act in late 1893, most of his main objectives had been reached. Economic harmony in the villages had to some extent been regained, and the more aggressive elements of British revenue policy curbed. The fortress of laissez-faire economic thought had been challenged in the name of a more pragmatic sensitivity to the traditional values of rural society. A socially varied group of respected men in the towns had been given increased responsibility, and the gap between government and society had been tentatively narrowed. The Deccan Agriculturists' Relief Act was the principal element in this trend, but it functioned in a broader context of both administrative problems and social theory which Ranade also addressed in the 1880's. It is these writings which give a clearer picture of his mature orientation toward the whole range of India's development.

Economic Development and Social Harmony

Ranade's ideas on the course of Maharashtra's development and the types of leaders who would preside fell into two general areas, economic development and political liberalization. Economic policy problems of the 1880's concerned for the most part the rural economy; his critique of these policies restated Ranade's social values with regard to the mofussil. They in turn were closely intertwined with his criticisms of British economic imperialism and led directly back to his demand for a gradual devolution of power into Indian hands. His discussion of political development largely focused on the towns and cities, where modern representative politics were first being introduced in his time. Ranade's assessment of the elite composition of urban areas differed somewhat from his interests in the countryside, as did the details of harnessing British political power to India's true needs.

Ranade's most systematic writings in the years after the famine concerned economic development. Here he faced the acute challenge: How can capitalistic development and agricultural innovation occur rapidly without upsetting the balance of Maharashtra's social interests? How should governmental policies be framed so as to balance progress and harmony and integrate the contrasting roles of the various rural classes? By now Ranade had studied several European societies with some care, for the purpose of gaining comparative insights into economic development. In the early 1880's he frequently cited England, France, Germany, and Russia as examples of progress, and almost invariably he used these examples in defense of a hardy, independent peasantry. He agreed with the Utilitarian advocates of ryotwari settlements that the government could have considerable leverage on the peasants' character. He pointed to the Russian serfs as evidence that "the ryot once emancipated and set on his feet and inspired with a sense that the land is as absolutely his as his home or clothes, there need never be any apprehension of his running into debt again and not practising thrift."[28] Similarly, the Prussian land reform legislation early in the century had demonstrated that judicious governmental action on the peasants' behalf could liberate their economic energies. The ryots as much as anyone else could become small-scale capitalists, for the Prussian legislators had "laid hold of the principle of individual and independent property in the soil as the cardinal point of their reform. . . . The great principle underlying all reform was 'to remove whatever had hitherto hindered the individual from obtaining that degree of well-being which he was capable of reaching by exertions, according to the best of his ability.'"[29]

Ranade's commitment to encouraging individual initiative was in fact more fundamental than his commitment to ryotwari settlements. It could just as well be linked to a defense of the landowning class, as in fact it was in many of his writings of this time. In his eyes the most objectionable social impact of the Utilitarian settlements, in Maharashtra and elsewhere, was the way in which they undermined all the leading classes of traditional society without setting up any new leaders in their place.

In contrast, the earliest British land settlements around India had taken much more careful account of the existing stratification. Ranade praised the social conservatism of the early British rulers' policies, in contrast to the levelling impact of Utilitarian policies.

> This tendency to innovation and the levelling up of oriental institutions to the requirements of the most radical theorists in Europe was in its full swing before the Mutinies, and the annexation policy and the denial of adoptions were only the political phases of this same spirit. The fearful blaze of that period of troubles opened the eyes of the ruling authorities to the great mistakes that had been committed, when the conservative traditions of the first conquests, the policy associated with the memories of Elphinstone, Munro, Malcolm, and Metcalfe, was given up for new-fangled ways of thought and revolutionary action, recommended by men like Bird and Thomason in the North-Western Provinces, and in our Presidency by Goldsmid, Hart, Cowper, and Willoughby.30

Without a capitalist class Maharashtra would be demoralized by "the uniformly dead level of poverty in a Rayatwari settled district." The traditional landholding class of the Desh held the secret of future development, as the small minority in society which possessed the essential attributes of leadership: "intelligence, wealth, thrifty habits, knowledge, and power of combination."31 Indian society in 1880 contrasted unfavorably with European not only in the condition of its peasantry but in the power of its gentry as well.

> If this country sadly wants a proud and independent yeomanry as the backbone of its strength and prosperity, it no less equally needs the leading and the light of propertied men. A complete divorce from land of those who cultivate it is a national evil, and no less an evil is it to find one dead level of small farmers all over the land. High and petty farming, with an upper ten thousand of the holders of large landed estates, and a vast mass of peasant farmers, this mixed constitution of rural society, is necessary to secure the stability and progress of the country.32

Here was the core of Ranade's theory: the traditional society of the Desh, with its carefully constructed hierarchy, provided the most certain basis for economic modernization. In this setting the landholders would exploit wisely patterned incentives from the government without abrogating their responsibility to village society as a whole.

Ever since the advent of British rule the social and economic position of the Maharashtrian landholding class had been vexed. Many of them had been given the rights to land revenue, or inam rights, during the last years of the Peshwas. Many of these grants were legally questionable, reflecting the turbulent conditions of the times. Beginning in Elphinstone's time district officers made sporadic efforts to reclaim spurious inams, and in 1842 the Inam Commission was established to conduct a thorough survey. In 1852 it was given full legal power to decide the validity of all inam grants, the rights on which many landed proprietors based their power in rural society.33 The commission's task was officially stated in positive terms: to give permanent validity to those grants which had been properly contracted under the Peshwas. But it held the power to undermine the financial basis of the rural gentry if it wished, and after 1852 Englishmen and Indians alike attacked it as carrying out a deliberate campaign of social levelling. One English friend of the inamdars referred to the commission as "machinery of confiscation," whose desire to grasp more tax revenue could easily lead to social chaos.[34] In 1861, under pressure from the governor of Bombay, the commission offered to liquidate its work by imposing a small assessment on all inams which had not yet been examined, and end further inquiries into their validity.[35] By 1874 the commission formally ended its work, having had less actual effect on the inamdar class than many had feared. As late as 1910 large amounts of inam land were still free of taxation,[36] but a legacy of distrust and apprehension remained.

Ranade referred to its effects with indirect expression of relief at the end of its work, during the tensions of 1878: "It is the good fortune of this Presidency that, notwithstanding the Inam Commission and the survey settlements, there are still left in the country a considerable middle class and a rich minority, who have not been yet levelled to the low status of the pauper tenantry of Government. In Madras, this levelling process has been complete, and this explains the fact of its unrelieved misery."[37]

For questions of economic development, however, references to a middle class and a rich minority obscured a crucial distinction in Maharashtrian society. These terms could refer either to the indigenous landholders or to the moneylenders, most of whom were intruders into the traditional social order. The moneylending class in the Desh included some indigenous Deshastha Brahmins, who were closely tied to the village system of mutual responsibilities. But during the previous century, and especially as a result of British revenue policies and courts, this class had been greatly augmented by an influx of Gujarati Banias and Marwaris from regions to the north.[38] As outsiders who tended to return their profits to their ancestral districts they had little interest in improving agriculture in Maharashtra. The most frequent complaints against them were that they charged excessive interest, they rarely gave receipts for loans and frequently wrote fraudulent contracts, they exercised corrupting influence in the courts, and they demanded repayment of debts with no thought for the borrower or the prosperity of his lands. The fury of the ryots in 1875 had been directed almost entirely against the Banias and Marwaris. The Relief Act had been primarily intended to curb their powers, and Ranade considered this to be necessary, since events of recent years were "visibly tending to the impoverishment of the old proprietors and transferring the lands into the hands of strangers and nonresidents, who generally belonged to the mercantile and trading classes, and bought up the land for no other attraction than its character as a paying investment."[39] Ranade shared the general Maharashtrian bias against Marwaris and Banias, writing in 1883 that "the substitution of home-made and closely related savkars for men of foreign birth cannot be regarded as a calamity, seeing that the new savkars are bound to be more humane and more compromising than the strangers."[40]

The degree of Ranade's commitment to the landholders as a class who could reconcile social harmony with economic progress is perhaps best illustrated by his views on one of the most controversial issues in India in the early 1880's, the question of the Permanent Settlement. The appropriate role for the landed aristocracy in India's development had been a constant subject of debate in government councils ever since 1858, and among the British the party which defended the gentry interest had scored some notable victories.[41] One of their hopes in the 1870's was to extend the permanent settlement of the government's revenue claim to the rest of India, in addition to Bengal. This system, designed to eliminate the disruptive effects of periodic government assessments of land revenue, could in theory be just as well applied to a region of peasant proprietors as to a region dominated by a landed class. But ever since Cornwallis' time it had been linked with a belief in the virtues of a gentry class, in the program of Whig liberals. Ranade stood squarely in this tradition, as did many of the leading men of Bombay Presidency, both British and Indian. The attacks on the Inam Commission were only one symptom of this. The dominant trend in Indian opinion in Bombay was illustrated by Native Opinion's view of the Bombay system in 1874. The Utilitarian bureaucrat, it insisted, desires "to put its finger into everything; and this appetite, unceasing in its operation is at the bottom of all these popular outcries [against extension of the Permanent Settlement]. Until the whole of India is blessed with a permanent land revenue settlement the country will have no peace."[42] The traditional rights of society's rightful leaders as well as the harmony of social life seemed at stake.

Although the Bombay government did not formally discuss the question of a permanent settlement in its Relief Act deliberations, public debate continued unabated. The most detailed plan was presented by William Wedderburn, the Englishman with whom Ranade was most closely associated in the early 1880's. Wedderburn published a tract in 1880, entitled A Permanent Settlement for the Deccan,[43] in which he proposed the revival of something akin to the old Maratha system. Rather than having to make cash payments to the government at planting time, when money was most dear, the ryots would pay a fixed percentage of the crop to the leading men of the community: landholders, savkars, pensioners, vakils, and others. They in turn would pay the government a fixed sum which would not vary from year to year. The government would be assured of a predictable annual income, and the symbiotic interests of the village community would be strengthened.[44]

Ranade supported Wedderburn's plan as a "modified permanent settlement," in which the permanent element was the percentage of the crop which the ryot was obliged to release. The great virtue of this system,

Ranade maintained, was that it would eliminate the need for tax remissions in poor seasons, giving the government a stable annual income and the people an unfluctuating revenue demand. The government would not need to meddle arbitrarily in the economy, and men of wealth would be free to invest their capital productively. "Impelled by the magic of property . . . the Zemindars in posse are expected to apply themselves heart and soul to the improvement of the soil, 'supplying the cultivators with superior seed and manure and machinery.'"[45]

Many others in India were far less rhapsodic than Ranade about the selflessness of the zamindars; it was agreed in most quarters that under the Cornwallis Settlement they had oppressed their tenants with unprecedented severity.[46] In the early 1880's legislation was introduced in the Bengal Legislative Council to limit the zamindars' powers. Commenting on the bill in 1883, Ranade granted that the zamindars, like the savkars of Maharashtra, might need some restraint. But the zamindars at least were an organic element of Bengali society, and Ranade anticipated that the bill would deprive them of their economic power and initiative. If the bill were passed, the landlords would be ruined and the ryots would be thrown into helpless dependence on the government, whose power to disrupt society he feared even more. Executive and judicial machinery would regulate the economy; this was a sure formula for economic disaster and political oppression.[47]

Writing in this vein Ranade gave little indication of awareness that the Bengali zamindars' performance had been less than economically progressive or socially harmonious. For this he was roundly criticized by other authors. In response he reiterated that for Maharashtra he desired no social upheaval like the one Bengal had undergone after 1793, for in Maharashtra the landlords were already the ancient respected class on the land. Therefore, "no new class of farmers or middle-men will be artificially created to cause annoyance to the Ryots, and suspicion to the officials."[48] Returning then to his usual belief that a benign government could assist the peaceful transition of rural administration and mediate class conflict if it arose, Ranade concluded: "If differences subsequently spring up between class and class, as they have on occasion sprung up in Bengal, the government can interfere as a mediator, and right matters by protecting the weak against the strong."[49] Here was an echo of traditional Hindu political thought: the ruler should intervene in society whenever it was necessary to readjust the harmonious balance of social groups. To Ranade this could provide a tangible link between past and future, similar to the link which the Deccan Agriculturists' Relief Act embodied.

One other major issue of the early 1880's clarified Ranade's views on the relation of government action to the pattern of social power in the mofussil. It also illustrated the conditions under which he believed the landowning class could fulfill its potential to lead rural society into an era of progress. Development capital was inadequate in the mofussil; the perennial problem in the Deccan was to make funds available to the farmer at low cost. Here Ranade saw an opportunity to link the wealthy interests of Poona and Bombay with rural society, which heretofore had rarely been accomplished either economically or politically. As early as 1858 some district officers had suggested that the government establish agricultural loan facilities in the villages, but the Bombay Raj had steadfastly refused to commit the large amount of capital necessary in such an undertaking.[50] The debate was renewed in the late 1870's when Wedderburn revived the demand for government-financed agricultural banks, which would provide loans at low interest rates with long periods of repayment.[51]

Ranade joined the discussion in 1878. Wedderburn's scheme was likely to founder on the lack of capital available to the government, so Ranade suggested that the government should not use its own capital but should guarantee private investment funds against loss, as it had for private British investment in railway construction.[52] This would complement the judicial relief provided for the countryside by the Relief Act. If the state "subsidizes or guarantees private banks against risk during the first few experimental years and enables them to rid the peasantry of their ancestral debts, and if at the same time it allows the land revenue to be redeemed or permanently settled at a moderate figure once and for all, it will provide an ample fund for agricultural relief improvement."[53] Private capital, from mofussil towns but especially from Bombay, was available if the government at first provided guarantees against failure, which no private agency could do.

Ranade's proposal was backed by a loose organization of Poona savkars, many of whom joined leading members of the Sarvajanik Sabha to found the Poona Committee for the Establishment of Agricultural Banks in the early 1880's. Beginning in late 1882 they petitioned the government to lend its guarantees to the proposed credit facilities. But laissez-faire opinion still prevailed among the British; it assumed that any government regulation in this area would stifle free enterprise. The India Office in London vetoed the plan.[54] In the balance of all these attempts to influence government policy, Ranade and his associates could measure only limited and unsatisfactory successes. The regime's potential for what they considered destructive intervention remained as great as ever, and this wariness ran throughout Ranade's administrative writings as another unifying thread.

The Political Role of Social Elites

One of the salient elements of Ranade's opposition to unbridled free-enterprise economics on the land was his view that the laissez-faire ideal of minimal government had led India to a new authoritarianism parallel in its effects to the oppression which it had once been meant to overcome.

Instead of releasing the productive forces latent in the economy, it had produced steadily deepening poverty and social fragmentation; for it involved an aggressive and systematic attack on the former social and legal system. "The perpetual interposition of civil courts and revenue authorities can only result in paralyzing private efforts, and increasing the sense of dependence on the state as the only regulator of private rights, than which nothing can in the end prove more prejudicial to all classes concerned."[55] Not only did the "revolutionary action" of the Utilitarians threaten existing social patterns; it also embodied the threat of despotism inherent in any imperial regime. Appealing to pre-British precedents, Ranade equated Utilitarian aggressiveness with the claim of Muslim governments that the state was ultimate owner of the land, leaving tenants only tenuous rights to their holdings. The British must not repeat the authoritarianism of the earlier Muslims, but should renew the more moderate claims of Hindu governments over their subjects' wealth. At this point Ranade enunciated what was to become a stock nationalist myth of the Maratha past as not only paternalist but responsible.

> The Government must retrace its steps, forget its Mahomedan antecedents of absolutism, and return to the old Hindu traditions, where the king's power was restrained in all directions by the rights of the people, among whom the king was more of a father and a manager than a conqueror or a sovereign lord, and cultivated land belonged in absolute right to private owners who paid as tax a fixed share of the produce to the king like any of his other subjects for the expenses of protection.[56]

This had also been the crucial assumption behind Ranade's work to establish the arbitration courts in Poona and the Desh. The panchayat courts which Elphinstone had used in the 1820's had placed local initiative where it properly belonged, in the hands of influential Indian representatives, not British officers. Those courts had withered under the early Utilitarian systems, and by now, "from one end of India to the other, it is the same sad tale of old institutions decayed, old ties broken up, old associations severed by the hand of violent innovation."[57] New strategies must now be used to recapture old patterns of influence and prestige.

Ranade clarified his strategy for Maharashtra's political development when Lord Ripon promulgated his Local Self-Government Bill of 1882. The effort to increase Indian participation at the lowest levels of government was part of a trend toward decentralization which Lord Mayo had initiated in 1870. For the sake of fiscal economy and local political revival, Mayo had decentralized the finances of several departments, stating at the time that decentralization "in its full meaning and integrity will afford opportunities for the development of self-government, for strengthening Municipal institutions, and for the association of Natives and Europeans to a greater extent than heretofore in the administration of affairs. . . . The Local Governments and all their subordinates will enlist the active assistance, or at all events, the sympathy of many classes who have hitherto taken little or no part in the work of social and material advancement."[58] These principles inspired hopes among Indians, but in the following decade they foundered against the opposition of provincial governments, which made little effort to increase Indian representation. Against this bureaucratic resistance Ripon renewed the challenge on May 18, 1882, declaring his desire to place political responsibility in the hands of those most directly concerned with its use.

> The establishment and development and practical working of self-government . . . is . . . a great object of political education to be obtained, and therefore we may well put up with even disappointments and annoyance rather than sweep away those principles which are calculated in the end, as they become better known, and as the people become more accustomed to work them, to confer large benefits upon the community in general. I, therefore, desire . . . to see the powers and independence of local bodies increased and extended, wherever it may be possible, although we are aware we can only proceed gradually and tentatively in that direction.[59]

Ripon was aware that the growing class of Western-educated Indians had been alienated from the Raj under Lytton's regime. To reverse this trend, Ripon suggested that the Municipal Committees for urban areas and the Local Fund Committees for the mofussil be reconstituted with a majority of non-official members, many of whom should be elected by their local constituencies rather than nominated as before. He went beyond this to a controversial attack on the power which the district collector exercised as committee chairman to veto any legislation. Wherever possible, he requested, even the committee chairmen should be non-official.[60]

Ranade, like most Western-educated Indians, supported the general outline of Ripon's proposals. An advocate of decentralization himself, Ranade agreed that under the Raj "power is too much centralized in the heads of different departments, and is dissociated from local knowledge and sympathy, as also from all participation of the popular voice in its decisions."[61] He immediately perceived that the local and district committees offered new hope of influence for the descendants of the Peshwas' officers. "Under the old rule, the native District officers, the Vatandar Deshmukhs and Deshpandes, discharged the function of being the advisers of the agents of the Central Government in local matters, and this function will be no less usefully discharged by the additional native members,"[62] many of whom would come from the same social classes as before. A mixed system of representation would assure local committees of the balanced proportion of leading classes, and it would revitalize the operations of government at the level which counted most.[63]

Ranade had begun to equivocate, however, on the vital issue of elected representatives. He favored evolution toward self-rule, but only if popular suffrage guaranteed India rational and efficient leaders. His experience with the political conditions of princely states and his view of the inefficiency of pre-British regimes contrasted with his admission that for all its faults the British Raj operated rationally. For the present period of India's political apprenticeship, even partial self-rule would be an unwise experiment unless educated and experienced Indian administrators could be found to fill elective posts. In sum, Ranade was wary about the prospects for electing worthy men to all the posts which might be open under Ripon's directive. From that time on, he began to resist trends toward rapid expansion of representative politics, in an increasingly paternalistic distrust of popular movements. His commitment to excellence and efficiency led to a growing embarrassment; he who had begun the process of representative politics in Poona would spend his last years resisting the pace of its advance.

In one of his most unexpected policy statements Ranade opposed Ripon's plan for non-official majorities on local committees and for the abolition of the district collector's veto. Under Ranade's more cautious alternative, local boards would have official majorities with the district collector still chairman so as to assure the government the veto power in local affairs "on those few occasions when government may reasonably feel that, in the interests of the people themselves, the unanimous opinion of their local representatives should be for a time set aside. Under the present circumstances of the country, we hold that, whatever may be said against it on the grounds of abstract theory, practically government for a long time to come must possess the power alluded to above, and on occasions exercise it in the interests of the people themselves."[64]

Ranade saw the mechanism of special constituencies as an effective means of increasing the influence of the complex social elite of the Relief Act and his economic writings, and in April 1882 he proposed a comprehensive plan for local government. Based on his experience with mofussil towns and villages, his plan expanded on Ripon's principles. He began with a scheme for gradually increasing non-official representation on town and rural councils, emphasizing that they were "the foundations upon which the superstructure is to stand, and unless the foundations are well laid, the superstructure must of necessity tumble down sooner or later."[65] For the ten cities of the Presidency whose municipal councils already had some elected members, Ranade proposed that fifty percent of the commissioners henceforth be elected. Their constituencies should be limited to the wealthier taxpayers, so as to ensure a responsible, intelligent and elite electorate, as was the practice in England. For each district committee Ranade proposed two special constituencies for wealthy landholders. He defended his position against those who might consider it reactionary by the paternalistic assertion that the inamdars "do not represent the class they belong to so much as their tenants who to a great extent have eventually to pay the Local Fund Cess. . . . The Inamdars moreover as a class, but more especially the larger ones among them, are an intelligent body and are the natural leaders of their respective local committees."[66] He was at pains, however, to balance the conservative landed interest with an equal number of reserved seats for the educated classes, "represented by the list of jurors and assessors of the district, the graduates of the University resident within the district, and the pleaders practicing within the district." He made no reference to the commercial classes as a category separate from landholders. Between them the educated members and the landed interests would constitute the half of the district committees not directly controlled by officialdom. This reliance on the strategy of reserved seats was designed to encourage cooperation among disparate groups; it rested on his assumption that they were likely to function harmoniously if given the chance. It never occurred to Ranade that this method of objectifying factional differences might clarify and intensify the conflicts among them. When later years produced results opposite from those he anticipated, Ranade was led to somber disillusionment.

But as yet this was not on the horizon. If city and district committees functioned well, provincial legislative councils could later be made more representative. Even now the Bombay Legislative Council could be made more responsive to popular interests if its Indian members were elected instead of appointed by the government. Under existing arrangements, he asserted, Temple and Fergusson had both habitually nominated the most conservative landholders, men who avoided any criticism of the government.[67] "During the last four or five years systematic . . . attempts have been made to impair the usefulness of our Legislative Council by ostracising . . . the really independent non-official element from the Council, and substituting in its stead persons whom a well-known Bengali gentleman characterized the other day as 'magnificent nobodies.'"[68] Ranade's caution in approaching the elective principle was again evident as he proposed that provincial council elections be indirect; municipal and district committees should constitute the constituencies for the higher council. Direct popular rule was not yet advisable in the circumstances of Indian society. "The masses of the people themselves are . . . incapable of choosing the fittest men to be their representatives in the Legislature, but those who manage the local affairs of these masses, and who possess their confidence, ought undoubtedly to be in a position to choose as deputies for the people generally the fittest to be their representatives in the Legislature."[69] After all this, his assurance shortly thereafter that sooner or later "the people of this country must rise to the status of a self-governed community, and learn to control their own affairs in subordinate alliance with England," struck his readers as an innocuous afterthought.[70]

The Bombay government reacted with surprised pleasure that the voice of the Sarvajanik Sabha should request caution. Governor Fergusson recognized the value of Ranade's support. Resisting rapid democratization, he wrote to Ripon in October 1883 insisting that bold changes were not desired even by the usually impatient Sarvajanik Sabha. "Only last year the journal of the Sarvajanik Sabha of Poona, which was supposed to be far advanced, in asking for a measure of representation, conceded voluntarily that Government must have a majority on the Boards."[71] Fergusson was opposed to increasing Indian representation in local political councils, and drafted bills which provided for nominated majorities on local committees and made the district collectors chairmen of the committees. The collectors' position was further strengthened by the power to nullify any election.

Ripon was forced to agree to these major qualifications to his resolution. Even after his capitulation the Bombay government did not put the system into effect until 1885, the year after Ripon and Fergusson left India. Furthermore, Fergusson's government made no serious consideration of changes in the legislative council. His successor, Lord Reay, made more popular appointments, including Ranade; hence Indian criticism of the legislative council was blunted. But no changes of procedure were introduced at this level until the Indian Councils Act of 1892. It was, however, within the legislative council and other high-level official bodies that Ranade most effectively pressed his demand that Indians be given greater influence within the administrative services. In this work the conservative implications of his belief in education and efficiency were less evident, and he seemed to his Poona constituents still the champion of the popular interest.

The Powers of Indian Officials

On several occasions during the 1880's the Government of India reconsidered the pattern of powers held by its hierarchy of officials, as far down as the village police. Here was one final arena in which Ranade felt constrained to defend the claims of the local elites. Village police, for example, had traditionally been empowered to carry arms, but during the political unrest of 1878 Lytton's government withdrew that right under the new Arms Act. By its provisions Indians but not Englishmen were required to have permits even in those cases in which the government sanctioned firearms. Second only to the Vernacular Press Act, the Arms Act was resented by the Indian political associations as racially discriminatory. The Sarvajanik Sabha denounced it as depriving the people of the right of self-defense and thus contributing to the dacoities of the following year. It requested the revival of the old system of arming the patils and using villagers as official night watchmen. Self-protection rather than a general disarming was the route to security in the villages.[72] The sabha's plea was ignored by the government, even under Ripon, and opposition to the Arms Act later became the subject of annual resolutions by Congress.

The powers of village officers were being eroded in other ways as well by the Bombay government. Until 1874 village police had been supervised only informally by district officials. The British revenue officers with whom the police worked in maintaining land records could charge the village police with inefficiency or dishonesty only in the civil courts. The revenue service won an important victory in 1874, when a new law stipulated that disputes would henceforth be appealed only to senior officers in the revenue department. In 1885 another bill was introduced into the legislative council, further threatening the village officials' position.[73] Until then, they had been paid for their services by the traditional system of hereditary land and money grants, or vatans. The new bill imposed strict penalties for failure to carry out their duties, punishing any misconduct with forfeiture of office. For any serious infraction all sharers in the vatan, including both the patil and his assistants, should forfeit both money and property interests, even though this contravened the liberal principle of individual responsibility and might well cause the ruin of influential families.

Ranade had received his first appointment to the Bombay Legislative Council that year.[74] On the council he was appointed to the committee which reviewed both the new bill and the law of 1874. In this position he unsuccessfully opposed the bill, which he saw as a dangerous bureaucratic encroachment on the vatandars' rights.[75] He insisted that the proposed penalties for even small infractions were unduly harsh. He condemned the idea of collective responsibility by urging that for any offense only the individual concerned should be penalized, not the other officers of the village.[76] In summary, he charged that British oppression had caused the decline of the local officials; revenue officials "too often make the Vatandars more wretched and helpless than the meanest Rayat in the land, and tend to convert the Vatan into a badge of slavery, and make its tenure more uncertain and burdensome than that of any other kind of property."[77] Once again he compared the British regime unfavorably with its less oppressive Maratha predecessors, who had carefully preserved local self-rule by respecting the vatandars' position. The only solution, Ranade advised, was for the government to return to the vatandars their traditional powers, while allowing their offices to change hands without restriction. Here was the essence of his strategy: an attempt to infuse new initiative into the traditional village leadership, but not so rapidly as to disrupt the social order. "It is high time to infuse new blood into these effete classes. Enlarge the sphere of families from whom selection for office has to be made. Leave the way open to strangers to enter in, and revive the energies of these classes, many of whose members have now ceased to be useful in the interests of general improvement."[78] Once again his strategy balanced a call for liberal innovation with a Burkean social conservatism.

Concerning the higher levels of administration, Ranade defended the claims of his own educated class. He joined the chorus of criticism against civil service regulations, which provided that competitive examinations for entrance into the Covenanted Civil Service would be held only in London, and that after 1876 the maximum age of eligibility for the examinations was nineteen. As Ranade put it, under Lytton's regime the Raj had "discarded the pledges and promises of successive proclamations and Parliamentary Acts in regard to the concession of real equality to all classes of Her Majesty's subjects."[79] Like most of the government's critics Ranade supported the claims of the educated class against the Statutory Civil Service as well. Lytton established the Statutory Service in 1878 chiefly to recruit the scions of aristocratic families. Rather than submit them to competitive examinations, in which they almost invariably fared worse than other Indian candidates, Lytton directed the provincial governments to appoint up to one-sixth of each year's civil service recruits from the aristocracy. Ranade, defending the principle of open competition which favored the educated class, condemned the Statutory Service as a reversal of the parliamentary decrees enjoining equal treatment of all civil service candidates.[80] Against the dubious advantage of a few young aristocrats serving poorly in low-paid subordinate positions, Ranade insisted that the more competent educated class had suffered a great loss in both moral and political status.

In this Ranade's stance was identical with that of his counterparts in Bombay. But there was a perceptible difference of emphasis between them. The Bombay spokesmen had few direct contacts with the mofussil, while Ranade was engaged month by month in the effort to revitalize mofussil leadership. When the Aitchison Commission of 1886 reviewed the Statutory Civil Service, most of those who testified in Bombay condemned that service without qualification.[81] Ranade, while agreeing that the statutory officers were held in general contempt, nonetheless suggested that some places should be reserved for scions of aristocratic families. In his plan, if competitive examinations failed to produce enough successful candidates in any year to fill available positions, the remainder should be appointed from the existing statutory officials or other aristocratic families.[82] This was a shrewd mechanism, leaving an opening for the sardars without depriving the educated class of any opportunity. But it was more clever than workable, and no one else seriously considered it. In his preoccupation with reconciling all parties to a situation, Ranade at times like this produced plans of conciliation that were so elaborate as to be politically impracticable. In the 1890's this became one of the fatal weaknesses of his Moderate approach to political life, a tendency to equivocate over great conflicts.

In retrospect it is clear that the coherence of Ranade's "plan," of his ability to foresee all the historical implications of his work, must not be overemphasized. The many statements which he issued in this period from 1878 to 1886 were not so much elements of a monumental vision as the pragmatic efforts of a man who encouraged activity at every point.

He did this regardless of whether any given group's background was Brahmin or non-Brahmin, urban or rural, Indian or British. The great controversy of his later years revolved around his contention that even the British could contribute to India's development. On this question he was to find a majority of the Brahmin community firmly opposed to him in the 1890's. But under Ripon and Dufferin this notion seemed self-evident. He confidently assumed that there was no objection to associating with the Raj in local government and administration. The dilemmas of acting as both Indian spokesman and government agent had not yet become insuperable. Given the proper education and professional training, Indians could harness the Raj to their benefit. The requisite education, the key to modernization, was itself largely the gift of the Europeans. The 1880's were also the decade when Ranade's educational efforts in Poona bore fruit.

Notes

[1] On the official debates regarding revenue administration, the rural economy, and DARA, see Kumar, Western India, pp. 203-226.

[2] Bombay Government, Report of the Committee on the Riots in Poona and Ahmednagar, 2 vols. (Bombay, 1876), I, 107-110.

[3] Ibid., p. 112.

[4] Gazetteer of the Bombay Presidency, XVIII, Part I, 129-130; Bombay Government, Report of the Administration . . . for 1878-79 (Bombay, 1879), p. xxvi.

[5] Official correspondence referring to his appointment praised the intimate knowledge of rural conditions which he had gained in organizing the work of the Sarvajanik Sabha in the previous ten years. Bombay Government, Judicial Department Proceedings, 1881, XV, No. 5415.

[6] Letter of May[?] 6, 1886, Ilbert Papers, Eur D 594/16.

[7] Government of India, Home Department, Judicial A Proceedings, September 1887, Nos. 282-288, pp. 6, 15.

[8] DARA II, 219.

[9] Ramabai Ranade, Reminiscences, p. 136.

[10] India Office Library, Private Papers: William Lee-Warner, Deccan Riot, Series II, pp. 223-224.

[11] Ibid., p. 223.

[12] Kumar, Western India, pp. 198-203.

[13] India Office Library, Private Papers: William Lee-Warner, Political and Miscellaneous, Series V: 1890-1894, p. 495. For the extent of pressure on the savkars, see Kumar, Western India, pp. 215-217.

[14] DARA I, 387-396. West's views were given added weight by the first official review of the act's effectiveness. This study, conducted by H. Woodward, was presented on June 25, 1883. See DARA I, 356.

[15] Minute of June 1883, DARA I, 399.

[16] Native Opinion, January 26, 1879, pp. 51-52; May 4, 1879, pp. 280-282; and June 8, 1879, pp. 356-357, give some detail of the courts' founding, Wedderburn's role in encouraging their proliferation, and the government's willingness to incorporate them into the Relief Act.

[17] M. G. Ranade, "The Deccan Agriculturists' Bill," JPSS, II (October 1879), 55.

[18] Private Papers, II, p. 201; Gazetteer of Bombay, XVIII, Part 3, 30.

[19] Poona Sarvajanik Sabha, "Representation on the Deccan Agriculturists' Bill," JPSS, II (January 1880), 108-109.

[20] Ranade, "Deccan Agriculturists' Bill," 54.

[21] Private Papers, II, p. 216.

[22] Kumar, Western India, p. 222.

[23] DARA I, 464-473.

[24] Ibid., 398-399.

[25] Ranade was faced with the concurrent task of defending the village munsifs, whose early work he also found popular in the mofussil. Significantly, their best work had been primarily in the towns, among traders and shopkeepers, which was not their original purpose. Nonetheless, Ranade felt that the requests for more munsifs which he had received in several market towns justified a systematic extension of their work into commerce as well as agriculture. Ibid., 299. The government rejected this request as representing interference with the free flow of

trade where there was not clearly an urgent need. Bombay Government, Judicial Department Proceedings, 1893, pp. 234ff.

[26] DARA II, 84.

[27] Ranade's note on the report of the review commission, October 18, 1892, DARA II, 319. Ironically, Ranade was now in the position of protecting the conciliators from the addition of new powers which might hinder their work. The commission of 1892 recommended that their decisions be given legally enforceable status, but Ranade objected that this would deprive them of their informal, persuasive character and thus destroy the villagers' confidence in them. Their authority must rise organically from their position in the community; legitimacy could not be imposed from the outside. Ranade's advice was again heeded, and their status remained unchanged. Ibid., 320.

[28] M. G. Ranade, "Emancipation of Serfs in Russia," JPSS, V (October 1882); reprinted in EIE, p. 275.

[29] M. G. Ranade, "Prussian Land Legislation and the Bengal Tenancy Bill," JPSS, VI (October 1883); reprinted in EIE, pp. 283-284.

[30] M. G. Ranade, "The Law of Land Sale in British India," JPSS, III (October 1880); reprinted in EIE, pp. 314-315. The resulting dislocation was doubly galling because it stood side by side with tax concessions to English planters in Assam and the Nilgiri hills. M. G. Ranade, "A Protest and a Warning Against the New Departure in the Land Assessment Policy," JPSS, VI (April 1884), 54.

[31] M. G. Ranade, "The Agrarian Problem and Its Solution," JPSS, II (July 1879), 18.

[32] Ranade, "Prussian Land Legislation," EIE, pp. 308-309.

[33] Basic documents for the early history of the inam investigations are in "A Selection of Papers Explanatory of the Origin of the Inam Commission," Selections from the Records of the Bombay Government, New Series, No. 30 (Bombay, 1856).

[34] Robert Knight, editor of the Bombay Times, who defended many of Elphinstone's policies in the 1850's and 1860's. See his The Inam Commission Unmasked (London, 1859).

[35] Metcalf, Aftermath, p. 238.

[36] Keatinge, Rural Economy, p. 30.

[37] Ranade, "Famine Administration in the Bombay Presidency," 15-16.

[38] Karve, Maharashtra-Land, p. 81.

[39] Ranade, "Law of Land Sale," EIE, p. 316. For similar views circulating within the government, see Kumar, Western India, p. 213.

[40] Minute of August 2, 1883, DARA I, 398.

[41] See Metcalf, Aftermath, ch. v.

[42] Native Opinion, June 28, 1874, p. 408. And see V. N. Mandlik's defense of the gentry interest in ibid. throughout 1864-1866.

[43] W. Wedderburn, A Permanent Settlement for the Deccan (Bombay, 1880).

[44] See Ranade's analysis in "Mr. Wedderburn and His Critics," 20-21.

[45] Ibid., p. 21.

[46] Bipan Chandra, "Two Notes on the Agrarian Policy of Indian Nationalists, 1880-1905," IESHR (April-June 1964), pp. 143-174.

[47] Ranade, "Prussian Land Legislation," EIE, pp. 296-299.

[48] Ranade, "Agrarian Problem," 16.

[49] Ranade, "Law of Land Sale," EIE, p. 352.

[50] Kumar, Western India, p. 193.

[51] B. K. Ratcliffe, Sir William Wedderburn and the Indian Reform Movement (London, 1923), pp. 37-41; and Wedderburn, Permanent Settlement.

See also Kumar, Western India, ch. vii; and Ian J. Catanach, Rural Credit in Western India, 1875-1930 (Berkeley, 1970), pp. 28-31.

[52] M. G. Ranade, "Land Law Reform and Agricultural Banks," JPSS, IV (October 1881), 48, 50.

[53] Ranade, "Emancipation of Serfs," EIE, p. 275.

[54] For a fuller account of the banks and their fate, see Catanach, Rural Credit, passim.

[55] Ranade, "Prussian Land Legislation," EIE, p. 302.

[56] M. G Ranade, "Proposed Reforms in the Resettlement of Land Assessments," JPSS, VI (January 1884), 19-22; and Ranade, "A Protest," pp. 44-46.

[57] M. G. Ranade, "The Central Provinces Land Revenue and Tenancy Bills," JPSS, III (April 1881), 2.

[58] Quoted in M. G. Ranade, "Administrative Reforms in the Bombay Presidency," JPSS, IV (April 1882), 6n.

[59] Quoted approvingly, ibid., p. 19.

[60] S. Gopal, The Viceroyalty of Lord Ripon (London, 1953), p. 92.

[61] M. G. Ranade, "A Note on the Reorganization of District Administration," JPSS, VIII (January 1886), 4.

[62] Ibid., pp. 11-12.

[63] M. G. Ranade, "Local Government in England and India," JPSS, V (April 1883); reprinted in EIE, pp. 260-261.

[64] Ranade, "Administrative Reforms," p. 44.

[65] Ibid., p. 20.

[66] Ibid., p. 43.

[67] Ibid., p. 23.

[68] Ibid., p. 7.

[69] Ibid., pp. 49-50.

[70] M. G. Ranade, "The Agitation in Regard to the Native Magistrates Jurisdiction Bill," JPSS, V (April 1883), 30.

[71] Fergusson to Ripon, October 7, 1883, Ripon Papers I S 290/8.

[72] Poona Sarvajanik Sabha, "Dacoit Letters," April 25, 1879, JPSS, II (July 1879), 71.

[73] Bombay Government, Proceedings of the Council of the Governor of Bombay, 1885, meeting of July 22, XXIV, 10; Kumar, Western India, ch. iv.

[74] Bombay Government, Judicial Department Proceedings, 1885, No. 1212.

[75] Ranade, "Local Government," EIE, pp. 258-259; and "The Hereditary Officers Act Amendment Bill," JPSS, VIII (October 1885).

[76] Bombay Government, Proceedings of the Legislative Council, 1886, meeting of October 6, pp. 95ff.

[77] Ranade, "Hereditary Officers," p. 17.

[78] Ibid., p. 23.

[79] Bombay Government, Proceedings of the Council of the Governor of Bombay, 1885, meeting of July 22, XXIV, 10.

[80] M. G. Ranade, "The Native Civil Service Correspondence," JPSS, IV (January 1882), 25, 28-32.

[81] H. L. Singh, Problems and Policies of the British in India 1885-1898 (Bombay, 1963), p. 42.

[82] Government of India, Report of the Public Service Commission, 1887, IV: Bombay Presidency, 143.

Chapter 6

EDUCATION AND POLITICS IN POONA, 1880-1890

> We will not comply with the fashion of those who criticize the actions of Government, and in the very same breath . . . add a set of routine compliments to their motives. --Mahratta

The caution which Ranade evinced in pressing Indians' claims to a role in local administration and government were one expression of his concern with the prerequisites of responsible self-rule. In the midst of this campaign Ranade continued his efforts to develop English education in Poona. Liberal Englishmen and Indian university graduates were in substantial agreement that constitutional political action among Indians must rest on the cultural foundations which Western education provided. During Fergusson's administration in the early 1880's this commitment was further reinforced, for Fergusson gave public support to both public and private plans for educational development. Under this encouragement Ranade renewed his educational efforts after his return to Poona in early 1881. The pattern of his work gave further insights into his view of the cultural changes which were prerequisite to India's progress.

Education and Social Renewal

By 1881 Ranade was Poona's most influential educator. His efforts spanned from primary education of women and non-Brahmins to a plea before the Aitchison Commission for educating a privileged few Indians in England.[1] This latter was an extension of a campaign which he carried out through the Sarvajanik Sabha in 1882 to finance higher education in England for Indian students, on the pattern of Chinese and Japanese efforts of the time. The sabha asked for contributions from princes, landholders, and Bombay millionaires for the purpose of sending ten students annually to Europe or the United States for technical or industrial management training. Emphasizing the invigorating influence of the West, the sabha's letter stated: "A nation's destiny for good or evil hangs on its rising generation and when the best of them are trained and qualified by a rich experience of all that is noble and powerful in the civilized world, India under such leadership will certainly be rescued from its present helplessness, [and] a new life will beat in the old members of the social body."[2]

This was controversial rhetoric for a city still dominated by Brahmin traditionalists who saw the threat to their own position. Ranade faced steady criticism whenever his efforts broke new ground, and nowhere was this more true than in his establishment of Western-oriented primary and then secondary schools for Brahmin girls. He and his wife Ramabai founded a primary school for women in 1881, which at first only the wives and daughters of social reformers attended. Its regular teachers were women, but influential reformers sometimes gave talks to encourage young ladies to emerge from the seclusion of their homes. The school gained important support from Pandita Ramabai, the controversial champion of women's education from Bombay whom the Ranades had first worked with in Bombay in 1880. Although a Chitpavan Brahmin herself, she had provoked orthodox hostility by marrying outside her own caste and later making all-India lecture tours to encourage Western education.[3] In 1882 she and the Ranades together founded the Arya Mahila Samaj, a social service organization for women which was in effect an extension of the work of the Prarthana Samaj.[4] Pandita Ramabai was to prove a liability to the Brahmin reformers a decade later, when she openly converted to Christianity. But in the 1880's she was tolerated by the orthodox.

In September 1882 Ranade was given an opportunity simultaneously to publicize women's education and to defend the virtues of Hindu civilization when the Hunter Education Commission visited Poona. The commission had been constituted earlier that year by the government of India to examine the educational system and present a plan for revising its structure. It spent several days in Poona reviewing the schools and colleges there. Its chairman, W. W. Hunter, was one of the most popular British officials in Indian circles. At the opening meeting in Poona, Hunter pointedly reproved the educators of Poona for doing far less than was done elsewhere to promote women's education. Shortly thereafter Hunter visited the Arya Mahila Samaj, and Ranade took the opportunity to defend the city's record. A local newspaper paraphrased his reply to Hunter:

> There is no race in India which allowed such freedom to women, or which was more liberal in its treatment of women, of course within traditional Indian limits, than the Mahrattas. Their women went out freely, they had their own way, and they moved about in the public streets without restraint. . . . This state of things was not at all the result of English education. This liberty had been allowed from times long before the English went there. The advent of English rule only strengthened the motives which justified the further extension of this liberty.[5]

By interpreting the social history of Hinduism in this manner, Ranade strengthened his position as defender of Poona against outside criticism and at the same time used Hunter's reproof as a means of legitimizing his own frequently criticized work.[6]

Proceeding from there, Ranade and other social reformers founded the Huzur Paga School, a girls' high school, in July 1884. It was immediately attacked by the orthodox party in Poona, who saw it as a further threat to traditional Hindu values. As always in his educational ventures of this period, Ranade gained influential support from sympathetic Englishmen in Poona. William Wedderburn agreed to become chairman of the Huzur Paga School.[7] This led a few months later to the completion of the edifice of women's education, when Ranade and friends founded the Poona Female Training College. At each stage Ranade insisted that government had a positive supporting role to play in the modernization of education. The schools were to accept a maximum of government aid, since adequate financing was not otherwise available. Ranade's constant associate, V. A. Modak, had written his agreement to Ranade in February 1884, stating that boys' schools had been given government aid at first "in the different districts of the Presidency when education was in its infancy; and I do not see any reason why female education in its infancy, as it at present is, should not receive the same liberal and stimulating encouragement from the State. If the object of Public Instruction is the enlightenment of the people for the purposes of better Government, this object is very inadequately fulfilled by confining the educational efforts of Government mainly to the education of boys."[8]

But even this work for women's education was inadequate in the eyes of the more radical reformers of Bombay. In August 1883 an anonymous writer in Bombay chided the educated elite for taking no interest in the troubles of the masses. He praised the work of Ranade and Bhandarkar within its own sphere, but insisted that it was narrowly elitist in emphasis. "Could they do no more for the people than at present? Poor Gunnesh Joshi was just showing the way when his invaluable life ran short of a sudden. India wants more people's men."[9] This view from Ranade's friends in Bombay struck him at a sensitive point, for he was then in the midst of his campaign to ameliorate the condition of rural society.

In January 1884 he called a meeting of "influential Native gentlemen" to establish an organization for non-Brahmin education, the Deccan Association. Its purpose was to finance higher learning for a select number of Maratha and Kunbi students. Backed by Wedderburn, the association's managing committee included the leading members of the Sarvajanik Sabha and several prominent social reformers from Poona. In its first study of mofussil education the association reported that new government schools in towns and villages were as yet inoperative. It stated that "the Maratha and Kunbi population form the muscle and bone of native society," yet these castes were ninety-seven percent illiterate. "The chronic poverty, improvident habits, aversion to seek new occupations, and supine acquiescence in degradation are some of the inevitable consequences, and as these classes form the majority of the population, their helplessness cripples all national efforts at progress."[10]

The association's primary effort was to collect funds to provide several low caste students with college scholarships each year. Appealing as usual to the sardars and princes for money, the association declared paternalistically that "it is the peculiar duty of the educated and enlightened Maratha Sovereigns, . . . to extend their generous aid in helping this fallen class of their fellow countrymen."[11] Sayajirao Gaikwad, the young ruler of Baroda, who was a Maratha by caste, became the chief financial patron of the association, while Ranade presented the third largest contribution. By 1888 the Deccan Association was financing the high school education of forty-four Marathas and the college education of four others.[12] Stressing the work of the association as unifying the factions of Hindu society, Ranade asserted: "In the interest of the whole community, we refuse to be split up into bisectional jealousies. We shall work for all by the help of all classes."[13] His hope for the emergence of a mixed elite drawn from a variety of castes and classes was predicated on the unity of Hindu society.

The task of financing advanced training for the landholding castes of the Desh in the otherwise solidly Brahmin schools of Poona faced numerous political complications in the middle years of the decade, since fiscal conservatives in Dufferin's government were attacking the Hunter Commission's plea for an expansion of grants to education. The commission's recommendations were unfortunately timed, coming in the wake of rapid increases in imperial expenditures in the early 1880's, especially for railroads and military works. In February 1886 the government of India formed a "Committee appointed for the purpose of examining expenditure, whether imperial or provincial, with a view to finding out what economies are therein practicable."[14] The committee was first constituted with only official members, but Indian protests led to Sir Courtenay Ilbert's suggestion that one non-official Englishman and one Indian be appointed.[15] While Dadabhai Naoroji was initially considered for the Indian position, the choice finally fell on Ranade, partly because of Dadabhai's advancing age.[16]

Poona greeted the appointment enthusiastically, as a new honor to its leading citizen. After securing temporary leave from his work for the Relief Act, Ranade left for the committee's headquarters at Simla in March 1886. After intensive study of administrative documents unavailable to the general public, Ranade found himself in a minority on the committee, disputing its majority recommendation that the Bombay government should cut back expenditures on public works and education. His protest against reducing education grants was expressed publicly by the Sarvajanik Sabha in an evaluation of the committee's work, in which they suggested that the financial crisis was caused not by famine works but by rapidly rising military expenses for British imperial policy. Since these expenses were not open to question, the committee's work was misdirected. The article opined that if savings were to be made in education and public works the educational inspectors should be Indians, not Englishmen, and the Public Works Department should appoint many more Indians.[17] Fortunately for this point of view, the Bombay government successfully resisted the committee's recommendations, in effect producing a victory for Ranade's position.[18]

The experience gained through his appointment to the committee was matched for Ranade that spring with another honor. Fearing that the government might severely curtail its support of education, the alumni of Bombay University met on April 16, 1886, to found the Bombay Graduates Association. Its first act was to elect Ranade, its most illustrious representative, as president. In the Bombay pattern, it was modeled after an all-British association, the Bombay Education Society, which had long supported a variety of educational ventures.[19]

The first purpose of the new association was "to point out the openings, in Government service, to which graduates may reasonably lay claim,"[20] and to increase the influence of the graduates' views by organizing united action among them. The founders explained that "It is . . . during the last decade that people are beginning to realize the advantages of joining hands and gaining strength by combination."[21] Their first major resolution was a protest against the danger that the government might follow the Finance Commission's recommendation and close Deccan College for the sake of economy. Vowing that the liberalism of the government was best expressed in its support of higher education, the association stated that "any attempt either to reverse that policy or to prematurely limit its obligations will be calculated to create mistrust among the people."[22]

Education and the Cultural Renaissance

Until this point Ranade and the liberal reformers of his generation who provided him support had dominated the educational and political life of Poona. The precedents which they established for public life went virtually unchallenged, for there was yet no organized opposition to those with experience of European education. Yet through their work of political education and cultural revival the liberal reformers were laying the foundation for more radical movements which would ultimately challenge their political leadership. That the political polarization did not occur until after 1890 reflected the fact that Ranade and the liberals were the founders and elders of the literary revival, and that in literary matters all political factions shared similar goals.

Ranade's efforts to establish new schools in Poona borrowed heavily from Western organizational forms and frequently conveyed liberal social values. But his work just as often emphasized a commitment to the vernacular culture and its values. In this he followed the work of his older associates and their British mentors from as far back as 1850. Together they had encouraged Marathi translations of Western and Sanskrit books through the Marathi and Gujarati Book Committees of the Students' Literary and Scientific Society which were actively at work when Ranade arrived in Bombay. Lokahitawadi had helped found their parallels in Poona, while Krishna Shastri Chiplunkar, the finest Marathi stylist of his generation, wrote many of the Marathi translations of the 1850's and 1860's. He was well placed for this work because he presided over the Poona headquarters of the Dakshina Prize Committee, the government's main effort in the literary field. Chiplunkar and other members of Young Poona had agitated in the late 1840's for more productive use of the Dakshina Fund; in response, the government established the committee in 1851 for the purpose of publishing both Marathi translations and original Marathi writings.[23] The annual awards of the Dakshina Prize Committee constituted still further support for the close circle of journalists, writers, educators, and social reformers whom Ranade joined in the 1860's. From 1866 onward Chiplunkar was editor of the committee's monthly journal, the Shālāpatrak, or Marathi School Paper, which published prizewinning Marathi writings and literary correspondence.

Ranade was associated with this work during his year as Marathi Vernacular Translator for the government, when he was responsible for recommending Marathi works worthy of government-subsidized publication. In conjunction with this work he joined forces with those who had opposed the elimination of Marathi and Gujerati from the compulsory university syllabus in 1864, and proclaimed in 1867 that although modern Marathi writing had little substance as yet, "the present . . . is full of promise, and there is every likelihood that before long the Marathi language will be in a position to take the first rank among the cultivated languages of Modern India."[24] Aside from this, however, he was not directly involved in the literary revival until the middle 1870's, when he was working closely with Chiplunkar and Lokahitawadi. When he and Lokahitawadi were together in 1878 they jointly initiated a new translation society, the Marāṭhī Granthottejaka Maṇḍalī (Society for Promoting Marathi Books). As their announcement expressed it in the January newspapers, they hoped to solicit one thousand subscribers whose contributions would finance publication of Marathi writings on a wide spectrum of subjects.[25] The subsequently appointed managing committee included Chiplunkar and others. They succeeded in attracting over five hundred subscribers, and their work continued for some five years before money and enthusiasm lagged.[26]

Although no one could foresee it at the time, the complementary effort of the same men was to bear greater long-range fruits. That May in Poona, Ranade and Lokahitawadi organized the first gathering of the Mahāraṣṭra Sahitya Pariṣad (Literary Society of Maharashtra), which in later years became a great annual conference.[27] Ranade was proclaimed its first president, and although few details of the first meeting have survived, he has ever since been remembered as the founder of Maharashtra's modern literary renaissance.

As organizers Ranade and the liberals played a seminal role in the growth of modern Marathi literature. But as writers and critics themselves, aside from Krishna Shastri Chiplunkar, they more often served as targets for younger men of greater literary talent and more radical nationalist views. The standard-bearer of the younger generation, lionized throughout the late 1870's, was Chiplunkar's son, Vishnu Shastri, who proclaimed in 1874 that pride in Hindu civilization must be not a side effect but the essence of India's resurgence. Born in Poona in 1850, Vishnu Shastri knew as a boy all of his father's notable associates.[28] He entered the government high school there in 1861 and advanced five years later to Deccan College, where he studied under Professor William Wordsworth, the most influential English educator in Maharashtra after Alexander Grant. After finishing his B.A. there he became a teacher in the Poona High School in 1873, under the irascible pro-British headmaster, M. M. Kunte.

It was here that the young Chiplunkar's opposition to the Westernized reformers quickly crystallized in the form of almost vitriolic critical essays. Kunte had recently published his own Marathi poems, written in the idiom of daily speech rather than in highly Sanskritized style. In unison with older shastris and others who disapproved of Kunte's esthetic tastes, Vishnu Shastri risked charges of insubordination by publishing critiques of Kunte's poetry and that of other liberal reformers. These essays were incorporated in his new Marathi periodical, Nibandhamālā (The Garland of Essays), which immediately became the classic document of modern Marathi prose, and were largely responsible for his transfer from Poona to Ratnagiri on the coast in 1875. In these essays, Vishnu Shastri elaborated a view of both Western and Marathi literature which reiterated the primacy of indigenous standards. One of the most famous essays in Nibandhamālā was an article of 1878 denouncing his father's and Ranade's disparagement of the poet Moropant. Ranade had judged that Moropant's poems lacked a sense of awe and humility before God. Vishnu Shastri insisted that Ranade was incapable of comprehending the devotional fervor which was Moropant's great strength.[29]

Nor were his writings all; with Ranade's efforts as a model, Vishnu Shastri founded in January 1880 the Kāvyetihāsa-sangraha, a periodical designed to rediscover and publish the classics of Sanskrit and Marathi poetry. Though short-lived, it became a model for later revivals of Marathi culture. Later in the same year he founded the Chitrashala Press to publish nationalist works; the building where the press was housed soon became an important meeting place for Poona's young militants.[30]

When his father and his only son both died in 1878, Vishnu Shastri had been left with weakened family ties; he was then free to pursue his more independent career. He was disillusioned with the government schools; as early as 1872 he had written that government education made both students and teachers unpatriotic and destroyed their moral fiber.[31] In 1879 he resigned from government service, pleading "supreme disgust of the drudgery of a Government school life" as the final cause of the break.[32] Shortly thereafter he established a new high school, in the wake of a government resolution giving grants-in-aid to all indigenous schools offering any secular education. The British hoped this would stimulate private efforts to supplement the overextended government schools.[33] Government money available in 1880 to private schools, however, was miniscule; it was far overshadowed by its contributions to mission schools, which were viewed with suspicion by Chiplunkar and his friends.[34] Vishnu Shastri resolved to open a new school entirely independent of the government. Calling for teachers with patriotic fervor willing to work for minimal pay, Chiplunkar attracted young graduates, including Bal Gangadhar Tilak, Mahadev Ballal Namjoshi and Vaman Shivram Apte, to join him.[35] Together they opened the New English School in January 1880, with the explicit intention of competing with government high schools. Apte, who became headmaster of the school, outspokenly attacked the mission schools for their Christian teachings and the government schools for their emphasis on English language and culture.[36] Chiplunkar condemned the lack of moral training in government schools and the poor moral example set by teachers. Both expressed a Hindu view of education which considered that a student must not only learn ideas and facts but also absorb a quality of life through intimate association with his guru.

The quality of indigenous high schools in Maharashtra at the time was so poor that an independent school whose teachers were among the finest graduates of Deccan College immediately established its reputation. Despite its lack of sanctioned credentials and its few small rooms in a borrowed home, the school attracted many students from the government high school, antagonizing Principal Kunte.[37] Other older reformers too were alarmed at the belligerent, anti-government stance of Chiplunkar and his associates. They appealed to Ranade to use his influence to dampen their spirits. Ranade, however, respected the young teachers' patriotism and financial sacrifice. He praised their efforts, saying, "Public work has, so far, been mostly carried on by government servants, who have naturally treated it as their sparetime work. This young group means to make it the mission of its life. That is a further step for the advance of our public life. We must encourage it, not be sceptic about it."[38] They were, after all, pursuing a variant of his own ideals.

Ranade was one of the principal financial contributors to the school in its early years. Chiplunkar, in turn, consciously followed an ideal of public service established by Ranade a decade earlier. Vishnu Shastri had been in Poona in 1870; he knew the difference that Ranade's presence had meant. He criticized Ranade respectfully, out of a sense of common Brahmin culture, in contrast to his contempt for the radical social criticisms and literary crudity of Jotiba Phule, Poona's leading low caste reformer. In a letter to a friend, Vishnu Shastri asserted, "In my estimation a Rao-Bahadur knocked down successfully is an infinitely more creditable game than all Dayanandas and Jotibas put together. If my tone is more respectful towards the Rao-Bahadur [Ranade] than towards the great author of Gulāmagirī [Phule] that is due to the unspeakable difference between the first man of the age and the sorriest scribbler with just the clothing of humanity on him."[39] The new educational radicals made the political implications of their experiment clear to their students. Chiplunkar and Gopal Ganesh Agarkar, who joined the school a year after its inception, frequently exhorted their classes to use their education for patriotic public service.[40] Poona, the historic home of the Peshwas, provided an appropriate atmosphere, for the school derived a sense of destiny from its surroundings. G. S. Sardesai, who later became one of the most respected historians of Maharashtra, entered the school in 1885. He later reminisced, "The first sight of the hallowed capital of the Peshwas, of which I had read and heard so much, filled me with peculiar awe and reverence, giving rise to a sense of homage and tremor directed towards many an illustrious name, not only of the glorious Maratha rulers of the past, but of more recent and renowned figures like the two Chiplunkars . . . Ranade, Kunte, and more particularly Tilak and Agarkar."[41] This brand of patriotism was calculated to embarrass the older leaders of the city, for Chiplunkar openly criticized those who served the alien government while sounding like patriots. V. K. Rajwade, another historian of Maratha times whose later writings were deeply influenced by Ranade's historical studies, wrote, "Mr. Ranade whose name has been beyond doubt the name of a saint to me was then no hero of mine. Along with others, I, too, enjoyed the ridicule poured on him by our teacher [Chiplunkar]."[42]

The New English School was the first successful high school whose leaders were unincumbered by connections with the government. It was the institutional foundation of the long effort to displace the alien government entirely, not simply to cooperate with it as Ranade and his generation did. The effects of this autonomy were soon clear, for out of the New English School came the first demand in Maharashtra for svarājya, or self-rule, for India. The school suffered a blow when Chiplunkar died on March 17, 1882, at the early age of thirty-one. Leadership passed to Tilak and Agarkar, still in their middle twenties, who shared Chiplunkar's militance. As Tilak wrote in his obituary of Chiplunkar:

> Nothing preyed upon the heart of Vishnushastri so much as our country's political bondage and poverty. The degradation of our countrymen agonized his heart. . . . He was full of pride for the Hindus, for their religion and their institutions, for everything, in short, that could claim to be "Hindu.". . . He was not the man to hesitate to use any means calculated to destroy the country's political dependence, and lead her into the haven of happiness under political Swarajya.[43]

This statement taken alone was a misleading indication of the relations between Tilak's associates and the older generation led by Ranade, on whom they continued to rely for support in their educational ventures. Chiplunkar had been guarded in his acceptance of Western education, but the younger men who assumed leadership after his death were more fully Westernized in their own thought. V. S. Apte defined the group's commitment to Western education as the basis for renewing Indian society, in terms which echoed Ranade's beliefs. "We have undertaken this work . . . with the firmest conviction and belief that of all agents of human civilization, education is the only one that brings about the material, moral and religious regeneration of fallen countries and raises them up to the level of the most advanced nations by slow and peaceful revolutions. And again, in order that education may produce the highest beneficial results which all writers of whatever country or belief agree in ascribing to it, it is absolutely necessary that it should be in the hands of the people themselves."[44]

There was general praise for the New English School for its low cost and its high standard of education. From the first its students won competitive prizes against the best students in Bombay. A boldly successful experiment in self-help, this was the most important of the institutions parallel to but independent of government which Ranade encouraged. But the school continued to need a firmer financial basis and a supporting organization. This was remedied in 1884 with the help of the influential liberals in Poona, both Indian and English. On October 24, 1884, Ranade presided over a meeting called for the purpose of "promoting education by means of private independent institutions," which founded the Deccan Education Society.[45] William Wedderburn was made chairman of the Managing Council; Ranade, Bhandarkar, and K. T. Telang joined Principal Apte, Tilak, Agarkar, and M. B. Namjoshi on the council, uniting the two most powerful factions in Poona behind the New English School.[46] The younger men, who dominated the committee of life members, retained power over the administration of the school, however. They controlled tuition rates and government grants and made most policy decisions.

The Deccan Education Society took its first major step on January 2, 1885, when it founded Fergusson College, Poona's first alternative to the government-run Deccan College. The new college was named for the governor of Bombay, who gave the inaugural address. Fergusson emphasized the need for privately sponsored education and praised the record of the New English School. He went further to suggest that "There is no social fact without its political side: and the opening of such a college as this under the present circumstances and prospects of India is unquestionably of great political importance."[47] William Wordsworth, who had been principal of Deccan College from 1862 to 1874 and principal of Elphinstone College since then, added his view of the political implications of the new college. He stated that it could exploit Ripon's willingness to open more positions in government to qualified Indians and that ultimately such colleges paved the way to self-rule.

In 1887 the Bombay government proposed that Fergusson College assume the responsibility for running Deccan College. Government influence over the colleges would be restricted to inspection of their educational standards. The Deccan Education Society recognized the opportunity, but they were reluctant to accept any government surveillance. They appealed to Ranade, who advised that they should accept the offer only if it were accompanied by an outright grant of Rs. 25,000 and included no commitment to hire European professors. Ranade's suspicions of official intentions were proved correct when the Bombay authorities then asked that the society hire two European professors and add three officially nominated members to its managing board. With Ranade on their side, the society demurred and the negotiations broke down.[48] Lord Reay, Fergusson's successor, desired to dissociate government further from direct responsibility for education and withdrew its annual grant of Rs. 3,000 to the society; it was restored six years later.[49] Through events such as these the young educators were confirmed in their distrust of cooperation with the government.

The Two Factions in Journalism and Politics

Relations between the older and younger men were by turns harmonious or strained as their educational purposes converged or differed. A similar pattern was evident throughout the 1880's in the field of journalism, in which again Ranade's generation had established the powerful precedent of the Journal of the Sarvajanik Sabha; but the younger men were intent on launching their own organs, more militantly nationalist in tone. Concurrent with the founding of the New English School, Chiplunkar and his co-workers established two new weekly newspapers, Kesari and Mahratta, in January 1881. It was a time of rapid expansion in the number and circulation of vernacular newspapers,[50] and the Marathi-language Kesari (The Lion) rapidly became the foremost newspaper in Maharashtra. It was addressed to the large Marathi-reading population which hitherto had been largely excluded from political debates. Chiplunkar was a regular contributor in the year before his death, and Agarkar served as editor for its first six years.[51] Mahratta in turn was pointed toward the English-reading public and the government; under Tilak's editorship until 1891, it presented a similar political stance. It was intended to carry the political criticisms in the Sarvajanik Sabha's Journal one step further, to an uncompromising defense of Indian interests against the British. It repeated many of the older journal's views, but its tone was decidedly more aggressive. Mahratta contended in its introductory editorial that foreign rulers never understood the subject people and hence could not be the best rulers, however benign their intentions. In an indirect thrust at Ranade and his friends, the editorial concluded: "We will not comply with the fashion of those critics who criticize the actions of Government, and in the very same breath with which they point abuses, they add a set of routine compliments to their motives."[52]

Direct criticisms of the sabha appeared in the first year of publication. On the basis of powerful journalism which voiced another common set of public views, the young editors demanded some influence over the sabha's work. Tilak wrote that hitherto a few enlightened men's opinions had been the basis of the sabha's actions, but now the oligarchy must broaden its base and admit new voices into its circles. "Now that the commons, whose interests the Sabha tries to watch have begun to feel, to watch and to move, it is but necessary that the Sabha should mould its procedure accordingly."[53] Mahratta questioned why the sabha had not acted on certain questions of urgent public concern, leading from this to direct prodding of the sabha's leading figures. When a correspondent suggested that one secretary of the sabha handled only correspondence and the other signed papers but did no work, Mahratta published the accusation. It stated that the assertion might not be true, but concluded that the sabha certainly had not been working hard of late.[54] But significantly, it carefully avoided such censure of Ranade. The extent of its criticism was illustrated when it mocked a speech of Ranade's for his "much might be said on both sides" approach.[55] Impatient with his equivocation, the editors nevertheless respected his preeminent position. Agarkar had gone so far as to talk at length with Ranade before beginning to publish Kesari; he began the venture after gaining Ranade's complete support.[56]

The area of policy in which the sharpest early conflicts arose was the affairs of the princely states. The Sarvajanik Sabha had consistently defended the autonomy of the states, in return for the financial and moral support of the princes. Its support of Baroda in the crisis of 1875 had been unequivocal, and in 1877 it petitioned the imperial darbar to form an Indian parliament with the princes as the upper chamber. On the other hand, Ranade and the sabha understood that the qualification of the states for serving as an Indian House of Lords would depend on their ability first to rule their own houses. This would call for radical reforms in many states which were notoriously corrupt and mismanaged, as the Baroda affair had shown.

In a series of articles on the princely states around 1880, Ranade revealed a major dimension of his vision of modernization, both political and social. Expanding on his plans for British India, he made it abundantly clear that the touchstone of his policy was the standards of public life in the contemporary Western world, not the glories of traditional India. When he was busy defending Baroda against the danger of annexation by the British, Ranade had little time to criticize their internal administration. But by 1880 he felt free to state his view of the princes publicly. He now described them as "at present in too many cases, being the source of annoyance and trouble to their own people and to the Paramount Power, and the laughing stock of the world for utter helplessness and the most depraved voluptuousness."[57] Ranade found the cause of their condition not only in the character of the rulers but also in the system by which they ruled. Especially in these years, when several of the princes were boys controlled by regents, Ranade felt that the basic trouble lay in "the system of absolute rule which prevails everywhere, . . . the temptations of which prove in too many cases so overpowering as to wash off the varnish of [the princes'] education in a few years, and leave the state none the better, often much the worse, for the care taken of the Chief during the minority."[58]

With this in mind Ranade defined the reforms which he believed could revive the administration of the states, taking as his model the principles of British constitutionalism. Here again, as in his other writings of these years, he took the opportunity to enumerate the social classes which could supply India's future leadership. The first step in the development of constitutional rule should be the promulgation of a Council of State, which would limit the despotic power of the prince and serve as a training ground for administrative personnel.[59] Pursuing his long-standing effort to adjust viable Indian traditions to the new era, Ranade hoped that the council could serve this function. He proposed that all laws and taxes should be passed by a council of the important sardars, merchants, priests and others, who were "the natural leaders," and not the "panderers and pimps and jesters and bad women" who now thronged the courts. The old Hindu texts on politics and the course of Maratha history he cited as demonstrating the importance of the councils, which "keep up uniformity, they conserve past traditions, and act as buffers against the evil effects of personal changes."[60] Ranade was less precise about which political traditions were worth preserving than about which classes should preserve them. The native governments should foster local self-government, as the British Raj had begun to do. This would provide positions of responsible power for the local patils, the district authorities, and the great sardars, who were the repository of ancient India's strength and traditions.[61]

Ranade saw that not all of the changes to a modern policy could be tailored to existing political traditions.[62] The idea of popular control over the government, he alleged, had been present in India's distant past but long since forgotten. Under present circumstances no prince ever voluntarily divested himself of power, so the British Raj would have to step in and enforce constitutions on behalf of the people. Only when public opinion had been educated to oversee its rulers could the Raj withdraw its supervisory function. In the meantime Ranade firmly believed that a benevolent paternalism was the only appropriate policy for the British to follow in their relations with the states. In order to curtail the duration of this era the Sarvajanik Sabha pressed its policies on a few states it hoped would become models for others to follow. It urged Sayajirao Gaikwad, at the time of his investiture as ruler of Baroda in 1881, to foster the political education of his people, adding that true constitutionalism could come only gradually, as the people became more advanced in the arts of modern civilization.[63]

This philosophy was sharply challenged by Mahratta, which declared in its first issue that it would be loyal under all circumstances to the states against encroachments by political officers of the Raj.

> With reference to Native States our policy will always be for the uninterfered continuance of such States. History will bear us out when we say that the decline of a Native State commences from the moment the English come in close contact with it; for it has been observed that the decline arises chiefly from the inordinate influence the Politicals are allowed to exercise. Our attempts, therefore, will always be directed at shielding the Native Princes from the uncalled-for interference on the part of the Politicals and exposing the latter to the public gaze.[64]

The bold patriotism of this position was an extension of the previous defense of Malharrao Gaikwad by the Sarvajanik Sabha. The difference from the policy of the Sarvajanik Sabha was that Mahratta made little note of the states' need to modernize their administrations.

Within a year the young editors found a cause to defend when a dispute arose in Kolhapur. Kolhapur, as the seat of Shivaji's descendants, was a state whose ruler commanded a patriotic following throughout Maharashtra. The present ruler was weak and indecisive, allowing a corrupt court to flourish. Charges were circulating in Bombay that the raja was losing his sanity. Kesari and Mahratta came into possession of several letters purportedly written by the dewan, M. V. Barve, implicating him in plans to remove the raja from his throne. The letters were reprinted in Mahratta in January 1882, together with a denunciation of Barve's treachery. When Barve learned of the publication, he denied the authenticity of the latters and instituted a defamation suit against the editors, Tilak and Agarkar. On January 27 a meeting was held to raise money for the Native Press Defence Fund, with some five thousand people present. One speaker accused Barve of attacking the freedom of the whole native press in the dangerous time when the Vernacular Press Act was still operative; many people rallied to the defense of what they considered the righteous crusade of Tilak and Agarkar.[65] Nonetheless, the two were convicted, on the grounds that the letters were forged and that Tilak had not taken sufficient precautions to verify their authenticity.[66] The two men were given four-month jail sentences. At the end of that time they were hailed as martyrs. A great crowd met them at Poona railway station and cheered their return. They were now becoming the spokesmen of popular opinion against all officialdom, whether English or Indian.[67]

The Barve case illustrated the close link in the minds of the editors between the issue of the Native States and that of a free press. Journalistic freedom was essential to their campaign against official oppression. The question was especially vital at the time the new newspapers were founded, for Kesari fell under the regulations of the Vernacular Press Act. Opposition to the act in Poona had been led by the Sarvajanik Sabha, which raised the question afresh upon Ripon's arrival in India. In a memorial to the government of India in February 1881, the sabha asserted that the act "cast an undeserved suspicion upon the loyalty of the

Vernacular news-papers, that it prevented the free discussion of official measures which, under the circumstances of an alien rule like that which obtains in British India, is so necessary in the interests of both the governed and the governing classes, that it checked from the sense of ignoble fear the growth of a healthy public opinion, and that it invested petty local authorities with a power of vexatious interference which cannot fail to demoralize them."[68]

In itself this statement closely represented the views of Kesari and Mahratta, but the younger men were not satisfied. The Journal of the Sarvajanik Sabha, a decorous quarterly, held immunity from the act which Kesari, a weekly newspaper dedicated to political agitation, could not claim. The Kesari group suspected that the sabha was not fully committed to the principle of a completely free press. Their feelings were set forth in opposition to a memorial which the sabha issued praising the new administration of Baroda, especially the dewan, Ranade's associate Sir T. Madhavrao. A Mahratta editorial criticized him as autocratic and notoriously distrustful of a free press. It taunted the sabha's memorial, saying that "no mention is made of the introduction of a free press into the estates of the kingdom."[69] In its eyes Madhavrao resembled Barve of Kolhapur in his efforts to stifle free criticism. The sabha by its silence tacitly approved the attitude of these regimes. The issue lost its cutting edge only after the repeal of the Vernacular Press Act, which coincided with the Barve crisis.[70]

The following year brought a temporary end to the conflict between the Kesari group and the sabha. At that time the first of a series of political issues arose in which their interests were identical. The major controversy of Ripon's viceroyalty began in February 1883, with the presentation of the Ilbert Bill before the Viceroy's Council.[71] The bill was designed to remove the disqualification of Indian judges in the mofussil from trying Europeans. Until this time, Englishmen had been allowed to transfer cases from the mofussil to Presidency courts under English judges. The practical import of the bill would be to give Indian mofussil judges jurisdiction over only a small number of such cases, which would involve only a few senior Indian judges in the near future. Hence the substance of the bill was far less important than the principle it embodied, which Sir Henry Maine had articulated three years earlier. "Men are nothing so like one another as in their appreciation of what is justice. I trust that no English statesman will ever convince himself that there can be two ideals of justice for India, but, if he does, he must persuade the English Parliament to agree with him."[72]

Ripon's council firmly supported the bill, failing to anticipate the storm of opposition which immediately broke in the non-official British community. The bill came in the heyday of racial antagonism between British and Indians; and it embodied a principle of equality which non-officials strictly rejected. Demonstrations, speeches, petitions, and editorials ensued in cities throughout India, galvanizing Indian politicians into counteraction.

Three years before, when Ranade had sentenced the Englishman Murray to eight months imprisonment for stealing Rs. 40 of clothes from his Indian servant,[73] the Bombay Anglo-Indian press denounced him for his harshness and injustice. Mahratta had sprung to Ranade's defense. Reminding its readers that "it has been the fashion of Anglo-Indian Journalists to throw unmerited aspersions on native officials and thus prejudice the minds of the higher authorities," it praised Ranade for his courageous and evenhanded justice in the face of such opposition.[74] When the Ilbert Bill appeared, the Times of India strongly opposed it, publishing a series of articles castigating native judges, including Ranade, and native journalists like Agarkar. Again Mahratta defended Ranade as an eminent Indian judge who sedulously upheld the laws of the empire.[75] Thus united against a common opponent, the Indian community of Bombay and Poona organized mass meetings in support of the bill. The Bombay branch of the East India Association sponsored a meeting on April 28 defending the Indian judges. It adopted a memorial stating, "It is impossible to suppose that any one of these Magistrates--most of whom must necessarily have been educated in England and have thus come into social contact with Europeans--could entertain any hostile prejudices against the English people."[76] On May 19 the Sarvajanik Sabha followed suit in a crowded meeting in Poona which denounced all racial distinctions in the Civil Service.[77]

Ranade was not present at the Poona meeting, for his professional position was too directly involved to permit him to organize public demonstrations. He was busy behind the scenes in maintaining communications between the British and Indian communities, since feeling on both sides was running high, and by May it was clear that the government was being forced to compromise. Bombay took the lead in establishing a conciliatory position as regards the bill. The personal friendships built up over the years at Deccan College and Elphinstone College provided the basis of this work. Principal Wordsworth of Elphinstone College held the trust of the educated Indians; he had defended them in the Bombay Gazette when the bill was introduced. He made his position clear by writing, "The Native Civil Service cannot permanently be retained on a footing which imposes on its members a galling consciousness of inferiority to their colleagues of European birth."[78] His home became the center for meetings which produced a moderate and coordinated policy among both English and Indian leaders in Bombay. During the height of the crisis he held a dinner party to which he invited members of the government and English barristers, as well as leading Parsis, Muslims, and one Hindu, Ranade.[79] As he later wrote to Ripon:

We have a formal discussion after dinner, and no single individual of any nationality objected to the principle of the Bill, though some objections were urged against some of its details. But we were all much impressed with the singular ability and moderation with which the Native gentlemen stated their views. For myself I could not help contrasting the fatuity of a policy which would alienate or humiliate men of this stamp, so anxious to stand well with us and to tread in our steps, with one which endeavors, in a spirit of magnanimous confidence, to associate them more closely with ourselves, and strengthens at the same time their self-respect and their respect for us.[80]

Ranade prided himself, as did his associates, on the superior quality of their conduct as contrasted with the hysteria of the Anglo-Indians. Seeing the conflict as essentially a moral struggle, he wrote that the non-officials had now shown their true character by defending European racial superiority and rule by force. In contrast, "The outraged nation magnanimously resolved not to follow the dastardly example set to them, and strong in the justice of their cause, their leaders have, in constitutional gatherings held in all our great towns, raised the voice of calm and determined protest."[81]

Throughout 1883 conflict within the government and the English community developed, and Ripon's position was steadily eroded. On January 25, 1884, a compromise bill was enacted. Europeans in the mofussil were still required to submit to the authority of district judges, whether English or Indian, in criminal cases involving penalties of three to twelve months' sentences. For these cases, however, the defendant could demand a trial by a jury the majority of whose members could be Europeans. In all more serious cases jurisdiction lay directly with the Presidency High Court. Hence the principle of racial equality, though not denied, was eviscerated. The Indian community was dismayed by the result; as one report stated, "There was but one feeling in regard to the ultimate compromise--intense dissatisfaction."[82] But Indian leaders were already committed to accept the law out of admiration for Ripon's heroic fight.

One lesson which the affair impressed upon Ranade was the importance of sympathetic opinion within the British government as a bulwark against the unbending Anglo-Indian community and its bureaucratic sympathizers. Ranade saw the situation as corroborating his basic view of conditions in India. "The educated minority of the native population with their free press, and their associations unconsciously sympathized with by the mass of their countrymen, represent the soul of Indian Liberalism, and their strength lies in the justice of their claim. Arrayed against them are the mighty forces of the official hierarchy, supported by the non-official phalanx of their countrymen here and the great reserve of power and prejudice stored in the large vested interest of their mother country."[83] More clearly than ever his defense against the threat of hostile British elements was taking on an elitist tone. The educated classes of India had demonstrated their responsibility and effectiveness in public life; they had thus earned the right to speak for the true interests of the populace. By implication, this might be so even under the unforeseen circumstances when the populace resisted the adoption of its own true good.

The Last Round of Unity

Ranade's view that indirect representation of India's interests was appropriate under foreseeable circumstances lacked the ring of militant nationalism which Tilak and his associates demanded. Ranade was known for his wariness of direct elections expressed at the time of Ripon's Local Self-Government Bill. This was only an application at the local level of the belief in indirect representation which the Sarvajanik Sabha put forth during the English election campaign of 1880. The sabha feared that a Tory victory would perpetuate Lytton's policies in India and perhaps even bring back Sir Richard Temple as viceroy. Under the circumstances it had seemed urgent to appeal to the basic generosity of the British electorate to elect the Liberal party. As the Journal expressed it, "On no previous occasion was the welfare and progress of India so dependent upon the choice of the electors of Great Britain and Ireland. The policy of domination and mastery which has been in the ascendant for the past four or five years has inflicted upon India such repressive and retrograde measures as the Vernacular Press Act and the Arms Act."[84]

To Ranade and his associates it was evident that the political system which influenced their lives stretched directly from their municipal council in Poona to the imperial government in London and the Parliament of the British people themselves. The political philosophy which they followed was attuned to correspondingly broad horizons. A year later, Ranade elaborated his defense of this work in the summary lecture of the Poona Elocution Gathering, entitled "Are We Represented in the British Parliament?" There was a juridical quality in his argument, as Mahratta paraphrased the speech.

> What is the end of all representation? That subjects should be enabled to state their grievances through their delegates before their Sovereign or Sovereign Body. If, then, owing to the peculiar constitution of Great Britain, Indian questions are enthusiastically taken up and discussed in the British Parliament, why shall we not say, that although we do not ourselves elect and send our delegates, we are in a kind of round-about way represented?[85]

An accompanying editorial in Mahratta implied that Ranade's outlook was both tortuous and disingenuous; it stated that Indian questions would be treated very differently in Parliament if Indian representatives were present. The writer, presumably Tilak, maintained that India was not even indirectly represented in Parliament.[86]

Ranade's optimistic tone reflected his satisfaction with the Liberal victory in England. Acceptance of indirect representation was also for him a realistic approach to the political patterns of his time. In his early years Indians had been given almost no direct role in official policy formation. The first Indian appointments to the viceroy's Legislative Council were made in 1862; the Bombay Council had no Indian members for years longer. The most that Indian politicians could hope for was a sympathetic understanding of their views by English members of the government such as Bartle Frere. Concurrently, in the non-official life of Bombay Presidency, the first clearly representative mechanism appeared with the membership regulations of the Sarvajanik Sabha. Even this, however, was not considered as important a claim to representative status as was the articulation of popular needs. The sabha's members specifically represented only the citizens of Poona, whereas they claimed from the first to represent the needs of the people of all Maharashtra to the government. The work of their first decade centered about the defense of the interests of all classes in the Desh, especially the ryots, who had no experience in the ways of modern politics. In the mofussil, where tradition still counted heavily, Ranade by 1880 supported the landowning class on district councils as the appropriate representative of the ryots' interests.

In the cities, where political trends were developing more rapidly, Ranade emphasized the right of the university-educated class to political leadership. This too was a moral claim, based on their putative ability to represent popular needs most effectively. In contrast to the sycophantic aristocrats who were frequently appointed to imperial councils, the leaders of the educated class articulated India's genuine interest. Since they had no ascriptive right of leadership, they at least could claim the requisite training and experience in modern politics.

As long as the Western-educated class presented a united front to the government, Ranade's leading position was unimpaired. But this unity was gradually eroding during the 1880's. The <u>Kesari</u> group was assuming a more militantly nationalistic stance, extending less equivocally the anti-British criticisms which Ranade had first uttered in the previous decade. The younger men expressed the immediate demands of local groups, rather than interpreting the long-range self-interest of India in imperial affairs, as Ranade was attempting. The young educators and editors were gaining a clearer sense of the political potential of discontented groups in Poona and the surrounding districts. They had little patience with English party politics, and even less confidence in the political generosity of the Liberal party. It was clear even from the Local Self-Government debate that the English people, and even the viceroy Ripon, could not overcome Fergusson's reluctance to grant real power to Indians. Fergusson's warning to Wilfred Scawen Blunt one evening in Bombay that "the Government of India was a despotism of a paternal and beneficent character, which was day and night working for the people's good and any agitation would only impede its efforts,"[87] would not have startled Tilak.

Tilak expressed his view of Ripon's scheme in an article of May 11, 1882, in <u>Mahratta</u>. He pleaded with the Sarvajanik Sabha to demand a larger number of non-official representatives on local councils. But at this juncture his specific proposals followed Ranade's at most other points. He hoped to construct a broader base of support by giving local representation to the trading classes, as well as the educated class.[88] He further advanced the proposal that elections should be based on town franchise, not town and rural votes. He demonstrated his growing interest in developing an electoral power base by requesting immediate urban franchise to be followed by rural franchise only as education spread. By implication this would allow time for the growth of educated leaders with an outlook similar to his.[89] Agreeing with the Sarvajanik Sabha that "the great object of the introduction of the principle of Local Self-Government is the political education of the people," he nonetheless wished to pursue self-government more militantly. He criticized the sabha for making only mild demands on a government entirely unwilling to relinquish any of its power.[90] As the Ilbert Bill controversy grew more bitter, Tilak attacked "the central sun" of the Sarvajanik Sabha, Ranade, for supporting the Bombay self-government bill and taking a conciliatory stand on the Ilbert Bill, against the virtually unanimous views of the native press.[91]

Tilak was already exploring the possibilities of electoral politics as a means of broadening popular political action, whereas Ranade remained congenitally uneasy with this democratizing trend. This was a fundamental difference in their approaches to the question of mass nationalism; in the 1890's it would become the touchstone of a complex power struggle between Moderates and Militants. But throughout the 1880's factional lines in Poona were still unclear; during this decade there were not two but three factional tendencies active in the city. The oldest was led by aging government servants like M. M. Kunte, principal of Poona High School, and K. L. Nulkar, chairman of the Sarvajanik Sabha, who almost invariably gave decorous support to government policies. Ranade's generation, also mostly lawyers and government servants, had led the campaign of criticism against the government in the 1870's, sometimes to the alarm of the older men. Even in the 1870's there seems to have been subtle competition for leadership in the Sarvajanik Sabha between its rising star, Ranade, and its official head, Nulkar, who disliked Ranade's outspoken criticisms of government. It was rumored that Nulkar was used by official interests as a counterpoise to Ranade in the political circles of Poona.[92] The Tilak-Agarkar group, younger and more militant still, had little formal contact with the government, preferring the independence of teaching and journalism as a base for unrestricted opposition to government actions.

The first test of the three generations' loyalties appeared in the Poona Municipal Corporation. Before 1885 the corporation had been dominated by official appointees, who worked alongside a minority of appointed non-officials, some of whom were Indians. The municipality's work was not politically sensitive, as it was responsible only for local administration, such as sanitation, epidemic regulations, and water supply. Nevertheless, great interest was generated when the first fruits of

Ripon's self-government scheme, elections to the local council, were held on December 1, 1885.[93] The younger men, or "popular party," saw an opportunity to challenge the influence of the older men, who supported the official interest. Eager to gain a voice in local government, they supported a slate of non-official candidates. Ranade actively worked for the "popular party" and its candidates, against the opposition of his old friend, M. M. Kunte. As the campaign developed, feelings on both sides ran high, and Kunte organized ward meetings at which he made sharp personal attacks on Ranade and the younger men. Ranade, fearing that the government would take the argument as a sign that Poona was not yet ready for representative government, unexpectedly attended a meeting at which Kunte spoke. Kunte petulantly ignored him and left the meeting hurriedly. Ranade followed, joined him in his carriage, and returned from a long ride having convinced Kunte not to oppose the popular party actively.[94]

Mahratta opposed Kunte, with veiled sarcasm calling him less self-sacrificing than others. Their preferences included Professor M. S. Gole of Fergusson College, the sardar T. N. Rajmachikar, and D. V. Gokhale, former editor of the reformers' newspaper, Dnyan Prakash. Factional barriers between Ranade's and Tilak's generations were not clearly delineated yet.[95] Despite the work of the Sarvajanik Sabha in organizing rallies and distributing pamphlets, the officially supported candidates, including Kunte, won the election. A supporter of the official party wrote to the Times of India afterwards, claiming that the political associations had shown themselves to be "mere tools and organs of the discontented and half-educated enthusiasts of this land."[96]

The growing factionalism of Poona affairs resembled the challenge of Bombay society which Ranade had seen years before. Henceforth the search for unity not only in social but in political affairs as well became a more pronounced theme of his work. He had praised the effectiveness of organized agitation since the Baroda affair of 1875; the Ilbert Bill fight among the British had shown him and his contemporaries the need for strong organizations among Indians to counteract Anglo-Indian influence.[97] In the following two years this lesson was applied in various parts of India in the effort to forge an organization of national political unity. The Indian National Congress was the result, convening for the first time at the end of December 1885 in Bombay, barely one month after the Poona local elections. It had originally been intended that the Congress would meet in Poona because of the national reputation for organization which the Sarvajanik Sabha held among political reformers, but an outbreak of cholera in Poona in early December forced the change of location. Nonetheless, unity was at hand, and Ranade was to play an important though shadowy role in the early development of the Congress organization.

As an officer of the government Ranade was not permitted to become an official member of the Congress, but no regulation prevented his attending its annual sessions as an honored guest and adviser. Surendranath Banerjea typified many comments on Ranade's role by writing: "He was a constant figure on the Congress platform as a visitor, and he was the power behind the throne, guiding, advising and encouraging the Congress leaders."[98] Such praise conceals the precise nature of Ranade's role, yet it suggests the general esteem in which his administrative experience was held. He attended the first Congress in 1885 and participated briefly in its floor debates. In this session he was a mediocre parliamentarian, raising awkward difficulties for resolutions proposed by his associates, S. H. Chiplunkar and K. T. Telang. Resolution II proposed the abolition of the Council of the Secretary of State for India, since Chiplunkar and others felt that it was dominated by retired Anglo-Indians whose experience of India was outdated. When debate ended and the measure was approved, Resolution III was presented, advocating considerable expansion of the powers of the provincial legislative councils. Only then did Ranade speak, suggesting in an impromptu manner that the resolution needed to be presented in far greater detail, presumably on the model of his local government scheme of 1882, if it was to be of use to the government. He then proposed a moderation of the earlier resolution: perhaps the Supreme Council should not be abolished but expanded by the addition of elected members.[99] Subsequent comments from the floor suggested that Ranade's idea was a circuitous compromise, coming too late in the day. Ranade was unheeded and both propositions were supported unanimously.

Little is known of Ranade's role in the second session of the Congress, except that he undoubtedly attended as an observer.[100] In the Madras Congress of 1887, however, he played an important part in the formation of the Subjects Committee. The Congress agenda had previously been arranged by a small group which met unofficially at the home of Allan Octavian Hume. Some congressmen felt that a more orderly and democratic procedure was needed. When the Congress meetings began, Ranade was staying with M. B. Namjoshi, who had been an active member of the Sarvajanik Sabha since its inception and more recently a close associate of Tilak. The evening before the opening session, the Bengali leader, Bipin Chandra Pal, discussed with Ranade and Namjoshi the complaint that Hume and a handful of Bengalis were again controlling the agenda. When Pal demanded that this autocratic faction be replaced by a committee representing various provinces, Ranade agreed in principle but warned against an open split in public. Instead, he quietly gained the support of Hume and the Congress president, Ranade's close friend and legal associate Badruddin Tyabji, for the formation of a Subjects Committee. Duly formed the next day, the committee became the chief executive group of the Congress until 1906, when it was replaced by the All-India Congress Committee.[101] From that time on, Ranade was usually present at Subjects Committee meetings, as well as at plenary sessions of the Congress.[102]

Ranade's efforts to retain a show of unity in the Congress displayed the conciliatory role that was congenial to him in public life. The stresses which resulted from uniting many different regional and ethnic groups under one banner were enormous; by the late 1880's Ranade's efforts were designed chiefly to prevent splits within the political movement. The danger of communalism in politics was becoming clear, as Sir Sayyid Ahmad Khan led a sizable section of Muslim opinion which opposed Badruddin Tyabji's cooperation with the Congress. Sir Sayyid denied the boast of the Congress that it represented all of India and refused to participate. While many Congress Hindus were becoming publicly angered with Sir Sayyid, Ranade saw that there were wider dimensions to the factional threat. He spoke publicly against the threat posed to the Congress by Hindus' myopic hatred of Sir Sayyid and his followers, warning of others as well who worked against its unity. In a speech of May 21, 1888, he told his listeners that "even some individuals among ourselves are practising Ahmadism," and pointed to selfish interests among Hindu groups within the Congress.[103] His warnings against communalist tendencies among both Hindus and Muslims were an oracle of a bitter conflict which awaited him in the 1890's, testing to the extreme his ability to channel political conflicts within parliamentary bounds.

Ranade's most lasting support for the parliamentary and pro-British tradition in the Congress politics was indirect. It resulted from his sponsorship of his protégé G. K. Gokhale, who led the Moderate wing of the Congress until 1915. In the late 1880's Ranade assiduously took the young Professor Gokhale to the Congress meetings and introduced him to the political leaders of other provinces as "a young man of great promise who . . . was destined to be one of the foremost men of India."[104] Gokhale was to carry Ranade's philosophy into the highest levels of politics and administration in the 1890's, but with less of the stoic fortitude which sustained Ranade in his declining years. When Gokhale entered politics the incipient split between Moderates and Extremists was still not clearly formulated in the political arena. The fundamental issues around which the two camps developed an irreconcilable conflict were not in the first instance political but social. It was only after 1890 that the conflict which had begun with the founding of the New English School came to dominate the entire structure of political life in Maharashtra. But by then, fundamental conflict over the relations of an alien government to its subject population could not be avoided.

Notes

[1] Government of India, Report of the Public Service Commission, 1887, IV: Bombay Presidency, 143.

[2] Poona Sarvajanik Sabha, "An Appeal to Princes," JPSS, IV (January 1882).

[3] See Helen S. Dyer, Pandita Ramabai: The Story of Her Life (London, n.d.).

[4] Ramabai Ranade, Reminiscences, pp. 101-104.

[5] Mahratta, September 17, 1882, pp. 4-5.

[6] Ranade's evaluation of the commission's work was summarized in a letter, probably written in 1887, to Pherozeshah Mehta. He wrote that the commission had framed a magnificent national education system, well suited to present conditions. He especially praised the strength of government-private cooperation, which the Deccan Education Society would not have done. In Mehta Papers.

[7] Mahratta, July 20, 1884, pp. 3-4.

[8] Modak to Ranade, February 18, 1884, in private collection of N. R. Phatak.

[9] Article by "Atha," Indian Spectator, August 19, 1883, p. 4. The writer's views reflected a growing trend in Bombay Presidency during the 1880's toward concern for technical education and education for the agricultural castes. See the discussion in Ellen E. McDonald, "Social Change in Late Nineteenth Century Bombay: 1858-98" (Ph.D. diss., University of California, Berkeley, 1965), pp. 160ff., 252ff.

[10] Deccan Association, An Appeal for the Promotion of Education Among Marathas, etc. (Poona, 1886), p. 2. Other information on the association comes chiefly from Appeal.

[11] Ibid., p. 4.

[12] McDonald, "Social Change," p. 255.

[13] Mahratta, May 2, 1886, p. 5.

[14] Bombay Government, Judicial Department Proceedings, 1886, 88, No. 534.

[15] The Sarvajanik Sabha held a meeting on May 28 claiming that the commission must have non-official members in order to gain a balanced view. Bombay Gazette, March 1, 1886, p. 5.

[16] See Ilbert to Reay, February 3, 1886, in Ilbert Papers, Eur D 594/10. Once again Ranade's appointment caused some difficulty within the government, for Ilbert had to defend him against the old suspicions of 1879 as well as to argue that he was better qualified than any available English Covenanted Civil Servant. Ilbert to Godley, February 16, 1886, and Ilbert to Reay, February 10, 1886, Ilbert Papers, Eur D 594/10. These letters indicated that many members of the government had not been impressed with Ranade's writings on economics and administration, probably considering them to express the special interests of one community.

[17] Poona Sarvajanik Sabha, "Reply to the Finance Committee's Circular," September 30, 1886, JPSS, IX (October 1886-January 1887), 1, 4, 27, 33.

[18] W. W. Hunter, Bombay: 1885 to 1890 (London, 1892), p. 351.

[19] Bombay Graduates' Association, First Annual Report (Bombay, 1887), p. 48.

[20] Mahratta, April 25, 1886, p. 1.

[21] Ibid.

[22] Bombay Graduates' Association, Report, p. 11.

[23] Bombay Government, General Department, 1849, Vol. 16.

[24] Ranade, "Remarks on the Marathi Catalogue," in MW, p. 11.

[25] For details, see Dnyanoday, February 21, 1878, p. 97; and April 4, 1878, pp. 170-171; or Native Opinion, January 27, 1878, pp. 58, 64; and March 3, 1878, pp. 135-136.

[26] It did provide a link, though, with the Deccan Vernacular Translation Society, which Ranade and many other literati of Poona founded in 1894 as a memorial to Lokahitawadi, who had recently died. Within a decade this organization had a large-scale publishing operation. See Report of the Deccan Vernacular Translation Society for the Year 1901-02 (Poona, 1903).

[27] See Maharashtra Sahitya Parishad, Hirak Mahotsava (Poona, 1970), pp. 13, 26. The society met again only in 1885, and held similar meetings annually from the late 1890's. Since 1905 its tradition has been uninterrupted and its conferences have been attended by all the important figures of Marathi literature. For a brief history, see pp. 13-28.

[28] Biographical details are found in N. C. Kelkar, Indian Worthies, pp. 119-143. In addition to his father, his uncle Sitaram Hari Chiplunkar was for many years secretary of the Sarvajanik Sabha.

[29] The essay is analyzed at length in G. T. Madkholkar and S. N. Banhatti, Viṣṇū Kṛṣṇa Ciplūnkar (Vishnu Krishna Chiplunkar), (Bombay, 1934), pp. 269ff.

[30] Kelkar, Indian Worthies, pp. 149-151.

[31] N. C. Kelkar, Life and Times of Lokamanya Tilak, tr. D. V. Divekar (Madras, 1928), p. 85.

[32] Kelkar, Indian Worthies, p. 144.

[33] S. Gopal, The Viceroyalty of Lord Ripon (London, 1953), pp. 172-174.

[34] In 1880 the Bombay government aided nine missionary high schools with grants of Rs. 38,000; but only one native school, with Rs. 4,500. Nine other native schools were not considered of high enough quality to aid. P. M. Limaye, The History of the Deccan Education Society (Poona, 1935), Part 1, p. 42.

[35] For the enthusiastic response of Bombay Hindus, see Native Opinion, May 19, 1878, pp. 307-308.

[36] Limaye, History of the Deccan Education Society, pp. 43-46.

[37] Kelkar, Indian Worthies, p. 147.

[38] S. L. Karandikar, Lokamanya Bal Gangadhar Tilak (Poona, 1957), p. 55.

[39] Kelkar, Indian Worthies, p. 160.

[40] Limaye, History of the Deccan Education Society, Part 1, p. 17.

[41] Ibid., Part 2, p. 108.

[42] Ibid., Part 2, p. 96.

[43] Ibid., Part 1, p. 20. For an analysis of Chiplunkar's strident but inspiring political views, see N. R. Inamdar, "Political Thought of Vishnushastri Chiplunkar," Journal of the University of Poona, Humanities Section, No. 31 (1969), pp. 15-24.

[44] Limaye, History of the Deccan Education Society, Part 1, pp. 71-73.

[45] Deccan Education Society, Report (Poona, 1885).

[46] As they had learned from their experience with the Sarvajanik Sabha, they invited the native princes of the region to lend their prestige and financial support by becoming patrons of the society. The Maharaja of Kolhapur was elected the first president. See ibid., pp. 1, 61; Limaye, History of the Deccan Education Society, Part 1, p. 56.

[47] G. P. Pradhan and A. K. Bhagwat, Lokamanya Tilak: A Biography (Bombay, 1958), pp. 30-31.

[48] Limaye, *History of the Deccan Education Society*, Part 1, pp. 95-99.

[49] Hunter, *Bombay*, pp. 51-67, gives Reay's policy in the context of earlier education policy in Bombay. See also Limaye, *History of the Deccan Education Society*, Part 1, p. 99.

[50] For detail, see Ellen E. McDonald, "The Modernizing of Communication: Vernacular Publishing in Nineteenth Century Maharashtra," *Asian Survey* (July 1968), pp. 589-606.

[51] Limaye, *History of the Deccan Education Society*, Part 1, pp. 33-34; and see *Kesari-Mahratta: Lokamanya Tilak Special Centenary* Issue (Poona, 1956), pp. 110-111, for a complete list of editors of both newspapers.

[52] *Mahratta*, January 2, 1881, p. 1.

[53] *Mahratta*, January 8, 1882, pp. 3-4.

[54] *Mahratta*, April 23, 1882, p. 4.

[55] *Mahratta*, May 14, 1882, p. 7.

[56] From a letter by N. G. Chandavarkar to *Times of India*, August 6, 1920, reprinted in S. V. Bapat, ed., *Lokamānya Tilak yāñcyā āthavaṇī va ākhyāyika* (Reminiscences and Recollections of Lokamanya Tilak), 3 vols. (Poona, 1924-28), I, 270.

[57] M. G. Ranade, "A Constitution for Native States," *JPSS*, II (January 1880), 17.

[58] *Ibid.*, p. 2.

[59] M. G. Ranade, "Sir Salar Jang's Administration," *JPSS*, III (October 1880), 45.

[60] Ranade, "A Constitution," pp. 78-80.

[61] *Ibid.*

[62] Ranade, "Salar Jang," p. 47.

[63] Poona Sarvajanik Sabha, "Suggestions to His Highness the Gaikwad of Baroda Regarding the Future Constitution of Baroda," *JPSS*, IV (January 1882), 26. These comments were especially pointed toward Sir T. Madhavrao, the dewan, who was becoming a close friend of Ranade in these years and who, four years later, joined Ranade in founding the National Social Conference.

[64] *Mahratta*, January 2, 1881, p. 1.

[65] *Mahratta*, January 29, 1882, p. 2.

[66] Ranade's role in the affair was disputed. Tilak's protégé and biographer, N. C. Kelkar, asserts that the letters were taken to Ranade for his opinion on their authenticity and that he kept them for one month, guaranteeing that they were genuine. At the trial he refused to testify on their authenticity in Tilak's defense, presumably because this would in effect destroy a fellow government officer. Consequently Tilak was jailed and Ranade's true loyalties were exposed. Kelkar, *Tilak*, I, 137-138. Agarkar's biographer, M. D. Altekar, insists that Ranade never saw or kept the letters, and that he consequently never deserted Tilak. M. D. Altekar, *Gopāḷ Gaṇeś Āgarkar* (Bombay, 1916), pp. 85-89.

[67] Pradhan and Bhagwat, *Tilak*, pp. 22-25.

[68] Poona Sarvajanik Sabha, "A Representation to the Government of India on the Subject of the Vernacular Press Act," February 11, 1881, *JPSS*, III (April 1881), 58-59.

[69] *Mahratta*, January 8, 1882, p. 3.

[70] Gopal, *Ripon*, pp. 70ff.

[71] See Christine Dobbin, "The Ilbert Bill," *Historical Studies, Australia and New Zealand* (October 1965), pp. 87-102.

[72] Quoted in Gopal, *Ripon*, p. 136.

[73] Phatak, *Ranade*, p. 325; Mankar, *Ranade*, I, 51-52.

[74] Mahratta, January 23, 1881, p. 4.

[75] Mahratta, June 10, 1883, p. 1; June 24, 1883, pp. 1-2.

[76] Mahratta, April 29, 1883, p. 3.

[77] Mahratta, May 20, 1883, pp. 2-3.

[78] Quoted approvingly in Mahratta, March 4, 1883. Reay summarized Wordsworth's position two years later when he wrote that he "has a very strong hold on the Brahmin community especially those he has educated whilst he was at Poona. He may be considered the English champion of educated Native opinion here." Reay to Cross, Secretary of State, November 26, 1886, Cross Papers, Eur E 243/48.

[79] A few orthodox Hindus, who could not accept the dinner invitation, arrived later in the evening.

[80] Wordsworth to Ranade, September 9, 1883, Ripon Papers, I S 290/8.

[81] Ranade, "The Agitation in Regard to the Native Magistrates Jurisdiction Bill," p. 24.

[82] Gopal, Ripon, pp. 161-163.

[83] Ranade, "The Agitation in Regard to the Native Magistrates Jurisdiction Bill," p. 25.

[84] Poona Sarvajanik Sabha, "An Appeal to the Free Electors of Great Britain and Ireland from Their Fellow Subjects, the Unrepresented Millions of the Inhabitants of India," March 19, 1880, JPSS, II (April 1880), 132-133.

[85] Mahratta, May 15, 1881, pp. 1-2.

[86] Ibid.

[87] W. S. Blunt, India Under Ripon (London, 1909), p. 220.

[88] Mahratta, June 11, 1882, pp. 4, 5.

[89] Mahratta, May 7, 1882, pp. 2-3.

[90] Ibid.

[91] Mahratta, November 11, 1883, pp. 3-4.

[92] Kelkar, Tilak, II, 88.

[93] As early as October 1877 the Sarvajanik Sabha had been pressing the governor to establish municipal elections in Poona; the scheme was nothing new. See Native Opinion, November 4, 1877, pp. 697-698.

[94] Gokhale, Late Mr. Justice Ranade, pp. 26-29.

[95] Mahratta, November 11, 1885. Mahratta did oppose the Moderate, K. P. Gadgil, later Gokhale's associate and a bitter enemy of Tilak, but their stated reason for opposing him was that as a nominated corporator, Gadgil had refused to attend many meetings.

[96] Times of India, December 30, 1885, p. 5.

[97] Ranade, "Administrative Reforms," p. 30. At that time he concluded: "Bureaucratic governments will do little of their own motion, and people must never cease to be importunate in their representations and demands, for that is the only way in which they can succeed in attaining their object." Ranade remembered the Baroda Affair of 1875 as an example of the decisive role of popular agitation. In a speech in Surat four years later, he praised the effectiveness of concerted public opinion and criticized his audience for not organizing a sabha there. He contrasted the annexation of Oudh a generation earlier, which went without public protest, with the decision not to annex Baroda, for which he took credit for the sabha's campaign. See Minute of Ravenscroft, Government of India, Home Judicial A Proceedings, August 1880, Nos. 203-205.

[98] S. Banerjea, A Nation in Making, new ed. (Oxford, 1963), p. 46.

[99] Indian National Congress, Report of the Proceedings, 1885, p. 28.

[100] Ranade travelled from Poona to Calcutta in November 1886 and remained for some time, presumably to attend the Congress. Ramabai Ranade, Reminiscences, pp. 138-139. Ramabai indicates elsewhere, on p. 320, that Ranade attended every Congress through 1899.

[101] B. C. Pal, Memories of My Life and Times, II: 1886-1900 (Calcutta, 1951), 35-40.

[102] Indian Nation Builders (Madras, n.d.), p. 8.

[103] Reported in Varhad Samachar, May 21, 1888; reprinted in SMHFM, II, 178-179.

[104] Speech by Motilal Ghose, March 2, 1915; quoted in P. Dutt, Memoirs of Moti Lal Ghose (Calcutta, 1935), p. 313.

Chapter 7

SOCIAL REFORM AND THE ROLE OF GOVERNMENT, 1884-1891

> Even in the most free countries the majority only determines the choice of those individuals to whose guidance it will submit. --Ranade

The political conflicts of the 1880's in Poona expressed differing assessments of the need to defend Indian institutions against the British. But they were differences of degree only, and the issues at stake were not as yet divisive enough to cause irreparable damage to the unity of Indian political interests. Polarization between Ranade's Moderates and Tilak's Extremists did develop during the 1880's, not at first over educational or political policies but over issues of social reform. Faced with the alternative guidelines for social development which Indian and Western traditions offered, the leading public figures of Maharashtra gravitated into different factions, each of which presented its own formula for action. The ensuing debate centered on two distinct but related questions: whether or not Hindu society should be gradually reformed along the lines of Western liberalism, and whether or not there was ever justification for an alien government's initiating changes. As the leading figure in the high caste social reform movement of the time in Maharashtra, Ranade found himself the focus of yet another turbulent conflict.

Government and the Rights of Women

The decade began uneventfully in Poona, for aside from women's education the social reform movement had been quiescent since the death of Vishnu Shastri Pandit in 1875. Leadership had passed to Ranade, who had never shared his older friend's delight in public confrontations. Ranade had seen during the widow-marriage campaign that there were no shortcuts to reform of Brahmin traditions, for direct attacks on orthodox thought had only polarized the community to the reformers' detriment. Moreover, Ranade had disqualified himself from leading this crusade by failing to marry a widow himself.

By 1880 public debate was shifting from the problem of enforced widowhood to that of child marriage, the major cause of widowhood. In many parts of India it was common practice among the upper castes to have girls married before they reached puberty.[1] An Age of Consent Act passed by the government of India in 1860 defined the age of ten as the minimum legal age for consummation of marriage, but the act had not been enforced.[2] In Poona a movement began in the early 1880's which contended that the existing legal minimum was too low to prevent early childbearing and the consequent physical debilitation of future generations. At a public meeting on May 19, 1881, speakers agreed that the shastras posed no serious barrier to raising the marriage age, and a petition was circulated on which some two hundred men pledged not to marry their daughters before age ten or their sons before age sixteen.[3] There was general agreement that Hindu society must reform itself in order to prevent government interference in matters intimately touching family life.

In an editorial the following week Tilak joined those who agreed on the need for change. While warning as usual against outside interference in Hindu marriage practices, he emphasized that existing practices were evil and the community must take action in line with its other efforts at self-improvement.

> If we want that we should be proficient in the art of self-government, the first qualification we should show is the <u>ability</u> to manage our own business among ourselves, and particularly that business which will be better regulated by ourselves than by the passing of an act or resolution. . . . Let our people, therefore, form associations, frame rules, and restraints for themselves and do all they can to check . . . this evil custom [of child marriage].[4]

As yet there was no sense of immediacy in the discussion, for no one anticipated any rapid shift in the public mood. The atmosphere changed abruptly in August 1884, when Behramji Malabari published <u>Notes on Infant Marriage in India</u>.[5] Malabari was editor of the <u>Indian Spectator</u>, the mouthpiece of the Parsi reformers in the 1880's. He was already known in Bombay for his outspoken social criticisms, and publication of the <u>Notes</u> brought Malabari instant fame in many parts of India. His argument rested on a sense of moral outrage; he appealed to the public conscience rather than to legal principles or tradition. Portraying child brides as brutally exploited by their husbands' families, he cried: "The country cannot rise unless its millions are lifted to a higher moral atmosphere and social responsibility. And this will not happen until we have a system of heart-education side by side with head-education."[6] He demanded immediate and decisive government intervention to end child marriages. When he sent copies of the <u>Notes</u> to many government officials and leading Indian spokesmen, he precipitated a debate over whether the government should raise the legal age of consent and what a new minimum might appropriately be.

A familiar problem in the history of the Raj had presented itself once again. The British had long been committed not to interfere in the essential religious and social practices of their subjects. But on certain occasions they had set aside this general principle in the name of an overriding dedication to principles of common morality. The most celebrated precedent for this had been the official abolition of sati in 1829. Ram Mohan Roy had initiated a campaign, of which Malabari's was in some regards a repetition, to arouse massive indignation against the practice of widows' self-immolation on their husbands' funeral pyres. His cause had achieved a controversial victory in 1829 when the new viceroy, Bentinck, agreed to intervention on the basis of "the paramount dictates of justice and humanity."[7] The campaign to enlist government aid succeeded, but only at the cost of stimulating orthodox Brahmins to organize counter organizations of their own, resentful of alien intrusion into spheres which they considered legitimately their own.

A more immediate precedent in Bombay had arisen in the early 1860's, this time over an Indian demand not for legislative but for judicial action against a presumed outrage against common morality by Hindu traditionalism. This cause célèbre, the Maharaj libel case of 1862, appeared when Karsondas Mulji, a Gujarati Bania reformer closely associated with the Maharashtrian reformers of Bombay, published in his newspaper an exposé of the Maharajas, or hereditary priests of the Vallabhacharya sect. Karsondas charged that the Maharajas posed as incarnations of the god Krishna and encouraged female devotees to worship them by submitting to sexual intercourse. Jagunathjee Maharaj, one of the priests, thereupon sued Karsondas for libel in the British courts, denying all his charges. Other reformers took the side of Karsondas and demonstrated the truth of his assertions.[8] Sir Joseph Arnould, the presiding High Court judge, found in favor of Karsondas, setting aside the general reluctance of Bombay courts to interfere with indigenous religious customs by appealing to abstract morality. "The principle for which the defendant and his witnesses have been contending is simply this, that . . . when practices which sap the very foundation of morality, which involve a violation of the eternal and immutable laws of Right, are established in the name and under the sanction of Religion, they ought, for the common welfare of society, and in the interests of Humanity itself, to be publicly denounced and exposed."[9]

Arnould's judgment placed the government in the role of ultimate defender of morality, to which reformers might appeal for support against their own social traditions. Hindu reformers were elated with the outcome, but on all sides there remained a residue of conviction that it was far preferable to reform Hinduism from within rather than resorting to alien authority. The British in effect agreed, for the Maharaj libel decision stirred up latent but strong hostility among the orthodox majority of the population. For the next quarter century the British carefully avoided further intervention in the internal conflicts of Hinduism.

It was against this background that Lord Ripon reacted cautiously to Malabari's Notes. He wrote to Malabari expressing personal sympathy with the proposed reform, but he felt powerless to move until a clearer expression of public support emerged. He wrote, "I shall rejoice if the results of your inquiries should show that there exists an opening for the Government to mark in some public manner the view which it entertains of the great importance of reform in these matters,"[10] meaning that his beleaguered forces could not afford to take action at the time.

Ranade's first reaction to receiving a copy of the Notes was tentative support for legislation. In a lengthy reply to Malabari, Ranade stated that there was no doubt in principle about the justification for state action: legislation on social reform was acceptable as long as it represented the most enlightened views of Indians themselves. Earlier in the year Ranade had maintained with regard to the Ilbert Bill that the educated class were the spokesmen of India's political interests; he now claimed a similar right on questions of social reform. Faced with the fact that prevailing custom ran counter to the values of the Westernized minority, Ranade claimed that the educated class represented not so much the immediate interests as the long-range needs of the people. Paternalistically, he wrote that "even in the most free countries . . . the majority only determines the choice of those individuals to whose guidance it will submit."[11]

Aware that the social reform movement needed whatever support it could find, he was eager to mobilize all available liberal forces, whether English or Indian. Hence he presented an inflated estimate of the power of the social reformers by arguing that private efforts had already prepared the ground for legislation. "One reason why State action is now urgently called for, is that [education and public opinion] have been working for a considerable time past, and they have prepared the ground sufficiently to make State action intelligible and beneficial."[12] In order to assure that new legislation would be received by the public as legitimate, not despotic, Ranade proposed his familiar tactic of associating influential Indians with new legislation as members of a commission to certify the age of brides and impose fines on families of child brides. "I would make over the fines to the heads of the castes . . . or to Local Boards and Municipalities, whose members, elected by the people, may safely be honoured" with this new power.[13] Ranade did not oppose bureaucratic solutions to social conflicts; he opposed solutions imposed from the outside by British bureaucrats.

Despite this contrived position Ranade had some support on the basic principle of government intervention from militant young social reformers in Bombay. Chief of these was N. G. Chandavarkar, who vowed that "where a social custom is grossly of a perverse nature, opposed to all sense of decency and humanity, whether a majority wishes for a change in it or not, the State ought to put it down."[14] He and a few Hindu associates gave Malabari their full support. Others, however, even in the intimate circle of social reformers, opposed official action in this instance as a self-defeating strategy. R. G. Bhandarkar, who was to change his mind two years later, now warned that this campaign could only harden the prevailing orthodox opposition, and many Bombay reformers agreed with him, even though they were personally sympathetic with raising the marriage age.

When Malabari's Notes first appeared, Ranade and others thought that the evils of child marriage were presented in exaggeratedly lurid colors. However, Ranade's own awareness of how slowly Indian society was reforming itself by its own volition was sharpened by Malabari's moral perception. With the publication of "State Legislation in Social Matters" in 1885, Ranade joined Malabari in the front ranks of militant reformers.[15] In contrast to the previous year he now contended that the evil of child marriage was widespread and insidious. A numerical survey alone could not tell the whole story, he contended, for child marriage was indirectly responsible for the sorrows of widowhood and other social evils. Child brides and widows could hardly speak for themselves, as they were secluded within their households far from the light of the public streets. Only the liberal reformers truly represented them in the public debate; hence the reformers must be accepted as the true representatives of the Hindu community.[16]

Ranade had been insisting with regard to civil administration that the state was already interfering in society in numerous ways and that properly guided it could play a productive role in the modernization process. This was a tacit corollary to his new contention that the state already regulated certain social and religious practices. As an example he pointed out that the legal abolition of sati had originally been based on moral principles, not majority demands, but later gained popular support. In such situations, "the State in its collective capacity represents the power, the wisdom, the mercy and charity, of its best citizens," and follows their initiative. Under these circumstances it is entirely unnecessary to distinguish alien from self-rule. The alternative to government action would be to "let us remain as we are, disorganized and demoralized, stunted and deformed, with the curse of folly and wickedness paralyzing all the healthy activities and vital energies of our social body."[17] In contrast to the more radical nationalists, Ranade assumed by now that the basic conflict in Indian affairs was not between British and Indians but between progressives and reactionaries, whatever their nationality.

In 1885, however, interest was diverted from the Age of Consent debate to another area of women's rights, the issue of whether a wife should be legally compelled to live with her husband. It was raised by the marriage of Dadaji Bhikaji to Rakhmabai, the daughter of Dr. Sakharam Arjun of Bombay. The father refused to send Rakhmabai to Dadaji during his own lifetime, since she was still a young girl. When he died, leaving her a considerable inheritance, Dadaji asked the courts to compel her to live with him. She was now publicly unwilling, rejecting him as illiterate, consumptive, and uncouth.[18] In self-defense Dadaji published a pamphlet in which he claimed that Rakhmabai's mother was preventing her departure for fear of losing her deceased husband's estate.[19] The conflict soon reached the newspapers and became a battleground for women's rights. A lower court upheld Rakhmabai on the grounds that she had married Dadaji without her consent and therefore could not be forced to live with him. The High Court, on appeal, reversed the decision and agreed with Dadaji that Hindu Marriage law made no provision for the wife's consent.[20] Rakhmabai, a well-educated and independent young woman, was adamant; she still refused to live with her husband, preferring to risk imprisonment. Her stand prompted many leading citizens of Bombay to organize a Rakhmabai Defence Committee under the chairmanship of Principal Wordsworth to raise funds for her further defense.[21]

Ranade joined the committee and championed its efforts in Poona.[22] In a speech in the Spring Lecture Series there in May 1887, he defended the questionable position that a Hindu marriage was not valid without the consent of the bride, and that the law should not establish any penalty for a wife's refusal to live with her husband. Tilak called this argument a bald misrepresentation of the shastras, unworthy of Ranade's education and position.[23] In a _Kesari_ article in June he refuted Ranade's contention by demonstrating that the smritis enjoined husbands to protect their wives but assumed that husbands also possessed their wives. Attacking Ranade's revisionist legal efforts, Tilak claimed that Ranade had no right to interfere with the dharmashastra. He suggested that Ranade should advocate reforms on the proper grounds of morality and not pretend an artificial reverence for tradition.[24] The Rakhmabai controversy ended late in 1887 when Dadaji decided not to pursue his claims against his wife, and the issue quickly subsided. Yet some damage was already done; the conflict had reinforced social dissensions in Poona.

All-India Reform: The National Social Conference

Malabari had never expected an easy success in his battle against the forces of darkness. As early as his _Notes_ he anticipated the need for a nationwide campaign for women's rights, suggesting the formation of "a national association for social reform with the existing societies as branches," to serve as a coordinating body for social reform.[25] By 1885 he launched an effort throughout India to elicit popular support for new legislation on the marriage age. From this time onward the social reform movement became national in scope. Its character changed as dramatically as the political movement changed with the founding of the Indian National Congress in the same year. Hitherto a few reformers had fought for specific changes in Hindu society, but the issues varied from one province to another. Communication among the reformers was restricted to newspaper reports and personal correspondence such as that which the members of the Samaj movement carried on. The appearance of Malabari's _Notes_ marked the first national social debate, for officials and reformers from all parts of India joined the discussion of marriage practices. It was also a time of organizational efforts. When the Congress was founded in 1885 many leading reformers hoped the new organization would deal with both political and social issues. Shortly before the first

Congress met, <u>Kesari</u> reported to its readers that the new association would deal with both "the rights which must be obtained from the government" and also "vitally important social questions."[26]

The relation of political to social advance was not a simple one. Many felt that if the Congress was to develop strength, it must concentrate on those political issues which had already elicited a united national position and leave the divisive social issues to another platform. As president of the Congress in 1886, Dadabhai Naoroji argued that the Congress was a political organization whose diverse membership could not confront the social issues which were specific to individual castes and regions. Dadabhai made clear his own commitment to social reform, stating that "it does not follow . . . that the delegates here present . . . are not doing their utmost to solve those complicated problems on which hinge the practical introduction of those reforms."[27] N. G. Chandavarkar, one of the most zealous social reformers, reported that the Congress delegates "all agreed that our primary object was union; that questions on which all felt alike ought alone to be taken up by the Congress; and by following such a course alone could we hope to unite all and make them see the necessity of social reform."[28] Almost simultaneously, K. T. Telang, another of Ranade's close associates in Bombay, delivered a speech entitled "Must Social Reform Precede Political Reform?" which provided the Congress with its most powerful justification for excluding social controversies from its debates. Telang rested his case on a contrast between the Congress' opposition on political questions and the opposition in social controversies. As political opponents "we have a government by a progressive nation, which is the benign mother of free nations. . . . On the other side, we have an ancient nation, subject to strong prejudices; not in anything like full sympathy with the new conditions now existing in the country."[29] The Congress must forge unity first in the area where some success was most likely, against the more pliable opponent. In the event, the Congress maintained a policy of leaving social reform to its members on an individual basis.

The government was critical of the decision in the Congress to avoid social questions. Lord Dufferin, the viceroy, had originally encouraged the founding of the Congress, presuming that it would promote social causes. When the Congress emerged as an exclusively political agitation, his hopes were dashed. In a speech of 1887 he retorted: "I cannot help expressing my regret that they should seem to consider such momentous topics [as social reform], concerning as they do the welfare of millions of their fellow-subjects, as beneath their notice."[30]

The social reformers were especially sensitive to criticism of this sort. Since the Congress officially had resolved not to debate social questions, the social reformers led by Malabari and the Brahmo Samaj answered critics by organizing social reform meetings to accompany the Bombay and Calcutta congresses. At the third Congress, held in Madras in 1887, the social reformers gave permanent structure to their work by establishing the National Social Conference. From that year onward the Social Conference met concurrently with the Congress each year and used the same facilities. This informal but close cooperation accomplished two objectives. It allowed liberal Congress delegates to attend the conferences conveniently so as to support social reform without jeopardizing political unity. And since the Social Conference was a non-political organization, men like Ranade who were reformers and also government servants could assume direct leadership of an all-India organization.[31]

Delegates to the first Social Conference elected the south Indian reformers Sir T. Madhavrao as president and Dewan Bahadur R. Raghunathrao as general secretary. Madhavrao soon afterward decided to oppose the Age of Consent agitation and withdrew from the Social Conference, and Raghunathrao's health declined. Ranade was left as the dominant figure in the all-India social reform movement for the ensuing thirteen years. He was disappointed that the Congress refused to take direct responsibility for liberalizing Indian society, believing that the demand for political advance could be justified only on the basis of a parallel movement of social reform. He was left, then, with the task of associating his Social Conference closely but informally with the work of the Congress. As general secretary of the Social Conference from year to year, Ranade made annual introductory addresses at the conference in which he outlined its work and character. He never failed to stress that the need for social reform was if anything even greater than the need for political advance. The Congress was unified and disciplined in its work, for "in the Congress we meet as citizens of one empire, subjects of one sovereign--obeying the same laws, liable to pay the same taxes, claiming the same privileges, and complaining of the same grievances." In contrast, the Social Conference must be loosely organized and decentralized because of local differences in social problems.[32]

Since most of the social issues of the day were of local interest and the delegates to the conference were extremely varied in their backgrounds, Ranade chose to leave the conference organization in an informal state, largely dependent on his personal coordinating efforts.[33] Through the Social Conference Ranade attempted to coordinate and encourage a loose alliance of the many and diverse organizations which were attempting some sort of social liberalization. Reluctant to exclude anyone who would join, Ranade was searching as always to rally all possible allies in the work of modernizing his society.

The associations which contributed most actively to the annual sessions of the conference were the voluntary intercaste reform groups which had begun to proliferate during the previous decade. In 1887 social reform associations were organized in Sind and Ahmedabad, probably as adjuncts of local branches of the Prarthana Samaj.[34] Their example, publicized by the National Social Conference, led to the formation of similar organizations elsewhere. The associations typically required pledges of their members binding them to such vows as abstinence from alcohol, not marrying their daughters before a certain age, and support for widow marriage and women's education. The Social Conference cooperated with individual caste associations. The Kayastha Conference in north India, for example, had recently been formed to discuss the possibility of sanctioning interdining and other liberal practices among the subcastes of Kayasthas. Other conferences of individual castes or caste clusters in north India were also beginning to meet to discuss possible reforms in their caste practices, chiefly concerning the rights of women.[35]

Ranade was aware that reforms undertaken by caste associations would be conservative and cautious. He warned his listeners that they "cramp and narrow the sympathies of those who belong to them, and the sphere of action is restricted within very defined limits." But under existing circumstances, in which all efforts at social reform were welcome, he believed that the caste associations "cannot fail to effect considerable change for the better in the social condition of the country, if only these separate caste movements work together for the common good."[36] Some of his younger associates, like Chandavarkar, were unconvinced by Ranade's familiar rhetorical optimism, but for the time being they cooperated with his patient efforts to stimulate the conservative reform groups.

A third possible ally of a conservative stripe was the more progressive native princes. Ranade's active efforts to gain the support of the princes for social reform reached back to 1870, when he joined the Bombay delegation to Baroda which tried to enlist the Gaikwad's support for widow remarriage. Twenty years later he was able to show that the great states like Baroda and Mysore were actively working for reform. He took the change to indicate that Indian society as a whole was beginning to modernize. "If the heart of the nation can be traced anywhere in its ancient strongholds, you will certainly see it strongly entrenched in the Native States. If any movement stirs the Native States, which are impervious to your political and industrial propaganda, that is a sign that the heart of the nation has been touched."[37] The rulers in the progressive states were incorporating social reform organizations by legislation, which the government of India was not effectively doing, and beginning to change specific practices within individual castes in their domains. Ranade saw all of this as vindication of his patient, moderate opposition to high caste traditions.

There was yet a fourth and more startling potential ally in conservative society, the shastris themselves. Through careful negotiations with the leaders of the orthodox camp, reformers like Ranade were attempting to gain their support for specific items on the reform agenda. By 1890 the campaign to curtail marriage expenses was being organized, and Ranade was able to state with pleasure that "even the Delhi Pundits found it necessary to yield to the spirit of the times by taking up the cry of the reformers against extravagant expenditure on marriage and other occasions."[38] Three years later, in 1893, he announced that the Shankaracharya of Sankeswar had pledged his support for the campaign to end excessive bride-price payments, ill-matched marriages between old men and young girls, and temple prostitution.[39]

There were massive obstacles in the way of organizing one conference to coordinate the activities of such varied groups in society. Each type of organization had different purposes and procedures; each had different values and represented a different orientation to traditional society. Although he never admitted it publicly, the almost mechanical optimism of Ranade's social reform addresses betrayed the constant drain on his energy which this work demanded. In the effort to articulate a common set of values for all constituents of the Social Conference, Ranade saw no alternative but a middle course of encouraging each organization in its own terms.[40] Only two lines of reform were unacceptable. The first was hollow lip service. In a speech shortly before the 1891 conference, he ridiculed those who agreed verbally that reforms were desirable but took no positive action. Presumably referring to Tilak and his followers, Ranade described these men as saying that "they should preach reform but that they should in practice only drift into reform, which means that we should close our eyes, shut our mouths, tie down our hands and feet. . . . Things should be allowed to take their own course."[41] These, he argued, were not true reformers, for without hard work no reforms ever resulted.

Second was the method of reform by rebellion. With the Brahmo Samaj and Maharashtrian reformers like Agarkar in mind, Ranade stated that the conference did not sanction this approach, since it meant a sharp rupture with Hindu society.[42] Here was an assertion of some significance, for it defined the limits of Ranade's willingness to challenge Hindu traditionalists. From the time he joined the Prarthana Samaj in Bombay in 1867, he had been steadfastly committed to working for reform from within the Hindu fold so as to avoid the social isolation of the Brahmo Samaj. As long as Ranade was the guiding figure in the Social Conference, he gave it a cautious and conciliatory character, emphasizing tactics and short-term goals rather than militant principles.

An English visitor who observed the conference one year preserved a memory of Ranade's presence on the platform which reveals that his style and his substance were well matched.

> Mr. Ranade was a man notoriously indifferent to appearances. His physique was rugged, with one drooping and watery eye. He dressed in anything, just a long black coat, frayed linen projecting from the sleeves, short, ill-cut white trousers. . . . He appeared on the platform, leaning on a knotted stick, standing in silent thought for near ten minutes completely indifferent to his audience. Then he began, slowly at first, gradually warming to his subject, and spoke

for an hour and a half. . . . Without a note, without a pause, he poured forth a stream of learning and sound sense, holding his audience enthralled though he had none of the art of the orator. It made it easy to understand the unseen influence he exercised on the best minds with which he was brought into contact.[43]

Ranade could give the impression of being totally oblivious to his public impact, yet he gauged his appeal carefully. He required more steadfast effort from himself than from any of his followers and he appealed to the reasonableness of men. This he reinforced with an artless and almost ingenuous moral purity. His audiences were impressed and stimulated, even when they chose to ignore his appeal for action. This was the dilemma which Ranade increasingly recognized: beyond his indefatigable administrative efforts, how could he provide the moral inspiration which would lead men to self-sacrificing action?

The Spiritual Basis of Reform

Ranade was becoming increasingly preoccupied with the relation of the reform of outward society to the refinement of the inner man. The longer he struggled to preserve a traditional personal discipline while loosening the social restrictions of Hinduism, the more he believed that the reformers' slow progress was at base caused by their own moral weakness. To those in the conference who feared that society at large was too powerful, Ranade was admonishing: "The thing to be reformed was their own self, heart and head and soul, their own prejudices were to be removed, their superstitions to be eradicated, their courage to be strengthened, their weaknesses to be conquered, in fact their character to be formed again so as to suit the times, so as to fit with the spirit of the age."[44] He chose to employ a Butlerian vocabulary, but it only thinly disguised the traditional Brahmin analysis that a man's power over the external world arose from the force of his internal austerity.

In his own life Ranade drew on the devotion of the bhakti saints, singing the abhangas of Tukaram and Namdev morning and evening. He even joined the devotees of Tukaram on their annual pilgrimage to Pandharpur, though few Brahmins were among the pilgrims. How frequently he went is not known, but as the pilgrims marched through Poona one year when he could not join them, he watched them pass with tears in his eyes and said, "How blessed and meritorious must Tukaram have been in life, since three hundred years after his death, hundreds and thousands of people are chanting his name and singing his praises! How could his words have such an effect without divine grace?"[45]

On his trips through India on official duties, Ranade sought out the great pilgrimage centers. In 1886 as he travelled from Simla to Calcutta he stopped at Hardwar at the head of the Ganges and fell into a reverie at his first sight of the holy river. Continuing on down the river, he stopped in Benares for a ritual bath in the Ganges and visited the holiest temples of the city.[46]

Ranade the social reformer was not content to allow religious discipline to remain a purely personal matter. For years he had used the Prarthana Samaj as the organizational vehicle linking personal piety and social reform.[47] In 1887 the social reform effort was given an all-India organization through the National Social Conference, and a year later a similar step was taken on the religious side with the founding of the All-India Theistic Conference. It was designed to encourage cooperation among the theistic samajes, to propagate theism, and to encourage philanthropy. Its links with the Social Conference were close, for it too met simultaneously with the annual congresses and Ranade dominated it as president from 1888 to 1892 and again in 1896.[48]

Like other reformer-saints before and since, Ranade derived his public influence to an important degree from the spiritual earnestness which he projected. The citizens of Poona were well aware of this, for in his later years they fell increasingly into the habit of honoring him as a rishi for the times, or a man who combined great wisdom with saintly austerity. Ranade expressed this in several ways in his educational work, for despite his insistence on a modern curriculum he attempted to preserve moral quality in students' lives. He customarily financed the education of four or five boys who lived in his home, and he saw to it that their daily studies included religious material as well as the regular curriculum.[49] As adviser to various educational experiments in Poona he made a similar emphasis. He praised the founders of the New English School when they attempted to revive moral training in the schools. Again, when he was asked by the Bombay government to comment on the moral fiber of the vernacular schools, he criticized existing policy for not allowing religious teaching in Hindu schools. He repeated his adherence to government neutrality in education but favored the recruiting of volunteer shastris to teach classical Hinduism in the schools. Stressing the moral content of their teaching, he dismissed the problem of sectarian conflicts among the shastris, and wrote that "unless supported by the religious sanction, lessons in moral training and discipline can never take root. The 'greatest good of the greatest number' philosophy never made a man moral or virtuous."[50]

As Ranade's search for moral revival grew in the 1880's, he considered again the religious roots of Hinduism. In his summary of one Elocution Society lecture in 1884 he described the flowering of astronomy and philosophy in the distant past of Hinduism; expressing great admiration for Brahmin religion, he urged his listeners to renew their own respect for their past.[51] It seemed to some onlookers that Ranade had become disenchanted with the Prarthana Samaj. <u>Mahratta</u> wondered why Ranade should criticize Christianity so harshly when the Prarthana Samaj borrowed heavily from it. A month after his lecture, <u>Kesari</u> printed an article entitled "Ranade Is Converted," stating that he seemed ready to desert the samaj and return to orthodox Hinduism so as to infuse public life with Hindu piety.[52] This was a misreading of Ranade's mind, for he was no closer to a desertion of reformed theism than ever. But he was attempting to build bridges of communication with the orthodox community. The orthodox knew him as a critic of the dharmashastra and consequently charged that he was nāstika, one who rejected the authority of the Veda and dharmashastra. Ranade's increased fervor on behalf of the religious spirit was in part an effort to counter that misrepresentation. Yet his spiritual fervor, expressed preeminently through his adherence to bhakti, was being challenged by Tilak and the younger men of the Deccan Education Society.

The 1880's were a time of rapid change in the English education system. Deccan College, where the young radicals were trained, exemplified the changes. Bishop Butler and the old preceptors of moral education were being replaced by Mill and Spencer, the rational sceptics of mid-nineteenth-century England.[53] The vogue of Mill and Spencer was popularized in Poona by Professor Selby, the agnostic champion of the younger teachers who were replacing Wordsworth's generation.

On May 11, 1885, Ranade attended a debate at Deccan College whose topic was whether morality necessitates a religious underpinning. When Mill and Spencer were invoked to show that the older beliefs of natural theology were unnecessary and unscientific, Ranade became visibly upset and turned on Tilak and the other young educators. He questioned the worth of Christian thinkers whose works produced a decline of religious belief; in contrast, he praised the Aryan philosophers of India for their metaphysical depth and religious confidence. Under attack himself from the orthodox as an atheist reformer, Ranade accused Tilak, Agarkar and others of treading of religious and moral traditions. Tilak responded by asserting that although Ranade was the greatest man in Poona, he had no right to denigrate the mightiest minds of the age. More concerned as yet with education than with religion, Tilak eagerly defended the rationalist social thinkers whom he revered. Remarking on Ranade's rare loss of composure, in its next issue Kesari impiously suggested, "If India had been independent and if Madhavraoji [Ranade] had been the Pope, we think he would have started the crusades."[54] All of this might have signified little in itself had it not soon become closely intertwined with hotly controversial social and political issues.

But Ranade linked piety with politics the moment he first responded to Malabari's crusade to raise the age of consent in 1884. Even before he was certain that legislation could be beneficial, Ranade knew that social improvement necessitated prior religious determination. "It is only a religious revival that can furnish sufficient strength to work out the complex social problems which demand our attention. Mere considerations of expediency or economical calculations of gains or losses, can never nerve a community to undertake and carry through social reforms --especially a community like ours, so spellbound by custom and authority."[55] His dilemma was that most men considered themselves religious, but they meant many different things by that and derived from it many conflicting lessons concerning public life. All of them ultimately brought their religious commitments to bear on the age of consent struggle. In the process Ranade's public standing was permanently weakened.

The Age of Consent Bill and Mass Movements

Almost as soon as Malabari announced his demand for new legislation two hostile camps emerged. Opposition to government intervention in Hindu religious practices was led by a coalition of Westernized nationalists and conservative shastris. The shastris still could compel the reformers to debate the traditional question, whether any reform of marriage age was acceptable, and on traditional grounds the authority of the Sanskrit texts. In both Bengal and Maharashtra the shastris protested that the Hindu lawbooks commanded that a girl be married before reaching puberty so that at the time of her first menstruation the garbhādhāna or ceremonial impregnation by her husband could take place. If the government were to establish an age limit of twelve, it would be regulating not a social custom but a jealously cherished religious rite. The moral strength of Hinduism seemed at stake.

Ranade was reluctant to engage in a debate on dharmashastra, predicting impatiently that hopeless confusion would result from an exercise in quoting irreconcilable texts.

> The confusion caused by inconsistent Smriti texts and judicial authorities on ancient Hindu Law and custom furnishes the strongest argument for a definite improvement based on ancient lines by way of codification on the subject by the legislature. There is not a custom, however absurd, which cannot be defended by some strong text of ancient law. The usual practice of reconciling texts, intended for different ages and countries, and the loss of the spirit of true criticism, have benumber the power of judgment.[56]

He and the other reformers much preferred to return to the more ancient Vedas so as to demonstrate that they were in fact more orthodox than the shastris. "The Shastris profess veneration for the past, but their allegiance is given not to the venerated Vedic past, but to the more modern transformations represented by the developments of the Puranic period, and owing to a false rule of exegesis, they try to distort the old texts so as to make them fit in with what is hopelessly irreconcilable with them."[57] This was identical with the reformers' approach during the widow-marriage controversy. It was shared by Dayananda Saraswati in the Punjab and by other reformers throughout India. Ranade contended that the Vedic period had been one of social flexibility, and he specifically praised the early period for its liberal attitude toward women's rights. "The Aryan society of the Vedic . . . period presents the institution of marriage in a form which recognized female liberty and the dignity of womanhood in full, very slight traces of which are seen in the existing order of things."[58]

Yet he could not resist the appeal to dharmashastra quotations where they might prove useful. Quoting texts which favored the age of twelve for the marriage of girls, he suggested in 1885 that twelve for girls' and eighteen or twenty for boys' marriage age might well gain consensual support. A year later he mused that consummation of marriage might well be left even to the ages of sixteen and twenty-five, respectively.[59]

The question of a proper marriage age was soon displaced, though, by the question of government interference on behalf of any specific age. In Poona Tilak immediately appeared as the defender of Hinduism against intrusions by an alien, despotic power. In the summer of 1884 he published a detailed defense against outside interference. He opened with a barbed reference to Ranade's second marriage and a plea for more Karsondas Muljis and Vishnu Shastri Pandits, who would bring forth social changes by their own courageous example.[60] This point was central for the moral fiber of society: men like Ranade who failed to embody their marriage ideals had no right to lead society. Furthermore, the reformers' claim to speak for the public was invalid, since the great majority of Hindus did not even understand Ranade's position, much less sympathize with him. The population as a whole was in no way prepared for reform. "They are in the fullest conviction that when they marry their children at an early age, they perform one of their solemn duties, enjoined by custom and by religion; and that there could arise no evil from such performances."[61]

Tilak was shrewdly exploiting his awareness of the increasing gap between the elitist politics of the Moderates and the weakness of Moderate politics, its distance from the very masses for whom it putatively spoke. But this was more than simply a strategy of conflict: at the same time Tilak was becoming aware that without a mass basis, Congress could never increase its effective political power beyond a token minimum. And if the populace associated Congress exclusively with the social liberals, its support would never be forthcoming. Thus he agreed with prevailing opinion in the Congress that social reform should not be allowed to influence political priorities. With this in mind he regularly attended the Social Conference in its early years so as to counteract the militant reformers. Shortly before the conference of 1888 he warned that the conference must proceed slowly in its reforms or it would precipitate united opposition to both its work and that of the Congress. He suggested that "the National Congress is fighting for reform of a moderate kind--for an improvement in what already exists. Let us be equally moderate in social reform and we are sure to get many men to go along with us."[62]

Ranade had already attempted to reassure Tilak with a reference to Herbert Spencer, over whose religious views they had quarrelled a year before at Deccan College. Both men were agreed on the conservative implications of Spencer's evolutionary social thought, and, calling Spencer "the great living philosopher of the age," Ranade interpreted him as showing that social evolution must be gradual. "For the carrying on of social life, the old must continue so long as the new is not ready, this perpetual compromise is an indispensable accompaniment of a normal development."[63]

Tilak was not to be placated, for he never shared Ranade's instinct for mediation, and he sensed by now the possibility of massive popular support for his position. The resulting polarization appeared first within the ranks of the Deccan Education Society, when Agarkar publicly declared his support for legislation. The members of the society became embroiled in the conflict and almost unanimously opposed Agarkar. While some favored voluntary change, most professed total orthodoxy and opposed any change in marriage practices, even voluntary. Tilak soon found himself leading the orthodox forces as well as those who preferred voluntary reform.

In 1886, when Ranade's protégé Gokhale joined the Life Members, he added important strength to the Agarkar camp, and helped to precipitate a struggle over control of the society. The issue which finally split the society was its original principle that the members should not engage in non-academic work. The newspapers Kesari and Mahratta were originally begun as one expression of national education, but with the founding of Fergusson College, it became difficult to pursue the newspaper work within the society. The newspapers were sold in 1886, but both Tilak and Agarkar continued to write for Kesari. The conflict between the two over the marriage age of girls became so bitter that in October 1887 Agarkar resigned from Kesari and founded his own newspaper, Sudhārak (The Reformer). Gokhale for his part continued outside work in violation of the strict principle of the society. Tilak protested when Gokhale accepted the post of secretary of the Sarvajanik Sabha in July 1890 to work more closely under Ranade. In the Life Members' meeting of the Deccan Education Society that October, Tilak forced a majority vote which censured Gokhale's work with the sabha. Thereupon, Agarkar proposed similar motions against himself, Tilak, M. B. Namjoshi, and Principal Apte for their outside work; these were likewise passed. The factional conflict between reformers and orthodox clearly underlay this competition. Tilak decided to resign from the society, despite majority support in the Deccan Education Society for the social issues which he was pursuing in Kesari.[64] He was now fully independent and prepared to build a personal following on the basis of Age of Consent antagonisms.

The conflict in Poona was intensified by the growing success of Malabari's efforts to gain signatures throughout India on petitions favoring the Age of Consent revision. He carried his crusade simultaneously to England, where he rallied the support of many of the most powerful figures in the country. In 1888 his forces adopted a new tactic. One of Ranade's close associates in the administrative work of the Social Conference was Malabari's friend and biographer, Dayaram Gidumal. It was Gidumal who proposed that the marriage age be changed by a simple revision of the penal code making twelve, not ten, the minimal legal age for consummation.[65] Gidumal, a judge like Ranade, saw this tactic as a means of limiting the field of argument to a legal technicality and accomplishing the desired reform by sidestepping the orthodox opposition. In 1889 the government took note of Gidumal's suggestion and began informally to reconsider the question of legislation. In support, Ranade proposed a resolution drafted by Gidumal at the Social Conference of December 1889, which encouraged both government action and private efforts simultaneously. It stated that "cohabitation before the wife is twelve years old should be punishable as a criminal offence, and that every effort should be made by awakening public conscience to the grave dangers incurred to postpone the completion of marriage till the age of fourteen at least."[66]

As Malabari's position gained adherents, Tilak broadened his opposition to legislation. In an attempt to gain allies among the cautious reformers he briefly joined Ranade's friends in August 1890, circulating an ambiguously worded petition which declared that girls should not be married until the age of ten to fourteen, boys should not be married before the age of sixteen or more, and that marriage expenses should be strictly curtailed.[67] Tilak also maintained personal pressure on Ranade, appealing to Ranade's latent wariness of government intervention. Tilak's associate, G. V. Kanitkar, wrote to Ranade opposing legislation on the basis of Mill's principle that government should never interfere where individuals could work more effectively, a principle which Ranade had invoked in other contexts. Ranade replied that in this case the principle did not apply, for "society with us has not passed through the stage of authority and command."

> The individual is not as strong to help himself and others [as in Europe]. . . . We are not barbarians certainly, but we are priest-ridden--we are caste-ridden. Authority is supreme in settling the smallest details of our life in all departments. In such a state of society the expectation that each individual will possess sufficient independence to work out his destiny by the higher law within us is of course anticipating events by decades. In the meanwhile we cannot afford to wait. The fringe of society may be able to help itself, but it is, after all, a fringe--and the mass is inert and spell-bound.[68]

Whatever Ranade's theoretical musings, Tilak had gained the initiative in Maharashtra. Throughout the second half of 1890 he attacked Malabari, paving the way for the first mass meeting in Poona against the bill, on October 26. In a speech that day, shortly after his resignation from the Deccan Education Society, Tilak warned that the people would not accept any reform in which they could not follow their social leaders, and he proposed that no legal change be accepted which did not conform to popular practice.[69]

Faced with virulent opposition to the bill, Ranade began to waver in his support of legislation. For him the bill's primary function was to provide a clear standard for the public to emulate; its educational function would be vitiated if it stimulated opposition to all reforms. He wrote to Telang and Nulkar at one point, suggesting that perhaps the law should honor orthodox sentiment by making puberty the legal minimum; even that would be a step forward from the retrograde limit of age ten. Yet this would have vitiated the principle of the bill, which was to establish moral rather than traditional grounds for marriage age. Chandavarkar later commented sadly that Ranade's "spirit of toleration led him at times to make weak compromises which jeopardised principle."[70]

Ranade attended the Social Conference in Calcutta that year and was impressed again by the force of opposition in Bengal. Despite the fact that the Age of Consent was the single dominant issue, Ranade still maintained that the chief function of the conference was not to join partisan conflicts but to organize and educate public opinion. He had wanted the conference to mobilize a broad coalition of reformers, both radical and cautious, but this issue had accomplished precisely the opposite, splitting high caste society into hostile camps and dangerously isolating the reformers. He had also come to believe that his enthusiasm had overreached the limits of the conference's prerogative, for the conference had been pledged from the first to avoid partisan political issues. Hence this year he staged a strategic retreat by asserting that public opinion was already formed and that a bill was shortly to be introduced in the imperial council; therefore it would be improper for the conference agenda to include a resolution on the subject. The strongest resolution which could pass against Ranade's determination to conciliate the opposition was one calling for members of social reform associations to postpone marriages; it added the weakening clause, "as far as possible." Tilak was present and became angered at this new expression of the reformers' equivocation in their standards for themselves. He forced the conference to omit the clause.[71]

But by this time the reformers were within sight of nominal victory. They still controlled the voluntary associations which for two decades had conveyed their views to sympathetic ears within the government. Malabari's campaign had produced great pressure favoring the bill, while Gidumal's suggestion had narrowed the proposed change to what seemed a minor revision of the penal code. It only remained to rally enough fervor within the English community and among the Hindu reformers in order to repeat the success of the Karsondas Mulji campaign of 1863. Public opinion in Bombay had been deeply influenced by the Rakhmabai case. Calcutta then responded in a wave of moral outrage in 1890 when news became public that a ten-year-old Hindu bride named Phulmoni Bai had died after forceable intercourse with her thirty-five-year-old husband, Hari Maiti.[72]

A majority of the imperial legislative council were committed to action when Sir Andrew Scoble formally introduced a bill in January 1891 to raise the minimum age of marriage to twelve years. They had decided that the demands of common morality in this case overruled the government's pledge not to interfere with Hindu religious customs. Lord Lansdowne, the viceroy, summarized the council's opinion when the bill was passed on March 19 by stating that "In all cases where demands preferred in the name of religion would lead to practices inconsistent with individual safety and the public peace, and condemned by every system of law and morality in the world, it is religion, and not morality, which must give way."[73]

The victory was bought at a dangerously high price for the reformers, however. In Poona, Tilak was losing a battle but gaining a strategic advantage. He could not boast the reformers' access to government circles, but he was developing an alternate strategy of cutting the reformers off from popular support. From January to April 1891 he published a stream of articles in <u>Kesari</u> opposing the bill in the sharpest terms. He charged bitterly that the proponents of the bill had "ceased to be Hindus," and were "high-paid Government servants only, . . . traitors to their government and their country."[74] Patriotism had become the overriding issue in the public debate, after a decade of tentative probings.

Tilak and the orthodox also joined forces to organize mass meetings. The first was held at Madhav Bag in Bombay, attracting ten thousand people in support of a resolution against the bill. Then on February 15 a meeting in Poona gained twenty-five hundred signatures on a similar petition. Tilak was joined in Poona by leaders of the orthodox party, including Ganesh Shastri Mavlankar, who had been the defendant in the widow-marriage trial twenty years before, and Balasaheb Natu, who was to lead the orthodox in the 1890's.[75]

Attempting to counter these developments, Bhandarkar and the Sarvajanik Sabha organized a meeting in Poona on March 1 which was intended to rally supporters of the bill. Tilak attended, resolved to propose amendments to the resolution which would nullify its intent. Many opponents of the bill followed him and attempted to enter the courtyard where the meeting was held. As the threat of a riot grew, Tilak retired to a nearby building and claimed no connection with the proceedings when police pleaded with him to calm the orthodox crowd.[76] The meeting ended in total confusion, with bitterness rising on both sides.

Throughout these months Ranade was remote from the conflict in Poona. After the Calcutta conference he gladly withdrew from a controversy which he had found increasingly distasteful. He was scheduled to tour the Sholapur and Ahmedabad districts on a survey for the Deccan Agriculturists' Relief Act, thus removing him temporarily from the Age of Consent controversy. This was fortuitous, for his compromise in Calcutta had left him unable to work decisively for either side. He was planning to arrive in Poona in late February, which would have brought him into the midst of the fray, but just before his return he contracted near-fatal cholera.[77] For the ensuing two months he was absent from public life; he thus avoided the publicity which Gokhale, Bhandarkar, and other reformers suffered. This served him well in the struggles of the 1890's, for he preserved his reputation for being above partisan fighting. The most virulent criticisms from the orthodox were left for his subordinates.

It was G. K. Gokhale above all who began to bear the brunt of the orthodox attacks, for he was emerging as Ranade's closest lieutenant among the younger man. As secretary of the Sarvajanik Sabha he was intimately involved in organizing the reformers' campaign to support the Age of Consent bill, but he was by nature introspective and fastidious, repelled by the turbulence of crowds. He was depressed at the conflict within the Deccan Education Society and disgusted by the demagogy and strife of the March 1 meeting. On March 3 he wrote to Ganesh Yankatesh Joshi, the rising economist of the Sarvajanik Sabha:

> The conduct of "leading men" of Poona, which culminated in the disgraceful rowdyism of Wednesday last has fairly sickened me. It has exercised a deciding influence on my wavering mind, and I am now most exceedingly anxious to be relieved of the necessity of keeping up any kind of connection with them. I have found that their attitude towards the Sabha is of a piece with that elsewhere. None of them would care to do the least work for the Sabha. Almost everyone of them would find fault with the work done by others, and what is worse, obstruct that work as much as possible. I am longing for the time when I shall have nothing to do directly with those people.[78]

Gokhale yearned to retire from political life and return to full-time teaching at Fergusson College, but his departure would have seriously weakened the Sarvajanik Sabha and the reform party. Ranade intervened and dissuaded him from withdrawing, since Ranade's health was still dangerously affected and he relied on his protégé's energy more than ever.

Tilak was still not silenced, for the popular response to his campaign had been heightened by the frustrated realization that their voice had been ignored by the government and its supporters. Tilak had begun to explore the notion that the Hindu people could protect their social, religious and political interests only through a political movement so broad that the government must necessarily listen. On March 22 he called for a "grand central organization," based on "self-preservation, self-protection, and self-support," to counteract the reformers' activities in England. He claimed that "we have been mischievously and shamelessly represented as a nation of savages and the sudharaks [reformers] have shamelessly testified to it. Let these sudharaks therefore form themselves into a separate nationality. . . . We ought no longer to allow to be amongst us those of our fellow-countrymen who are really our enemies but who pose as our friends. The time has come when we should divide."[79]

The organization did not materialize for another four years, but the groundwork was laid through the merging of social and political conflicts, which was precisely what the Congress had tried to avoid. Political unity was thus endangered, for the social reformers now faced the accusation that their attempts at modernization were a threat to Hindu civilization itself. As these charges drew increasing support in the early 1890's, Ranade and his associates became the chief targets. It would soon be abundantly clear that they had only the most fragile mass following and therefore stood at a crucial disadvantage with the radicals.

Notes

¹Dayaram Gidumal, Behramji M. Malabari (Bombay, 1888), p. 18, quotes census figures for 1881 as stating that in Bengal some 14 percent of girls under ten years of age were married. In Bombay the figure was 10 percent, somewhat lower.

²Heimsath, Indian Nationalism, p. 161.

³Mahratta, May 22, 1881, p. 2.

⁴Mahratta, May 29, 1881, p. 1.

⁵The Notes were reprinted in Government of India, Home Department, Selections from the Records, No. CCXXIII, Serial No. 3. Heimsath, Indian Nationalism, p. 152, gives a fuller analysis of the contents.

⁶Quoted in Gidumal, Malabari, pp. 191-192.

⁷Metcalf, Aftermath, pp. 26-27; Heimsath, Indian Nationalism, p. 75.

⁸Report of the Maharaj Libel Case (Bombay, 1862), pp. 202ff.; B. N. Motiwala, Karsondas Mulji (Bombay, 1936), pp. 36ff.

⁹Maharaj Libel Case, p. 234.

¹⁰Gidumal, Malabari, p. cxii.

¹¹Quoted in Mahratta, August 31, 1884, pp. 3-4.

¹²Dayaram Gidumal, The Status of Woman in India (Bombay, 1889), pp. 91-92.

¹³Ibid., p. 94.

¹⁴Chandavarkar, Speeches and Writings, pp. 40-41.

¹⁵Malabari, who led the fight in Bombay and elsewhere in India, was disqualified as a Parsi from leadership in Poona. He was delighted to have Ranade accept that position: "Mr. Ranade . . . is perhaps the ablest Native judicial officer in India; few know as I do what marvelous sagacity and acumen that man possesses." Gidumal, Malabari, p. 192.

¹⁶M. G. Ranade, "State Interference in Social Matters," RSR, pp. 92ff.

¹⁷Ibid., pp. 105-106.

¹⁸Kellock, Ranade, pp. 86-87.

¹⁹[Dadaji Bhikaji], An Exposition of Some of the Facts of the Case of Dadaji vs. Rakhmabai (Bombay, 1887), p. 2.

²⁰Kelkar, Tilak, I, 188.

²¹The full membership is given in Government of India, Home Department, Judicial Proceedings, September 1887, No. 298.

²²Rakhmabai's cause coincided with Ranade's campaign to defend the property rights of women. The dominant tradition of Hindu law in Maharashtra held that women could not hold property except through the men of their families. Considering this a cruel abrogation of women's rights, Ranade joined the campaign to provide legal guarantees for women's rights. In 1885 he argued before the Bombay Legislative Council on the question of vatandars that women should be eligible to inherit vatan rights. He attested that "daughters, sisters, and their sons are not such remote and strange heirs as some appear to imagine. . . . To a childless Hindu, the existence of a daughter or her son is a source of consolation. . . . His affection for them, and their dependence on him, are as strong and legitimate as in the case of male heirs." Ranade, "Hereditary Officers," pp. 24-26. Ranade, who had one daughter and no sons, expressed an element of his own interests in this statement; it suggests an important reason for his willingness to defend Rakhmabai against the majority of his community.

²³Mahratta, May 29, 1887, pp. 2-3.

[24] Kesari, June 7, 1887; March 29, 1887.

[25] See Heimsath, Indian Nationalism, p. 152.

[26] Reported in Sahyādrī, December 1885; reprinted in SMHFM, II, 5-6.

[27] Report of the Proceedings of the Indian National Congress of 1886, p. 3.

[28] SMHFM, II, 35-36.

[29] K. T. Telang, Select Writings and Speeches (Bombay, 1916, 1930), I, 287-288.

[30] Quoted in Banerjee, Indian Constitutional Documents, II, 91-92.

[31] Heimsath, Indian Nationalism, p. 190.

[32] MW, p. 116.

[33] The organization of the conference was exemplified in 1893 when Ranade held a preliminary meeting of the leading social reformers during the Congress meetings. Ranade read the reports of the social reform associations for the year; then the small group present mutually decided the agenda for the conference. Report of the Seventh Social Conference (Lahore, 1893), pp. 3-4.

[34] Gidumal, Malabari, pp. 222-224.

[35] See the annual reports of the Social Conference; see also Dobbin, Urban Leadership, ch. x, for rapid concurrent developments in Bombay.

[36] MW, pp. 164-165.

[37] MW, pp. 95-96, 128, 135-136.

[38] MW, p. 102.

[39] MW, p. 128.

[40] MW, pp. 87-88.

[41] MW, pp. 111-112.

[42] MW, pp. 114-116.

[43] Sir Stanley Reed, "My First Year in India," Times of India Annual, 1925.

[44] MW, pp. 110-111.

[45] Agashe, Third Anniversary, p. 10.

[46] Ramabai Ranade, Reminiscences, pp. 157, 172.

[47] As early as 1877, when the Subodh Patrika, the newspaper of the Prarthana Samaj, initiated English-language columns, it announced that rather than pursue political questions it would concentrate on social and religious revival. "There are so many grave shortcomings in the society to which we belong, so many moral drawbacks to the progress of our young men, such utter indifference to religion, . . . that we shall best satisfy our own feelings, if we assign to ourselves the humble duty of being serviceable in this new sphere," December 2, 1877, p. 1.

[48] In 1898 the Theistic Conference actually met in Ranade's home, although this was a sign of its declining strength. By then its numbers were dwindling, as annual conferences had not proved the most effective way of encouraging spiritual fervor. Shinde, Theistic Directory, pp. 43-46.

[49] Ramabai Ranade, Reminiscences, p. 109.

[50] Letter to Bombay Government, May 5, 1888, in Private Papers, IV, 124-125.

[51] Mahratta, June 1, 1884, p. 1.

[52] Mahratta, May 17, 1885; Kesari, June 6, 1885.

[53] McDonald, "Social Change," p. 469.

[54] Mahratta, May 17, 1885; Kesari, May 12, 1885; Altekar, Agarkar, pp. 126ff.

⁵⁵Gidumal, Status of Women, pp. 120-121.

⁵⁶M. G. Ranade, "State Interference in Social Matters," RSR, pp. 109-110.

⁵⁷M. G. Ranade, "The Sutra and Smriti Dicta on the Age of the Hindu Marriage," RSR, p. 28. This article was revised from an earlier draft, published in 1885 as the introduction to A Collection Containing the Proceedings which Led to the Passing of Act XV of 1856, ed. N. K. Vaidya (Bombay, 1885). The earlier version discussed the historical rise and fall of women's rights and the libertarian arguments for and against state action in greater detail than the later version.

⁵⁸Ibid., p. 29.

⁵⁹Ibid., p. 49.

⁶⁰Mahratta, August 8, 1884.

⁶¹Mahratta, December 14, 1884, pp. 1-2.

⁶²Mahratta, December 23, 1888, p. 3.

⁶³Mahratta, December 11, 1887, pp. 5-7.

⁶⁴Pradhan and Bhagwat, Tilak, pp. 41-48.

⁶⁵Heimsath, Indian Nationalism, p. 161.

⁶⁶Chintamani, Indian Social Reform, Part II, p. 6.

⁶⁷SMHFM, II, 201; Stanley A. Wolpert, Tilak and Gokhale (Berkeley, 1962), pp. 61-62.

⁶⁸Letter of February 2, 1890, in Mankar, Ranade, II, 212-214.

⁶⁹Kelkar, Tilak, I, 191-193.

⁷⁰Chandavarkar, Speeches and Writings, p. 350.

⁷¹M. G. Ranade, speech at fourth Social Conference, Calcutta, 1890, in Chintamani, Indian Social Reform, Part I, pp. 16-17; Heimsath, Indian Nationalism, pp. 167-168.

⁷²Wolpert, Tilak and Gokhale, pp. 50-54.

⁷³See Heimsath, Indian Nationalism, pp. 170-173.

⁷⁴Mahratta, March 15, 1891, p. 2.

⁷⁵Mahratta, February 22, 1891, pp. 2-3.

⁷⁶Kelkar, Tilak, I, 196-199; Wolpert, Tilak and Gokhale, pp. 56-57.

⁷⁷Ramabai Ranade, Reminiscences, pp. 180-192.

⁷⁸Gokhale to G. V. Joshi, March 3, 1891, Gokhale Papers, V, 203/270.

⁷⁹Mahratta, March 22, 1891, p. 3.

Chapter 8

THE CRISIS OF THE MODERATES, 1891-1897

> There is something in the race
> which is unequal to the strain
> of sustained exertion. --Ranade

After 1890 Ranade faced growing harassment of his effort to harmonize all aspects of national development. His ability to coordinate the whole range of public life was becoming a thing of the past, as younger men organized alternative programs to challenge him. The Moderates were becoming one organized faction in the social and political conflicts of Maharashtra, conserving its influence against that of others. As the decade wore on, Ranade found himself vacillating between leadership of the Moderate school and mediation among contending factions. The complexities of his situation developed through three interlocking conflicts: the antagonism between radical social reformers and militant orthodox Hindus, the growing communal tension between Hindus and Muslims, and most absorbing of all to participants, the intensifying hostility between Hindu nationalists and the British Raj.

Ranade had always found the role of mediator congenial, but as the 1890's progressed he found himself more frequently than ever on middle ground, under fire from all sides. In political and social conflicts his efforts to mitigate the destructive passions of the times were increasingly unsuccessful. But he did manage with considerable success to insulate the more specialized dimensions of his work from the turbulence of the market place. His efforts to maintain cooperation between British and Indians for economic and administrative development were only peripherally influenced by the evolving power struggle in Poona.

Economic Development

Many of Ranade's campaigns for reform and development took the form of concentrated efforts lasting three to five years each; this was one method by which he achieved over a forty-year career the notable breadth of his work. This was nowhere clearer than in the field of economic development, where he concentrated his planning efforts during the early 1890's. A decade earlier his numerous articles on the social and economic modernization of rural life had established his long-range strategy of development. As the 1880's wore on he could show little solid achievement either in rural capital development or in urban industrialization; during the late 1880's there was a virtual hiatus in his economic writings, as he concentrated his attention on political and social reform movements. After 1890 he turned once again both to publicizing and to organizing industrialization.

In a series of articles and speeches on economic affairs from 1891 to 1893, Ranade illustrated the need to mobilize all available assistance, whether British or Indian, in order to alleviate India's chronic economic stagnation. Even a decade earlier he had been a critic of laissez-faire economics, at a time when non-interference in the economy was a principle almost universally shared by British administrators. At the time, Ranade's attack had been pragmatic and piecemeal, but by 1892 he constructed a more general basis in his best-known essay, "Indian Political Economy." Taking his cue from the schools of national economics which had grown up in continental Europe and the United States since the 1870's, Ranade attempted to demonstrate that whatever the abstract virtues of classical economics, in practice these theories applied at best only to the special historical circumstances of recent England.[1] In the very different situation obtaining in India, social conditions precluded the functioning of an English-style economy. In India men did not act solely on the basis of individual economic interest, capital and labor were not free to gravitate to the place of maximum profit, and the mechanisms of a competitive market were not free to work efficiently. Beyond this Ranade questioned whether the welfare of the individual entrepreneur should be considered the great goal of society, at the expense of social welfare and political strength. The moral objection to unfettered capitalism was clearer in his mind by now.

In place of political economy Ranade called for a return to pragmatic solutions of India's economic difficulties. He was at heart not a theorist so much as a reformer; his sorties into the realm of theory were meant to clear away obstacles to action. By this time there were increasing signs that the pragmatists were gaining adherents among his English contemporaries as well. In the administrative reforms of the Deccan Agriculturists' Relief Act the pragmatic approach was demonstrating its effectiveness within the limited scope of its ambitions. Conversely, the chronic lack of agricultural capital, which the act was not designed to alleviate, remained a pressing difficulty. Ranade, Wedderburn and others had failed to convince the government of the need for agricultural banks in the early 1880's, but the issue had never lapsed entirely. Interest within the government revived slowly in the early 1890's; Ranade returned to the attack in 1891 with a new demand that the government actively provide the credit for agricultural loans which otherwise could only come from local moneylenders. Consistent with his attacks on the theory of classical economics, he marshalled a broad array of precedents from European and American economics to demonstrate the vivifying influence of government banks for agricultural development.[2] Here was an area in which private capital, however abundant, could not possibly organize on the scale needed; government intervention seemed essential. Nor would this development in any way constitute an intrusion on cherished Hindu social practices; it would not precipitate popular hostility in the way the Age of Consent act had. Ranade was never to see the fruits of his effort, for it was three years after his death that the government passed the Indian Cooperative Societies Act of 1904, in which some of his proposals appeared as law.[3]

There was no need to wait, however, for a cautious government to act in the complementary field of industrial development. As early as his famine report of 1878 Ranade had indicated that industrial development was a potential solution for rural poverty and overpopulation. Had industry been stronger then in the Deccan, private resources for famine relief would have been more adequate to the need.[4] In 1878 his view had been linked to support of Dadabhai Naoroji's Drain theory, which condemned the British for extracting vast resources from the Indian economy to finance the Raj. Although Ranade continued to subscribe to Dadabhai's views, by 1890 he was wary about some of Dadabhai's followers, who used the Drain theory in a doctrinaire way to excuse their own inaction. To Ranade, India's economic stagnation had always seemed to have a moral dimension: the lethargy of the Indian people. It was on these grounds that he criticized the Drain theory now. Too many were using the notion that India was losing its wealth to England as both a political weapon and an excuse for taking no initiative themselves. He now suggested that Indians leave the debate over the Drain to the politicians and address themselves to active industrial development.[5] He had reached a tacit and amicable parting of the ways with Dadabhai: the political defense could be safely left in Dadabhai's hands, while Ranade pursued constructive work.

Ranade's main line of action was his role in the founding of the Industrial Conference of Western India in 1891. In 1889 Lord Dufferin had suggested that the Congress initiate industrial development,[6] but the Congress had already chosen to limit its field of action to issues of direct political import. The disinterest of the Congress notwithstanding, there was already a beginning of industrial development around Poona. For some years Ranade and Namjoshi had actively encouraged both English and Indian capitalists to found small-scale industries there. But by 1890 there was growing criticism from the Tilak camp against Anglo-Indian cooperation. The swadeshi movement, which Ranade had helped to organize in the 1870's, was now fueled by the nationalist assumption that India must accomplish its own industrial development without outside help or interference.

This anti-British view could become politically explosive, interfering with the pace of industrialization. The Industrial Conference was designed to counteract this trend, and in the early 1890's its spokesmen were both Indian and British.[7] S. Beauclerk, president of the first annual conference, made it clear that politically sensitive questions such as the Drain debate and the swadeshi movement were to be excluded from the conference agenda as the price of English participation.[8]

Ranade concurred; to him Indian self-help was essential, but not to the exclusion of productive forces from outside. In his speech to the first conference he expressed a fear of entangling economics with politics, in a statement reminiscent of several of his Social Conference speeches. "The programme of the Congress gatherings is avowedly Political. Here we eschew Politics altogether, for there is really no conflict of interests between the Rulers and the Ruled, who all alike desire to promote the Industrial and Economic Progress. . . . Here, on the Economical platform, all shades of opinion, all differences of views on Social, Political, and Religious subjects, may unite and co-operate."[9]

Ranade, always careful to touch both sides of an issue, warned his audience that cooperating with English entrepreneurs and soliciting the aid of the government were strictly secondary. The basic work must be accomplished by Indians themselves, for without this India would remain in the familiar stagnation in which foreigners dominated the Indian economy by virtue of their greater energy and skills.[10] In other words, the swadeshi campaign too had both its strengths and its excesses; Ranade refused to take an anti-nationalist position as he had over the Age of Consent, for Tilak and Namjoshi were now leading the swadeshi forces.[11] It was a considerable achievement to maintain contact in the field of economic development while simultaneously the two sides were being pulled further apart over social issues.

The Orthodox Counterattack

Ranade's efforts to maintain influence among the political nationalists and socially orthodox of Poona, which had been severely disrupted over the Age of Consent, were renewed in 1891 when he began his retreat from reliance on the government in social matters. He believed himself to be as patriotic as any Indian, but there were treacherous political implications to his working principle of cooperation between Indians and Englishmen. Hence he redoubled his efforts to work with the conservative forces in society, although these efforts were doomed to increasing frustration. Echoing the call of Tilak and his friends, Ranade began to place renewed emphasis on self-help as the path to social regeneration. His conciliatory moves shortly before the passage of the Age of Consent Bill were followed by other moves in the Social Conference, where he had never taken a militantly liberal position. In the conference of December 1891, Ranade noted the campaign to gain voluntary pledges against infant marriages and ill-assorted marriages, which he and Tilak had both joined in Poona in the summer of 1890.[12] Three years later, although he praised social legislation in British India and the Native States, he emphasized that "the work of social reform cannot be an act of state. It is chiefly valuable when it is the work of the people."[13] Reminding his listeners that legislation was useless unless it was implemented by dedicated workers, Ranade pointed out as exemplary the work of caste and voluntary associations in India. It was in such groups that Ranade now professed to see the great hope for a revivified India.

Sensing that his position in Indian circles had been compromised, Ranade made new efforts after 1890 on other fronts to regain the confidence of the Hindu community. One opportunity came when a Christian evangelist, Dr. Pentecost, gave a series of fifteen lectures in Poona in September 1891. The missionary attempted to demonstrate that belief in Christianity was both a necessity for eternal salvation and the most serviceable religion for this life. Ranade attended the lectures and gave summary remarks at the end. Attempting to counteract the partisan ardor of the speaker, Ranade gave a historical survey of the contributions to civilization made by Greece, Rome, Judaism, Christianity, Islam, Buddhism and Hinduism. He ended with a defense of Hinduism, expressing the hope that in a purified form it would prove worthy of becoming the future universal religion.[14] The theme of Hinduism as the coming world religion was by this time a common refrain from Bengal to Maharashtra, so that Ranade's defense of Hinduism on the platform of the religious opponent gained enthusiastic support in the Poona newspapers.

At the same time, Ranade pursued his association with the missionaries, primarily in the interests of his educational work. He and Ramabai had maintained these contacts from the time her own education began, and it was taken for granted that they would lend their presence to prize-giving ceremonies and other functions at the schools. On October 14, 1890, they attended a function at the Panch Howd Mission, the Anglican missionary center in Poona, with some seventy men and a few ladies. The usual round of essays and speeches was followed by a social hour at which the sisters of the mission served tea and biscuits. Some guests drank the tea but others merely accepted it, drinking none because of their caste's dietary restrictions.[15] Unfortunately, the event coincided with the height of the Age of Consent controversy. Unlike similar previous teas, which the public had rarely noticed, this event became a cause célèbre in the Brahmin community of Poona, raging for a year and a half.

The first public reaction came six months after the tea, when a detailed account appeared in the Marathi newspaper, Pune Vaibhava (The Glory of Poona). The article charged that those who attended had broken caste regulations and should therefore be ostracized until they did proper penance.[16] The author of the article was Gopal Vinayak Joshi, a man of some notoriety in Poona. Once converted to Christianity and then reconverted to Hinduism, Joshi had become a gadfly in Poona.[17] A few years previously he and a few friends had ridiculed their political opponents by dressing a donkey in clothes and parading it through the streets of the city.[18] As the sensationalist editor of Pune Vaibhava, Joshi was known for his capricious and vituperative attacks on public figures. In the article on the tea-drinkers he asked rhetorically: "How can the people of Poona tolerate the fact that these [public leaders] drank to their hearts' content tea served by the fair and tender hands of the nuns but actually prepared by low born Mahars! Is it because these people are high officials? Or do the priests keep quiet because they look forward to a dozen rich feasts in the year and plenty of dakshina from these people?"[19]

Sensing that Joshi's article could provide a rallying point for the orthodox against the reformers, Tilak's associate, Balasaheb Natu, urged that those who did not deny the charges should be ostracized. Proceedings began much as they had twenty years before in the widow-marriage affair. Public meetings of the orthodox declared forty-two outcasted. Before long both sides called on the Shankaracharya to adjudicate the dispute, each side hoping to gain his support. He soon discovered that there were different categories of offenders. The first group had not sipped tea and were dismissed by the inquiry. A second group had taken tea but shortly afterward applied to the Shankaracharya, willing to do prayaścitta (ritual penance) so as to be readmitted to caste. This group included Tilak, who openly admitted having drunk tea. Finding himself unexpectedly linked with the reformers under orthodox attack, Tilak agreed to journey to Benares to do penance. The orthodox leaders had been excoriating Tilak as well as the other reformers, but his expiation ended their attacks on him.[20]

The core of the controversy concerned a third group: those who did not deny their offense but refused to do penance. This group included Ranade, who was long accustomed to social ostracism. Although Ranade had not drunk the tea, he refused to desert his friends, on the grounds that reformers must stand together in mutual defense. When the outcasting was generally accepted and many people refused to deal with the Ranades, he was better prepared than he had been at the time he was first ostracized in 1870. He was now supporting four Brahmin priests who were willing to carry on the necessary family ceremonies for the outcasted families. For twenty months he and a few friends refused to submit to penalties in which they did not believe. Hence the isolation of their families became steadily more acute. Wives of the reformers could not visit their families, and festive ceremonies were difficult to carry on. In the wedding season of 1892, Ranade's friend Nagarkar[21] returned from Poona to his village to celebrate two weddings in his family. Arriving there, he was prevented from entering his family home or sharing their meals. The family was in turmoil over his adamant refusal to perform prayaścitta. Under pressure from his father to repair family harmony, Nagarkar decided with others to relent if Ranade would join them in penance. As always in crises, Ranade was touched more deeply by family pressures than by his public commitments. Remembering painful crises with his own father over social reforms, Ranade advised Nagarkar, "I would make my father happy despite the disgrace to me."[22] He decided to join the group doing penance, regardless of criticism from the militant reformers. The group resolved that if they could extract a reasonably small penance decree from the Shankaracharya they would perform prayaścitta together. In May 1892 the group applied to him to determine a proper penance. The Shankaracharya imposed a token fine on each of Rs. 11, which they gladly paid, taking this to be a victory for them against the much harsher demands of the orthodox party.[23]

In explanation of the significance of his abrupt change of position, Ranade wrote a long letter to the <u>Bombay Gazette</u>, in which he discussed his view of the issues at stake. Against the charge of cowardice he pointed to the fact that for his remarriage work since 1870 "and for my associating freely with those of my friends who visited Europe, and for my connection with the Prarthana Samaj, I have continued to this day to be regarded as an excommunicated person."[24] He justified the reformers' original appeal to the Shankaracharya by stating that the orthodox attacks against the reformers were so violent and based on such absurd charges that it was imperative to "remove the dispute from the lynch-law tribunals to the regularly-constituted courts . . . the ecclesiastical heads of the community." Ranade revealed the juridical aspect of his view of the matter by claiming that such an appeal was sanctioned by the courts of British India. "The jurisdiction of the Acharya in such caste matters is a recognized fact, and the courts themselves have upheld his decisions in many cases." It was especially important that the Acharya had appointed his shastris and not members of the orthodox faction in Poona to judge the case. Ranade insisted that "the Acharya in this case was not the oppressor or the tyrant he is alleged to be. . . . He was an arbitrator between two factions, one strong in numbers, the other strong in a just cause."[25]

Finally, Ranade believed that the substantive issue at stake between the two sides was trivial; the quarrel was far greater than the Panch Howd tea justified. There were certain questions which to him represented cardinal principles of social reform, including widow marriage. In contrast, drinking tea with Europeans was not worth a major conflict with the orthodox party. He feared that resisting a minimal penalty would simply prolong a pointless and damaging agitation. Using the recognized caste authorities was for Ranade a lesser evil than allowing lawlessness to continue.

Ranade may not have anticipated the vehemence of criticism which now appeared among his erstwhile supporters in the reform camp. Militant reformers saw his action as a desertion of the cause. They were reminded of his marriage to Ramabai years before and of his vacillation in the critical months of the Age of Consent campaign. The <u>Subodh Patrika</u>, organ of the Prarthana Samaj in Bombay, charged that men who themselves would not have yielded to orthodox pressure did so when Ranade repented. It deplored the day of "such utter moral prostration in the country that one of the most highly educated and clear-headed of Hindus occupying a high position, justly respected by all, and the leader of reform for a quarter century, tamely submits to orthodoxy."[26]

On the other hand, Ranade had support from some reformers. One wrote to the <u>Bombay Gazette</u> explaining that the whole furor was an aftereffect of the Age of Consent battle, in which unscrupulous orthodox adherents used a minor incident as a means of totally discrediting the reformers. When most other reformers backed down under the pressure, Ranade's only reasonable course was to join them, for otherwise he and his supporters would have been isolated from society, and their reform movement destroyed.[27] Another letter referred to the penance imposed on Krishna Shastri Chiplunkar in 1870 for eating in a European home. At that time Chiplunkar was compelled to shave his head and pay a fine of Rs. 500 before being readmitted. That the Shankaracharya, under severe pressure from the orthodox, imposed only a token penalty in 1892 was considered a great advance.[28]

Thus, while all of Ranade's efforts had been calculated to preserve unity in the reform camp, his penance had split the reformers' ranks. To the steadfast reformers his actions betrayed his condemnations of the reactionaries during Malabari's crusade, yet to the orthodox party he remained an unrepentant opponent. Ranade's influence over events in Poona was slipping; he was painfully aware of his inability to control the various factions as he once had. On June 5, 1892, he spoke to the city at Hirabag in an effort to explain his position. Poona audiences had long been accustomed to hear Ranade muse introspectively about the meaning of events, but on this occasion he revealed the inner tensions in his life with extraordinary candor. Suggesting that his own turmoil reflected that of Indian society at large, he pointed out the difficulties of acting under the conflict of "two ideals of life, of two civilizations, of two modes of thought, acting upon us forcibly and calling on all to make the choice of alternative courses. . . . Those who surrender themselves to one of these influences have their course of life comparatively smoothed for them. A considerable body amongst us cannot, however, claim this advantage, if indeed it is an advantage at all to do so. We cling to the past, we are drawn to the present. Both have their claims on us, and we seek to re-concile these claims as best we can by not breaking abruptly and finally with either."[29]

Ranade saw the Hindu reactionaries of Poona as one of the threats to this creative tension, for they rejected the politics of dispassionate reason which he espoused. He was especially troubled about the mob turmoil of recent weeks, having come to believe that mass meetings and mass movements endangered progress. Quoting Sir Francis Bacon, one of the seminal intellectual influences of his youth, he warned that the idols of the market place, which inflamed popular passions, were "operative for mischief in their action on large masses of men who take up their notions on imperfect information and hasty generalization, and prescribe tests which are intolerant of all departure from conventional rules and class standards."[30] Unwittingly he allowed a note of hauteur to appear as he warned against the dangers of turmoil.

Ranade's difficulties were inadvertently compounded in 1893 when he further alienated the orthodox through his educational work. Pandita Ramabai, Maharashtra's foremost crusader for women's education, had opened a home for widows in Bombay called the Sharada Sadan. In November 1890 the school moved to Poona, where it caused considerable controversy.[31] Ranade, C. N. Bhat, R. G. Bhandarkar, Lokahitawadi, and K. L. Nulkar, among the foremost reformers of the older generation, were on the board of directors. They provided buildings and funds for the school and worked actively to promote its work with widows. They were not, however, responsible for the education within the school, which many regarded with suspicion. Pandita Ramabai was receiving financial support from Protestant mission groups in Boston, and after a time she admitted to being a Christian convert. Many Hindus feared that she was attempting to proselytize her students. She avowed publicly that although she held Bible study classes, the girls were not required to attend. This did not satisfy the public, because it soon became evident that Ramabai was effectively teaching Christian doctrines to her students under pressure from the mission boards. Ranade, Bhandarkar and Bhat were finally obliged by public pressure to dissociate themselves from the Sharada Sadan. On August 13, 1893, only one year after the end of the Panch Howd controversy, they went through the embarrassment of resigning publicly. They issued a joint statement of explanation to the newspapers:

> Pandita Ramabai has always shown her active missionary tendencies by asking the parents and guardians of the girls to allow them to attend her prayers and, in one case at least, to become Christians themselves, [and] we are assured that two of the girls have declared to their elders that they have accepted Christ. Such a departure from the original understanding cannot fail, in our opinion, to shake the stability of the Institution and alienate the public sympathy from this work. We are sorry our individual remonstrances with the Pandita Bai have proved of no avail. If the Sadan is to be conducted as an avowed proselytizing institution we must disavow all connection with it.[32]

For Ranade this was a demoralizing retreat because Pandita Ramabai had been his chief co-worker in educational reform for over a decade, as well as a close friend of his family. It was discouraging to see barriers placed between him and his friends at the Panch Howd Mission and the Sharada Sadan; a source of support for his beleaguered reform efforts was thereby removed.

As he always had, Ranade faced a challenge by forming a new organization to strengthen his supporters' work. This time it was the Deccan Social Reform Association, founded in 1893. The new association was an outgrowth of earlier voluntary reform organizations. As in the others, membership was voluntary and intercaste; each member pledged to cooperate in the work of marriage reform, women's education, "domestic reform in such customs and manners as are injurious to the society," and intermarriage among those subcastes which dined together. Each member was bound to support the vows made by the association as a whole; any member who broke his pledge was liable to be fined for his infraction. The association was formed a year after the Panch Howd penance and was designed to achieve a collective opposition to the power of the orthodox. The charter stated specifically that "taking prayashchitta or performing any similar religious rites, on account of [following] the pledges agreed to by the member, shall be taken as an admission of the infraction of the pledge, and shall be dealt with accordingly."[33] Ranade approved heartily of this new form of voluntary collective effort, for it was more in tune with modern life than traditional collective groups in Hindu society. He explained to the Social Conference that the new association relied "not so much upon the sanction of caste rules or the religious sense of duty, but upon trust in the honour of members," which was a weaker but more honorable sanction.[34] It was groups such as this which he hoped would ultimately lead the way, however slowly, to an era of liberalism for Hindu society. As he put it in one of his best-known rhetorical flourishes: "The change we should all seek is . . . a change from constraint to freedom, from credulity to faith, from status to contract, from authority to reason, from unorganised to organised life, from bigotry to toleration, from blind fatalism to a sense of human dignity. This is what I understand by social evolution, both for individuals and societies in this country."[35]

Communalism and the Political Struggle

Ranade was aware that his vision judged not only the Hindu factionalism of Poona but also a wider communal conflict of which the tension between liberal and orthodox Hindus was only one expression. The traditionalists' reassertion of the greatness of Hindu civilization was directed at the social reformers and with even more concentrated hostility at the alien government of the British. Ranade opposed this trend, pleading for continued receptivity to influences from the West. In one Social Conference address he interpreted the history of Indian civilization in these terms:

> The history of this great country is but a fairy tale, if it has not illustrated how each invasion from abroad has tended to serve as a discipline of the chosen race and led to the gradual development of the nation to a higher ideal. . . . The nation has never been depressed beyond hope of recovery, but after a temporary submerging under the floods of foreign influences, has reared up its head--absorbing all that is best in the alien civilization and polity and religions.[36]

As the 1890's progressed, it became more and more difficult to isolate any area of public life from inexorably growing tensions. From Bombay there were politically oriented reactions when Ranade agreed to the Panch Howd penance. The socially advanced but politically cautious

Parsis argued that Ranade's penance demonstrated the stranglehold of reactionary casteism, which was using reform politics for its own ends. An article in Rast Goftar called educated Hindus "ultra-radical as politicians, and bigoted reactionaries in social matters. They would have slavery at home and liberty abroad. They would invite and uphold the tyrannical exercise of its power by the caste hierarchy, while they would cry their loudest for political emancipation. It is these glaring inconsistencies in their character that have made us oppose the extravagances of their political pretensions."[37]

The British community echoed similar consternation. The Bombay Gazette expressed its astonishment that "eleven otherwise intelligent and enlightened Brahmin gentlemen have thus placed their neck under the foot of their spiritual leader, [men] whose names we should have expected to find associated with anything rather than so strange a surrender to sacerdotal coercion."[38] Ranade of all men should have resisted the orthodox tyranny, since he represented India's greatest hope for advancement. His intellectual and moral reputation and his professional standing would surely protect him from the petty tyranny of the caste leaders. The writer accused Ranade and C. N. Bhat, another district judge who had submitted with him, of helping to rebuild the barriers of caste and Brahmin supremacy, which were again on the ascendant: "The tyranny of classes or cliques, which seemed to be put out of sight during political discussions . . . is as strong as ever it was. . . . More than ever self-government in this Presidency is a process of government by a dominant caste, that things are arranged so that everything shall work for the greater good of the Brahmins."[39]

The writer's fear of Brahmin tyranny was a mild reflection of the anti-Brahmin sentiment in the British community which answered the resurgence of Hindu orthodoxy. The changing atmosphere was indicated in the governor's office. Lord Reay retired in 1890, having established himself as strongly sympathetic to Indian political ambitions. His successor was Lord Harris, a conservative who soon became unpopular over the politically sensitive question of legislative representation for Indians. The Congress and other political groups had long agitated for broader Indian representation in the legislative councils, especially for the educated class. A parliamentary review of India's constitutional status resulted in the India Councils Act of 1892, which provided that Indian membership in the councils should be increased somewhat. Directives from the viceroy, Lord Lansdowne, made many of the new positions elective. In Bombay the question became that of defining constituencies. Harris, less favorable to Indian political activity than Lansdowne, stated that there should be three representatives of the landed aristocracy, two urban representatives of the trading classes, one member of the Bombay Council, and one representative of Bombay University. As part of the Central Division, Poona would be represented only by the Deccan sardars; there was no hope of direct representation for the Sarvajanik Sabha.[40] The sabha and the Bombay Presidency Association organized meetings protesting the bias against their interests. Harris reacted in a note to Lansdowne, reporting that "those busy bodies, the Poona Sarvajanik Sabha and the Bombay Presidency Association, are very angry. . . . The former has held a meeting (public so-called) and passed an impertinent resolution that we had deliberately evaded the intentions of the Act. I think they will have to be made to retract before any notice is taken of their protests."[41] The controversy simmered until 1895, when the municipalities of the Central Division, including Poona, were given one elected representative.

As yet the communal conflict was only two-sided, involving government and Hindu political interests. But in 1893 the previously latent Hindu-Muslim conflict flared up in Bombay, adding impetus to the three-way communal struggle which ultimately split the subcontinent in half. In this milieu mass political movements soon emerged, shifting the base of political power from the council chamber into the streets. During that summer the worst riots in many years broke out between Muslims and Hindus in various parts of India. There was widespread rioting in the Salem district of Madras, but its impact on Bombay was perhaps less than that of a smaller riot nearer home in Junagad state of Kathiawar. In Bombay the most recent communal trouble had been the 1874 riots between Muslims and Parsis.[42] Hindu-Muslim competition had not yet broken into violence. But within the rise of new industries there, thousands of Muslim Pathans and Hindu Marathas moved to Bombay, working and living in close proximity. On August 11, 1893, rioting broke out between these two groups and continued for four days. Some eighty people were killed, 530 injured, and 1,505 arrested.[43] The riots ended only after Bombay authorities called a joint meeting of Hindu and Muslim leaders and organized a parade of unity in which they marched.[44] The causes were not clearly understood, but Harris placed the blame on the Hindu cow-protection societies, which had been growing over the past few years.[45] Hindu newspapers reacted indignantly. <u>Dnyan Prakash</u> asserted that the government deliberately fomented the riots, pitting one race against another for its own political advantage.[46]

Tilak led the protest in Poona. Enjoying widespread support after the Age of Consent controversy and the Panch Howd affair, Tilak was looking for means to mobilize popular action in political affairs, which he still considered to be the province of a few cautious intellectuals. In the subsequent campaign the depth of his challenge to Ranade, the Moderates, and the political patterns to which they were committed became clearer with every step. On September 10 Tilak addressed a meeting in Poona which was attended by some seven thousand people, the largest public gathering since the Age of Consent protests. He introduced a resolution which denied that the cow-protection movement was in any way responsible for the riots, and called the government guilty of handling communal relations incompetently.[47] He knew at first hand that government officials had reacted with no clear policy to the recent riots in Yeola in Nasik district, and he understood the unpopularity of the special police which Harris had newly established in Bombay.[48] He added shortly in Kesari that Hindus and Muslims could live amicably only if each community asserted its rights boldly and strengthened its own traditions.[49]

Tilak was more interested in strengthening Hindu solidarity than in conciliating either the Muslims or the government. One week after the Poona meeting he sponsored the first modern Ganesh festival. An old Hindu festival honoring the birth of the elephant god Ganesh, or Ganpati, it had been popular in the time of the Peshwas. Under the British it had declined to the status of personal worship in the home. Many Hindus joined the Muslims in their annual celebration of Mohurram when they honored the grandsons of Muhammad by constructing replicas of their tombs and carrying them through the streets of Poona in a gala parade to the river. But now, in 1893, Tilak announced that Hindus should no longer participate in Mohurram but should revive the Ganesh festival with similar festivities and processions. The Ganesh festival was inaugurated in September, drawing many Hindus away from the Muslim festival. There were no riots that year in Poona, and Tilak praised participants for encouraging Hinduism without disturbing Islam. Governor Harris, reluctant to find anti-British sentiment where it did not exist, shared the view that in this form the festivities were not offensive to the Raj.[50] But other British spokesmen raised once again the spectre of a Brahmin conspiracy against British rule.

Communal tensions remained high, for there was little formal communication between Hindu and Muslim leaders. Ranade attempted to deal with this difficulty as early as the Social Conference of December 1893, when he sponsored a resolution favoring the formation of Hindu and Muslim panchayats comprised of the most influential leaders of each community. These committees would take responsibility for their communities' actions and negotiate with each other regarding each other's religious processions and other rights.[51] This was consistent with Ranade's many attempts to organize the leading elements of Indian society as quasi-official mediators between government and the people. In the new conditions of market-place politics, it was also an implicit attempt to keep political decisions in the hands of established leaders, not subject to the enthusiasms of a crowd.[52] As the Ganesh celebration of September 1894 drew near, many feared communal outbreaks. There was danger of provocation from Hindu melas, or singing groups, composed of young men whom Tilak had organized to sing patriotic and religious songs. The festival lasted ten days, and for the first eight there was no trouble. On the evening of the ninth day a mela sponsored by the orthodox leader, Sardar Tatiasaheb Natu, passed a mosque singing. The Muslim worshippers rushed from the mosque and a riot resulted in which one Muslim died and approximately a dozen men were arrested.[53] No further violence occurred in Poona, although there were subsequent riots elsewhere.

The Sarvajanik Sabha had attempted to remain neutral in the controversy, hoping to avoid further exacerbating the political and communal fissures in Poona. But now it felt compelled to speak, and in a memorial to the Bombay government it followed Ranade's lead in attempting to eliminate nationalist politics from the issue. Denying rumors that the unrest had any political implications, the sabha insisted that "the misunderstandings have had no other than a religious root. The dispute has been solely between two sections of the ruled and in no way whatever between the rulers and the ruled."[54] In order to avoid further exacerbations of relations between rulers and ruled, it turned once again to Ranade's standard strategy of using local elders as a buffer between the formal governmental process and the people. "The help of the leading members of these communities should be more freely and unreservedly sought than has yet been attempted in this presidency." Sensing the erosion of its position as the effective spokesman of the city, or at least of the Hindu community, the sabha in effect requested the Bombay government to renew its support of the sabha's role.[55] In the following months its vulnerability in the face of factional conflict became ever more painfully evident.

Factions and Elections

The communal riots subsided after early 1895, but they assured that new conflicts in the future would be less easily resolved than before. Tilak understood that his growing organizational power, cemented by religious loyalty, could give him unprecedented political strength. One path to influence lay in the elective system which had grown over the previous decade. In the annual municipal elections in Poona in 1895, factional candidacies were more clearly delineated than ever before, and in the test of majority votes Tilak's candidates won two new seats in the Corporation.[56]

In the provincial legislative council as well, there were new opportunities. In 1895 Harris' successor Lord Sandhurst declared that one council member would henceforth be elected by the District Local Boards in the Central Division, which included Poona.[57] Tilak sought to gain the seat as a means of consolidating his power. His major opponent, S. B. Jathar from Varhad in southern Maharashtra, was a liberal reformer, government official, and close associate of Ranade. As the election date drew near, the campaign in Poona became heated, for there it was a clear-cut conflict between Tilak's Extremist camp and the Moderate reformers represented by Jathar, whom the Sarvajanik Sabha outspokenly supported.[58] Tilak, sure of success, campaigned intensively. He appeared at one meeting organized by Jathar's supporters and asked, "What has Jathar done for the Public? In Varhad affairs he has been useless." One observer demanded that Tilak have more respect for older men, fearing that he was equally contemptuous of Ranade; Tilak brushed aside his complaint.[59] Tilak's confidence was well founded, for when the election results were announced in late May, he had won a stunning victory, polling thirty-five votes to Jathar's two.[60] No clearer indication of organizational strength in the Desh was needed.

The forces of Tilak and Ranade faced another test of strength shortly after the legislative council election. On July 14, 1895, the Sarvajanik Sabha held its annual meeting for welcoming new members and electing its officers for the following year. Until this time Ranade had always exercised a dominant influence, but Extremist attacks on the sabha had increased. Mahratta was fond of attacking the Moderate-led Managing Committee as "a body of monopolists who were unwilling to take note of what was going on around them."[61] Tilak was now ready to challenge their power. Officers were elected by the full membership of the sabha, and membership was open to anyone who had the support of fifty citizens of Poona. Under this elective system Tilak mobilized his mass support to bring many new members into the sabha, where they summarily voted the old officers out of power. In a move to placate Ranade's men they allowed Gokhale to remain as joint-secretary, and the new Managing Committee of thirty-five members admitted ten incumbents, including V. M. Bhide and S. B. Jathar. But Tilak's associate, Annasaheb Patwardhan, was elected chairman, and a substantial majority of the committee was loyal to Tilak.[62] Gokhale, who had less tolerance of political competition than Ranade, decided to retire from public life. He charged that Tilak's men had voted against the Moderates out of spite against his guru Ranade, who for twenty-five years had "done all the real work of the Sabha." He called them men "who cannot bear the thought of Mr. Ranade wielding so much influence even in political matters . . . men who simply hate Mr. Ranade for his opinions in social and religious matters."[63]

The danger facing Ranade's associates was that with the decline of their influence in Poona, the polarization between Extremists and Moderates was tending toward a polarization between Poona and Bombay.[64] Bombay was still related to the rest of Maharashtra largely through Poona. The all-India influence of Pherozeshah Mehta and his friends would be reduced if Poona moved irretrievably into the Extremist camp. Since Ranade and Gokhale were the Moderates' vital link with Poona, throughout that turbulent year the Bombay strategy was to encourage the unity of all political factions in Poona so as to salvage the Moderates' position. Mehta and Ranade together pleaded with Gokhale to remain with the Sarvajanik Sabha at least through the end of the year. He finally agreed, though with considerable reluctance, knowing that in December the Congress was to hold its annual meeting there for the first time, placing Poona in the vortex of all-India politics.

In order to maintain unity in Poona for the success of the Congress, Ranade had suggested in March that the Poona Congress Committee be reorganized and broadened; he warned his followers not to exclude Tilak. He nominated Tilak as secretary of the Congress Working Committee and offered to let him choose a joint-secretary from the Moderate group. Tilak shrewdly chose K. P. Gadgil, whose charter membership in the Poona Association twenty-eight years before had made him a leading member of the Moderate circle. Gadgil, however, could be as partisan as Tilak, so there was considerable danger of quarrels when the orthodox community refused to collect funds for the Congress if the Social Conference were associated with it.[65] When this first became clear, Tilak rebuked the orthodox, but a few months later he changed his mind.

Tilak was more than ever sympathetic with the orthodox position. In January he had written an article in Kesari summarizing the first ten years of the Congress, criticizing it for being the creature of a small group of men with little popular following. This weakness, he suggested, could only be overcome by the growth of stronger local organizations and mass support for the Congress.[66] In Poona there was a large potential following for a political organization, but it could only be mobilized by an appeal to Hindu orthodoxy, and this was impossible as long as Ranade's Social Conference met with the Congress. By the summer Tilak began to support the orthodox position. At the time of the Sarvajanik Sabha defeat in July, Ranade found himself under concerted attack from the orthodox majority of Poona.

Ranade's position was made still more uncomfortable as he suffered further attacks from radical social reformers. After 1890 discontent with his cautious, diversified approach to reform had steadily grown, and with the death of his colleague Telang in 1893, Ranade was losing some of his support. He gave a memorial speech on Telang that year, in which he defended the necessity of moving slowly so as to encourage all possible reforms.[67] At about the same time, he wrote to a militant reformer who was willing to cut himself off from Hindu society by following the example of the Brahmo Samaj. Ranade argued with him, "You are not strictly correct when you think that men like Mr. Telang paused and halted from want of earnestness or from fear of offending people. Those who live in the past secure popularity. Those who bury their past attain ease. Men like Mr. Telang and others obtain neither ease nor popularity by the very fact that they can neither hold by the past nor forget it altogether."[68]

The attitude of Ranade and Telang seemed like equivocation to men like R. G. Bhandarkar. Bhandarkar was fully committed to Western social values; he stated frequently in the 1890's that Ranade was too optimistic about Hinduism's ability to reform itself and too patient with those who moved slowly. In December 1894 they both spoke to the Madras Hindu Social Reform Association before the opening of the Congress session. Ranade sought to cheer his audience by asserting that even the slow progress visible in social reform represented an awakening. On this basis he appealed to them to take new hope and renew their efforts.[69] Bhandarkar spoke the following day, commenting drily, "I agree with my friend the Honorable Mr. Justice Ranade in thinking that there has been an awakening. But he has allowed us the option of being satisfied with it. I exercise the option and declare that I am dissatisfied with it. The lamp has been lighted; but the light is flickering, and in view of the attitude of even our educated brethren, it is just as likely to my mind that it will be blown out as that it will blaze."[70]

Bhandarkar found a receptive audience, for the young social reformers of Madras were restive under Ranade's leadership. In 1890 they had founded the journal <u>Indian Social Reformer</u> through which they prodded Ranade to take firmer action throughout the 1890's. As early as 1892 they challenged the Social Conference to break with the Congress, which they saw as an endless round of futile debates. "If it is still insisted to hold the Conference with the Congress, then the future of the Conference is not hopeful. It is only another way of proclaiming to the world that the Conference cannot stand on its own legs."[71] Taking this position, the reformers of Madras by late 1895 joined the orthodox Hindus in opposing Ranade's efforts to maintain the link between the Congress and the conference.

By mid-October Ranade faced two equally intolerable dangers. On the one hand, the conference might be forced away from the Congress; in his mind this would seriously weaken both movements. On the other hand, maintaining the close connection between the two threatened to split the political association into two warring camps. He still was unwilling to compromise with popular sentiment in Poona; on October 16 he wrote to the South Indian reformer, K. Subba Rao, asserting stoically that in Poona "the struggle has commenced in right earnest between the two parties. We do not desire the struggle, but it cannot be helped. . . . It is a genuine struggle between earnest men, and though we may be outnumbered now, I have faith from my personal knowledge of 30 years that we must win in the end."[72]

There was increasing confusion over the crucial decision of who should be empowered to decide the conference question. The Moderates under Ranade attempted to remove the decision from the crosscurrents of Poona, where they were being outmaneuvered. They proposed the formation of a Congress Reception Committee to deal with administrative details of the session. The committee was to be composed of 225 members, not only from Poona but also from those districts which helped to finance the meeting. The Reception Committee would make the final decision on whether or not to allow the Social Conference to use the Congress facilities.[73]

The Extremists were willing to consider this alternative as long as they could be assured of maintaining effective control through large-scale support in Poona itself. Ranade and the Moderate Congress leaders of Bombay attempted to convince Tilak "not to go in for a sectional meeting of extremists,"[74] but after a few days of equivocation Tilak yielded to pressure from Poona orthodoxy and demanded that a public meeting of the citizens of Poona be empowered to make the decision.[75] A mass meeting on October 22 enthusiastically voted that "in the opinion of the Poona public the Social Conference is not popular owing to its deliberation and sectional character and the time has now come when the public confidence in the National Congress should not be allowed to be shaken by the cognate relation which is now believed to exist between the Congress and the Conference."[76]

The Moderates charged that the meeting had been unruly and that both Tilak and Namjoshi had made inflammatory remarks in their speeches. <u>Indu Prakash</u> criticized Tilak's implication that the social reformers were destroyers of Hindu religion and nationality and "his wild statement that the great masses are so disgusted with the thinkers and leaders of reform in social matters that they are justified in declaring themselves absolved from all binding of following even their political lead."[77] It charged the Extremists with using the strategy of the Sarvajanik Sabha affair: taking control on the basis of mob support. It warned of dire consequences "if stones and bricks break the hoary head of our saintly sage Mahadev Govind."[78] But the central question was no closer to resolution. <u>Mahratta</u> claimed that the reformers had promised that anyone paying Rs. 50 could vote for the Reception Committee which would make the final decision. The reformers, sensing defeat ahead, attempted to alter the resolution of the October 22 mass meeting so as to allow proxy votes; this the orthodox viewed as a breach of promise.

The conflict by this time had destroyed the Working Committee. The "Conferenceites" under Gokhale and Gadgil then unilaterally formed a new committee with Jathar as chairman to continue preparations for the Congress meetings.[79] They feared that without the new organization Poona would never be ready for the Congress and would face the humiliation of having the assemblage moved elsewhere, as it had been ten years before. Telegrams had already begun to arrive from Satara and Nagpur offering to sponsor the Congress.[80] Faced with the breakdown of the Working Committee, Tilak resigned, claiming that the committee was dominated by unscrupulous reformers. Ranade felt now that Gokhale's group had to work alone, and he deplored the "irresponsible and unsteady action on the part of Mr. Tilak and others."[81]

On October 26 the Bombay leaders once again attempted to mediate by suggesting that a Reception Committee be formed with seven secretaries: three from Bombay, Gokhale and Gadgil, and Tilak and another of his choosing.[82] They also resolved to invite Surendranath Banerjea from Bengal, as an outsider, to be president of the Congress meetings; they deputized Ranade to write him.[83] When news of the invitation became known in Bengal, the Bengali leaders began attempts to end the conflict in Poona, most of which took the form of pleas to preserve the unity of the Congress at any cost.[84] Motilal Ghose wrote to Tilak and Namjoshi, his fellow editors, saying that he was using his influence on Surendranath to pressure Ranade to remove the conference before a showdown vote was taken.[85] Ranade approached Surendranath a second time and found that "he apparently holds back from fear of the bitterness of party feeling here."[86]

Meanwhile the anti-conference forces were moving ahead. Mahratta returned to the accusation that the reformers were government lackeys, writing on November 10 that "the mischief of the official class has permeated to the ex-officials and in their closing years they want to do a service to the country . . . by changing its popular character. . . . It is an official cry that we cannot make any political progress without Social Reform."[87] On the same day, the Extremists held another meeting which some ten thousand people attended. It renewed the demand that the Social Conference quit the Congress, resolving that the conference derived an unjustified semblance of popular support from its connection with the Congress.[88]

Mass meetings were now accompanied by violence. In early November two reformers, W. B. Patwardhan and his friend Limaye, were attacked and beaten on the streets of Poona.[89] Shortly afterward they received anonymous letters threatening murder and warning that "although the reformers are forgiven for whatever they have done hitherto, they should conduct themselves with great caution hereafter, as, otherwise, it would be our sad and painful duty to put them to the sword."[90] Under these mounting pressures, Ranade began to waver.

At the same time, an orthodox adherent, S. V. Date, attended the meeting on November 10 and threatened to burn the Congress pandal if the conference were not removed. K. P. Gadgil consequently took the unpopular step of turning to the police, from whom he requested special guards to patrol the Congress site. Mahratta contemptuously revealed the story to its readers as an indication that the reformers were now afraid of the public. It still hoped that Ranade could be pressured into backing down, and it requested him to remove the Social Conference before more violence occurred.[91]

By now many people were blaming the zealots on both sides for the conflict, calling for an end to the dispute at any price. On November 25 Indu Prakash for the first time placed blame on Gadgil as well as Tilak.[92] It was publicly declared that Surendranath had told Ranade that he was willing to accept the Congress presidency only if it were supported by "a broad unanimity" of the people.[93]

Faced with these pressures, Ranade also confronted the fact that no one had been able to decide how the conference question should be resolved. In effect this left the question up to him, and a decision not to capitulate could only lead to further explosions. He had requested the views of the local Standing Congress Committees in the hope that they would support him strongly enough to enable him not to withdraw the conference. By his own standards his stratagem failed. He capitulated on December 1, announcing that although the local committees had voted twenty-eight to fourteen in favor of keeping the conference in the Congress pandal, most of the favorable votes also admonished him to do no damage to the interests of the Congress, and many other committees expressed no preference. He therefore decided to capitulate and withdraw the conference. In his frustration he wrote to the militant reformers of Madras, from whom he had expected firm support, exclaiming, "I am sorry for . . . those friends who, after having encouraged me with hopes, held back and counselled peace at any price. It is a general weakness of the Nation."[94]

Mahratta hailed Ranade's decision as statesmanlike, noting that in Maharashtra public meetings in several towns had clearly opposed the conference.[95] There and in Bengal the opposition to the conference was strongest. Significantly, it was in these two provinces that the Congress movement held its greatest strength. Preparations now proceeded without further major incidents, but the danger of violence remained. Ranade arranged for a separate pandal to be erected on the grounds of Fergusson College and took careful precautions to see that neither the pandal nor the conference was disrupted. He exercised strict control over the distribution of tickets to the conference, allowing only sympathizers to attend. Conference sponsors had to foil at least one attempt to burn the pandal.[96]

The Poona delegation to the Congress was dominated by Tilak yet was representative of the different factions. It was chosen at a mass meeting on December 22 at which some demanded that the reformers be given no place. But S. G. Jinsivale, an orthodox professor of Sanskrit and a leading Extremist, insisted that unity of the Congress demanded more equitable representation. Tilak agreed, and the meeting followed their suggestion, electing Gokhale and other reformers.[97] The Congress meetings opened on a note of forced amity, then went about their business. Surendranath stated in his presidential address, "I cannot help expressing my sense of admiration at the conciliatory attitude so strikingly displayed by Mr. Justice Ranade. . . . It averted a crisis which might have proved disastrous to the best interests of the Congress."[98]

Ranade's own attempt to summarize the lessons of the year's events was revealed in the address by V. M. Bhide, chairman of the Reception Committee. Bhide had been a leading figure in the Sarvajanik Sabha since its outset. His health was now failing, so he allowed Ranade to write his speech, and Gokhale read it.[99] It was in substance a manifesto of the Moderate philosophy; its dominant note was the unity which had been precariously preserved. A hundred years before, India fell into internecine conflict so deep that England easily became her master. England must not be condemned for the achievement of uniting India, but gratefully praised:

> Fortunately for us, our affairs have been entrusted to the safekeeping of a power which has won a world-wide reputation as the mother of great nations and the liberator of mankind. Brought up by such a discipline . . . we have benefited by the education that we receive and by the material civilization which annihilates time and distance, and brings us together to feel a common interest in our own elevation.100

Attempting to assuage all sides, Ranade nonetheless wrote from the assumptions of the Moderates. He again revealed his distaste for the crowd in politics by insisting that the cause of unity could only be preserved "by the moderation and business-like character of our deliberations, by our mutual toleration of each other's feelings and prejudices." The combination of his oblique denigration of Hindu nationalism and his preference for thoughtful restraint over demagogy revealed one reason for his inability to rally support locally for the Social Conference.

The attitude underlying this stance was Ranade's lifelong preoccupation with the moral underpinnings of politics. In the stress of recent events this puritanical streak had come to the surface. Not long before, he had discussed with Gokhale his conviction that India's great weakness was its inability to work cooperatively for the common good. When Gokhale asked whether he was not discouraged over the slow progress of the Social Conference, Ranade replied, "Not that the work is hollow, but the faith in these men is shallow. Wait for a few years. I see a time coming, when they will ask the same question about the Congress, which, at present, evokes so much enthusiasm. There is something in the race which is unequal to the strain of sustained exertion."101 This note of discouragement was becoming more frequent in Ranade's public statements. Describing the challenge of forging unity out of the conflicting strategies within the Congress, he warned the assembled delegates:

> Many people among us do not sufficiently realise how hard this struggle is naturally bound to be. They seem to imagine that we can pass from the old world to the new . . . without budging an inch or sacrificing anything. The sooner they abandon visions such as these, the better it will be for them and for us all. There will be struggles, our consciences accusing and excusing night and day, castes and creeds in conflict with one another in endless directions. Such struggles are inevitable and people who are put out by the first signs of such differences are not the men from whom we can expect success in such high tasks.102

In his own judicious way Ranade was lecturing to the people of Poona, who for many years had been his students in the conduct of public life. Most of the audience did not know, however, that Ranade had written the speech, and they expected him to denounce the tactics of Tilak's group. When the Social Conference opened, many who otherwise might not have attended did so in anticipation. Ironically, the conference therefore had a better attendance than usual. In his opening speech Ranade tried not to vilify the Extremists but to heal the wounds of conflict. Somewhat inconsistently with his earlier position he stated that "the two assemblies . . . had nothing whatever to do with each other. Their organizations are separate, their modes of work are separate, their publications and objects are separate," but convenience suggested that both meetings be held together, since many delegates attended both. It was thus inconsequential that they should now be separated.[103]

Ranade used the conflict as a lesson in the proper methods of carrying on political life. He spoke of the reform movement in other parts of India as specializing in a single type of reform. In Bengal the Brahmo Samaj, which dominated the movement, had chosen the extreme course of breaking off from Hindu society. Maharashtra was the only region, Ranade explained, where the reform movement was versatile enough to pursue all lines of reform simultaneously. The heated arguments there came as a result of disagreements within the movement. "The peculiar feature of the movement in the Presidency is that we want to work on no single line, but to work on all lines together and above all not to break with the past and cease all connections with our society. . . . We have the different Samajes, but somehow or other there is something in our nature which prevents us from bodily moving into another camp. We do not desire to give up our hold on the old established institutions. Some might say this is our weakness--others think in it consists our strength."[104]

Ranade's efforts at conciliation and his almost desperate optimism disarmed his listeners. In fashioning a graceful retreat he regained his personal popularity in the city.[105] But there was no doubt that political initiative had decisively passed to the opposition.

The Aftermath

Ranade hoped that with the end of the Congress meetings calm might return to Poona. The hope rested upon Tilak's choice of initiatives in the Sarvajanik Sabha. Unfortunately, trouble developed when political conditions were least able to withstand new pressures, just as in the 1870's. This time the disaster was double: bubonic plague, which reached Bombay from the Middle East in 1896; and a new famine in Maharashtra, the worst since the 1870's. The earlier famine had precipitated a new Famine Code, which incorporated many of the Sarvajanik Sabha's views as to the rights of the people to government aid. Since that time the work of the sabha in times of food scarcity had changed. In 1896 Tilak followed precedents set by Ranade and the sabha in the 1870's by organizing a campaign to instruct the people in their rights against the government. Under the new code the sabha was able to point out precisely the areas in which government actions failed to live up to the legally defined standards.[106] In a sense this criticism was less radical than the famine reports of the 1870's, which had asserted governmental responsibilities where none formally existed. But the tenor of Tilak's protests was more combative. The new Sarvajanik Sabha issued such peremptory demands to the government that Bombay's worst fears of Brahmin sedition were stimulated. In early 1897 the governor issued the declaration which Ranade had long feared. "The Poona Sarvajanik Sabha as at present constituted must cease to be recognized as a body which has any claim to address Government on questions of public policy."[107]

The Moderates under Ranade's lead had anticipated the breakdown of communication with the government. The older generation, who represented the leading Moderates of Maharashtra, met in early October 1896 at Ranade's home on Cumballa Hill in Bombay.[108] Having failed to influence Tilak's sabha in any way toward moderation, they resolved to form a new association to continue the work of the old Sarvajanik Sabha, and agreed that Ranade should write the manifesto.[109] On November 14, 1896, they established the Deccan Sabha to perpetuate the work of the Moderate party. In the manifesto Ranade expressed the reasons for its birth, giving the Moderates' interpretation of recent events.

> The Sabha always aimed at securing the co-operation of all classes and it scrupulously avoided identifying itself with any preponderant sectional interest. Recently, however, the conditions which ensured this balance of judgment have been to a large extent disturbed: . . . sectional interests have now obtained an ascendancy, which, added to the general spirit of reaction, has alienated the sympathies of those whose long association with the Sabha was principally instrumental in building up for it whatever prestige it possesses and securing to it the measure of success it has achieved as an intermediary between the Government and the people.[110]

In defining the principles on which the new association would function, Ranade demonstrated how far the political atmosphere had changed in the years since the founding of the Sarvajanik Sabha. Political experience in Maharashtra had matured greatly under Ranade's leadership; the principles by which British constitutionalism prospered were more widely understood. Ranade epitomized them in these words: "Liberalism and Moderation will be the watchwords of this Association. The spirit of Liberalism implies a freedom from race and creed prejudices and a steady devotion to all that seeks to do justice between man and man, giving to the rulers the loyalty that is due to the law they are bound to administer, but securing at the same time to the ruled the equality which is their right under the law."[111] A note of defensiveness and fatigue was apparent, for these guidelines were being set aside by the Extremists. The enthusiasm and optimism of the earlier days were missing from Ranade's description of moderation.

> Moderation imposes the conditions of never vainly aspiring after the impossible or after too remote ideals, but striving each day to take the next step in the order of natural growth by doing the work that lies nearest to our hands in a spirit of compromise and fairness. After all, political activities are chiefly of value not for the particular results achieved, but for the process of political education which is secured by exciting interest in public matters and promoting the self-respect and self-reliance of citizenship.[112]

To its opponents in Poona the manifesto sounded like an apology to the government for Extremist patriotism. <u>Mahratta</u> accused the Deccan

Sabha of being a clique of wornout pensioners in league with Anglo-Saxon journalists and bureaucrats.[113] It was they, not Tilak's supporters, who represented a minority faction in Poona. Kesari spoke of the sabha as "Ranade's Mela."[114] Mahratta charged that for years the Sarvajanik Sabha had been a tool of Ranade's own views, allowing no dissent from his personal methods. "Many members of the Sarvajanik Sabha naturally grew weary of this despotism and were not willing to change a public institution into a pliant and willing instrument of anybody however gifted and high in source he may be."[115] The most sensitive point of all lay in Ranade's linking Tilak's followers with "the general spirit of reaction" in Poona. To them the phrase seemed an insinuation of political disloyalty, the sort of veiled charge which hitherto had been made only by Anglo-Indian journalists. Ranade of all men should have known how destructive it was to charge political associations with disloyalty without substantiating the charge: it was Ranade who had first made Poona a center of political activity and had suffered most from similar charges about his work.[116]

Throughout the Kesari and Mahratta editorials there ran a bitterness which expressed Tilak's sense of betrayal. He had not anticipated Ranade's move and now berated him for founding a competitive sabha, undercutting the very organization which he had nurtured and led for many years. If there was a disingenuous quality in Tilak's argument, it was matched by his genuine dismay that the split had passed beyond the hope of repair. Ranade too felt the pain of old loyalties irreparably severed. He ended the Deccan Sabha's manifesto with the sombre admission that "the rupture of old ties, in the case of some, as dear and strong as any ties could be--is always painful, but there are occasions when public duty requires even this great sacrifice."[117] His own efforts to broaden the base of political influence had led inexorably beyond the limits which he sanctioned and decisively undermined his own position. Tilak had not, as most commentators assume, brought "the masses" into political action in any systematic way. But he had introduced new techniques of political mobilization which Ranade believed would destroy the delicate system of political participation and restraint which he had spent a lifetime helping to construct. In the last years of his life Ranade spent little time in Poona; he was at home only in Bombay.

[1] For the following argument, see M. G. Ranade, "Indian Political Economy," EIE, pp. 1-42.

[2] M. G. Ranade, "The Re-organization of Real Credit in India," EIE, esp. pp. 66-69; M. G. Ranade, "Netherlands India and the Culture System," EIE, pp. 80, 96, 104.

[3] See Kumar, Western India, pp. 250-253; and Catanach, Rural Credit, pp. 48-55.

[4] Ranade, "Famine Administration in the Bombay Presidency," p. 20.

[5] Ranade, "Industrial Conference," p. 200.

[6] Ganesh Vyankatesh Joshi, Writings and Speeches (Poona, 1912), pp. 743-753.

[7] Sir George Birdwood, who sat simultaneously on the Executive Council of the Bombay Government, was the first president. The managing committee included both Ranade and G. H. Deshmukh. See Industrial Association of Western India (Poona, 1892), Appendix, pp. 1, 7-8.

[8] Report of the First Industrial Conference, held at Poona on August 24-27, 1891 (Poona, 1891), pp. i-iii.

[9] Ranade, "Industrial Conference," p. 193.

[10] Ibid., pp. 198, 207.

[11] Kellock, Ranade, p. 122.

[12] MW, p. 103. He had substantial grounds for hope in the effectiveness of this movement, for it had rapidly spread throughout the Bombay Presidency and into northern India.

[13] MW, pp. 122, 136.

[14] Parvate, Ranade, p. 62.

[15] Ramabai Ranade, Reminiscences, p. 193.

[16] See Ranade's letter in Bombay Gazette, May 28, 1892.

[17] Kulkarni, Parmanand, p. 195.

[18] Joshi's wife was the celebrated Dr. Anandibai Joshi, the first Indian woman to travel to the United States when she went there for her advanced medical training. Parvate, Ranade, p. 117.

[19] Ramabai Ranade, Reminiscences, p. 193.

[20] Kesari, May 17, 1892.

[21] Probably R. D. Nagarkar, who joined the reform leaders in the fight against Tilak in 1895.

[22] Ramabai Ranade, Reminiscences, p. 201.

[23] Bombay Gazette, June 8, 1892. The orthodox zealots agreed with their interpretation. On June 19 they met, condemned the settlement as unsatisfactory, and refused to accept it as binding. Indian Spectator, June 26, 1892. At this point, however, there was little more they could do than protest; their cries were generally ignored.

[24] This and the following quotations are from Ranade's letter to Bombay Gazette, May 28, 1892.

[25] Ranade clarified his views through several opinions he handed down after he joined the Bombay High Court the following year. See Appaya v. Padappa, ILR, 23 Bombay 122; and Keshavlal v. Bai Girja, ILR, 24 Bombay 13.

[26] Subodh Patrika, May 29, 1892. See also letter from "Reform," Bombay Gazette, May 31, 1892.

[27] Letter from "Steady Reform," Bombay Gazette, June 4, 1892.

[28] Letter from "A Hindu," *Bombay Gazette*, June 8, 1892.

[29] M. G. Ranade, "Mental Prepossessions," reprinted verbatim in *Indian Spectator*, June 26, 1892, pp. 513-516.

[30] *Ibid.*, p. 513.

[31] N. Macnicol, *Pandita Ramabai* (London, n.d.), p. 77.

[32] The text of the resignation note is in D. S. Sarma, *The Renaissance of Hinduism* (Benares, 1944), pp. 135-136; and in "Ramabai and Her School for Hindu Widows," *Indian Magazine and Review*, XXV (January 1894), 49-50.

[33] *Report of the Seventh National Social Conference*, Appendix L, pp. 132-134.

[34] *MW*, p. 139.

[35] *MW*, pp. 116-117.

[36] *MW*, pp. 115-116.

[37] Quoted in *Bombay Gazette*, June 2, 1892.

[38] *Bombay Gazette*, May 25, 1892.

[39] *Bombay Gazette*, May 25, 1892.

[40] Richard Cashman, *The Myth of the "Lokamanya": Tilak and Mass Politics in Maharashtra* (Berkeley, 1975), pp. 64-66.

[41] Harris to Lansdowne, April 9, 1893, Harris Papers, E 256.

[42] See *The Bombay Riots of 1874* (Bombay, 1874).

[43] Cashman, *Myth of the "Lokamanya*," p. 66.

[44] Karandikar, *Tilak*, p. 112. The document in which Ranade and others dissociated themselves from Pandita Ramabai was published on the third day of the rioting. It was a time when their solidarity with Hindu society was a matter of great urgency.

[45] Wolpert, *Tilak and Gokhale*, pp. 65-66; P. C. Ghosh, *Indian National Congress* (Calcutta, 1960), pp. 68-71.

[46] Reported in Kelkar, *Life and Times*, p. 228.

[47] Karandikar, *Tilak*, p. 112.

[48] Kelkar, *Life and Times*, pp. 230-231.

[49] Karandikar, *Tilak*, pp. 112-113. In a city which was over ninety percent Hindu, this argument was potentially inflammatory. Ranade and the Bombay leaders were reported to have written Tilak before the meeting asking him to cancel it; he refused to drop the meeting but moderated his attack on the government for the time. *SMHFM*, II, 201.

[50] For a detailed analysis of the political and social significance of the festival, see Cashman, *Myth of the "Lokamanya*," ch. iv.

[51] Ranade, in *Report of the Seventh National Social Conference* (1893), p. 26.

[52] Tilak's dislike of Ranade's elitist method of linking bhakti religion with Moderate politics was brought out in a *Kesari* article, September 8, 1896, when he wrote, "Instead of singing devotional songs in the Prarthana Samaj, it would be better if people, such as judges, would describe the importance of bhakti in the Ganpati festival hall." Quoted in Cashman, *Myth of the "Lokamanya*," p. 79.

[53] *Ibid.*, p. 92.

[54] Poona Sarvajanik Sabha, "Memorial to Government on the Music Rules," November 29, 1894, *JPSS*, XVII (January 1895), 32.

[55] A year later when the new viceroy, Lord Elgin, stopped in Poona, Ranade wrote a memorial which a delegation from the sabha presented, making the same suggestions once again. "An Address of Welcome to Lord Elgin," November 9, 1895, *JPSS*, XVIII (January 1896), 13.

[56] Sarma, *Renaissance of Hinduism*, p. 138.

⁵⁷Kelkar, Life and Times, pp. 267-268.
⁵⁸Indu Prakash, May 27, 1895, p. 3.
⁵⁹V. K. Rajwade, in Bapat, Tilak, III, Part 1, 193-194.
⁶⁰The third candidate for the seat was D. S. Garud, from Nagpur, where he gained enough votes to place second. When Tilak was jailed for sedition in 1897, Garud replaced him on the council.
⁶¹Mahratta, July 21, 1895, p. 3.
⁶²Ibid.
⁶³Gokhale to G. V. Joshi, February 8, 1896, Gokhale Papers, V, 203/207.
⁶⁴For the influence of this trend on all-India politics over the following decade, see Gordon Johnson, Provincial Politics and Indian Nationalism: Bombay and the Indian National Congress 1890 to 1915 (Cambridge, 1973), ch. iii.
⁶⁵Karandikar, Tilak, pp. 124-125.
⁶⁶Kesari, January 8, 1895.
⁶⁷M. G. Ranade, "The Telang School," RSR, pp. 135ff.
⁶⁸Mankar, Ranade, I, 109-110.
⁶⁹Ranade, speech at Madras Hindu Social Reform Association, 1894, quoted ibid., p. 111.
⁷⁰Speech of December 27, 1894, in R. G. Bhandarkar, Collected Works (Poona, 1933), II, 516.
⁷¹Natarajan, A Century of Social Reform, p. 88.
⁷²Quoted in K. Subba Rao, Revived Memories (Madras, 1933), pp. 248-249.
⁷³Mahratta, September 29, 1895, p. 4.
⁷⁴Ranade to Mehta, November 11, 1895, Mehta Papers.
⁷⁵Ibid.
⁷⁶Mahratta, October 27, 1895, p. 5.
⁷⁷Indu Prakash, October 28, 1895, p. 3.
⁷⁸Ibid.
⁷⁹Mahratta, October 27, 1895, p. 4.
⁸⁰Karandikar, Tilak, p. 126; Mahratta, November 3, 1895, p. 5.
⁸¹Ranade to Mehta, November 11, 1895, Mehta Papers.
⁸²Karandikar, Tilak, p. 127.
⁸³Banerjea, A Nation in Making, p. 128.
⁸⁴Mahratta published extensive extracts from the Bengali press during this period. Most of the articles took this stand.
⁸⁵Karandikar, Tilak, p. 128n.
⁸⁶Ranade to Mehta, November 11, 1895, Mehta Papers.
⁸⁷Mahratta, November 10, 1895, p. 3.
⁸⁸Mahratta, November 24, 1895, p. 1.
⁸⁹It later became clear that the assailant was D. H. Chapekar, a young orthodox firebrand who murdered the British official, Rand, two years later. Chapekar's autobiography, which reveals the details, is republished in SMHFM, II, 935-1015.
⁹⁰Ibid., p. 980.
⁹¹Mahratta, November 17, 1895, p. 4.
⁹²Indu Prakash, November 25, 1895, p. 3.

[93] *Amrita Bazar Patrika*, quoted in *Mahratta*, December 8, 1895, p. 4. Ranade later confirmed this view at the Social Conference. *MW*, pp. 152-153.

[94] Ranade to K. Subba Rao, December 1, 1895, reprinted in Rao, *Revived Memories*, pp. 250-254.

[95] *Mahratta*, December 1, 1895, pp. 3-4.

[96] Chapekar's autobiography, in *SMHFM*, II, 981-982.

[97] *Kesari*, December 24, 1895; and *Sudharak*, December 23, 1895, paraphrased in Bombay Government, *Report on the Native Papers Published in the Bombay Presidency*, week ending December 28.

[98] S. N. Banerjea, *Speeches and Writings* (Madras, n.d.), pp. 14-15; *Report of the Proceedings of the Indian National Congress for 1895*, pp. 7-8.

[99] The assurance that Ranade wrote the speech is in N. C. Kelkar, *Pleasures and Privileges of the Pen* (Poona, n.d.), p. 115, and in a speech by Gokhale in Deccan Sabha, Poona, *Golden Jubilee Celebration*, January 18, 1947.

[100] *Report of the Proceedings of the Indian National Congress for 1895*, pp. 7-11.

[101] Gokhale, *Speeches*, p. 779.

[102] Perhaps Ranade was addressing Gokhale personally, for at the end of the Congress Gokhale again attempted to retire from public life. As he wrote to G. V. Joshi, "I have . . . grown absolutely sick of the public life of Poona. Recent events have opened my eyes very wide indeed and I am anxious to be relieved of all public responsibilities and to lead hereafter an entirely retired life. . . . There is so much that is selfish and ignoble here that I would fly from it to the farthest extremities of the world, if I could." Gokhale to Joshi, February 8, 1896, Gokhale Papers, V, 203/273. He added that "a great deal depends yet on the wishes of Mr. Ranade, for I don't wish to do anything that would in any way displease him." Ranade's pleas persuaded him to remain in public life, where he was already emerging as Ranade's successor.

[103] *MW*, p. 154.

[104] *MW*, pp. 159-160.

[105] See the account of the conference in G. Deshpande, *Mājhī jīvanakathā* (The Story of My Life), (Bombay, 1960), pp. 76-77.

[106] N. Rath, "A Note on the Famine Inquiries of the Poona Sarvajanik Sabha," *Thought Currents in Maharashtra 1850-1920* (Poona, 1962), p. 39.

[107] Quoted in *SMHFM*, I, 152. For a detailed account of the famine and its political consequences, see Cashman, *Myth of the "Lokamanya,"* ch. vi.

[108] *Mahratta*, November 22, 1896, pp. 7-8.

[109] Deccan Sabha, *Golden Jubilee*.

[110] The Manifesto is reprinted in full in *SMHFM*, II, 847-849.

[111] *Ibid.*, pp. 848-849.

[112] *Ibid.*, p. 849.

[113] *Mahratta*, November 15, 1896, p. 4; and November 22, 1896, p. 2.

[114] *Kesari*, November 15, 1896, p. 1.

[115] *Mahratta*, November 15, 1896, p. 3.

[116] *Mahratta*, November 22, 1896, pp. 7-8.

[117] *SMHFM*, II, 849.

Chapter 9

BOMBAY: THE LAST YEARS

> Be you humble and seek the
> favor of saints. If you want
> to meet God, this is an easy
> way. --Tukaram

The competition for power and influence which Poona witnessed in 1895 was not to be resolved in an uneasy compromise such as Ranade had always been willing to accept before. He could no longer decisively influence mass movements there, for they were now that province of the coalition of political extremists and socially orthodox. Indeed, Ranade had never attempted to mobilize mass support through public meetings; he was wary of the threat which this style of politics posed to orderly constitutional processes. His reputation in Poona was of a different order. The breadth and penetration of his public pronouncements had earned him the popular sobriquet of "rishi"; the piety and dignity of his personal bearing reassured the instincts of a populace which feared rapid cultural change. Further, in an age when the British rulers maintained a stance of racial superiority, his many achievements were a constant reminder that Indians could compete with Englishmen in any area of public life.

The copestone of Ranade's official career was placed in position in November 1893, when the government announced that he would leave his post with the Deccan Agriculturists' Relief Act to join the High Court of Bombay. His close friend, K. T. Telang, had been the first Indian judge on permanent appointment to the court, the highest judicial office available to any Indian in the government. When Telang died, Ranade was the popular choice for the position. He was at Sholapur on tour when the announcement appeared. Before he left, the citizens of Sholapur presented him with an address of congratulations. They echoed the feeling throughout Maharashtra by proclaiming at a meeting in his honor that "Your nomination to the Local High Court, while it is a most fitting recognition of your eminent abilities and long and distinguished service is a great honour to the whole native community."[1]

Ranade immediately returned to Poona to find a jubilant city awaiting him. Its most respected leader, he was now to be its first representative in the highest judicial post of the Presidency. His friends wanted to organize a full week of receptions and celebrations, perhaps as a means of strengthening the popular strength of the Moderates in the face of Tilak's growing mass appeal. Ranade took no interest in the tactical possibilities of the situation and warned his friends half seriously: "I am afraid of you all. You always go to extremes. You lose all sense of proportion. Once you take up something, whether it is good or bad, you go on and on with it. . . . Whatever you intend to do in this case, do it with a sense of proportion."[2] When his advice failed to sober them, Ranade slipped away one night to avoid a mass farewell at the railway station. He could scarcely have known how prophetic his words would seem two years later.

From that time onward Ranade's home was in Bombay, and after 1895 he rarely left the coastal city except for holidays in the hills. He continued to maintain close contact with Gokhale and other friends who now led the Moderate faction in Poona, but he was primarily absorbed in the far wider range of affairs of the greater city, the nerve center of the Presidency administration. This suited him well, for in his last years his predilection for the stable channels of legislative council, meeting hall, and administrative office was more pronounced than ever. Here he was able to reestablish the range of action which had characterized his middle years and to provide his work with its ultimate philosophical rationale.

The Many Facets of Politics

After 1893 Ranade's confidants were the Saraswat Brahmin Chandavarkar, the Parsis Mehta and Wacha, and the Muslim Tyabji--all lawyers with advanced degrees from Bombay University. Although he himself no longer served on the Bombay Legislative Council after 1893, his closest friends did by turn. As the only man of Poona among them, Ranade channeled to them the views of the moderate political associations of Poona. The most constant issues were, as always, those of rural finance. The government still had not acceded to either of his principal demands: lower tax rates and mechanisms of rural credit. Ranade remained Poona's leading contact with the government on these issues, applying pressure wherever he could.[3]

In 1896 the monsoon failed in the Desh, bringing on the first serious famine since Governor Temple's time. The Deccan Sabha was founded just as the famine began. Its main work over the next four years was a repetition of the Sarvajanik Sabha's famine relief work of the 1870's. The new sabha carried out detailed surveys of rainfall, crop production, and health conditions which it sent to the Bombay government. It directed its criticisms of lax administration at the Indian-controlled local boards for not having improved village wells, and at the government for not providing adequate relief works.[4] Ranade assisted Mehta in raising questions in the Legislative Council regarding what the Indians felt were unduly severe labor demands on famine relief projects. He also suggested that private famine relief be encouraged, as in the 1870's, but be placed under committees of prominent citizens in the towns and subdistricts.[5] Neither the problems nor Ranade's solutions had changed greatly since the early days of his career.

An extension of the dispute over financial administration arose in 1896 when Parliament responded to pressure from its pro-India wing by forming the Welby Commission. The commission was empowered to study Indian finance, with a special eye to the hitherto forbidden nationalist assertion that too high a percentage of the Home Charges was being paid by taxes raised in India. Dadabhai Naoroji was the only Indian member of the commission; as the great publicist of the Drain Theory, he was an appropriate choice. When the commission decided to call witnesses from India to testify, Sir James Peile, who as a member of the Bombay Council twenty years before had opposed Ranade, now proposed that he be summoned. Dadabhai enthusiastically supported the idea. He wrote to Ranade in June 1896, urging him to make the trip. "You have an opportunity now to do the greatest service you can to our poor country that you will have in your life-time. Come and support me in your own able way. . . . If this want of honour, honesty and righteousness of the British Indian authorities--and the terrible misery as a result--be made clear to the British public . . . what may not happen to our good?"[6]

Sir James Westland, Finance Member of the Viceroy's Council, objected. He had served with Ranade on the finance commission of 1886 and had formed a low opinion of his abilities in the realm of finance. Westland asserted that "he will not be regarded from the European point of view, as a representative of Native feeling and opinions; they will not get over their notion that a High Court Judge is above politics of the kind." Furthermore, Ranade would "not be accepted as an exponent of their views by the Native party, so far, at any rate, as financial matters are concerned, for he has taken no lead in such matters."[7]

Under these circumstances the Bombay government did not release Ranade for the trip; Gokhale was chosen in his place. It was an extraordinary opportunity for Ranade to sponsor Gokhale, and it was a major step for Gokhale toward filling Ranade's place in the councils of British India. Wacha endorsed the choice happily; he considered Gokhale "a good supporter and such an able exponent of the views of Mr. Ranade--[who is] the man who could speak with the greatest authority and confidence on each and every part in detail of Indian administration."[8] Ranade placed his studies of Indian finance before Gokhale and coached him rigorously for weeks. When Gokhale sailed for London, Ranade sent with him a letter of introduction to Wedderburn, explaining that "he has been acting under my advice for the last eight years, and I have found that he possesses a very high order of natural talent and scholarship." He praised Gokhale as one of the finest speakers in Maharashtra, but warned that because of Gokhale's youth Wedderburn and Dadabhai might be well advised to rehearse and correct Gokhale's testimony once more.[9] Gokhale's presentation was confident and exhaustive, running to 191 pages of written text.[10] He was praised by many, including Wedderburn, who told him afterwards, "Your evidence will be much the best on our side. Let me congratulate you on the signal service which you have rendered to your country. Our minority report will be based practically on your evidence."[11]

Gokhale's success was mixed with intense embarrassment that spring. The Welby Commission's results, slow to appear, were overshadowed by a new political explosion which centered on Gokhale. An outbreak of plague had appeared in Bombay the previous year; by now it had reached epidemic proportions in Bombay and Poona. Schools and businesses were closed as many people fled the tainted cities to more distant locations. Faced with severe and immediate danger, the British authorities took what measures they could to prevent the spread of the plague. They prohibited pilgrimages and established special police to prevent unrest. To coordinate the plague administration the Bombay authorities appointed W. C. Rand as plague commissioner for Poona. Rand, an efficient but authoritarian officer, soon antagonized the local population. He saw his duty as strict enforcement of health regulations, including police inspection of homes which were suspected of harboring plague victims. The police were instructed to remove victims to quarantine hospitals regardless of the protests of their families.

There was no more sensitive question than police oppression. As the police went about their work, protests arose charging that they were taking victims to death hospitals where families could not even visit them, and that the police were violating the sanctity of the women's quarters.[12] The Sarvajanik Sabha under Tilak's leadership fired a series of memorials to Bombay denouncing Rand and his officers. The Deccan Sabha joined him in the protest. From February to May 1897 their notes to the government became increasingly bitter in criticism of the plague administration.[13] Finally, Gokhale precipitated an uproar, announcing in London that his friends had sent him positive evidence that famine police had molested several women in their Poona homes. In the ensuing sensation, Gokhale was challenged to reveal the sources of his evidence. Under pressure he retreated and publicly apologized for the charges.[14] Many Indians assumed that his informants in Poona feared police reprisals if their identity became known. It was known at the time that Ranade had influenced Gokhale's decision; he later told a friend that Gokhale was willing to adhere to his charges but that in the interests of conciliation Ranade had advised him to apologize.[15] In effect, Ranade asked Gokhale to risk his public career to avoid a disastrous conflict in Poona. Gokhale was demoralized, especially as he was soon after outcasted by the orthodox Chitpavans for having crossed the ocean. Again he wanted to retire to full-time teaching, and again Ranade dissuaded him, demanding of his protégé the tenacious fortitude that he himself had always shown.

Tensions between the government and its subjects were reaching dangerous proportions in the fight over the plague and famine administration. Ranade discouraged nationalist attacks against the administration, much as he had discouraged Gokhale from revealing the evidence against the police. In May Patwardhan and Deodhar, editors of <u>Sudharak</u> since Agarkar's untimely death in 1895, attacked the plague administration in articles which seemed to the British politically disloyal. In protest Principal Selby of Deccan College resigned as chairman of the Deccan Education Society, in which they all were life members. Patwardhan and Deodhar in turn resigned to prevent Selby's departure. Ranade was again caught in the middle; he attempted to conciliate the two sides so as to prevent a breakdown of relations between British and Indians. He and Bhandarkar persuaded Selby not to resign, on condition that the society's life members abstain from politics for one year, that Deodhar and Patwardhan apologize in print, and that Sudharak return to its original character as a social reform newspaper.[16]

It seemed in some Poona circles that Ranade had adopted a harsh anti-nationalist stance, but until the end of his life, three years later, he remained a trusted adviser in many aspects of Poona's affairs. Shortly before he died he was elected to the Deccan Education Society's governing council with the highest vote of any candidate, surpassing even Selby, Mehta, and Bhandarkar.[17] He also continued his role as adviser to the native princes on political and administrative affairs. He had friends or acquaintances in many states, from whom he obtained regular reports of their administrations. His associations were well known, and his adversaries used the fact to circulate rumors that Ranade wanted to obtain an appointment as dewan in an important state--for a high price. Ranade learned of the rumors and wrote indignantly to a friend, "The rumors . . . are all false. Do you think that after having been a Judge of the High Court, I would ever be willing to dance attendance on young Maharajas? Those who set up such reports have no idea of the independence we enjoy and have no imagination to understand how difficult it is for us to reconcile ourselves to the subordination which a Dewanship implies."[18]

The continuities with Ranade's earlier life were nowhere clearer than in his relations with Tilak. The two men had steadfastly disagreed since the 1880's. In the following decade they opposed each other in contests for popular support in Poona. Yet until Ranade died, relations between them remained, if not cordial, at least respectful. They continued to share common interests on long-range issues of political development and cultural revival, even though mutual respect was not always easy to cultivate. Tilak denounced Ranade so bitterly in 1896 for forming the Deccan Sabha that some of Ranade's friends urged him to prosecute Tilak for libel, in order to teach Tilak's followers the proper limitations of political invective. Ranade refused, no doubt remembering the consequences of the libel prosecution in 1871. He said with characteristic self-effacement, "Even if I myself have fully thought and decided about the character of my acts and from your viewpoint and mine they seem proper, I can not testify that they are totally without fault."[19] He reminded his followers that Tilak was as patriotic as they, and that a quarrel would weaken the Indian position in the eyes of the government.

A few days later Tilak went to Ranade's home to ask for information on a different matter. When Ranade gave him the material he was denounced by friends who could not understand why he helped Tilak after such intemperate public attacks. Ranade explained that the quarrel over the Deccan Sabha bore no relation to the other research which he and Tilak were pursuing.[20]

The two men's sense of common purpose on fundamentals was demonstrated in an indirect but dramatic fashion in late 1897 by Ranade's most significant decision as a member of the High Court. During his seven years on the court, Ranade handed down several decisions defining the limits of constitutional political agitation.[21] He had joined the court at a time when Hindu-Muslim riots were greatly feared, and leading Hindus were especially wary that the government might impose strict police regulations or press censorship, thereby constricting political movements under the guise of controlling communal tensions. Ranade unexpectedly found himself in a position to limit the government's field of action when he passed judgment in the Kahanji sedition case. As the riots subsided in Bombay in August 1893, Kahanji, a Hindu editor, published a poem he had written, which included the lines, "Fight again for your country's good./ Brave, brave are the Kamatis."[22] He was arrested and convicted in the district court for provoking riots. When the case was appealed to the High Court, Ranade reversed the decision, declaring Kahanji innocent. He argued that the British district judge had taken the two lines out of context and had misconstrued them. The complete text was in fact conciliatory, stressing the tragedy of the riots. Ranade pointed out that Kahanji had admitted the poor judgment of the two lines in question before the trial began, and had omitted them in a second edition. Further, the poem was published in Gujarati, which none of the rioters understood. No copies were distributed among the rioters; after the poem's publication there were no subsequent riots.[23] The effect of Ranade's judgment was to restrain the government from other prosecutions during the communal troubles, for Governor Harris later wrote that in the Kahanji case Ranade had upset the government's initiative:

> The finding and the reasons for it caused considerable surprise to most people, whether lawyers or laymen . . . and this decision discouraged Government from prosecuting the authors of what Government might regard as inflammatory publications, except upon the most confident opinion from their legal advisors. . . . I should also think it quite possible that the effect of this judgment was by no means to discourage editors of vernacular papers from inserting editorials and letters certainly not calculated to promote peace.[24]

The old spectre of press censorship, once buried by Ripon, was emerging again under stress of political conflict.

The judicial precedent set in 1893 was inadequate to deal with the complex events in 1897. On the evening of June 22, 1897, the governor held a party in his Poona mansion to honor the sixtieth anniversary of Queen Victoria's accession to power. Rand, the plague commissioner, attended; and as he left the party he was attacked and murdered by the Chapekar brothers, who had attacked the liberals Patwardhan and Limaye in 1895. The brothers were soon captured and brought to trial. The political repercussions were immediate, for not only were the Chapekar brothers on trial but the Indian press was implicated under a section of the penal code which enabled prosecution for sedition or disaffection. For his recent articles in **Kesari**, Tilak was arrested on July 27 and tried for disaffection. Ranade was again involved, this time in proceedings against Tilak himself. On the day following his arrest, Tilak's lawyer applied to the High Court for his release on bail. Ranade and Justice Parsons refused to grant his release, on the grounds that the trial would begin two days later.[25]

Tilak's trial centered on the juridical question of the definition of disaffection. The limits of the statute were somewhat loosely defined in Section 124A of the Indian Penal Code: "Whoever by words either spoken or intended to be read, or by signs, or by visible representation, or otherwise excites or attempts to excite feelings of disaffection to the Government established by law in British India shall be punished with transportation for life, or for a term which may extend to three years, to which fine may be added, or with fine."[26]

Justice Strachey, who presided over the trial, followed a precedent set by the Chief Justice of Bengal in an earlier sedition trial by stating that "disaffection means simply the absence of affection. It means hatred, enmity, dislike, hostility, contempt, and every form of ill-will to the Government. 'Disloyalty' is perhaps the best general term, comprehending every possible form of bad feeling to the Government."[27] He succeeded in convicting Tilak, who was sentenced to eighteen months' rigorous imprisonment. But the jury's vote was split: the nine Europeans voted against Tilak and the three Indians voted in his defense. The ominous implications of this result were noted in the Indian press, which condemned the proceedings and Strachey's part in them as unbridled imperial oppression.[28]

Ranade played no part in the Tilak trial itself; it would be incidental to his story but for the fact that shortly thereafter Ranade presided with Justice Parsons over an identical case in which his views on Strachey's decision were made abundantly clear. The day after Tilak was arrested, the Natu brothers of Satara were arrested on similar charges for articles published in their Marathi newspaper, **Pratoda** (The Whip). They were accused of proclaiming that Indians should work actively for independence, by analogy with a Canadian separatist movement. Again the pivotal question was the legal application of the word "disaffection." Parsons commented that the term "cannot be construed as meaning an absence of or the contrary of affection or love . . . but is used in its special sense as signifying political alienation or discontent, . . . a feeling of disloyalty to the existing Government, which tends to a disposition not to obey, but to resist and subvert the Government." When Ranade and Parsons agreed on a decision, Parsons usually rendered the decision as the senior member of the court. This time Ranade presented an elaborate concurring opinion, prefacing it with the remark, "It seems necessary in the circumstances of this case that I should briefly state the reasons which lead me to [my] conclusion." He knew how deeply his non-official life involved him in the situation. Ranade presented a detailed survey of the English statute and common law precedents on rebellion, which differed radically among themselves in breadth of definition. He then argued that "disaffection . . . is a positive political distemper, and not a mere absence or negation of love or good-will. It is . . . a defiant insubordination of authority, or when it is not defiant, it secretly seeks to alienate the people and weaken the bond of allegiance. [It is] a feeling which . . . makes men indisposed to obey or support the laws of the realm, and promotes discontent and public disorder."[29]

This was a fundamental question for Ranade in that its proper resolution involved the establishment of the legal framework within which the nationalist movement would be carried out. It had both immediate and long-range implications for Ranade's own conception of proper political action; as such, it represented a culmination of one of his lifelong public concerns. In constructing a narrow and precise definition of disaffection, Parsons and Ranade paved the way for imposing a minimal sentence on the Natu brothers. They ruled that the defendants were guilty of the charges against them, but reduced the sentences imposed by the district judge to a minimum, in contrast to the sentence handed down to Tilak.[30]

Five months later, Ranade again presided over a celebrated political trial when the Chapekar brothers were tried for the murder of Rand. The elder brother, Damodar, was given a death sentence by the Poona district court, and the appeal went to Parsons and Ranade on the High Court. As there was little doubt of his guilt, the two judges dismissed the appeal.[31] This judgment, which balanced the Natu decree for Ranade, was not protested by the Poona press. Objections from Chapekar's supporters could be safely ignored, for by now Ranade's confrontations with the Extremists were past.

Ranade in these cases faced the major test of both the integrity of Indian judicial officers and his own belief in political organizing within the framework of constitutional process. He succeeded on the court in helping to define the limits of constitutional politics, but in his role as political adviser he found that channeling political pressures within orderly bounds was more than simply a judicial matter. It involved equally his ability to inculcate a commitment to constitutionalism among his followers. For this task, which he also addressed in the mid-1890's, he chose the new medium of historical scholarship.

The Reassessment of Maratha History

By the early 1890's Maharashtra's cultural revival was developing rapidly, encompassing not only the neo-orthodoxy which helped shape Tilak's political campaigns but intensive reconsideration of the region's historical legacy. The central figure of Maharashtrian history, around whom the new interpretations revolved, was Shivaji. Before 1890 the standard interpretation of Maratha history was the classic British view of the subject, Grant Duff's three-volume study published in 1824. Beginning around 1860, numerous scholars, both British and Indian, began systematic collection of historical documents on the Marathas and reconsideration of the meaning of Maratha history.[32] But before 1890 no new synthesis of Maratha history appeared, and no sustained efforts were made to convey the meaning of Shivaji and his successors to the Maharashtrian public.

Maharashtra's ignorance of its own traditions was expressed by the fact that Shivaji's tomb at the fort of Raigad had long since been left to crumble in disrepair. Ranade was evidently the first to attempt to repair the tomb as a historical monument. In May 1885 he organized a meeting of the sardars and leading citizens of Poona, which petitioned the Bombay government for funds to repair the tomb. Results were disappointing: Lord Reay, evidently wary of the political implications of Shivaji's memory, earmarked only Rs. 4 per year for the purpose. Ranade's associates themselves did not follow up their initial interest.

A decade later Tilak once again appropriated a tactic which Ranade had initiated and gave it more dynamic political meaning.[33] In May 1895 he convened a meeting designed to raise funds for the repair of Shivaji's tomb and to establish an annual festival parallel to the Ganpati celebration. By leading a pilgrimage to Raigad, as he first did in 1896, Tilak appropriated to his movement another powerful symbol of Hindu greatness. But there was considerable difference of opinion as to the meaning of the Shivaji tradition. Some accounts stressed the violence with which he led the Maratha struggle against the alien Muslims. This was the school of thought which provoked hostility within the Bombay government and indirectly contributed to the sedition cases of 1897. Tilak, on the whole, held to a more moderate school of thought regarding the meaning of Shivaji's life.[34] The moderates agreed that the memory of Shivaji was an important source of patriotic sentiment; as *Mahratta* put it, "pride and admiration for heroes is a principal element in the sentiment of nationality."[35]

This conflict of historical mythmaking provided the public context for one of Ranade's most notable academic efforts: his study of Maratha history. He sensed the need for a full-scale interpretation of Shivaji and his successors, grounded in careful historical research, which would encourage Maharashtrian patriotism but within the framework of liberal constitutional values. He and his friends began discussing the need to rewrite Maratha history as early as 1891.[36] It was not until 1900 that Ranade's *Rise of the Maratha Power* appeared in print. In the intervening decade he found time to pore over the rich archives of the Peshwas, with the purpose, as he wrote in the introduction to the book, of presenting "a clear view of the salient features of the history from the Indian standpoint, [and] to remove many misapprehensions which detract much from the moral interest and the political lessons of the story."[37] The result was a book which still stands as a seminal work of regional historiography, in part because of its deliberate liberal nationalist bias. The political lessons to which Ranade referred were embodied in a section on Shivaji and his successors which he wrote in 1894 and 1895 at the height of his struggle with Tilak. It was designed to demonstrate that Shivaji, not the British, laid the groundwork for liberal constitutionalism in India. "Like the first Napoleon, Shivaji in his time was a great organizer, and a builder of civil institutions, which conduced largely to the success of the movement initiated by him and which alone enabled the country to pass unscathed through the dangers which overwhelmed it shortly after his death, and helped it to assert its claim to national independence, after a twenty years' struggle with the whole power of the Moghul Empire."[38]

The chief repository of this strength, according to Ranade's interpretation, was Shivaji's council of state, or Ashta Pradhan. He consulted his ministers regularly, gave them civil as well as military responsibilities, and through them organized a government which dealt in an orderly and just manner with the many aspects of administration. Ranade likened the Peshwa to a prime minister, sitting at the king's right hand. He found counterparts for the other ministers in the officials of a modern government. This incipient constitutional order which Shivaji established was parallel to the modern viceroy's council, "a council of the highest officers of the State, sitting together to assist the king in the proper discharge of his duties."[39] Even after Shivaji's death the Maratha central authority both perpetuated national unity and avoided oppressive rule; the governmental structure enabled the leaders "to carry on the government and direct the national force without the advantage always of having any strong personal ruler at the head. . . . There was no such experiment of Federal Government on such a scale undertaken in this country under either Hindu or Mahomedan sovereigns."[40]

Later research has demonstrated that Ranade greatly overestimated the role of the Ashta Pradhan. As a group it met irregularly if at all. Shivaji's lieutenants included several powerful figures not mentioned as members of the council itself. Within a few years historians demonstrated that Ranade had read the present into the past too uncritically.[41] Yet when he presented his view it was enthusiastically greeted as evidence that Indians were capable not only of carrying out the responsibilities of representative government but also of establishing constitutional rule without the aid of Western models.[42] The swadeshi movement had not only an economic but a cultural dimension.

Like Tilak, Ranade was constructing new images of past national greatness as a means to the revival of Hindu initiative and self-respect. Ranade's images were conveyed through learned writings, while Tilak's were molded into festivals in the streets. Both men faced the vexing challenge of asserting Hindu greatness without eliciting anti-Muslim passions. While Tilak made little effort to avoid communal tensions, Ranade carefully attempted to reconcile the two communities with an image of mutual tolerance. It was not easy to provide this apologetic when he addressed Maratha history, for Shivaji and his successors had created and maintained Maratha power largely at the expense of the Mughal empire. They rallied their people to the slogan of svarajya, or national liberation, a term which the Extremists were reviving in the 1890's. Ranade insisted, on the basis of highly ambiguous evidence, that the svarajya which Shivaji envisioned was limited to the preservation of a Hindu polity in the region of Maharashtra. He did not wish to destroy other kingdoms but simply to take his rightful place alongside them.[43] This interpretation was the historian's gesture which matched the administrator's plea for Hindu-Muslim conciliation boards for music and processions.

Ranade's widest publicity for the message of communal harmony came from his annual speeches to the National Social Conference. He gave the question of Hindu-Muslim relations his most exhaustive treatment at the Social Conference of 1899, which was held in Lucknow, an old center of Islamic learning. Aware of the long-range danger of communal tensions, Ranade emphasized that both communities must share in a great effort to renew their old contacts. "In this vast country no progress is possible unless both Hindus and Mahomedans join hands together. . . . In the backwardness of female education, in the disposition to overleap the bounds of their own religion, in matters of temperance, in their internal dissensions between castes and creeds, in the indulgence of impure speech, thought and action . . . both communities are equal sinners."[44]

There was one bridge by which the two communities, setting aside their internal difficulties, might join in the great task of creating true national unity. The bhakti tradition had always fought against the degenerate practices and arbitrary barriers which caused communal antagonism, Ranade opined. "Caste, idolatry, polytheism and gross conceptions of purity and pollution were the precise points in which the Mahomedans and the Hindus were most opposed to one another, and all the sects had this general characteristic that they were opposed to these defects in the character of our people."[45]

As he had outlined to the Prarthana Samaj a quarter-century before, Ranade again proposed that a purified monotheism could provide both personal purity and national unity in a pervasively religious society. It would supply the religious basis for social reform and political advance

217

which Ranade had called for fifteen years earlier when he warned Malabari that only a great religious revival could provide the basis for genuine reform in India. This too was relevant to the political scene, for the construction of constitutional rule, although complex and time-consuming enough in itself, was not an end to be achieved in a vacuum. The whole range of social and religious life also demanded continued attention, and the work of Ranade's final years in Bombay revealed the last dimensions of his life's effort.

Women, the Lower Castes, and Social Unity

Throughout his career Ranade had seen the disabilities of high caste women as a primary focus in his social crusades. His seven years on the Bombay High Court provided yet another dimension for this work, in the form of many cases involving property law and social regulation. In the Bombay legal system Ranade inherited patterns which were already somewhat more liberal regarding women's rights than the codes in force elsewhere in India. In Bengal scholars had codified formal Sanskrit and Persian law as the dominant precedents for the judicial system. Hence by the nineteenth century that socially conservative province presented a conservative law code. The major Hindu codes of western India were somewhat more generous regarding women's rights in premodern times. Furthermore, the Bombay codifiers had been more receptive to customary law than in Bengal, and customary patterns were less restrictive toward women than the ancient Brahmin lawgivers.[46] Finally, in Bombay Ranade worked with a system which allowed greater discretion to trial judges than in Bengal.[47] This final element had enabled the Bombay court to enter a period of rapid liberalization after the middle 1870's under Chief Justice Westropp and Justices Raymond West and K. T. Telang.

When Ranade reached the High Court he was able to enforce moderately liberal rights for women within the framework of existing legal tradition. In one judgment he upheld the right of a widow to adopt a son without her deceased husband's prior authorization, when her own son died without an heir.[48] In another case, when a young widow sued for a share in her deceased father-in-law's estate, Ranade ruled that a widow should rightly share in her father-in-law's inheritance.[49] These decisions had the effect of slowly enhancing women's rights in the Bombay courts.

However, Ranade's rulings in cases involving widows were carefully limited in the range of their application. In one case he upheld a widow's right to bequeath both movable and immovable property, on the basis of her husband's written will. At the same time he made it clear that large areas remained in which a widow did not hold property rights.[50] A firm supporter of widow marriage, he nonetheless ruled against a widow's right to give her son away in adoption.[51] Only once did Ranade depart from a narrow procedural statement, in a case which echoed his own relations with his widowed sister. When a woman whose husband and father had both died claimed support from her father's estate against the claims of his second wife, Ranade ruled against her on the grounds that a married daughter was universally required to seek support from her husband's family. In this case the daughter, being indigent, had strong moral but no legal grounds for her plea.

> Every father of a family has a sort of moral duty to support his male and female relations; but there are certain persons so related in respect of whom the obligation is legal, and in regard to others the texts should be interpreted as being intended for exhortation and recommendation. . . . It is only the unmarried daughters who have a legal claim for maintenance. The married daughters must seek their maintenance from the husband's family. If this provision fails, and the widowed daughters returns to live with her father or brother, there is a moral and social obligation, but not a legally enforceable right.52

The overall effect of these and other decisions demonstrated that even in institutional structures where rapid reform was virtually unthinkable, changes could accumulate by slow accretion. However slowly progress might come in liberalizing society, forward steps were possible even in unexpected quarters.

Ranade's efforts on behalf of lower castes' rights demonstrated a similar commitment. His initial action during the 1890's to defend the lower castes occurred in the Bombay Legislative Council. In October 1890 the council passed the Bombay Municipal Servants Bill, which Ranade alone opposed. The bill was designed to discourage strikes by menial city employees to gain better working conditions. Its chief feature was to increase the size of fines and length of prison sentences for strikers. In his dissenting speech Ranade declared that the new penalties were excessively harsh. He pointed out that in effect the bill would strengthen the position of high caste municipal officeholders against low caste workers, an unnecessary and unjustified change.53 As in other areas of his life in Bombay, Ranade exploited his position in high-level governmental bodies to express otherwise undefended interests.

Ranade's efforts on behalf of low caste interests, however liberal for a Chitpavan Brahmin of his time, were never as outspoken as the efforts of his Saraswat friends, Bhandarkar and Chandavarkar. These two outspokenly considered the caste system as the greatest source of evil in Hindu society;54 they were uneasy with Ranade's cautious leadership of the Social Conference. The issues which Ranade confronted in the Social Conference were largely restricted to high caste practices. It was not until 1895, when the conference met in Poona under the presidency of Bhandarkar, that Ranade agreed to its first resolution expressing a broad condemnation of the evils of caste. Bhandarkar's influence was directly felt in the passage of the resolution, which singled out the lower castes for social uplift.55

Ranade was congenitally averse to intercaste conflict, and although he seems to have supported Jotiba Phule's non-Brahmin movement privately and cautiously, he could never subscribe to the militantly expressed antagonisms of the non-Brahmin leaders. Agreeing that caste barriers must be softened, Ranade preferred to appeal to the unity of the whole society on the basis of moral or spiritual fervor. This perspective was given new substance in the early 1890's when he became increasingly preoccupied with the inner qualities of a man as the essential key to his human worth. In the "Mental Prepossessions" speech of June 1892, Ranade denounced harsh stereotypes in which "the Sudra becomes often a type of all that is mean and dirty. The black skin becomes an emblem of a blacker inside nature."[56] At the time, this line of thought was little more than an aside in his effort to show how rigid stereotypes often did injustice to the complex position of the reformers.

A year later Ranade was more outspoken in a speech at the orthodox Brahman Sabha in Bombay. He had been invited in honor of his High Court appointment; one speaker emphasized his new post as a great achievement for the Brahmin community. When Ranade spoke he praised the personal qualities of self-control, austerity, purity, restraint of the senses, love of learning and teaching, and other qualities cited in the Bhagavad Gita which all Brahmins might honor. He went on to say that one who did not possess these qualities, though he was born of Brahmin parents, would disgrace them, and one who did possess them would be a Brahmin in fact if not by birth. He ended by urging his audience to look not so much to a man's caste as to his personal attributes.[57] The speech caused an uproar in orthodox circles, but Ranade stood firm.

In December of that year when Ranade and Bhandarkar were returning by train from the Congress meetings in Madras, a young English judge arrogantly usurped Ranade's seat. The High Court justice responded by squeezing into Bhandarkar's seat, and when the Englishman discovered Ranade's identity he attempted to apologize. Ranade's dignity had been injured, and for once he refused even to recognize the man's presence. Though Ranade would not retaliate, yet he felt the insult, for he later mused to Gokhale: "Is our own conscience clear in these matters? How do we treat members of the depressed classes--our own countrymen--even in these days? At a time, when they and we must all work hand in hand for our common country, we are not prepared to give up the privileges of our old ascendency, and we persist in keeping them down-trodden. How can we, then, with a clear conscience, blame members of the ruling race, who treat us with contempt?"[58]

The incident is similar to the racial discrimination that the young Mohandas Gandhi was experiencing on trains in South Africa at the time. The two men's reactions were similar: a sharp sense of disillusionment that the British system had room for racist tendencies, combined with a heightened awareness that the Hindu caste system embodied similar evils. Gokhale relates that during the mid-1890's Ranade was corresponding with Gandhi, although no trace of the correspondence survives.[59] Ranade is also recorded as having pleaded with a Bombay audience in 1895, shortly before Gandhi's return, to see that the social degradation which was permitted by legal racial discrimination in South Africa was no worse than the social discrimination of the caste system in India.[60]

This was the background against which Ranade constructed his new interpretation of Maratha history in the last years of the decade. Previous authors had seen the pre-British era almost solely from the traditional emphasis on political and bureaucratic trends. <u>The Rise of the Maratha Power</u> went much further in analyzing social and cultural history as well. The didacticism of Ranade's style was designed to illustrate his hope that the social changes then visible might evolve into a surge of national unity and self-strengthening such as he believed Maharashtra had experienced in the days of Maratha glory. It was generally agreed that Shivaji's military prowess had bound together the scattered elements of the Maratha people. In a vein of sentimental populism which had always informed his work, Ranade sought to show that the credit belonged not to Shivaji alone but to the whole Maratha nation. "It was not the outcome of the successful enterprise of any individual adventurer. It was the upheaval of the whole population, strongly bound together by the common affinities of language, race, religion, and literature, and seeking further solidarity by a common independent political existence."[61]

Ranade had made clear in many contexts that national movements of this sort in India could be bound together only by a new growth of religious fervor; he found support for his belief when he surveyed Maratha history and described an outburst of religious feeling in the fifteenth and sixteenth centuries. The key to this revival had been its popular character, a protest against Brahmin exclusiveness.

> This Religious Revival was not Brahminical in its orthodoxy; it was heterodox in its spirit of protest against forms and ceremonies and class distinctions based on birth, and ethical in its preference of a pure heart, and of the law of love, to all other acquired merits and good works. . . . At its head were Saints and Prophets, Poets and Philosophers, who sprang chiefly from the lower orders of society--tailors, carpenters, potters, gardeners, shopkeepers, barbers, and even <u>mahars</u>--more often than Brahmins.[62]

He praised the saints' fight for the vernacular language against the dominance of Sanskrit, as a means of making the cultural mainstream accessible to the whole populace. In summary, Ranade pointed out in a sanguine moment that "caste exclusiveness now finds no place in the religious sphere of life, and it is relegated solely to the social concerns of men, and even there its restrictiveness is much relaxed."[63]

Ranade was writing for his times, defending the position of the liberal reformers. His sponsoring of intercaste cooperation became clearer when in 1900 he published an "Introduction to the Peshwa's Diaries," in which he extended his analysis to cover the last decades before Maharashtra fell to the British. For the last years of Maratha rule the great question concerned the causes of Maratha downfall and the reasons for the dissolution of earlier Maratha unity. Ranade's view was now outspokenly anti-Brahmin. He wrote that the Peshwas dismissed Shivaji's policy of balancing the interests of different castes, both Brahmin and non-Brahmin. Instead, they gave virtually all high posts to Brahmins in hereditary tenure, betraying the cause of national unity. "Their return to the old Brahmanic ideals of exclusiveness and division sowed the seeds of decay, which ultimately hastened the downfall of the Confederacy."[64] His critics immediately objected to his analysis. Mahratta was representative; it argued that intercaste conflict did not contribute to the Maratha downfall. On the contrary, throughout the period Brahmins had earned their high positions by ability, except for the last chaotic years after 1800.[65]

On one level Ranade's reformist principles met resistance from the orthodox camp, which gave political Extremism its communalist leanings. On another level both camps were united on the need for a cultural revival to match political mobilization. Ranade's demonstration of the importance of cultural history has remained the facet of his historical writings which most influenced subsequent writers. Ranade's interest in the Maharashtrian cultural revival in his last years was more than academic musing. He played a leading role in the effort of the 1890's to invigorate the vernacular culture. The principal association sponsoring Marathi literary development was the Literary Society of Maharashtra, over which Ranade presided in its annual session of 1899. It was clear at this conference that both Moderate and Extremist nationalists were united in support of a cultural renaissance. During the meeting one member of the audience denounced Tilak, who was then in jail for sedition, and asked the conference to disavow all connections with him. Ranade immediately silenced the protest by insisting that Tilak's political views had no relevance for his devotion to Marathi literature. He was a great figure among Marathi writers and a great public servant; the association would commit a damaging mistake to reject him for his other views.[66]

The literary conference had as one purpose the hope of stimulating university graduates, who were well trained in the demanding literary standards of the West, to write in their own vernacular and thereby enrich its traditions. Ever since Marathi had been eliminated as a required subject for university examinations in 1867, the university had been training men who were only half literate in the vernacular. Under these conditions the cultural bridge between Europe and Maharashtra was weakened. Shortly after his arrival in Bombay in 1893, Ranade was elected to the University Senate, where he served until his death.[67] In the senate he carried out an intensive campaign for the reintroduction of Marathi in the required curriculum. He insisted that its removal had been disastrous for the development of the Marathi language and had left the university curriculum too exclusively Western in orientation. Asserting that "the divorce of Indian Universities and their graduates from all interest in the development of the Indian vernaculars is an evil of the first magnitude,"[68] he conducted a new survey of vernacular literature in 1898 to update his first survey of 1867. Ranade's data supported his contention that the vernacular culture was declining. He spoke of the early poet-saints as "essentially modern poets"; compared with their works there had been no distinguished writings since the British conquest. "The poetic fire has become extinct with the loss of political power."[69] If the needed revival were to take place, he contended, students must be heartily encouraged to put new emphasis on Marathi. Without this, Western education would never become firmly rooted in the lives of the students and their countrymen. The purpose of the university, which was to enrich vernacular culture by the study of the West, would thereby be vitiated. With a startling metaphor, he explained that "No mere foreign graftings can ever thrive and flourish unless the tender plant on which the grafting is to be made first germinates and sends its roots deep in its own indigenous soil. When the living tree is thus nourished and watered, the foreign manure may add flavour and beauty to it."[70]

Ranade became a leading member of a committee which in 1898 investigated this question and recommended that the vernaculars be reintroduced. When the University Senate considered the question in July, there were powerful groups opposed to the change, especially Bombay Parsis for whom Marathi was not native. When one speaker criticized Ranade for not making significant contributions to Marathi, Ranade was embarrassed and angered. He lost his usual composure, ridiculed the Christians for their Marathi translations of the Bible, and scoffed at the Parsis for lacking commitment to the problems of vernacular culture.[71] His campaign failed on that day, for the proposal was defeated by one vote. Three months after Ranade's death the proposal was reconsidered and passed, a posthumous tribute to his thirty years of effort.

The Religious Matrix

The effort to improve the condition of women, the campaign to construct bonds between Brahmins and non-Brahmins, Hindus and Muslims, the writing of relevant history, the infusion of new vitality into the vernacular language--all were facets of a complex effort to revitalize Indian society. But taken separately, they had only tenuous links with each other. Ranade became increasingly aware of the slow pace of change as the 1890's wore on. As early as the turbulent years of 1892 and 1893 his speeches were becoming more emphatic on the need for reformers to practice enthusiasm, patience, and fortitude. By 1895 the ranks of the reformers were thinning with the deaths of many of Ranade's friends. Telang, Lokahitawadi and Nulkar died in 1893; S. P. Pandit and S. H. Chiplunkar, two more confidants, died in 1894. Under the stress, his attention began to turn inward with increasing intensity to the need for moral and spiritual sustenance. In 1894 he gave a memorial address at the Prarthana Samaj on Telang's public service, in which his long-familiar stoicism and self-criticism rose to the surface. He inveighed against the discouraged reformers who believed that opposition in the Hindu community would defeat their best work. "Our difficulties . . . are in us, in our inertia, in our weakness, in our physical inability to sustain hard work, in our inaptitude to work long for great results by great toil. . . . We should learn to be men, stalwart puritan men, battling for the right, not indifferent nor sanguine, trustful but not elated, serious but not dejected."[72] Introspection had always been present in Ranade's public appearances, but now it was becoming the dominant note.

As always, he clarified his internal impulses by articulating their philosophical consequences. His search for a spiritual revival which would appeal to all classes of the population and support his cherished social reforms had come to rest not only on the bhakti poets but on the Vaisnavite philosophers as well. Journeying to Madras in 1894, he praised Ramanuja and the Vaisnavite saints as "the fountain sources of all the higher wisdom and spiritual elevation, that have distinguished the religious history of the last thousand years and more."[73] Here was an intercaste movement uniting all orders of society as devotees of the one God in whatever form he might take. Ramanuja, the greatest of them, repudiated the atheism of the Buddhists and Jains, and his successors overcame Brahminical exclusiveness through a religion of love. Surveying the whole subcontinent, Ranade pointed to Chaitanya in Bengal and Guru Nanak in the Punjab as worthy successors of Ramanuja. "[They] were the first social reformers. They felt compassion for the hard lot of the poor and disfigured widow, and did their best to carry comfort to her. They also took pity upon the fallen condition of the lower strata of the social system and conceded to them the privilege of admitting them into a community of faith with the higher classes."[74]

The teachings of Ramanuja cemented the link between devotional religion and social reform against a threat from yet another quarter. The curriculum in English-language colleges had changed significantly since Ranade's student days. Formerly its goal had been the perfection of individual character through the study of Bishop Butler and others. By the 1890's the secular thought of Herbert Spencer and John Stuart Mill was in the ascendant. Many in Ranade's generation saw the trend toward scepticism inherent in the natural sciences and Darwinian evolution as destructive of moral values and social commitment.[75] In a second discussion of Ramanuja in 1895, Ranade praised him for providing a philosophical answer to the agnostics. In Ramanuja's modified <u>advaita</u> system neither the human soul nor exterior matter has a separate existence, Ranade explained. Both are embedded in the Supreme Spirit, which provides unity and meaning for human existence. To Ramanuja's thought "may be traced the rise and progress of the Vaishnava Sects throughout India, which Sects have attained to a higher and truer conception of Theism than any of the other prevailing systems."[76] Ranade specifically posed the Vaisnavite tradition as superior to the socially and philosophically unacceptable system represented by the Shankaracharyas, who had opposed his own efforts at social reform.

In describing the essence of the Vaisnavite tradition Ranade presented a personal view. He had become in effect another innovator in the tradition, this time borrowing heavily from Christian ethics. He saw the essence of Vaisnavism as the assurance that a loving relation between a worshipper and his God was possible. "Above all, Indian Theism is built on the rock of the direct communion of the individual soul with the Soul of the Universe to which it is linked by the tie of faith, hope and love."[77] Here was an amalgam of the Upanishads and the New Testament.

In Ranade's mind this carefully modulated piety had nowhere been more highly developed than in Maharashtra, whose theistic tradition he and others have called "Bhagwat Dharma." Its two salient characteristics, he believed, were its pure devotionalism and its egalitarianism. The Marathi saints had employed the vernacular language against the entrenched position of Sanskrit among the orthodox pandits. For the first time poets made great religious traditions available to all men. As with the Bombay University curriculum, Ranade saw both a need and a historical precedent for the revival of vernacular culture. Using Marathi, the Bhagavata saints had allowed a place for the lower classes, women, and even Muslims within their number. In a five-hundred-year period there had been fewer Brahmin bhakti saints than non-Brahmins.[78]

Ranade identified the Prarthana Samaj as the latest expression of the tradition. Calling it Protestant Hinduism, he claimed that its legitimacy came from standing in the ancient tradition of protest against customs "which have an inveterate tendency to encrust the true spirit of our faith and to give a human coating which obscures from view the essentially divine element."[79] Characteristically, he had found a philosophy which served both his internal needs and his social crusades. He was clarifying a position for the Moderates which would be rooted in regional and national history yet would constitute effective opposition to the forces of obscurantism which threatened to dominate the Maharashtrian cultural revival.

A rich vein of thought, this was not dispassionate historical analysis so much as a new manifesto for changing times. Outside the Prarthana Samaj it found little support. <u>Indu Prakash</u>, which supported both social reform and Moderate politics, attacked Ranade's conception of Bhagwat Dharma as unrepresentative of Maharashtrian traditions. Calling the Prarthana Samaj unfaithful to the old movement, it asserted that the samaj was "the result of Western education and a second-rate imitation of Christian modes of worship and propaganda. . . . It is an aristocratic body caring little for the enlightenment of the masses."[80] It was precisely these tendencies within the Prarthana Samaj against which Ranade contended; his religious discourses were designed to convince the samajists as much as outsiders.

The Last Days

The formulation of a philosophy for the Prarthana Samaj and the completion of The Rise of the Maratha Power summarized Ranade's final views on the public life of Maharashtra. They contained his tenacious belief that there were sources of greatness in the Marathi character, however encrusted with layers of strangling custom. They further exemplified an effort of will in his last years to display a more encouraging public stance than he felt in private. The plague was taking a bitter toll in Bombay: schools were closed and the Provincial Conference of the Congress was cancelled in 1897, 1898, and 1899.[81] The reform associations likewise curtailed their work.[82] Nonetheless, Ranade steadfastly championed social reformers and continued to receive criticism for his caution. In 1899 he was chairman of a meeting honoring twenty-five years of the widow-marriage movement, at which the principal speaker was Professor D. K. Karve, the new champion of the widow-reform association and a man who had married a widow himself. When Karve finished speaking a young zealot in the audience denounced Ranade's presence as detrimental to the movement. Ranade replied with a long discussion of his marriage to Ramabai, which he prefaced by stating, "We are lame and weak persons. So I say to you my young friend: You lead us and we shall follow you with whatever strength and ability we possess in our frailty."[83]

Ranade was weary of the fight against religious dogmatism and ready to relinquish his leadership. Even the popular doctrines of the poet-saints and his variation on them in the Prarthana Samaj had failed to move men noticeably. He wrote to Gokhale in June 1899, admitting that "religious doctrine is powerless with the vast majority of men to reform their moral conduct." He had lost his public optimism, but his hope remained. He appealed again to an "intellectual puritanism, white, burning puritanism [which will] burn up all impurities. . . . Puritanism is not always intolerance and or fanatical but a self-respecting puritanism is our great want. Men should have settled beliefs which they don't want to question as they don't question gravitation."[84]

Ranade's relations with Poona were still strained. In his last years his patience with the factionalism of the city had expired. In mid-1899 he informed Gokhale from Bombay that another friend had written from Poona "in a strain which makes me despair of Poona, and induces me more than before to think of permanently settling here rather than be witness to such a change as that [sic] has come over Poona. . . . I am speaking of the moral change which gives me more pain than anything I have felt during my last thirty years of residence in Poona."[85] His efforts to revive the defunct Sarvajanik Sabha were of no avail, since he relied on friends like Gokhale, Jathar, and Nagarkar to do the work when their popularity in the city was at an ebb.[86]

The plague had taken toll among Ranade's friends and even within his own household. Several servants and students staying with him died in 1898 and 1899.[87] When his aunt died in late 1899, he wrote to Gokhale, "Though we have been living in the plague for the last three years and more this death has brought it more home to one's feelings than ever before."[88] He became steadily less interested in public affairs, withdrawing perceptibly from social life. He simplified his diet and regulated his daily schedule more rigorously.[89] In his personal religious rituals he redoubled his study of the Maratha saints, the Bhagavad Gita, and the Upanishads. In his private life he sought the solace of the bhakti poets; Tukaram especially grew in importance for him. Despite his physical weakness Ranade continued his daily work, commenting that he wished to work as much as possible before his next life.[90] He was gradually withdrawing from the world in a traditional Brahmin manner.

Nonetheless, he managed a few final public appearances. When Dadabhai Naoroji returned to India in November 1900, a testimonial greeted him. Ranade was the chief speaker at the meeting, adding his personal perspective to the occasion. His view of Dadabhai's contribution to Indian political life had changed markedly in recent years. He said now that Dadabhai's strength lay not in riches or aristocratic birth but in being a man of the people. On this basis he represented the age in which he lived, an age of reconciliation between Britain and India. Ranade seemed to be speaking more of his own vision than of Dadabhai's when he described the great work of reconciling Indians to reliance on continued British dominion in India as the path toward reconstructing India's place among the nations of the world. The task of reconciliation was to be carried out not only between India and England but among the many communities which made up the Indian nation.[91] The speech was a peroration for Ranade's own career.

In the following weeks Ranade became seriously ill.[92] He still hoped to attend the annual Social Conference which was to be held in Lahore in December, but his doctors persuaded him to let Gokhale present his address. The address was a final expression of the scope and limits of Ranade's social reform position. In it he emphasized again reform within the individual. He praised the Vedic age, when Brahmins and Kshatriyas sat at each other's feet, accepting each other not for accidents of birth but for moral stature and profound learning. This was the age of the Rishis, when the exemplars of society embodied wisdom and moral greatness.[93] Ranade then recounted the story of Vashistha and Visvamitra as a paradigm of social reform. Vashistha, the powerful Brahmin, was "a great exponent of Brahmin orthodoxy." He was wise and powerful, but he was also jealous of his position and refused to share it. Visvamitra was equally wise and pure, but he had been born a Kshatriya, so Vashistha held him in contempt. "Throughout the story Vishvamitra represents the view of those who try to admit the non-Aryans into the Aryan community and seek to elevate them." Visvamitra performed such austerities that even the all-powerful Vishistha was forced to recognize Visvamitra's right to become a Brahmarshi and share his power.[94] Ranade's ideal still embodied the Brahmin virtues, but he differed from the majority of his Brahmin contemporaries in believing that the lower classes could achieve the same stature through individual effort and that they should be given every encouragement. Because he was too weak to continue leading the Social Conference, Ranade wrote to Gokhale on his protégé's return from Lahore imploring him to assume the burden. So few young men came forward in these days, he wrote, that Gokhale was a great solace to him, the only one who was generous and strong enough to take over the work.[95] The need for a spiritual son to perpetuate his work was as urgent as ever.

After rallying his strength briefly, Ranade died a few days later, on January 16, 1901. The Bombay High Court met the following day to present eulogies to his memory, and then cancelled its session. Schools and public offices were closed that day for Ranade's funeral, and many people flocked to his bungalow. The Prarthana Samaj conducted a memorial service at the Brahmin burning ghat in the city; over a thousand people attended.[96] It was too late now to realize his friends' hope that Ranade would retire from government service to devote his time to public work. Dadabhai wrote to Ramabai on behalf of the Indian community in London: "The death of my highly esteemed friend Mr. Ranade is indeed a great loss to India and the loss is the more deplorable, as we were so very hopeful that his brilliant talents and great knowledge would now be more completely available for the good of India after his retirement from Government service."[97] In the atmosphere of mutual condolence, Ramabai answered, "Throughout his life he used to speak of you in terms which a pupil in India uses in speaking of a teacher."[98]

In Poona the dissident leaders Ranade left behind united in praising his selflessness and fair-mindedness, his elevation above petty party squabbles. <u>Mahratta</u> stated that "one particular party in Poona was known to identify him with itself. But so far as public work of a general kind was concerned Mr. Ranade, we know, was a man of no party." It invoked his magnanimity of 1895 as proof.[99] Gokhale mourned that his master, on whom he had leaned for advice and encouragement for many years, had left him.

> I feel as though a sudden darkness has fallen upon my life and the best part of the satisfaction of doing public work is, for the present at any rate, gone. Of course, I recognize that it is my duty, as it is that of so many others, to struggle, faintly it may be, but ever in faith and hope--trying in our feeble manner to uphold the banner unfurled by him.[100]

In his own way Gokhale did perpetuate Ranade's hopes, but in the political arena, not the social. The social movement was becoming more radical in its pursuit of social justice, and Gokhale had disqualified himself from this work by marrying a second wife while his first still lingered on her sickbed. Chandavarkar instead assumed leadership of the social movement. He was supported by Bhandarkar, who shared his opposition to caste society, and by K. Natarajan, the Madrasi reformer who had moved to Bombay in 1899 with his militantly liberal newspaper, The Indian Social Reformer.[101] Among non-Brahmins as well, a new militance was growing in Maharashtra around 1900, a movement which Ranade sympathized with but could never have supported actively.[102] His time was past; the generation after 1900 would have been less receptive to his leadership.

In the political realm the tensions Ranade had sought to avert grew inexorably after his death. Tilak, released from jail, steadily increased his political following, while Gokhale attempted to sustain a Moderate character in the political movement. Their failure to cooperate culminated in the Surat Congress of 1907, when Tilak's Extremists marched out of the meetings in protest against the Moderates' acquiescence in repression. This marked not so much the failure of the Moderate generation's work as it did an unavoidable extension of divergent tendencies which Ranade had precariously balanced. Tilak himself was aware of this in his obituary to Ranade in Kesari. He said that Ranade's death left an empty place in every household in Maharashtra, for his worth lay not in his work for any single movement, whether political, legal, social, or religious. He would be remembered and emulated for taking the lifeless and inert body of Poona and infusing each of its members with new life. He left no side of Maharashtrian life untouched. "The greatest quality of Ranade was his fervent faith that the condition of his country would surely improve and he believed, therefore, in making a ceaseless and unsparing effort. He was thus a true guru of the people."[103] Tilak had led the opposition to Ranade in Poona for many years and had displaced his power in that city. He was the one man best qualified to assess Ranade's role and significance for the younger generation. He made it clear that Ranade would be remembered for his versatility and learning and his inspiration to younger men. In this Gokhale concurred, telling the public on one occasion that Ranade could quickly discern earnest workers in public life: "He had a wonderful faculty in this respect and as a result, he was to many young men, scattered all over the country, like the central sun from whom they moved, each in his own orbit and at his own distance."[104]

The lionization of Ranade was already beginning. It would continue, transforming the man into legend. Some called him a great guru, remembering him as the teacher he had always considered himself. But more recalled him as a rishi, the man who brought into the contemporary world the old virtues of moral piety as well as depth of learning. Fewer remembered him as a Victorian gentleman, the crusader for women's rights and the defender of law, stability and intelligence in public life. All the memories contained portions of Ranade's legacy, yet none told the full story. The diversity of his efforts had left its mark on nearly every aspect of the public life of Maharashtra. His failure in his own eyes lay in his inability to sustain the balance which was indispensable to his vision of a revived India.

Notes

[1] Quoted in *Bombay Gazette*, November 6, 1893, p. 6.

[2] Ramabai Ranade, *Reminiscences*, pp. 212-217.

[3] See Ranade to Mehta, January 20, 1895, Mehta Papers. He no longer felt, however, that new ideas were basically his. In these last years in Bombay he left detailed analysis of financial questions to Gokhale and G. V. Joshi, the rising young Poona economist. His own role was as a link with Wacha and Mehta in Bombay. Ranade to Gokhale, February 13, 1899, Gokhale Papers, IX, 443/17.

[4] Deccan Sabha to Bombay Government, November 18, 1896, in Deccan Sabha, Poona, *Correspondence File, 1896-1920*.

[5] Ranade to Mehta, February 9, 1897, Mehta Papers.

[6] Dadabhai to Mehta, June 18, 1896, Mehta Papers.

[7] Westland to Elgin, June 29, 1896, Elgin Papers, F84/68.

[8] Wacha to Mehta, April 9, 1897, Mehta Papers.

[9] Ranade to Wedderburn, March 19, 1897, Gokhale Papers, IX, 443/10.

[10] The complete testimony is reprinted in *Speeches and Writings of Gopal Krishna Gokhale*, ed. R. P. Patwardhan and D. V. Ambekar, new ed., Vol. I: *Economic* (Bombay, 1962), 456-647.

[11] Gokhale to G. V. Joshi, April 16, 1897, Gokhale Papers, V, 203-279. Gokhale in turn gave credit to Ranade and Joshi, writing to Joshi that if honor "has been bestowed on me, I have received it only as your representative, and now I lay it at your feet and Rao Saheb's as our ancient honoured gurudakshina." *Ibid*.

[12] Wolpert, *Tilak and Gokhale*, pp. 83-84. The responsibility for this conflict seems to have been reciprocal, for few of Poona's leaders were willing to cooperate with the special police even at the beginning. Personal communication from Richard Cashman.

[13] See Deccan Sabha, *Correspondence File*.

[14] D. B. Mathur, *Gokhale, A Political Biography* (Bombay, 1966), pp. 24-34.

[15] Babu Piyush Kanti Ghose, editor of *Amrita Bazar Patrika*, in Bapat, *Tilak*, III, Part 2, 93.

[16] Limaye, *History*, pp. 156-158.

[17] Meeting of December 31, 1900, in Deccan Education Society, Poona, *Proceedings of Governing Body and Council*, from July 10, 1896, to August 9, 1911, p. 32.

[18] Ranade to Subba Rao, sometime in the 1890's. Quoted in Rao, *Revived Memories*, p. 256. See also M. Visvesvaraya, *Memoirs of My Working Life* (Bangalore, 1951), pp. 28-29.

[19] V. N. Deshpande, in Bapat, *Tilak*, I, 427-429.

[20] Conversation with N. R. Phatak, January 6, 1965.

[21] The question was ironically familiar to Ranade, as he had been in the vortex of the sedition controversy in the late 1870's. For fuller analysis of the constitutional questions involved, see Tucker, "The Proper Limits of Agitation."

[22] Queen-Empress v. Kahanji, ILR, 18 Bombay 758.

[23] *Ibid*.

[24] Quoted in *Mahratta*, September 5, 1897, p. 8.

[25] A new request for Tilak's release was granted, this time by Justice Badruddin Tyabji, who caused a sensation by his judgment. H. B. Tyabji, *Badruddin Tyabji* (Bombay, 1952), pp. 288-291. Tyabji had originally

been offered Telang's seat in 1893 but asked for special working conditions because of his poor health. His extraordinary demands were refused and the seat was offered to Ranade. Tyabji joined the court when the next opening occurred. See RNP, week of November 11, 1893, p. 14.

[26] This clause was quoted in ILR, 19 Calcutta 35, which was referred to in the Tilak trial.

[27] Queen-Empress v. Bal Gangadhar Tilak, ILR, 22 Bombay 112.

[28] Significantly, Ranade never sat with Strachey on a case in his seven years on the court.

[29] Queen-Empress v. Ramchandra Narayan [Natu], ILR, 22 Bombay 152.

[30] When the Natu decision was announced, there was little criticism from the British press. The Indian press praised Ranade's arguments as a vindication of the impartiality of the courts, which had been in question after the Tilak trial. One article announced that the Natu decision reestablished the integrity of British justice, stating that the "judges have got us back to what is both sound law and sound policy on this matter, and the whole country stands their debtor for it." Advocate of India, quoted in Mahratta, December 5, 1897, p. 7.

[31] Kelkar, Indian Worthies, p. 28; Pradhan and Bhagwat, Tilak, p. 120.

[32] See the author's "Ranade: The Historian as Liberal Nationalist," in A. R. Kulkarni, ed., Historians of Maharashtra, forthcoming.

[33] Cashman, Myth of the "Lokamanya," ch. v.

[34] For a detailed account of the violent and moderate schools of historical interpretation in this period, see ibid., pp. 101-108.

[35] Ibid., p. 105.

[36] R. V. Oturkar, in RMP, Introduction, p. i.

[37] Ibid., pp. ii-iii.

[38] Ibid., p. 63.

[39] Ibid., pp. 68-69.

[40] Ibid., p. 7.

[41] R. P. Patwardhan, in RMP, Introduction, pp. viii-ix.

[42] Mahratta, September 29, 1895, p. 4.

[43] RMP, p. 63.

[44] Ranade, speech at the thirteenth Social Conference, Lucknow, 1899, MW, pp. 226-228.

[45] Ibid., p. 225.

[46] Bernard S. Cohn, The Development and Impact of British Administration in India (New Delhi, 1961), pp. 37-38; G. S. Ghurye, Caste and Class in India (Bombay, 1957), pp. 185-186.

[47] The Raghunandan and Jimuta Vahan traditions of Bengal contrasted significantly with the Mitakshara and Mayukha codes on which the Bombay Codes were partially based. See N. G. Chandavarkar, "Bombay High Court Jubilee Celebration," Times of India, August 14, 1912, pp. 7-8.

[48] Gavdappa v. Girimallappa, ILR, 19 Bombay 331.

[49] Yamunabai v. Manubai, ILR, 23 Bombay 608.

[50] Motilal v. Ratilal, ILR, 21 Bombay 170.

[51] Panchappa v. Sanganbasava, ILR, 24 Bombay 89.

[52] Bai Mangal v. Bai Rukhmini, ILR, 23 Bombay 291.

[53] Bombay Government, Proceedings of the Council of the Governor, 1890, XXXI, 93ff.

[54] See, for example, Bhandarkar's speech on social reform at the Social Conference, 1894, in which he described a steady decline in Hindu

society for many centuries until the arrival of the British. Report of the Eighth Social Conference, pp. 54-62.

[55] Heimsath, Indian Nationalism, p. 197.

[56] Ranade, "Mental Prepossessions," speech at Poona Summer Lecture Series, June 5, 1892; reprinted in Indian Spectator, June 26, 1892, pp. 513-516.

[57] Parvate, Ranade, pp. 296-297.

[58] Gokhale, Late Mr. Justice Ranade, pp. 14-15.

[59] Gokhale, Speeches, p. 899.

[60] Ibid., p. 900.

[61] RMP, p. 3.

[62] RMP, p. 5.

[63] Ranade, "Hindu Theism," RSR, pp. 24-25.

[64] RMP, pp. 174-175.

[65] Mahratta, June 17, 1900.

[66] D. S. Yande, owner of Indu Prakash, in Bapat, Tilak, I, 272-273. Yande relates other incidents of cooperation between Ranade and Tilak in these years as well.

[67] Although he was widely supported for the position of vice chancellor in 1896, he never received that ultimate academic honor. Mahratta, May 3, 1896.

[68] Ranade, "A Note on the Growth of Marathi Literature," reprinted in MW, p. 53.

[69] Ibid., p. 24.

[70] Ibid., p. 14.

[71] Mahratta, July 10, 1898.

[72] Ranade, "The Telang School," RSR, p. 148.

[73] Ranade, speech at the eighth Social Conference, Madras, 1894, MW, p. 134.

[74] Ibid.

[75] Ellen McDonald writes: "The conflict between education as moral improvement and education as dispassionate inquiry into all subjects, regardless of their moral value . . . induced many to take refuge in Hindu tradition." "Social Change," p. 355. Ranade took refuge too, but in his own personal fashion.

[76] Ranade, "Hindu Theism," RSR, p. 12.

[77] Ibid., pp. 24-25.

[78] Ranade, "Hindu Protestantism," RSR, p. 200.

[79] Ibid., p. 199.

[80] Indu Prakash, May 3, 1895.

[81] Mahratta, April 30, 1899, p. 3.

[82] See annual reports of the National Social Conference, 1896-1900.

[83] Chandavarkar, Karve, pp. 81-82; Parvate, Ranade, p. 290.

[84] Ranade to Gokhale, June 24, 1899, Gokhale Papers, IX, 443/21.

[85] Ranade to Gokhale, September 18, 1899, Gokhale Papers, IX, 443/25.

[86] Ranade to Gokhale, December 6, 1899, Gokhale Papers, IX, 443/30.

[87] Ramabai Ranade, Reminiscences, pp. 244-245, 266.

[88] Ranade to Gokhale, September 18, 1899, Gokhale Papers, IX, 443/25.

[89] Ramabai Ranade, Reminiscences, p. 272.

[90] *Ibid.*, p. 285.
[91] *Mahratta*, December 2, 1900.
[92] Mankar, *Ranade*, II, 133ff.
[93] Ranade, speech at the fourteenth Social Conference, Lahore, 1900, *MW*, pp. 244-245.
[94] *Ibid.*, p. 243.
[95] Ranade to Gokhale, January 3, 1901, Gokhale Papers, IX, 443/39.
[96] *Bombay Gazette*, January 18, 1901, pp. 5-6.
[97] Dadabhai to Ramabai Ranade, January 31, 1901, Dadabhai Papers.
[98] Ramabai Ranade to Dadabhai, February 22, 1901, in Masani, *Dadabhai*, p. 425.
[99] *Mahratta*, January 20, 1901.
[100] Gokhale to R. P. Paranjpye, April 12, 1901, in Parvate, *Gokhale*, p. 28.
[101] Natarajan, *A Century of Social Reform*, pp. 109-113.
[102] Heimsath, *Indian Nationalism*, pp. 244ff.
[103] *Kesari*, January 20, 1901.
[104] Parvate, *Gokhale*, p. 30.

GLOSSARY

abhaṅga	A religious verse or hymn; notably composed by <u>bhaktī</u> saints.
advait	"Non-duality"; the school of Hindu philosophy postulating monism.
bhāgavat	A Vaishnava sect, or a devotee of a personal god; in Maharashtra, roughly equivalent to the <u>bhaktī</u> tradition.
bhaktī	The path to salvation through devotion to a personal god. In Maharashtra associated especially with the pilgrimage to the Vithoba temple in Pandharpur.
chauth (cauthāī)	Under the Maratha empire, regular payments exacted from tributary regions in return for protection against other enemies.
dacoity	Robbery.
dakshiṇā	Formerly a prize grant given by the Peshwa to learned Brahmins; converted by the British into a scholarship fund for students.
darbār	An official audience held by the ruler.
desh	country; in Maharashtra, the districts of the Deccan plateau above the coastal <u>ghāṭs</u>; the heartland of Marathi culture.
dewān	Chief minister of a Princely State.
dharma	Righteousness, duty.
dharmashāstra	Authoritative writings on Hindu morality, conduct and law.
dnyān	"Knowledge," especially transcendent knowledge of the Supreme Being.
Gaṇapati	Ganesh; the elephant god, popular in Maharashtra as the god of wisdom and good fortune.
garbhādhāna	In orthodox practice, the ceremony in which marriage is consummated.
ghāṭ	Mountain; specifically, the coastal ranges between the <u>desh</u> and the Arabian Sea.
gūrū	Hindu teacher or spiritual preceptor.
gūrūdakshiṇā	The traditional form of a student's homage to his <u>gūrū</u>.
haḷdī-kuṅkū	A traditional party among Maharashtrian women.
inām	Under the Maratha empire, a tax-free grant of the revenues of a parcel of land; in some cases continued under the British.
ināmdār	The holder of an <u>inām</u>.
jāgir (jahāgir)	Similar to <u>inām</u>, but in Maharashtra implied a larger-scale grant, often including some political and police powers.
jāgirdār	A landed aristocrat; the holder of a <u>jāgir</u>.
kārbhārī	An administrative officer in a Princely State.
karma-yogi	One who seeks spiritual merit through selfless performance of worldly responsibility.
khot	Collector of government revenues; hence, a landholder, especially in the Konkan.

kirtan	Songs, stories and moral homilies, usually based on the epics and myths of Hinduism.
kirtankār	A trained performer of kirtan.
Konkaṇ	The coastal district south of Bombay, home of the Chitpavan Brahmins.
kulkarṇī	Village accountant in charge of land records; in Maharashtra usually a Deshastha Brahmin.
lavād	Arbitration.
mahār	The numerically largest caste of ex-Untouchables in Maharashtra.
māmlatdār	Under the Marathas a revenue officer in charge of a tāluka; under the British, a salaried assistant revenue collector.
Marāṭhā	The cluster of non-Brahmin castes who own and till most of the land of rural Maharashtra. In former British usage, any Marathi-speaking person.
meḷa	A group of singers and dancers, at festival time.
mofussil (mufassil)	The rural area of a district surrounding a major center.
nyāyādhisha	Chief judicial officer of a Princely State.
panchāyat	A council of the elders of a caste or village.
pandal	A tent erected for large meetings.
pāthashālā	A traditional Sanskrit school.
pāṭīl	Village headman; in Maharashtra, usually a Maratha by caste.
Peshwa	Chief minister of the Maratha empire; from 1720 to 1818 the de facto ruler, hereditary in a Chitpavan Brahmin family, with center in Poona.
prāyashcitta	Penance imposed by Brahmin authorities for breach of dharma.
Pūrushasukta	A creation myth, found in Rig Veda 10.90.
rishī	A sage or seer; used broadly to indicate a man of exceptional wisdom, piety and self-discipline.
ryot (rayat)	A cultivator, peasant.
sabhā	An assembly, association, society.
samāj	See sabhā.
sannyāsi	An ascetic who has cast off worldly responsibilities in the search for spiritual enlightenment.
sardār	Formerly a military commander; more recently an important landholder; roughly equivalent to jāgirdār.
satī	The ritual self-immolation of a Hindu widow on her deceased husband's funeral pyre.
sāvkār (sowcar)	A moneylender.
Shaṅkarāchārya	Head of an important temple and monastery center, with final authority over dharma for the surrounding region.
shāstra	See dharmashāstra.
shāstrī	A Brahmin learned in the dharmashāstra.
sheṭ	A well-to-do merchant; in Bombay, usually Gujarati.
shrāddh	Religious ceremony performed by a son to honor his deceased father.

swadeshī	"Of one's own country," especially the nationalist strategy of boycotting British-made cloth.
swāmī	A learned and holy man; sometimes synonymous with <u>Shankarāchārya</u>.
swarājya	"Self-rule," especially home rule or independence.
tāluka	A subdistrict.
tapas	Heat, sometimes considered to contain magical powers, generated by the force of a man's meditation.
vakīl	Pleader, lawyer.
vatan	A grant of land or office; usually refers to hereditary village offices.
yoga	Meditation or spiritual self-discipline leading to union with the Supreme Being.

CHRONOLOGY OF RANADE'S LIFE AND WORK

1842 Born in Niphad, January 18.
1844 Moves to Kolhapur.
1851 Enters Kolhapur English School.
1854 Marries Sakhubai Dandekar.
1856 Goes to Bombay. Enrolls in Elphinstone Institution.
1859 Matriculates at Bombay University.
1860 Junior Fellow at Elphinstone College, until 1863.
1862 Receives B.A. Six months of severe eye trouble. Associate editor of Indu Prakash.
1863 Appointed Teaching Fellow at Bombay University, until 1866.
1866 May: Appointed Marathi Translator for Bombay Government, until 1867.
      Receives LL.B. Appointed karbhari at Akalkot.
1867 Transferred to Kolhapur, then back to Bombay. Joins Prarthana Samaj.
1868 Appointed Assistant Professor of English and History at Elphinstone College.
1869 Joins Bombay Association. Founding member of Managing Committee of Bombay Branch, East India Association. Joins Widow-Remarriage Association. Appointed Assistant Reporter of Bombay High Court.
1870 Joins Managing Committee of Bombay Association.
1871 Passes Advocates Examination. Appointed Judge of Bombay Small Cause Court.
      November: Transferred to Small Cause Court, Poona.
      Joins Poona Prarthana Samaj and Poona Sarvajanik Sabha.
1872 Organizes Sarvajanik Sabha's report on rural conditions.
1873 Father Govindrao moves to Poona.
      October: Sakhubai dies.
      Ranade marries Ramabai. Founds Elocution Society.
1874 Founding of Vedashastrottejaka Sabha.
1875 Govindrao dies. Ranade arranges visit of Dayanand Sarasvati.
1876 Famine in Maharashtra, until 1878.
1878 January: Transferred to Nasik.
      Founds Sahitya Parishad and Society for Promoting Marathi Books.
      Sarvajanik Sabha Journal begins publication.
1879 May: Transferred to Dhulia.
      Phadke's revolt. Deccan Agriculturists' Relief Act.
1880 Assists founding of New English School.
1881 January: Appointed Presidency Magistrate, Bombay.
      March: Returns to Poona Small Cause Court.
      Founds elementary school for girls in Poona.
      August: Appointed Joint Judge of Deccan Agriculturists' Relief Act; thereafter makes annual tours of mofussil until 1893.
1884 January: Founds Deccan Association.
      Founds girls' high school and Poona Women's Training College.
      October: Joins Managing Council of Deccan Education Society.
1885 Joins Age of Consent debate. Helps found the Congress.
      Appointed to Bombay Legislative Council, until 1886.
1886 April: First President, Bombay Graduates' Association.
      March: Appointed to Government of India Finance Committee.

	Travels to Simla, then through northern India to Calcutta.
1887	Founds Indian National Social Conference.
1888	President of All-India Theistic Conference, until 1892; again in 1896.
1890	March: Appointed to Bombay Legislative Council, until 1891. October: Attends Panch Howd Mission's momentous meeting.
1891	February: Contracts near-fatal cholera. Helps found Industrial Conference of Western India. March: Age of Consent Act.
1893	Founds Deccan Social Reform Association. Appointed to Bombay Legislative Council, until 1894. August: Communal riots in Bombay. Ranade resigns from Sharada Sadan. First Ganpati festival in Poona. November: Appointed to Bombay High Court. Elected to Bombay University Senate.
1894	Founds Deccan Vernacular Translation Society.
1895	December: Congress and Social Conference meet in Poona. April: Legislative Council elections in Poona.
1896	Founds Deccan Sabha. First Shivaji festival.
1897	Tilak sedition trial. Famine and plague.
1899	Elected President of Sahitya Parishad.
1901	Dies, January 16.

BIBLIOGRAPHY

I. Primary Sources

Books and Tracts by Ranade:

Dharmapara vyākhyāneṅ (Religious Discourses). Bombay: Nirnayasagar Press, 1902.

Essays on Indian Economics. 2nd ed. Madras: Natesan, 1906.

Miscellaneous Writings of the Late Hon'ble Mr. Justice M. G. Ranade. Published by Ramabai Ranade, with an introduction by D. E. Wacha. Bombay: Manoranjan Press, 1915.

A Note on the Decentralization of Provincial Finance. Poona: Dnyan Prakash Press, 1894.

Plea for Protection: Indian Sugar Industry. Three articles contributed by Ranade to Times of India, May-June 1899. Poona, 1942.

Religious and Social Reform. Ed. M. B. Kolaskar. Bombay: Claridge, 1902.

A Revenue Manual of the British Empire in India: An Epitome of the Fawcett Committee Report. Poona: Dnyan Prakash Press, 1877.

Rise of the Maratha Power. Bombay, 1900. A new edition, including Ranade, "Introduction to the Satara Raja's and the Peshwa's Diaries," and K. T. Telang, "Gleanings from Maratha Chronicles," is Bombay: University of Bombay, 1961.

Statistics of Civil Justice in the Bombay Presidency. Bombay: Times of India Press, 1873. Originally a series of articles printed in Times of India, 1871.

Statistics of Criminal Justice in the Bombay Presidency. Bombay: Times of India Press, 1874. Originally a series of articles printed in Times of India, 1873.

The Texts of Hindu Law on the Lawfulness of Remarriage of Widows, with a note on the "Punarbhu." 2nd ed. Bombay, 1870. Reprinted as "Vedic Authorities for Widow Marriage," in RSR, pp. 53-90.

Vyāpārasambandhī vyākhyāneṅ (Lectures on Trade and Commerce). Poona, 1873. A new edition, with introduction by N. V. Sovani, is Poona, 1963.

Articles by Ranade in Quarterly Journal of the Poona Sarvajanik Sabha:

"Famine Administration in the Bombay Presidency," I (July 1878), 1-31.

"R. B. Dadoba Pandurang and the Swedenborg School," I (January 1879), 43-46. Reprinted in MW, pp. 57-60.

"The Agrarian Problem and Its Solution," II (July 1879), 1-21.

"The Deccan Agriculturists' Bill," II (October 1879), 43-67.

"A Constitution for Native States," II (January 1880), 1-17.

"Sir Richard Temple," II (April 1880), 40-54.

Review of Henry Fawcett's Three Essays on Indian Finance, III (July 1880), 73-81.

"The Law of Land Sale in British India," III (October 1880). Reprinted in EIE, pp. 14-53.

"Sir Salar Jang's Administration," III (October 1880), 30-50.

"Hindu and Mohamedan Religious Endowments," III (January 1881), 1-16.

"Mr. Wedderburn and His Critics on a Permanent Settlement for the Deccan," III (January 1881), 17-36.

"The Central Provinces Land Revenue and Tenancy Bills," III (April 1881), 1-24.

"The Rulers of Baroda," III (April 1881). Reprinted in MW, pp. 60-65.

"Parliamentary Committee on Indian Public Works," IV (July 1881), 1-29.

Reviews of A. Mongredien, Free Trade and English Commerce; and L. Malet's letter on free trade and reciprocal tariffs, IV (July 1881), 50-56.

"Land Law Reform and Agricultural Banks," IV (October 1881), 32-58.

"The Central Asian Question," IV (January 1882), 1-20.

"The Native Civil Service Correspondence," IV (January 1882), 21-35.

"Butler's Method of Ethics," IV (January 1882). Reprinted in MW, pp. 65-90.

"Administrative Reforms in the Bombay Presidency," IV (April 1882), 1-56.

Review of Dadabhai Naoroji on the poverty of India, IV (April 1882), 69-76.

"Primary Education and Indigenous Schools," V (July 1882). Reprinted in MW, pp. 248-275.

"Higher Education--Its Claims on State Support," V (July 1882). Reprinted in MW, pp. 275-294.

"Emancipation of Serfs in Russia," V (October 1882). Reprinted in EIE, pp. 262-276.

"Forest Conservancy in the Bombay Presidency," V (January 1883), 1-18.

"Local Government in England and India," V (April 1883). Reprinted in EIE, pp. 230-261.

"The Agitation in Regard to the Native Magistrates Jurisdiction Bill," V (April 1883), 23-41.

"Prussian Land Legislation and the Bengal Tenancy Bill," V (October 1883). Reprinted in EIE, pp. 277-313.

"Proposed Reforms in the Resettlement of Land Assessments," VI (January 1884), 1-22.

"A Project and a Warning Against the New Departure in the Land Assessment Policy," VI (April 1884), 37-57.

"The Hereditary Officers Act Amendment Bill," VII (October 1885), 17-35.

"A Note on the Reorganization of District Administration," VIII (January 1886), 1-12.

"The Sutra and Smriti Dicta on the Age of the Hindu Marriage," XI (January-April 1889). Published in an earlier form as Preface to A Collection of All Proceedings . . . , ed. Pandit Narayan Keshav Vaidya. Bombay, 1885. Entitled "The Shastric Texts on the Subject of Infant Marriage," it appeared in Gidumal, Status, in the same form as in the Journal. Finally, it was republished with additional remarks on the progress of the remarriage movement in RSR, pp. 27-50.

"Netherlands India and the Culture System," XII (April 1890). Reprinted in EIE, pp. 70-104.

"The Re-organization of Real Credit in India," XIV (July 1891). Reprinted in EIE, pp. 43-69.

"Compulsory Vaccination in the Bombay Presidency," XIV (January 1892), 1-16.

"Indian Political Economy," XV (January 1893). Reprinted in EIE, pp. 1-42.

"Twenty Years' Review of Census Statistics," XV (April 1893). Reprinted in EIE, pp. 209-229.

"Decentralization of Provincial Finance," XVI (July 1893-April 1894). Reprinted under separate cover.

"Indian Foreign Emigration," XVI (October 1893). Reprinted in EIE, pp. 130-169.

"Mr. Justice Ranade on 'Matters Educational,'" XVI (April 1894). Reprinted as "Why Graduates Die Young," MW, pp. 291-315.

"Present State of Indian Manufactures and Outlook of the Same," XVII (October 1894). Reprinted in EIE, pp. 105-129.

"An Unwritten Chapter in Maratha History," XVII (January 1895). Reprinted as ch. xii of RMP.

"On University Reform: Examinations," XVIII (July-October 1895). Reprinted in MW, pp. 316-329.

"The Saints and Prophets of Maharashtra," XVII (April 1895). Reprinted as ch. viii of RMP.

"An Address of Welcome to Lord Elgin," XVIII (January 1896), 10-13.

Writings Drafted or Supervised by Ranade in Quarterly Journal:

"Famine Narratives," I (July and October 1878, and April 1879).

"A Letter to the Famine Commission Regarding the Famine Mortality in the Bombay Presidency," I (October 1878), 9-13.

"A Memorial . . . on the Bill to Amend the Vernacular Press Act," I (October 1878), 29-34.

"A Letter to the Government of Bombay Reviewing the Report of the Deccan Riots Commissioners," I (January 1879), 35-43.

"Representation on the Deccan Agriculturists' Relief Bill," II (January 1880), 103-119.

"Letters to Government on the Deccan Dacoities," II (July 1879), 68-77: and II (April 1880), 120-127.

"Suggestions to His Highness the Gaikwad of Baroda Regarding the Future Constitution of Baroda," IV (January 1882), 24-29.

"An Appeal to Princes," IV (January 1882), 30-33.

"Mr. Baxter and the Poona Sarvajanik Sabha," IV (April 1882), 39-45.

"Representations to Government of India . . . Criminal Procedures Code Amendment Bill," VI (July 1883), 4-10.

"Reply to the Finance Committee's Circular," IX (October 1886-January 1887), 1-35.

"Petition to Parliament Concerning the Mamlatdars' Indemnity Act," XII (April 1890).

Other Writings and Speeches by Ranade:

"The Jubilee Celebration of Queen Victoria," address to the students of Elphinstone College, 1897. Reprinted in A. T. Crawford, Our Troubles in Poona and the Deccan (Westminster: Archibald Constable, 1897), pp. 116-121.

"Currencies and Mints under Mahratta Rule," read before the Bombay Branch of the Royal Asiatic Society, February 16, 1899. Reprinted in MW, pp. 330-342; and in RMP, pp. 216-226.

Article in Bombay Educational Record, III (1867), reviewing "Sairandri" and "Ratna Prabha."

Articles in Bombay Educational Record, III (1867), reviewing "Dnyan Prasarak and Sarva Sangraha," "History of India in Marathi," "Keka Dursh," "Marathi Rudimentary Grammar," "The Bhoslays of Sattara," and "The License Tax."

Deccan Agriculturists' Relief Act. Ranade's writings as Special Judge are collected in DARA I and II, and India Office Library, Private Papers: William Lee-Warner (see below).

English Essay "Beta," written for Senior Scholarship Examination, May 1858, at Elphinstone College. In RDPI, 1858-59, pp. 53-56.

Essay for Senior Scholarship Examination, April 20, 1861, at Elphinstone College. In RDPI, 1860-61, pp. 105-106.

Essay Book, dated June 15, 1858. Contains essays submitted at Elphinstone College, 1858.

Essay Book, 1859. Contains essays and lecture notes at Elphinstone College.

"Introduction to the Peshwa's Diaries," read before the Bombay Branch of the Royal Asiatic Society, June 1900. Reprinted in MW, pp. 342-380, and in RMP, pp. 173-205.

"Introduction," The Speeches and Addresses of Sir H. B. Frere. Ed. B. N. Pitale. Bombay, 1870.

"Learning in the English Language," a Marathi speech in Nasik, August 18, 1878. Paraphrased in Phatak, Ranade, pp. 302-305.

Memorial in defense of Malharrao Gaikwad, adopted at a public meeting in Poona, January 15, 1875. Partially reprinted in Phatak, Ranade, pp. 220ff.

"Mental Prepossessions," speech at Poona Summer Lecture Series, June 5, 1892. Reprinted in Indian Spectator, June 26, 1892, pp. 513-516.

National Social Conference. Ranade's annual addresses are reprinted in each year's Report from 1887 to 1901, and collected as Chintamani, Indian Social Reform, Part II.

"A Note on the Growth of Marathi Literature, 1898," in MW, pp. 12-56.

Ranade et al. "Questions Regarding Social Reforms," circulated with Report of the Eighth National Social Conference, 1894. Reprinted in MW, pp. 143-150.

"Remarks on the Marathi Portion of the Catalogue." Catalogue of Native Publications in the Bombay Presidency, up to 31st December 1864. 2nd ed. Bombay, 1867. Reprinted in MW, pp. 1-11.

Review of government aid to Christian denominations in India. In Government of India, Ecclesiastical Department, Proceedings, May 1887, No. 13-23.

Speech at annual meeting of Bombay Branch, East India Association, 1871. Printed in its Annual Report, 1871.

Speech of V. M. Bhide, Chairman of Reception Committee for the annual meeting of the Indian National Congress, Poona, December 1895. In Indian National Congress, Report of the Proceedings, 1895.

Speech unveiling portrait of Dadabhai Naoroji, Bombay, November 11, 1900. Paraphrased extensively in Mahratta, December 12, 1900.

Private Papers, England:

    Viscount Cross, IOL Eur E 243.
    Lord Curzon, IOL Eur F 111.
    Lord Elgin, IOL Eur F 84.
    Sir James Fergusson, IOL Eur E 214.
    Lord Harris, IOL Eur E 256.
    Sir Courtenay Ilbert, IOL Eur D 594.
    Sir William Lee-Warner, IOL Eur F 92.
    Lord Lytton, IOL Eur E 218.
    Lord Ripon, British Museum I S 290/5, 7, 8.
    Sir Richard Temple, IOL Eur F 86.

Private Papers, India:

Gopal Krishna Gokhale, microfilm copies at National Archives of India, New Delhi, and Servants of India Society, Poona.

Sir Pherozeshah M. Mehta, microfilm copy at National Archives of India.

Dadabhai Naoroji, in the possession of Professor R. P. Patwardhan, Poona.
Bal Gangadhar Tilak, at Kesari-Mahratta Library, Poona.

Other Unpublished Materials:

Deccan Sabha, Poona. Correspondence File, 1896-1920.

McDonald, Ellen E. "Social Change in Late Nineteenth Century Bombay: 1858-98." Ph.D. dissertation, University of California, 1965.

Patterson, Maureen L. P. "Original Konkan Settlements, Spread and Present Distribution of Chitpavans." Paper presented at Maharashtra Studies Group Conference, May 1969, University of Chicago.

Roberts, John. "The Movement of Elites within the Bombay Presidency Under Early British Rule." Paper presented at Maharashtra Studies Group Conference, May 1969, University of Chicago.

Surlacar, J. M. "1857 in Maharashtra." Ph.D. dissertation, Bombay University, 1964.

Tucker, Richard P. "Ideologies of Intercaste Relations in Maharashtra, 1848-75." Paper presented at Maharashtra Studies Group Conference, April 1971, University of Minnesota.

_____. "M. G. Ranade: The Historian as Liberal Nationalist," in *Historians of Maharashtra*, ed. A. R. Kulkarni. Forthcoming.

Zelliot, Eleanor M. "Dr. Ambedkar and the Mahar Movement." Ph.D. dissertation, University of Pennsylvania, 1969.

Official Publications and Documents:

Bombay Government. *Catalogue of Native Publications in the Bombay Presidency, up to 31st December 1864*. 2nd ed. Bombay, 1867.

_____. *Catalogue of Native Publications in the Bombay Presidency from January 1, 1865 to June 30, 1867*. Bombay, 1867.

_____. *Judicial Department, Proceedings*: 1880, Vol. XXV, Nos. 797, 1257; 1881, Vol. XV, No. 71; 1885, No. 1212; 1886, Vol. LXXXVIII, No. 534.

_____. *Proceedings of the Council of the Governor of Bombay*: 1885, Vol. XXIV; 1890, Vol. XXVIII; 1893, Vol. XXXI.

_____. *Report of the Administration . . . for 1878-79*. Bombay, 1879.

_____. *Report of the Director of Public Instruction*. Annual volumes for 1847-48 to 1868-69. Bombay, 1848-69.

_____. *Report of the Committee on the Riots in Poona and Ahmednagar, 1875*. 2 vols. Bombay, 1876.

_____. *Reports on the Native Papers Published in the Bombay Presidency, 1884-1901*.

_____. *Selections from the Records of the Bombay Government. New Series, No. 30: A Selection of Papers Explanatory of the Origin of the Inam Commission*. Bombay, 1856.

_____. *Selections from the Records of the Bombay Government. New Series, No. 31: Correspondence Exhibiting the Results of the Scrutiny by the Inam Commission of the Lists of Deccan Surinjams, Prepared in 1844*. Bombay, 1856.

_____. *Selections from the Records of the Bombay Government. New Series, No. 132: Narrative of the Bombay Inam Commission*, by A. T. Ethbridge. Bombay, 1874.

_____. *Source Materials for a History of the Freedom Movement in India*. Ed. M. R. Palande. 2 vols. I: 1818-85; II: 1885-1920. Bombay, 1957-58.

Government of India. *Census of India*. 1901. Vol. IX-A, Part 2; 1911, Vol. VII, Part 1.

Government of India. Home Department, Judicial A Proceedings: August 1880, Nos. 203-205; June 1887, Nos. 189-192; September 1887, Nos. 282-288, 298-300.

_____. Report of the Public Service Commission, 1887. Vol. IV: Bombay Presidency.

_____. Selections from the Records of the Government of India, No. 342, Home Department Serial No. 20: Papers on the Deccan Agriculturists' Relief Act, 1875-94. 2 vols. Calcutta, 1897.

India Office Library. Private Papers: William Lee-Warner. Deccan Ryot, Series II.

_____. Finance, Politics, etc., Series IV: 1885-89.

_____. Political and Miscellaneous, Series V: 1890-94.

Indian Law Reports, Bombay Series. Vols. I-XXV (1877-1901).

II. Secondary Works

Published Works, English

Agashe, G. J. The Third Anniversary of Mr. Justice M. G. Ranade's Death. Address at Bombay Hindu Union Club, January 16, 1904. Bombay: Indu Prakash Press, 1904.

Ballhatchet, Kenneth. Social Policy and Social Change in Western India, 1817-1830. London: Oxford University Press, 1957.

Banerjea, Surendranath. A Nation in Making. Bombay, 1963.

Bapat, S. V., ed. Reminiscences and Anecdotes of Lokamanya Tilak. 2 vols. Poona: Jagadhitecchu Press, 1924-29.

Bhandare, L. S. Mahadev Govind Ranade: A Social Reformer. Reprinted from Journal of the University of Bombay (July 1942).

Bhandarkar, R. G. Collected Works. 4 vols. Ed. N. B. Utgikar and V. G. Paranjpe. [Bombay] Government Oriental Series, Class B, No. 1. Poona: Bhandarkar Oriental Research Institute, 1933.

Bhate, G. C. History of Modern Marathi Literature: 1800-1938. Poona: Aryabhushan Press, 1939.

[Bhikaji, Dadaji]. An Exposition of Some of the Facts of the Case of Dadaji vs. Rakhmabai. Bombay, 1887.

Blunt, Wilfred Scawen. India Under Ripon. London, 1909.

Bombay Association. Minutes of the Proceedings of the Founding Meeting. Bombay, 1852.

_____. Minutes of the Proceedings of the First Annual General Meeting. Bombay, 1853.

_____. Minutes of the Proceedings of the Second Annual General Meeting, January 1855. Bombay, 1855.

_____. Petition to Parliament, 1852. Bombay, 1852.

_____. Petition . . . relative to the British-Indian Government, 1853. Bombay, 1853.

_____. Minutes of a . . . Public Meeting . . . on March 5, 1868. Bombay, 1868.

Bombay Graduates' Association. First Annual Report. Bombay, 1887.

Bombay, University of. Matriculation Examination Papers in Marathi from 1859 to 1866. Ed. G. M. Pitale. Bombay, 1867.

_____. Papers for the First Examination in Arts in Marathi from 1861 to 1868. Ed. G. M. Pitale. Bombay, 1868.

Brown, D. M. "The Philosophy of Bal Gangadhar Tilak: Karma vs. Jnāna in the Gītā Rahasya." Journal of Asian Studies. XVII (1958), 197-208.

Butler, Joseph. *The Analogy of Religion, Natural and Revealed, to the Constitution and Course of Nature*. London, 1878.

Carpenter, Mary. *Six Months in India*. 2 vols. Bombay, 1868.

Cashman, Richard. *The Myth of the "Lokamanya": Tilak and Mass Politics in Maharashtra*. Berkeley: University of California Press, 1975.

Catanach, Ian J. "Agrarian Disturbances in Nineteenth Century India." *Indian Economic and Social History Review*, III (March 1966), 65-84.

──────. *Rural Conditions and the Cooperative Movement in the Bombay Presidency, 1875-1930*. Berkeley: University of California Press, 1971.

Chandavarkar, G. L. *A Wrestling Soul: Story of the Life of Sir Narayan Chandavarkar*. Bombay: Popular Prakashan, 1955.

Chandavarkar, N. G. "Bombay High Court Jubilee Celebration." *Times of India*, August 14, 1912, pp. 7-8.

──────. *Speeches and Writings*. Bombay: M. G. P. Mandali, 1911.

Chandra, Bipan. *The Rise and Growth of Economic Nationalism in India*. New Delhi: People's Publishing House, 1966.

Chintamani, C. Y., ed. *Indian Social Reform*. Madras: Thompson, 1901.

Cohn, Bernard S. *The Development and Impact of British Administration in India*. New Delhi, 1961.

Collet, S. D., ed. *The Brahmo Year-Book*. Annual vols. London, 1876-79.

Conlon, Frank F. *A Caste in a Changing World: The Chitrapur Saraswat Brahmans*. Berkeley: University of California Press, 1976.

Cotton, J. S. *Mountstuart Elphinstone*. Oxford: Clarendon Press, 1892.

"The Deccan Address to the Hon. Sir A. Grant." *Bombay Educational Record*, IV (November 1868), 338-342.

Deccan Association. *An Appeal for the Promotion of Education Among the Marathas, etc*. Poona: Aryabhushan Press, 1886.

Deccan Education Society. *Reports*. Poona, 1885-86.

Deccan Sabha (Poona). *Golden Jubilee Celebration, January 18, 1947*. Poona, 1947.

Deleury, G. A. *The Cult of Vithoba*. Poona, 1960.

Deshpande, P. Y. "Mahadev Govind Ranade." *Jīvan-Vikās*, III (March 1962), 39-42.

Digby, William. *The Famine Campaign in Southern India, 1876-78*. 2 vols. London: Longmans-Green, 1878.

Dighe, V. G. "The Renaissance in Maharashtra, 1818-70." *Journal of the Asiatic Society of Bombay*, n.s. 36-37 (1961-62), pp. 23-31.

Dobbin, Christine E. "The Ilbert Bill." *Historical Studies, Australia and New Zealand*, XII (October 1965), 87-102.

──────. *Urban Leadership in Western India*. Oxford: Oxford University Press, 1972.

Dongerkery, S. R. *A History of the University of Bombay, 1857-1957*. Bombay: Bombay University Press, 1957.

Dutt, P. *Memoirs of Moti Lal Ghose*. Calcutta, 1935.

Dyer, Helen S. *Pandita Ramabai: The Story of Her Life*. London, n.d.

Enthoven, R. E. *The Tribes and Castes of Bombay*. 3 vols. Bombay: Government Central Press, 1920.

Farquhar, J. N. *Modern Religious Movements in India*. New York: Macmillan, 1915.

Forjett, Charles. *Our Real Danger in India*. London, 1877.

Furber, Holden. *Bombay Presidency in the Mid-Eighteenth Century*. Bombay, 1965.

Gadgil, D. R. *Poona: A Socio-Economic Survey*. Part 1: *Economic*. Poona: Aryabhushan Press, 1945.

Galanter, Marc. "Law and Caste in Modern India." *Asian Survey*, III (November 1963), 544-559.

Gazetteer of the Bombay Presidency. Vol. XVIII, Parts 1-3, *Poona*; Vol. XX: *Kolhapur*.

Ghosh, P. C. *The Development of the Indian National Congress, 1892-1909*. Calcutta: Mukhopadhyay, 1960.

Gidumal, Dayaram. *The Life and Life Work of Behramji M. Malabari*. Bombay, 1888.

―――. *The Status of Woman in India*. Bombay, 1889.

Gillion, Kenneth L. *Ahmedabad*. Berkeley: University of California Press, 1968.

Gokhale, G. K. *The Late Mr. Justice Ranade*. Bombay, 1903.

―――. *Speeches*. Madras: Natesan, 1903. 3rd ed., 1920. An annotated, more complete edition is *Speeches and Writings of Gopal Krishna Gokhale*, ed. R. P. Patwardhan and D. V. Ambekar. 3 vols. Bombay, 1962.

Gopal, S. *The Viceroyalty of Lord Ripon*. London: Oxford University Press, 1953.

Gopalakrishnan, P. K. *Development of Economic Ideas in India, 1880-1950*. New Delhi, 1959.

Gordon, R. G. *The Bombay Survey and Settlement Manual*. 2 vols. Bombay: Government Central Press, 1917.

Gune, V. T. *Judicial System of the Marathas*. Poona: Deccan College, 1953.

Hambly, G. R. G. "Unrest in Northern India During the Vice-Royalty of Lord Mayo, 1869-72: The Background to Lord Northbrook's Policy of Inactivity." *Journal of the Royal Central Asiatic Society*, XLVIII (January 1961), 37-55.

Heimsath, Charles H. *Indian Nationalism and Hindu Social Reform*. Princeton: Princeton University Press, 1964.

Holmes, T. R. E. *History of the Indian Mutiny*. London: T. H. Allen, 1891.

Houghton, Walter E. *The Victorian Frame of Mind*. New Haven: Yale University Press, 1957.

Hunter, W. W. *Bombay: 1885-1890*. London: John Murray, 1892.

Hutchins, Francis G. *The Illusion of Permanence: British Imperialism in India*. Princeton: Princeton University Press, 1967.

Inamdar, N. R. "Political Thought of Vishnushastri Chiplunkar." *Journal of the University of Poona, Humanities Section*, No. 31 (1969), 15-24.

―――. "Political Thought in Journals in Maharashtra During 1818-1873." *Journal of the University of Poona, Humanities Section* (1968), 37-55.

Indian National Congress. *Reports of the Proceedings*. 1885-1901.

Indian Worthies. Vol. I. Bombay: M. G. P. Mandali, 1906.

Jacob, Sir George LeGrand. *Western India Before and During the Mutinies*. London: King & Co., 1871.

Jagirdar, P. J. *Studies in the Social Thought of M. G. Ranade*. Bombay, 1963.

Jambhekar, G. G. *Memories and Writings of Acharya Bal Shastri Jambhekar*. 3 vols. Poona: Lokashikshana Karyalaya, 1950.

Johnson, Gordon. "Chitpavan Brahmins and Politics in Western India in the Late Nineteenth and Early Twentieth Centuries." *Elites in South Asia*, ed. E. R. Leach and S. N. Mukherjee. Cambridge: Cambridge University Press, 1971.

_____. *Provincial Politics and Indian Nationalism: Bombay and the Indian National Congress, 1890 to 1915*. Cambridge: Cambridge University Press, 1973.

Joshi, Ganesh Vyankatesh. *The Late Mr. Justice Mahadev Govind Ranade: A Tribute to His Memory*. Poona, 1905.

_____. *Writings and Speeches*. Poona: Aryabhushan Press, 1912.

Joshi, V. S. *Vasudeo Balvant Phadke, First Indian Rebel Against British Rule*. Bombay, 1929.

Kale, V. G. *Gokhale and Economic Reforms*. Poona: Aryabhushan Press, 1916.

Kane, P. V. *History of Dharmasastra*. 5 vols. Poona: Bhandarkar Oriental Research Institute, 1930-62.

Karandikar, S. L. *Lokamanya Bal Gangadhar Tilak*. Poona: M. G. Shirali, 1957.

Karkaria, R. P. *India: Forty Years of Progress and Reform*. London: Henry Frowde, 1896.

Karve, D. G. *Ranade: The Prophet of Liberated India*. Poona: Aryabhushan Press, 1942.

Karve, Iravati. "On the Road: A Maharashtrian Pilgrimage." *Journal of Asian Studies*, XXII (November 1962), 13-30.

_____. *Maharashtra--Land and Its People*. Bombay: Government Press, 1968.

Keatinge, G. *Rural Economy in the Bombay Deccan*. London: Longmans-Green, 1912.

Keer, Dhananjay. *Mahatma Jotiba Phooley*. Bombay: Popular Prakashan, 1964.

Kelkar, N. C. *Life and Times of Lokamanya Tilak*. A translation and abridgment by D. V. Divekar of *Lo. Tilak yañce caritra*, vol. 1. Madras: S. Ganesan, 1928.

Kellock, James. *Mahadev Govind Ranade*. Calcutta: Association Press, 1926.

Kikani, L. T. *Caste in Courts*. Rajkot: Ganatra, 1912.

Kirtikar, K. R. *Two Addresses on the Theistic Movement in Western India*. [c. 1873].

Knight, Robert. *The Inam Commission Unmasked*. London: Effingham Wilson, 1859.

Kopf, David. *British Orientalism and the Bengal Renaissance*. Berkeley: University of California Press, 1969.

Kumar, Ravinder. "The Deccan Riots of 1875." *Journal of Asian Studies*, XXIV (August 1965), 613-636.

_____. *Western India in the Nineteenth Century*. London: Routledge & Kegan Paul, 1968.

Kunte, M. M. *The Reform Question*. 2 vols. Bombay: Indu Prakash, 1870-71.

Latthe, A. B. *Memoirs of His Highness Shri Shahu Chhatrapati, Maharaja of Kolhapur*. 2 vols. Bombay, 1924.

Lee-Warner, Sir William. *Protected Princes of India*. London, 1894.

Limaye, P. M. *The History of the Deccan Education Society*. Poona: Aryabhushan Press, 1935.

Majumdar, R. C., ed. *History of the Freedom Movement in India*. Vol. I. Calcutta, 1963.

Malabari, B. "Ranade and His Times." *East and West* (November 1903), pp. 1299-1311.

Malleson, G. B. *An Historical Sketch of the Native States of India*. London, 1875.

―――――, ed. *History of the Indian Mutiny, 1857-59*. 3 vols. London, 1880. Vol. II: *History of the Indian Mutiny*, by J. W. Kaye.

Mandlik, V. N. *Brief History of the Wattandar Khotes of the Southern Konkan District*. Bombay: Times of India, 1874.

Mangudkar, M. P. "Liberal Thought in Maharashtra." *Journal of the University of Poona*, IX (1958), 77-86.

Mankar, G. A. *A Sketch of the Life and Works of the Late Mr. Justice M. G. Ranade*. 2 vols. Bombay: Caxton, 1902.

Mankar, G. S., and J. Nanabhai. *Examination Papers . . . for Subordinate Judge, High Court Pleader . . . 1869-89*. Bombay, 1890.

Martin, Briton. "Lord Dufferin and the National Congress, 1885-1888." *Journal of British Studies*, VII (November 1967), 68-96.

Masani, R. P. *Evolution of Self-Government in Bombay*. London, 1929.

―――――. *Dadabhai Naoroji*. London: Allen & Unwin, 1939.

Masselos, James C. "Lytton's 'Great Tamasha' and Indian Unity." *Journal of Indian History*, XLIV (December 1966), 731-760.

―――――. *Towards Nationalism: Group Affiliations and Politics of Public Associations in Nineteenth Century Western India*. Bombay: Popular Prakashan, 1975.

Mate, M. S. *Temples and Legends of Maharashtra*. Bombay: Bharatiya Vidya Bhavan, 1962.

Mathur, D. B. *Gokhale: A Political Biography*. Bombay, 1966.

McCully, Bruce. *English Education and the Origins of Indian Nationalism*. New York: Columbia University Press, 1940.

McDonald, Ellen E. "English Education and Social Reform in Late Nineteenth Century Bombay." *Journal of Asian Studies*, XXV (May 1966), 453-470.

―――――. "The Modernizing of Communication: Vernacular Publishing in Nineteenth Century Maharashtra." *Asian Survey*, VIII (July 1968), 589-606.

McLane, John R. "Peasants, Money-lenders and Nationalists at the End of the Nineteenth Century." *Indian Economic and Social History Review*, I (July 1963), 66-73.

Mehrotra, S. R. "The Poona Sarvajanik Sabha: The Early Phase (1870-1880)." *Indian Economic and Social History Review*, VI (September 1969), 293-322.

Mehta, P. M. *Speeches and Writings*. Ed. C. Y. Chintamani. Allahabad: Indian Press, 1905.

Metcalf, Thomas R. *The Aftermath of Revolt: India from 1857 to 1870*. Princeton: Princeton University Press, 1965.

Minayeff, I. P. *Travels in and Diaries of India and Burma*. Tr. H. Sanyal. Calcutta, 1955.

Minocha, V. S. "Ranade on the Agrarian Problem." *Indian Economic and Social History Review*, II (October 1965), 357-366.

Mitchell, John Murray. *In Western India: Recollections of My Early Missionary Life*. Edinburgh, 1899.

Mody, H. P. *Sir Pherozeshah Mehta: A Political Biography*. 2 vols. Bombay: Times Press, 1921.

Moore, R. J. *Liberalism and Indian Politics, 1872-1922.* London, 1966.

Morris, M. D. *The Emergence of an Industrial Labor Force in India: A Study of the Bombay Cotton Mills, 1854-1947.* Berkeley: University of California Press, 1965.

Motiwala, B. N. *Karsondas Mulji.* Bombay, 1935.

Moulton, Edward C. *Lord Northbrook's Indian Administration, 1872-1876.* Bombay: Asia, 1968.

Mozoomdar, P. C. "Six Months in Simla." *Interpreter* (December 1886), pp. 113-124.

Naik, V. N. *Kashinath Trimbak Telang.* Madras: Natesan, n.d.

Naoroji, Dadabhai. *Baroda Administration in 1874.* London, [1875].

_____. *Poverty and Un-British Rule in India.* London: Swan Sonnenschein, 1901.

Natarajan, S. *A Century of Social Reform in India.* London, 1959.

Nowrozjee Furdoonjee. *On the Civil Administration of the Bombay Presidency.* London: John Chapman, 1853.

Pal, B. C. *Memories of My Life and Times.* Vol. II: *1886-1900.* Calcutta: Yugayatri, 1951.

Parvate, T. V. *Bal Gangadhar Tilak.* Ahmedabad: Navajivan, 1958.

_____. *Gopal Krishna Gokhale.* Ahmedabad: Navajivan, 1959.

_____. *Mahadeo Govind Ranade: A Biography.* Bombay: Asia, 1963.

Patterson, Maureen L. P. "Changing Patterns of Occupations Among Chitpavan Brahmans." *Indian Economic and Social History Review,* VII (September 1970), 375-396.

_____. "Chitpavan Brahman Family Histories: Sources for a Study of Social Structure and Social Change in Maharashtra." *Structure and Change in Indian Society,* ed. Milton Singer and Bernard S. Cohn. Chicago: Aldine Publishing Co., 1968.

Phatak, N. R., et al. *Rationalists of Maharashtra.* Indian Renaissance Institute, Essays and Monographs, No. 3. Calcutta: Renaissance Publishers, 1962.

Pradhan, B. P., and A. K. Bhagwat. *Lokamanya Tilak, A Biography.* Bombay: Jaico, 1958.

Raeside, Ian. "Early Prose Fiction in Marathi, 1828-1885." *Journal of Asian Studies,* XXVII (August 1968), 791-808.

Raghunathadas, Madhavadas. *Story of a Widow Remarriage: Being the Experiences of Madhowdas Rugnathdas, Merchant of Bombay.* Bombay: Khambata, 1890.

Ratcliffe, S. K. *Sir William Wedderburn and the Indian Reform Movement.* London, 1923.

Rath, N. "A Note on the Famine Inquiries of the Poona Sarvajanik Sabha." *Thought Currents in Maharashtra 1850-1920.* Poona: Poona University Press, 1962.

Reed, Sir Stanley. "My First Year in India." *Times of India Annual 1925.*

Report of the Deccan Vernacular Translation Society for the Year 1901-1902. Poona, 1903.

Report of the First Industrial Conference, held at Poona on August 24-27, 1891. Poona, 1891.

Report of the Maharaj Libel Case. Bombay, 1862.

Report of the Poona Sarvajanik Sabha on Matters Relating to India. Poona, 1873.

Report of the Trial of Wasudev Bulwant Phadkey . . . together with his diary and autobiography. Poona, 1879.

Rogers, A. *The Land Revenue of Bombay*. 2 vols. London: W. H. Allen, 1892.

Sarma, D. S. *The Renaissance of Hinduism*. Benares: Benares Hindu University, 1944.

Sastri, Sivanath. *History of the Brahmo Samaj*. 2 vols. Calcutta, 1911-12.

Seal, Anil. *The Emergence of Indian Nationalism*. Cambridge: Cambridge University Press, 1968.

Selby, F. G. *What Are We Here For? Address at Deccan College, March 20, 1894*. Poona: Kulkarni, Gokhale & Co., 1894.

Sen, Surendranath. *Administrative System of the Marathas*. 2nd ed. Calcutta: Calcutta University Press, 1925.

Shahani, T. K. *Gopal Krishna Gokhale: A Historical Biography*. Bombay: Mody, 1929.

Shils, Edward. *The Intellectual Between Tradition and Modernity: The Indian Situation*. The Hague: Mouton, 1961.

Shinde, V. R. *The Theistic Directory*. Bombay, 1912.

Singh, Bawa Chhajju. *The Life and Teachings of Swami Dayananda*. Part 1: *Saraswati*. Lahore, 1903.

Singh, H. L. *Problems and Policies of the British in India 1885-98*. Bombay: Asia, 1963.

Singh, Karan. *Prophet of Indian Nationalism: A Study of the Political Thought of Sri Aurobindo Ghosh, 1893-1910*. London, 1963.

Smith, George. *The Life of John Wilson*. London, 1878.

Smith, William Roy. *Nationalism and Reform in India*. New Haven: Yale University Press, 1938.

Sovani, N. V. "Ranade's Model of the Indian Economy." *Artha Vidnyāna*, IV (1962), 10-20.

Srinivasa Sastri, V. S. *Centenary of the Birthday of M. G. Ranade*. Madras: Law Journal Press, 1942.

──────. *Life of Gopal Krishna Gokhale*. Bangalore: Bangalore Printing & Publishing Co., 1937.

Students' Literary and Scientific Society. *Third Report*. Bombay, 1852.

Subba Rao, K. *Revived Memories*. Madras: Ganesh & Co., 1933.

Taleyarkhan, D. A. *The Revolution at Baroda 1874-75*. Bombay: Sorabjee & Co., 1875.

Telang, K. T. *Free Trade and Protection, From an Indian Point of View*. Bombay: Atmaram Sagoon, 1877.

──────. *Select Writings and Speeches*. 2 vols. Bombay: Manoranjan Press, 1916-30.

Temple, Sir Richard. *India in 1880*. London: John Murray, 1881.

Tucker, Richard P. "The Defense of Dharma in Maharashtra: The Redefinition of Orthodoxy Between 1830 and 1857." *Maratha History Seminar (May 28-31, 1970) Papers*, ed. A. G. Pawar. Kolhapur: Shivaji University Press, 1971.

──────. "From Dharmashastra to Politics: Aspects of Social Authority in Nineteenth-Century Maharashtra." *Indian Economic and Social History Review*, VII (September 1970), 325-346.

──────. "Hindu Traditionalism and Nationalist Ideologies in Nineteenth-Century Maharashtra." *Modern Asian Studies*, X (1976), 321-348.

──────. "The Proper Limits of Agitation: The Crisis of 1879-80 in Bombay Presidency." *Journal of Asian Studies*, XXXVIII (February 1969), 339-355.

Tyabji, Husain B. *Badruddin Tyabji*. Bombay: Thacker, 1952.

Vaidya, C. V. *On the History of Hindu Social Reform Agitation*. Social Reform Series, No. 1. Poona, 1890.

Visvesvaraya, Sir M. *Memoirs of My Working Life*. Bangalore, 1951.

Wacha, Sir Dinshaw E. *Shells from the Sands of Bombay, being my recollections and reminiscences 1860-75*. Bombay: Anklesaria, 1920.

Wedderburn, W. *Allan Octavian Hume*. London: T. Fisher Unwin, 1913.

──────. *The Indian Raiyat as a Member of the Village Community*. London, 1883.

──────. *A Permanent Settlement for the Deccan*. Bombay, 1880.

West, Sir Raymond. "Mr. Justice Telang." *Journal of the Royal Asiatic Society* (1894), pp. 103-147.

Wolpert, Stanley A. *Tilak and Gokhale*. Berkeley: University of California Press, 1962.

Yajnik, Javerilal U. *Writings and Speeches . . . with a short sketch of the biography*. Vol. I. Ahmedabad: Union Printing Press, n.d.

Zelliot, Eleanor. "The Nineteenth Century Background of the Mahar and Non-Brahman Movements in Maharashtra." *Indian Economic and Social History Review*, VII (September 1970), 397-415.

Published Works, Marathi

Bapat, S. V., ed. *Lokamānya Ṭiḷak yāñcyā āthavaṇī va ākhyāyikā* (Reminiscences and Recollections of Lokamanya Tilak). 3 vols. Poona, 1924-28.

Bhagwat, B. H. *Prārthanā mandīrācā saṅkshipta vṛttānta* (A Brief Account of the Prarthana Mandir, Bombay; with a list in English of the subscribers). Bombay, 1877.

Borvankar, Ramchandra Ganesh. *Gaṇeś Vāsudev Jośī urpha Sārvajanik Kākā yāñce caritra* (The Life of Ganesh Vasudev Joshi alias the Uncle of the People). Poona, 1924.

Chiplunkar, V. K. *Nibaṅdhamālā* (A Garland of Essays). 3rd ed. Poona, 1926.

Deshmukh, G. H. [Lokahitawadi]. *Śatapatre* (A Hundred Letters). Ed. S. R. Tikekar. Poona: City Book Stall, 1963.

Deshpande, G. *Mājhī jīvanakathā* (My Life Story). Bombay: Mouj, 1960.

Havaldar, G. R. *Rāvasāheb Viśvanāth Nārāyaṇ Maṇḍlik* (Rao Saheb Vishvanath Narayan Mandlik). 2 vols. Bombay, 1927.

Kelkar, N. D. *Lo. Ṭiḷak yāñce caritra* (The Life of Lokamanya Tilak). 3 vols. Poona, 1923-28.

Kesari-Mahratta. *Lokamānya Ṭiḷak janma-śatābdī viśeshāṅka* (Lokamanya Tilak Special Centenary Issue). Poona, 1956.

Kulkarni, P. B. *Māmā Paramānand āṇi tyāñca kālakhaṇḍa* (The Life and Times of Mama Parmanand). Bombay: Nirnayasagara Press, 1963.

Lokahitawadi. See Deshmukh, G. H.

Madkholkar, G. T., and S. N. Banhatti. *Vishṇū Krishṇa Cipḷūnkar* (Vishnu Krishna Chiplunkar). Bombay, 1934.

Maharashtra Sahitya Parishad. *Hirak Mahotsava* (Diamond Jubilee). Poona, 1970.

Mumbaī ethīl prārthanāsamājācī hakīkat (Account of the Prarthana Samaj of Bombay). Bombay, 1883.

Phatak, N. R. *Nyāyamūrti Mahādev Govind Rānaḍe yāñce caritra* (The Life of Justice Mahadev Govind Ranade). Bombay, 1925. Rev. ed. Poona, 1966.

Priyolkar, A. K. *Paramahamsa sabhā va tice adhyaksha Rāmchandra Bālkrishṇa* (The Paramahamsa Sabha and Its President Ramchandra Balkrishna). Bombay, 1966.

———. *Rāv bahādūr Dādobā Pāṇḍuraṅga* (Rao Bahadur Dadoba Pandurang). Bombay, 1947.

Punā asosieśan mhaṇje puṇyāntīl sārvajanik sabhā hyā sabhece nīyam (Rules of the Poona Association or the People's Association of Poona). Poona, 1867.

Punarvivāhottejak maṇḍalīcyā don sahāmahīnce riporṭ (The Two Half-Yearly Reports of the Widow Marriage Association, from 1st February 1869 to 30th January 1870). Bombay, 1870.

Puṇeṅ vedaśāstrottejaka sabhecā śake 1808 sālacā vārshika riporṭa (Poona Society for Promoting the Veda: Annual Report for 1883-84). Poona, 1884.

Puṇeṅ yethīl sārvajanik sabhecī racanā va nīyam (Poona People's Association: Procedures and Rules). Poona, 1870.

Ranade, Ramabai. *Āmcyā āyushyāntīl kāhī āṭhavaṇī* (Some Memories of Our Life Together). Poona, 1910.

Vaidya, Dvarkanath Govind. *Prārthanāsamājācā itihās* (The History of the Prarthana Samaj). Bombay: Prarthana Samaj, 1927.

Periodicals and Newspapers

 Bombay Educational Record, II-IV (1866-68).

 Bombay Gazette, 1862-1901.

 Deccan Herald, 1876-78.

 Dnyan Prakash, 1848-80, incomplete files.

 Dnyanoday, 1844-80.

 Elphinstone School Paper, I-V (1859-64).

 Indu Prakash, 1883-95.

 Journal of the East India Association, Bombay Branch, I-V (1867-71).

 Kiran, 1877-79.

 Mahratta, 1881-1901.

 Native Opinion, 1864-80.

 Quarterly Journal of the Poona Sarvajanik Sabha, I-XVIII (1878-96).

 Subodh Patrika, December 1877-January 1901, incomplete files.

 Times of India, 1861-1901, 1912.

INDEX

Agarkar, Gopal Ganesh, 135, 140-41, 146, 164, 167, 170, 210

Age of Consent controversy, 155-59, 168-75

Agricultural banks, 114-15, 180-81

Aitchison Commission, 122, 127

Akalkot, 31-32

All-India Theistic Conference, 166

Apte, Ram Dixit, 61, 74

Apte, Vaman Shivram, 134-36, 170

Arbitration courts, 107

Arjun, Sakharam, 159

Arms Act of 1878, 120

Arnould, Joseph, 157

Arya Mahila Samaj, 128

Arya Samaj (Bombay branch), 61

Ashburner, Lionel, 90, 95

Asiatic Society, Royal (Bombay branch), 18, 26

Atmaram Pandurang (Tarkhadkar), 43

Baji Rao II, 5

Banerjea, Surendranath, 148, 196-97

Banias, 2, 17, 23. See also Marwaris, savkars

Baroda State. See Gaikwad

Barve, Mahadev Vasudev, 140-41

Beauclerk, S., 181

Bengal Tenancy Bill, 114

Bentinck, Lord William, 157

Bhakti, 9, 14 n.28, 46, 165, 204 n.52, 221, 223-27
  as Bhagwat Dharma, 225
  See also Prarthana Samaj

Bhandarkar, Ramkrishna Gopal, 24, 48, 136, 158, 173-74, 187, 194-95, 211, 219, 220, 229

Bhat, C. N., 187, 189

Bhau Daji (Lad), 26, 87

Bhide, Vishnu Moreshwar, 70, 193, 198

Blunt, Wildred Scawen, 145

Bombay Association
  1852-54, 34-35
  revived in 1867, 35, 82

Bombay Education Society, 22, 41

Bombay Government
  Board of Education, 22
  High Court, 94, 207, 212-14, 218-19
  Legislative Council, 144, 208

Bombay Graduates Association, 131

Bombay Presidency Association, 190

Bombay University, 23-26, 42, 222-23

Brahman Sabha, 220

Brahmins
  Chitpavan, 4; occupations, 5-6; in Bombay, 17, 23; and widow remarriage, 48-51
  Deshastha, 3, 112
  Gaud Saraswat, 3, 5, 17, 23, 48-54

Brahmo Samaj, 44, 62, 164

Butler, Joseph, 45-46, 167

Canning, Lord Charles, 20, 86

Chaitanya, 223

Chandavarkar, Narayan Ganesh, 158, 161, 163, 172, 208, 219, 229

Chapekar, Damodar, 205 n.89, 213-14

Chiplunkar, Krishna Shastri, 70, 131-33, 186

Chiplunkar, Sitaram Hari, 148, 223

Chiplunkar, Vishnu Shastri, 132-35, 137

Chitrashala Press, 133

Dadaji Bhikaji, 159-60

Dadoba Pandurang (Tarkhadkar), 44

Daftardar, Vithoba Anna, 51-52, 98 n.23

Dakshina Prize Committee, 131-32

Dalhousie, Lord, 19, 85

Date, Shridhar Vithal, 197

Dayananda Saraswati, 61-62, 168

Deccan Agriculturists' Relief Act, 102-09, 173, 180
  conciliators, 107-09

Deccan Association
  of 1852, 71
  revived 1867, 72
  of 1884, 129-30

Deccan College, 58, 131, 136-37, 167
  See also Sanskrit College (Poona)

Deccan Education Society, 136-37, 167, 170, 211

255

Deccan Institute, 70
Deccan riots, 83
  Commission, 83, 104
Deccan Sabha, 201-02, 208, 210
Deccan Vernacular Translation
  Society, 70, 151 n.26
Deodhar, Sitaram Ganesh, 210
De Rozio, Henry, 43
Deshmukh, Gopal Hari, 42, 51, 70,
  75, 78, 131-32, 187, 203 n.7, 223
Deshmukh, Krishnarao Gopal, 53-54
Dhamdhere, Abasaheb, 69
Dnyaneshwar, 9, 14 n.28
Dufferin, Lord, 130, 161, 181
Durbar of 1877, 88-89, 138

East India Association, Bombay
  Branch, 36, 76, 87, 142
Educational policy, 22-24, 41-43,
  66-67, 69, 222-23
Elocution Encouragement Society, 55
  144, 166
Elphinstone, Lord, 19-20
Elphinstone, Mountstuart, 6, 20, 22,
  29-30
Elphinstone College, 20, 33
Elphinstone Institution (high school),
  23
Essays on Indian Economics, 179-82

Famines
  1876-78, 83-85
  1897, 200-02, 209-10
Fawcett Committee, 76-77
Female Training College (Poona),
  129
Fergusson, James, 94-96, 119-20, 136;
  Ranade on, 145
Fergusson College, 136, 198
Finance Committee of 1886, 130-31
Frere, Bartle, 20-22, 24, 31, 86, 145
  Ranade's evaluation of, 21, 31
Furdoonji, Naoroji, 76

Gadgil, Krishnaji Parashuram, 72, 194,
  196-97
Gaikwad
  princely family, 4, 51, 163
  Sayajirao, 4, 88, 129-30, 139
  Malharrao, 87, 140
Gajendragadkar, Narayanacharya, 52
Gandhi, Mohandas Karamchand, 220

Ganesh Festival, 191-92
Garud, Dhondo Shamrao, 205 n.60
Ghose, Motilal, 197
Gidumal, Dayaram, 171, 172
Gokhale, Gopal Krishna, 10, 47,
  149, 170, 174, 193, 198-99,
  209, 226, 228-29
Gole, Mahadev Shivram, 147
Grant, Alexander, 25, 28
Grant Duff, James, 28, 215

Hari Maiti, 172
Harris, Lord, 189-90
Hindu Religion, Society for the
  Protection of, 49-54
Howard, E. I., 23
Hume, Allan Octavian, 87, 148
Hunter Education Commission,
  128, 130
Huzur Paga School, 61, 128

Ilbert, Courtenay, 130
Ilbert Bill, 141-43, 146, 158
Inam Commission, 70, 111-12
Indian Cooperative Societies
  Act of 1904, 181
  See also agricultural banks
Indian Council Acts
  of 1861, 21
  of 1892, 189
Indian National Congress, 147-49,
  169, 226
Indian National Social Conference,
  162-63, 169, 171, 182, 191,
  194-95, 217, 227
Industrial Conference of Western
  India, 181-82

Jagirdar. See sardars
Jambhekar, Bal Shastri, 41, 48
Jathar, S. B., 192-93, 196
Jinsivale, Shridhar Ganesh, 198
Joshi, Ganesh Vasudev, 74-75, 78,
  89, 107, 129
Joshi, Ganesh Vyankatesh, 206 n.
  102
Joshi, Gopal Vinayak, 183

Kahanji Sedition Case, 212
Kalyanonnayaka Mandali. See
  Society for General Amelioration
Kanitkar, G. V., 171

256

Karve, Dhondo Keshav, 226
Kayastha Conference, 163
Keays, R., 71
Kelkar, Sadashiv Pandurang, 62
Khan, Sayyid Ahmad, 149
Kirtane, Janardan Hari, 8
Kirtane, Vinayak Janardan, 8, 12
Kolhapur, 4, 6-7, 19-20, 31-33
Kulkarni, 3, 14 n.20
Kunbi. See Maratha
Kunte, Mahadev Moreshwar, 25, 50, 54, 64 n.38, 133, 134, 146-47

Lansdowne, Lord, 189
Lectures on Trade and Commerce, 77-78
Literary Society of Maharashtra, 132, 222
Local self-government, 75, 145-47
　under Ripon, 116-20
Lokahitawadi. See Gopal Hari Deshmukh
Lytton, Lord, 83, 89, 92-94, 120-23

Macaulay, Thomas Babington, 22
Madhavrao, T., 88, 141, 162
Mahar, 5, 221
Maine, Henry, 141
Malabari, Behramji, 156-60, 167, 171, 218
Mamlatdar, 5, 7
Mankar, G. A., 33, 58
Maratha (Kunbi), 2, 4, 14 n.20, 17, 82-85, 129
　and DARA, 103-09
　and economic growth, 110-15
Marathi Granthottejaka Mandali
　See Society for Promoting Marathi Books
Marwaris, 2, 83, 112
　See also Banias, savkars
Mate, Vyankat Shastri, 52
Mavlankar, Ganesh Shastri, 173
Mayo, Lord, 75, 116
Mehta, Pherozeshah, 193, 208, 211
Mill, John Stuart, 30, 167, 171, 224
Modak, Vaman Abaji, 24, 60, 129
Moropant, 46, 133
Mozumdar, Pratap Chander, 44
Mulji, Karsondas, 157, 169
Murray Trial, 142

Muslims
　in Bombay, 17, 20, 23, 35, 142, 190-92
　in Desh, 72
　Ranade on, 116, 149, 217
Nagarkar, R. D., 184-85
Namdev, 165
Namjoshi, Mahadev Ballal, 134, 148, 170, 181, 196-97
Nanak, Guru, 223
Naoroji, Dadabhai, 35-36, 75, 77, 87-88, 130, 161, 209, 227
Natarajan, K., 229
Native General Library (Poona), 55, 70
Native Improvement Association, 41
Natu, Balasaheb, 173, 184
Natu, Ganesh Ballal, 73
Natu, Tatiasaheb, 191
New English School, 134-36, 166
Non-Brahmin Movement, 219-22, 229. See also Phule, Jotirao
Nulkar, Krishnaji Lakshman, 81, 146, 187, 223

Padmanji, Baba, 48
Pal, Bipin Chandra, 148
Panch Howd Mission, 183-85, 187
Panchayats, 6-7, 80, 107-08, 116
Pandit, Daji Krishna, 7
Pandit, Shankar Pandurang, 61, 223
Pandit, Vishnu Shastri, 42, 48-51, 60, 62, 169
Pandita Ramabai, 128, 187-88
Pant Pratinidhi, 74
Paramahamsa Sabha, 43, 48
Parmanand, Narayan Mahadev, 91
Parsis, 17, 23, 35, 142
　and education, 23, 223
Parsons, Justice, 213-14
Parvati Temple, 73
Patil, 14 n.20, 108
Patwardhan, Annasaheb, 193
Patwardhan, Wasudev Balwant, 197, 210
Peile, James, 209
Pelly, Lewis, 88
Permanent Settlement, 113-15

Perry, Erskine, 22, 69
Peshwas, 2, 55, 111
  Ranade on, 216, 222
Phadke, Vasudev Balwant, 91-93
Phayre, Robert, 87
Phule, Jotirao, 5, 134, 219
Phulmoni Bai, 172
Plague, 210, 226
Pollen, A. D., 105-09
Poona Association, 72-73
Poona High School, 70
Poona Municipal Corporation, 72, 146, 190, 192
Prabhu, 13 n.8, 17, 23
Prarthana Samaj, 10, 43-48, 60-62, 162, 164, 166, 185, 223-26, 228
Pratoda Case, 213-14

Raghunathrao, R., 162
Rajmachikar, Tryambak Narayan, 147
Rajwade, Vaijanath Kashinath, 135
Rakhmabai Case, 159-60, 172, 176 n.22
Ramanuja, 223-24
Ranade, Amritrao, 6, 9
Ranade, Bhaskarrao, 6
Ranade, Govindrao, 6-8, 10-11, 32, 58-60
Ranade, K. K., 92
Ranade, Ramabai, 57, 59, 105, 128, 226, 228
Ranade, Sakhubai, 10, 58
Rand, W. C., 210-13
Raste, Bapusaheb, 71
Reay, Lord, 58, 105, 137, 189, 213
Rebellion of 1857, 19-20, 72
Revenue systems, 80-83, 102-07, 109-15. See also Permanent Settlement, Utilitarianism
Ripon, Lord, 94-96, 116, 120, 141-43, 145, 157
Rise of the Maratha Power, 216-17, 221
Roy, Ram Mohan, 156
Ryot. See Maratha

Sahitya Parishad
  See Literary Society of Maharashtra
Sandhurst, Lord, 192, 201
Sanskrit College (Poona), 69
  See also Deccan College

Sardars, 4, 23, 30, 36, 63 n.15, 68-69, 72, 74, 81, 102, 112-20, 122, 145
Sardesai, Govind Sakharam, 135
Sarvajanik Sabha (Poona), 73-78, 81, 87-88, 92, 115, 127, 138, 140-47, 190-201, 210
  agrarian policies, 82-85
  and princely states, 85-89, 138-40
Sarvajanik Sabha (Sholapur), 84
Satara, 2, 19-21
  under Maharaja Pratap Singh, 86
Sathe, Mor Shastri, 71
Savkars, 83-85, 103-09, 112-15
  See also Banias, Marwaris
Sayajirao Gaikwad
  See Gaikwad, Sayajirao
Scoble, Andrew, 172-73
Selby, F. G., 167, 211
Sen, Keshub Chander, 44, 48
Shankaracharya of Karvir and Sankeshwar, 50-54, 64 n.41, 164, 184-86
Sharada Sadan, 187-88
Shastris, 49, 68, 74, 163-64
  See also Shankaracharya, Widow-Remarriage Association
Shet, 17, 20, 35
Shivaji, 2, 28, 215-17
  festival of, 215-17
Society for General Amelioration, 71
Society for Promoting Marathi Books, 132
Society for Promoting the Veda, 57
Spencer, Herbert, 167, 169-70, 224
Spring Lecture Series, 55, 160
Statistics of Criminal Justice in the Bombay Presidency, 78-81
Statutory Civil Service, 122-23.
Stephen, James, 78-79
Strachey, John, 213
Students' Literary and Scientific Society, 41-42, 44, 131
Subba Rao, K., 195
Swadeshi, 78, 181-82

Tara Bai, 7
Telang, Kashinath Trimbak, 33, 87, 136, 148, 161, 194, 207, 218, 223-24

Temple, Richard, 84
  Ranade on, 85, 92-96, 119
Thakurdwar Temple, 47, 51
Tilak, Bal Gangadhar, 134, 138, 140-41, 144-45, 156, 160, 164, 167, 169-75, 184, 190-202, 215, 222, 229
Tukaram, 9-10, 165, 227
Tyabji, Badruddin, 148, 208

Utilitarianism, 82, 110
  See also revenue systems

Vallabhacharyas, 157-58
Vatandars, 121-23
Vedasastrottejaka Sabha
  See Society for Promoting the Veda
Vernacular Press Act of 1878, 90, 140
Victoria, Queen, 86, 88
Vidyasagar, Ishwarchandra, 48-49
Vithoba, 1, 9

Wacha, Dinshaw, 26, 208-10
Wagle, Bal Mangesh, 24
Wedderburn, William, 113, 115, 128, 136, 180, 209
Welby Commission, 209-10
West, Raymond, 106-09, 218
Westland, James, 209
Westropp, Michael, 93-94, 218
Widow-Remarriage Association, 48-54
Wilson, John, 18-19, 22
Wodehouse, Philip, 83, 87
Women's education, 10, 42, 57, 127-29
  See also Pandit, V. S.; Ramabai, Pandita
Woodburn, A. F., 109
Wordsworth, William, 133, 136, 142-43, 160

Young Poona, 70, 72